# YOUTH MEDIA

Bill Osgerby's innovative introduction traces the development of contemporary youth culture and its relationship with the media, from the days of diners, drive-ins and jukeboxes, to today's world of iPods and the internet, examining youth media in its economic, cultural and political contexts. *Youth Media* explores:

- Youth culture and the media
- The 'fab phenomenon': markets, money and media
- Generation and degeneration in the media: representations, responses and 'effects'
- Media, subculture and lifestyle
- Global media, youth culture and identity
- Youth and new media

**Bill Osgerby** is a Reader in Media, Culture and Communications at London Metropolitan University and has written widely on youth culture, gender and British and American cultural history.

# ROUTLEDGE INTRODUCTIONS TO MEDIA AND COMMUNICATIONS

Edited by Paul Cobley *London Metropolitan University*

This new series provides concise introductions to key areas in contemporary communications. Each book in the series addresses a genre or a form of communication, analysing the nature of the genre or the form as well as reviewing its production and consumption, outlining the main theories and approaches that have been used to study it, and discussing contemporary textual examples of the form. The series offers both an outline of how each genre or form has developed historically, and how it is changing and adapting to the contemporary media landscape, exploring issues such as convergence and globalisation.

*Youth Media*
Bill Osgerby

*Videogames*
James Newman

*Brands*
Marcel Danesi

*Advertising*
Ian MacRury

*Magazines*
Anna Gough-Yates

*News*
Jackie Harrison

*Cyberspace*
Mikle Ledgerwood

# YOUTH MEDIA

*Bill Osgerby*

Routledge
Taylor & Francis Group

LONDON AND NEW YORK

First published 2004
by Routledge
2 Park Square, Milton Park, Abingdon, Oxon OX14 4RN

Simultaneously published in the USA and Canada
by Routledge
270 Madison Ave, New York, NY 10016

*Routledge is an imprint of the Taylor & Francis Group*

© 2004 Bill Osgerby

Typeset in Perpetua and Univers by
Florence Production Ltd, Stoodleigh, Devon
Printed and bound in Great Britain by
The Cromwell Press, Trowbridge, Wiltshire

*British Library Cataloguing in Publication Data*
A catalogue record for this book is available from the
British Library

*Library of Congress Cataloging in Publication Data*
A catalog record for this book is available from the
Library of Congress

ISBN 0–415–23807–2 (hbk)
ISBN 0–415–23808–0 (pbk)

# CONTENTS

# FIGURES

# SERIES EDITOR'S PREFACE

There can be no doubt that communications pervade contemporary social life. The audio-visual media, print and other communication technologies play major parts in modern human existence, mediating diverse interactions between people. Moreover, they are numerous, heterogeneous and multi-faceted.

Equally, there can be no doubt that communications are dynamic and ever-changing, constantly reacting to economic and popular forces. Communicative genres and modes that we take for granted because they are seemingly omnipresent – news, advertising, film, radio, television, fashion, the book – have undergone an alarming sea of changes in recent years. They have also been supplemented and reinvigorated by new media, new textualities, new relations of production and new audiences.

The *study* of communications, then, cannot afford to stand still. Although communication study as a discipline is relatively recent in its origin, it has continued to develop in recognisable ways, embracing new perspectives, transforming old ones and responding to – and sometimes influencing – changes in the media landscape.

This series of books is designed to present developments in contemporary media. It focuses on the analysis of textualities, offering an up-to-date assessment of current communications practice. The emphasis of the books is on the *kind* of communications which constitute the modern media and the theoretical tools which are needed to understand them. Such tools may include semiotics (including social semiotics and semiology), discourse theory, poststructuralism, postcolonialism, queer theory, gender analysis, political economy, liberal pluralism, positivism (including quantitative approaches), qualitative methodologies (including the 'new ethnography'), reception theory and ideological analysis. The breadth of current communications media, then, is reflected in the array of methodological resources needed to investigate them.

Yet, the task of analysis is not carried out as an hermetic experiment. Each volume in the series places its topic within a contextual matrix of production and consumption. Each allows readers to garner an understanding of what that communication is like without tempting them to forget who produced it, for what purpose, and with what result. The books seek to present research on the mechanisms of textuality but also attempt to reveal the precise situation in which such mechanisms exist. Readers coming to these books will, therefore, gain a valuable insight into the present standing of specific communications media. Just as importantly, though, they will become acquainted with analytic methods which address, explore and interrogate the very bases of that standing.

# ACKNOWLEDGEMENTS

The author and publisher gratefully acknowledge the following for permission to reproduce material: Pictorial Press for Figures 3.1, 4.1, 5.2, 5.3, 6.1 and 8.1. Every effort has been made to trace copyright holders. The author apologises for any errors or omissions in the above list and would be grateful to be notified of any corrections that should be incorporated in the next edition or reprint of this volume. For help in obtaining innumerable source materials, heaps of thanks go to Alan Chalkley at the Library of London Metropolitan University.

As ever, this book would not have been possible without the help and support of an army of people. I am especially indebted to Rebecca Barden and Kate Ahl at Routledge and, of course, to series editor Paul Cobley for their support . . . and not a little patience. In the course of completing this project I was lucky enough to have the continuing help and encouragement of all my family and friends. At London Met., Mike Chopra-Gant, John Gabriel, Stuart Isaacs, Gholam Khiabany, Marcy O'Reilly and Milly Williamson have been great to work with. Anna Gough-Yates deserves very big thanks for her support and for pointing me in the direction of invaluable sources and ideas. Thanks, too, to Martin Barker, Christian Bugge, Chris Bullar, Becky Ebenkamp, Alun Howkins, Rehan Hyder, Mary Celeste Kearney, Andy Medhurst, Lucy Robinson and Lyn Thomas. Gratitude also goes to George Osgerby, Jon and Julie Deadman, Sean 'Tiger Woods' Gregory, John 'Minigolf' McIver, Dave 'Diddyman' Quinn, and to Clive Gilling and all the Surfin' Lungs. And the usual huge thanks goes to Liz Davies for her infinite strength, patience and support. Thanks, too, to Joey the cat.

# 1

# INTRODUCTION
## Youth culture and the media

To see the lack of influence that real world patterns have on the youth market, all you need do is stroll through the shops and listen to the chi-ching of the cash registers. In the wake of the Christmas spending blitz, while many of us are struggling to scrape together enough change for an after-work pint, the young are still shopping. And, they are shopping for themselves, spending for all they are worth, buying up Nike, Kangaroo, Levis, Tommy, Diesel and Hobo. Some of us may wonder how they get the energy, others how they get the money. But if you're in marketing or business design, all you want to know is how you get their attention. . . . With phrases such as disposable income, brand awareness and brand loyalty linked to their spending patterns, it is little wonder that advertisers and marketers are engaged in a series of hit-and-miss backflips trying to answer the million-dollar question – what is cool?

(Michelle Warren, 2000)

## SELLS LIKE TEEN SPIRIT: YOUTH, CONSUMPTION AND MEDIA

Touted as the cutting-edge of streetwise style, Diesel's 55DSL fashion range made a big splash on its launch in Britain. One of the world's most profitable designer clothing companies, Diesel showcased its 55DSL line of jeans and sportswear in the UK during 2002 with the opening of a flagship store in London's trendy Soho and a multi-faceted advertising campaign that pitched 55DSL as the last word in urban cool. The development of the 55DSL label was a high point in Diesel's success story, but the launch of 55DSL was also indicative of broader developments in the commercial youth market and the role of the media in selling goods and services to young consumers.

Generally, Diesel's distinctive approach to business organisation and marketing was indicative of broad shifts in the media and consumer industries during the late twentieth century. The rise of Diesel as a leading international fashion group, for instance, embodied the increasingly 'global' scale of media and consumer enterprise. With the intensification of economic competition and deregulation of markets during the 1980s and 1990s, the media and consumer industries increasingly developed marketing strategies that extended across national boundaries in integrated and interconnected business networks. The growth of Diesel and its approach to marketing was exemplary. The creation of Italian designer Renzo Rosso, Diesel was founded in 1978 and quickly developed into an innovative fashion company, manufacturing jeans, casual clothing and a wide range of stylish accessories geared to the youth market. Positioning itself as a global brand during the 1990s, Diesel's worldwide marketing strategy epitomised the increasing 'internationalisation' of consumer industries. From its Italian origins Diesel quickly developed into a global business concern. By the end of the 1990s 85 per cent of Diesel's $330 million annual turnover was generated outside Italy, the company managing twelve subsidiaries across Europe, Asia and the Americas.

Diesel's approach to business organisation also epitomised broader trends. During the 1980s and 1990s a quest for greater efficiency saw many corporations pursue strategies of multi-sector integration, buying into related industries and bolstering sales through the cross-promotion of products. Diesel, for example, developed its own distribution system and retail outlets, the firm opening a worldwide chain of its own stores selling an array of goods bearing the 'Diesel' brand name. The Diesel empire also exemplified both the rise of more 'flexible' systems of business organisation and trends towards an international division of labour. In their efforts to reduce production costs and respond more quickly to market changes, many firms developed international networks of subcontracting and outsourcing configured around a central business 'core'. Diesel's operations, for example, were centrally managed from the firm's headquarters in Molvena (in northern Italy), but most production was outsourced to an army of small- and medium-sized manufacturing companies based throughout the world. The drive for greater business flexibility also relied on the deployment of new computer technologies in processes of production and retailing. And, again, Diesel was in the forefront. One of the first clothing companies to harness the marketing potential of new communications technologies, Diesel launched its own website in 1995, allowing customers to browse an online store and access virtual versions of the season's fashion shows.

Diesel's marketing tactics were also indicative of developments in media targeting. During the 1980s and 1990s the media and consumer industries increasingly moved away from attempts to target monolithic, undifferentiated mass markets. Instead, new, more flexible, techniques of production and delivery allowed goods and services to be aimed at a spectrum of more nuanced market segments. Diesel exemplified this, more focused, approach to marketing through its launch of distinctive fashion ranges geared to specific market 'niches' and 'lifestyles'. The core label, D-Diesel, focused on denim jeans and casualwear, gradually extending into new ranges of shoes, leather goods and fragrance. But Diesel also developed more specialised lines. In 1998, for example, the company launched StyleLab, a more up-market and unconventional collection aimed at young professionals who wanted the hip kudos of Diesel jeans, but who also sought an avant-garde style that stood out from the mainstream. StyleLab was aimed at consumers in their late twenties and thirties, but Diesel also prioritised a younger market. Through their 55DSL line (overseen by Rosso's young son, Andrea) the company targeted consumers in their teens and twenties with a fashion line that was configured as more rebellious, rougher-edged and defiantly 'street'. Diesel's approach to marketing, then, was not only exemplary in being informed by new developments in economy and media; it also demonstrated the rise of new techniques for the targeting of specific groups of young consumers.

Alongside Diesel's move towards market segmentation, the company's emphasis on design and advertising was also indicative of wider business shifts. Of course, since the late nineteenth century, advertising has been central to the operation of consumer industries. But, with the trend towards more flexible forms of production and the targeting of market 'segments', what are often termed the 'cultural intermediary' occupations – design, marketing, advertising – became increasingly influential. During the 1980s and 1990s, especially, the ambition to home-in on differentiated market 'niches' impelled manufacturers to associate their products with meanings and values that would appeal to particular groups of prospective buyers. The 'cultural intermediaries' played a pivotal role in moves towards this 'aestheticisation' of consumer goods and services. Market researchers and forecasting agencies, for example, were increasingly relied upon to monitor subtle shifts in consumer tastes as producers sought to 'get close to the customer'. Advertisers and designers also grew in importance, as firms sought to invest their goods with values and meanings that would foster a greater sense of identification between the consumer and the product.

This was a practice in which Diesel excelled. During the late 1990s the company scooped a bevy of prestigious awards for a series of iconoclastic ad campaigns that targeted an audience of young, sceptical and acutely media-literate consumers. In 1998, for example, Diesel won the Grand Prix at the Cannes International Advertising Festival for its 'For Successful Living' campaign which satirised traditional media themes, twisting familiar images in a way that was droll and playfully ironic. In a Western parody, for instance, one television commercial featured a handsome hero wearing Diesel jeans who is shot down by an ugly gunslinger wearing nondescript denims – the final scene concluding with the bad guy's echoing laugh and the slogan 'Diesel, for successful living'. Often intriguing, occasionally confusing, Diesel's ads required audience wit and involvement to be deciphered, so that those who understood the company's wry sense of humour could feel a sense of complicity between themselves and the brand.

The UK launch of Diesel's 55DSL label, especially, exemplified wider moves towards the 'aestheticisation' of consumer goods. In an effort to build up 55DSL's associations with the hippest end of the British youth market, Diesel recruited a specialised youth marketing agency – Freewheelin' Media – to oversee the promotion of the new label. A small, independent consultancy, Freewheelin' Media claimed to have their ear to the ground in the fast-changing world of youth culture. Working hard to position 55DSL as a brand for consumers who saw themselves as part of a hip and media-savvy style underground, Freewheelin's campaign for 55DSL steered clear of the glossy advertising strategies traditionally associated with big brand names. Instead, the 55DSL campaign drew on methods of 'guerrilla' marketing, deploying unconventional and unorthodox promotion strategies to build up the label's cachet among the intended consumer niche. Crucial to the campaign was a playing-down of 55DSL's corporate associations and the cultivation of a cultish, illicit aura around the label. The 'guerrilla' promotion of 55DSL, therefore, began quietly. Prior to the label's launch, low level manoeuvres were used to raise market awareness – with 30,000 stickers bearing the 55DSL logo (but, significantly, not the Diesel brand name) flyposted around London's coolest neighbourhoods as an enigmatic 'teaser'. Once underway, the campaign deployed further 'guerrilla' tactics, with a 'pirate' radio station – 55DSL FM – broadcasting the latest in drum 'n' bass and dancefloor breakbeat from Diesel's London store. In reality, the radio broadcasts were completely legitimate, but the pirate facade served to engender an image of daring subversion. A *55RPM* magazine worked in a similar way. Photocopied and laid out in the style of a 'fanzine', the deliberately crude appearance of *55RPM* was designed to enhance the label's 'underground' connotations, bringing 55DSL closer to its intended public. Other attempts to foster a maverick image quickly followed, 55DSL sponsoring both a posse of rough-and-ready skateboarders and a nationwide tour by an entourage of London rappers.

Overall, then, the success of Diesel pointed to much broader economic and cultural trends. The rise of the Italian fashion company as an international corporation exemplified the increasingly global scale of the contemporary media and consumer industries, while the scope of the Diesel empire was indicative of the complex webs of integration and synergy that have come to characterise modern business practice. Diesel's attempts to target a range of differentiated consumer groups, meanwhile, highlighted a shift from mass to niche marketing, while the company's innovative approach to promotion was constituent in a broader 'aestheticisation' of commercial culture that gave greater importance to the practices of designers, advertisers and marketers. But the centrality of *youth* within the world of Diesel was also significant.

The launch of Diesel's 55DSL fashion line testified to the continuing endurance of the youth market as a linchpin within the consumer and media industries. During the mid-twentieth century the youth market first emerged as a mainstay within developed economies and, despite the labour market shifts and economic recessions of the 1980s and 1990s, young people's spending power has remained a cornerstone within consumer and media enterprise. Hence 'youth media' have been a crucial means for the delivery of young audiences and markets to commercial producers – a factor central to any attempt to understand the development of modern youth culture and its attendant industries. Indeed, the late twentieth century saw a significant extension of the economic and cultural influence of the 'youth' market as producers and advertisers increasingly sought to associate 'youthful' values, attitudes and lifestyles with goods and media texts geared to a wider constituency of consumers. Beyond their 55DSL sales campaign, for example, Diesel's pitch to older market segments was also informed by the attitudes and styles of contemporary youth culture – the brand configuring itself as the essence of 'youthful' cool. The success of Diesel and the character of its promotions, then, suggested that the 'youth' market and 'youth media' were no longer the exclusive preserve of the young, but had come to represent a particular kind of consumer identity whose values and lifestyles could win broad cultural appeal.

The case of Diesel, its marketing strategies and cachet as the quintessence of cool, brings together many of this book's themes. Primarily, the book explores the complex relationships that exist in the production, circulation and consumption of media and cultural texts geared towards markets and audiences of young people. The book analyses the historical development and contemporary configuration of the commercial youth market, highlighting its relation to both the broader development of modern media institutions and to wider shifts in social, economic and political relations. Attention is given to the place of the youth market in the globalisation of consumer industries, the shift towards niche marketing and the growing importance of 'cultural intermediaries' in modern business practice. But consideration is also given to youth's relationship with the media and the various ways young people make commercial texts and products 'meaningful'. Recognition is given to young people's ability to be 'active' consumers who create their own identities through their practices of consumption, but issues of institutional power, control and inequality are also stressed. Generally, emphasis is placed on the way cultural meanings are always dynamic – continually formed and reformed as they circulate through (and feed back into) the various sites of production, representation and consumption.

As well as exploring the symbiotic relationships that exist between young people's cultural formations and commercial industries, this book also analyses media representations of young people and the way configurations of 'youth' have featured within wider media and political discourse. Here, attention is given to the various ways the media have constructed 'ideologies of youth' through the deployment of specific representational codes and modes of address. The constitution of ideologically-charged representations of youth, it is argued, has functioned as an important medium through which fundamental shifts in social boundaries and cultural relationships have been historically explored, made sense of and interpreted – not only by the media, but also by legislators, institutions of social control and a wide spectrum of cultural commentators.

## THEORISING YOUTH AND THE MEDIA

The media are a pervasive presence in young people's social and cultural experiences. In America, for example, research conducted by the Kaiser Family Foundation during 1999 suggested that young people's lives were dominated by their media usage – with the average American child growing up in a home with three TVs, three tape players, three radios, two video recorders, two CD players, one video game player and one computer (Rideout et al., 1999: 10). Not including any media used in school or for homework, the US researchers calculated that youngsters aged between eight and eighteen spent an average of nearly seven hours a day using a wealth of electronic media (television, videos, computers and video games) as well as movies, books, magazines and newspapers (Rideout *et al.*, 1999: 7).[1] European research also testified to the omnipresence of the media in young people's lives. In Britain, for instance, research conducted during the late 1990s by Sonia Livingstone and Moira Bovill (1999) found that young people aged between six and seventeen spent an average of five hours a day using some form of media. Of these five hours, around half the time (46 per cent) was spent watching television and a further fifth was spent listening to music, with videos, computer games and reading each accounting for around ten per cent of British youngsters' media usage (Livingstone, 2002: 76).[2] The media, however, not only occupy a central place in young people's social and cultural lives – they have also been crucial in shaping our concepts of youth as a distinct generational category.

Some form of transitional stage between childhood and adulthood has been common to most societies, but the features regarded as characteristic of this developmental phase have varied across time and between cultural contexts. Modern notions of 'youth' as a discrete life stage demanding special attention and supervision first took shape during the late nineteenth and early twentieth centuries. In the fields of psychology and pedagogy studies such as G. Stanley Hall's rambling opus, *Adolescence: Its Psychology and Its Relations to Physiology, Anthropology, Sociology, Sex, Crime and Education* (1904), helped popularise the notion of adolescence as a distinct phase of bio-psychological transformation that began with puberty and ended in mature adulthood. Hall's view of adolescence as an innately volatile period of identity formation (inevitably troubling for both young people and wider society) retains influence in branches of psychology. More generally, however, this approach fell from favour during the mid-twentieth century as empirical investigation cast doubt on notions of adolescence as an intrinsically traumatic phase of personal development.[3]

In place of inherent bio-psychological characteristics, theorists increasingly focused on the social and economic conditions that were believed to set youth apart as a discrete social group. During the early 1940s the American sociologist Talcott Parsons coined the term 'youth culture' to denote what he saw as a distinct generational cohort subject to common processes of socialisation. For Parsons, this 'youth culture' was a transitionary experience that performed a positive function for the social whole by 'easing the difficult process of adjustment from childhood emotional dependency to full "maturity"' (Parsons, 1943: 30). Other

American researchers followed his lead.[4] Erik Erikson's *Childhood and Society* (1950), for example, presented adolescence as a confusing (though not especially deviant) phase of identity formation, while in *Generation to Generation* (1956) S.N. Eisenstadt emphasised the way adolescent peer culture eased young people into their adult roles. James Coleman's *The Adolescent Society* (1961) was also influential, portraying a teenage culture whose attitudes and interests were markedly different to those of the wider adult world. In these terms it was not any innate biological or psychological 'storm and stress' that set young people apart as a generational group, but their distinctive social experiences, values and behaviour.

More recently, however, theorists have challenged notions of 'youth' as a universal social category. Instead, 'youth' has been understood as a relative, culturally constructed concept. Of course, the experience of ageing is a fundamental biological process and the physical transformations associated with puberty represent a tangible moment of transition from childhood to mature adulthood. But the social characteristics ascribed to the generational category labelled 'youth' have varied between different historical and cultural contexts. As David Sibley has argued, the boundary separating childhood and adulthood is imprecise and 'the act of drawing the line in the construction of discrete [age] categories interrupts what is naturally continuous' (Sibley, 1995: 35). Rather than being a consistent and unvarying stage in human physical and psychological development, therefore, the distinguishing features of 'youth' are the product of wider social, economic and political structures.[5] Or, as Sheila Allen put it:

> Age relations (including youth) are part of the economic relations and the political and ideological structures in which they take place. It is not the relations between ages which explain the changes or stability in society, but changes in societies which explains the relations between ages.
>
> (Allen, 1968: 321)

According to John Gillis (1974), modern notions of youth were originally delineated during the late nineteenth century, the outcome of a growing apprehension among legislators and reformers that the teenage years were a life stage distinguished by social and psychological vulnerability. As a consequence there followed a flood of protective legislation which, coupled with a new range of specialised welfare bodies and employment practices, marked out youth as a distinct social group associated with particular needs and social problems. Claire Wallace and Sijka Kovatcheva (1998) have also seen processes of industrialisation and the development of state agencies as central factors in the emergence of youth as a clearly defined stage in the life-course. For Wallace and Kovatcheva, concepts of youth developed as a facet of Western modernity and 'the development of the modern world associated with professional bureaucratic power, industrial society and enlightenment rationality' (1998: 10). From this perspective, the modern configuration of distinct age groups was the product of state bureaucracies, who developed age as a precise method of calibration in administrative practices that worked to define and control subordinate populations. According to Wallace and Kovatcheva, this bureaucratic calibration of age reached a high point with the expansion of state welfare and education systems after the Second World War. Indeed, in both America and Europe, the proliferation of welfare agencies and educational provision after 1945 was crucial in institutionalising 'youth' as a distinct age category. But wider social, economic and political shifts were also important.

Mid-century perceptions of 'youth' as a distinct social group were a response to a number of developments. On both sides of the Atlantic a post-war 'baby boom' ensured a burgeoning youth population throughout the 1950s and 1960s, while the expansion of consumer industries and the reconfiguration of traditional labour markets ensured buoyant levels of youth employment and boosted young people's spending power. In turn, the growth of youth's disposable income underpinned a huge expansion of the commercial youth market, so that by the late 1950s the range of products geared to the young was virtually boundless. The media and consumer industries scrambled to capitalise on youth's enhanced economic muscle, with filmmakers, record companies, magazine publishers and fashion houses all jostling to cash-in on the growth of teen spending. This exponential growth of the youth-oriented leisure and entertainment industries added force to notions of a distinctive adolescent peer culture. Indeed, intrinsic to Parsons' concept of 'youth culture' and Coleman's account of the 'adolescent society' was the assumption that the new fads, fashions and media pitched at the young were catering to a generational culture denoted by its preoccupation with leisure, style and conspicuous consumption. Increasingly, then, the characteristics that seemed to set 'youth' apart as a distinct cultural group were not their bio-psychological attributes, but their distinctive patterns of media use and practices of commodity consumption.

During the 1950s and 1960s notions of a new, hedonistic and distinctly 'teenage' form of consumerism were at the forefront of dominant accounts of social change. In both Britain and America 'teenage' culture was configured as the harbinger of a modern consumer culture in which the 'old' boundaries of class and economic inequality were perceived as steadily disappearing. The media and social theorists alike presented newly affluent 'gilded youth' as the vanguard of a liberated, exciting and pre-eminently classless modern society. In reality, however, inequalities of wealth and status remained (as they still remain) crucial determinants of young people's social experiences and life chances. Indeed, while notions of an integrated and homogeneous 'youth culture' dominated the sociology of youth during the 1950s and early 1960s, the influence of social class was never entirely evacuated. In America, for example, August Hollingshead's study of *Elmstown's Youth* (1949) described the activities of generationally-based cliques, but also acknowledged the ways that social behaviour was shaped by family and community background. In Britain researchers gave even greater recognition to the influence of socio-economic structures on young people's cultural experiences. David Downes' (1966) study of youths from London's East End, for example, highlighted the way social class affected young people's attitudes and aspirations, while Graham Murdock and Robin McCron found that teenagers' tastes in pop music and style were influenced by their class background, earlier researchers having 'seriously underestimated the importance of class inequalities in shaping adolescents' lives and in limiting their responses' (Murdock and McCron, 1973: 692).

During the 1970s class emerged as a pre-eminent theme in analyses of British youth culture. Especially influential in this respect was work produced by members of the Centre for Contemporary Cultural Studies (CCCS) at the University of Birmingham. Edited by Stuart Hall and Tony Jefferson, *Resistance Through Rituals* (1976) drew together work by various members of the CCCS team. Common to the contributions was a neo-Marxist reading of youth style (encompassing dress, music, language and postures) as a form of class-based resistance against a dominant culture. For the CCCS theorists the styles of spectacular youth groups such as Teddy boys, mods and skinheads represented gestures of symbolic defiance by disempowered working-class youngsters who resisted dominant power structures by creating oppositional subcultural identities. In these terms, the rebellious meanings encoded in subcultural fashion and music could be 'read' using methods of semiological analysis, with Dick Hebdige famously deploying an arsenal of semiotic theory, literary criticism and structural anthropology in his reading of 1970s punk as a 'style in revolt' (1979: 106).

Indicative of the influence of the CCCS team's work are the number of later studies framed as responses (or successors) to their subcultural analysis – for example, David Muggleton's notion of 'post-subcultures' (1997, 2000; Muggleton and Weinzierl (eds), 2003) or Andy Bennett and Keith Kahn-Harris's *After Subculture* anthology (2004). More recent analyses of youth culture still acknowledge social class as a mediating factor in young people's lives, but have generally moved away from the reductive and 'totalising' tendencies associated with the CCCS theorists' engagement with Marxism. Rather than privileging class relations, for example, feminist critics such as Angela McRobbie (1978, 1981) were quick to emphasise the importance of gendered identities and power structures within young people's lives, issues that had been sidelined within the original canon of subcultural theory. New analyses of the relationship between youth and ethnic identity have also been influential. Authors such as Les Back (1996), Paul Gilroy (1987, 1993a, 1993b) and Sanjay Sharma *et al.* (1996), for example, have explored the relations between structures of class and racism in late modern societies, and the strategies through which young people negotiate their identities between not only differences of age, gender and social class; but also through discourses of ethnicity and 'race'. Andy Bennett (1999b, 2000), meanwhile, has also drawn attention to the role of locality in shaping young people's identities and cultural expressions.

Other theorists have reconsidered the relationship between youth subcultures and the commercial market. For instance, whereas subcultural theorists such as Hebdige saw the market as exploiting and 'defusing' styles generated at 'street level' by authentic subcultures, Sarah Thornton's (1995) analysis of the late-1980s dance music scene emphasised the way subcultures were *locked into* a mutually dependent relationship with the media and other commercial interests. Theories of postmodernism and post-structuralism have also registered significant impact in the study of youth culture. During the early 1990s, for example, a collection of work spearheaded by Steve Redhead at the Manchester Institute of Popular Culture focused on the dimensions of fluidity and mutability within contemporary youth style (Redhead, 1990; Redhead (ed.), 1993; Redhead, Wynne and O'Connor (eds), 1997). Some theorists have gone so far as to argue that the concept of subculture should be abandoned altogether. Authors such as Bennett (1999a, 2000), for instance, have argued that firmly demarcated subcultural identities have been displaced by a profusion of more ephemeral 'neo-tribes' characterised by their fragmentation, flux and fluidity, while Steven Miles (2000: 6–7) has argued that the concept of youth *lifestyles* is now more useful than that of youth *subcultures* – with young people drawing on the products of consumer industries and the mass media not to 'resist' dominant culture, but to forge a meaningful sense of self in a world increasingly characterised by instability and risk.

Focusing on the relationship between youth and the media, this book charts the development of these different theoretical paradigms and the way they have responded to shifts in young people's cultural expressions and life experiences. It begins with an analysis of the changing political economy of 'youth media'. While the existence of a commercial youth market can be traced back to the nineteenth century, Chapter 2 argues that the mid-twentieth century marked an important phase in the development of young people as a distinct consumer group, with shifts in demography and labour markets pushing youth to the centre of the postwar consumer boom in both America and Western Europe. During the 1970s, 1980s and early 1990s economic recession and industrial restructuring eroded the labour markets that had underpinned the explosion of 'teenage' consumption during the 1950s and 1960s; with the result that young people's routes into full-time employment became extended and more unpredictable. Chapter 2 shows, however, that (rather than fading away into the cultural past) the youth market has remained a lucrative and influential business sector. Indeed, the 1990s saw something of a renaissance for the media and consumer industries geared to youth demand, and Chapter 3 explores the way the youth market has not only figured in recent shifts towards business conglomeration, synergy and internationalisation, but has also led the way in trends towards the 'niche' segmentation of consumer markets and media audiences.

The media's various constructions and representations of 'youth' are explored in Chapter 4. Attention is given to the way media and politicians alike have made recurring use of the themes and images of 'youth' as a medium for comment on broader social and political issues. Deployed as an 'ideological vehicle' where understandings of broader social changes are encoded, representations of 'youth' have *both* celebrated young people as the exciting precursor to a prosperous future *and* (sometimes simultaneously) vilified them as the most deplorable benchmark of cultural decline. The chapter explores the way young people have often been represented as the victims of harmful media 'effects', with a succession of 'media panics' citing the popular media as a cause of juvenile crime and delinquency. The role of the media *themselves* in the development of these concerns is also discussed, with particular attention given to the concept of 'moral panic' in which distorted media coverage is understood as an important factor in the escalation of social problems. But media and political rhetoric surrounding youth has never been entirely negative and Chapter 4 shows how, at particular historical moments, more positive configurations of youth have come to the fore – the early 1960s, especially, seeing the imagery of youth deployed (in both Britain and the United States) to promote visions of 'classless' consumerism and forward-looking, national vigour.

Chapter 5 examines the links between media representations of youth and broader political agendas. On both sides of the Atlantic, it is argued, media and political discourse have regularly constructed fearful representations of delinquent youth that have been mobilised to win support for authoritarian political programmes. Focusing on recent media representations of youth subculture, the chapter also assesses how notions of 'moral panic' might need revision in order to take account of the changing nature of the contemporary media. The chapter goes on to explore the more positive representations of youth that appeared in Britain during the late 1990s, with specific consideration of the Labour Party's efforts to mobilise concepts of 'youthfulness' in its vision of a dynamic and rejuvenated 'New Britain'. Chapter 5 concludes with a discussion of the sense of 'ironic detachment' that pervades much contemporary 'youth media'. The 'postmodern' proliferation and fragmentation of the media, it is argued, has meant that representations of youth are now shot through with ambivalence, ambiguity and contradiction.

In Chapter 6 the focus shifts to young audiences' engagement with popular media, with a critical survey of the key developments in the study of young people's patterns of media consumption. While theorists have generally moved away from seeing young people as the passive victims of exploitative cultural industries, the chapter shows there has been an on-going tension between the approaches of political economy and those of cultural studies. While the former has tended to emphasise dimensions of power and control within the market (occasionally sliding into overly pessimistic notions of a manipulated mass audience), the latter has stressed the capacity of consumers to construct their own cultures from commercial resources (sometimes slipping into excessively romantic accounts of symbolic 'resistance'). Attempts to bridge this theoretical divide have been notoriously problematic, but more recent studies of youth consumption have gone some way towards integrating the two paradigms – giving recognition to young people's active agency in the creation of their culture, but with an awareness that these processes take place within a wider field of economic and political power structures.

Issues of economic power and cultural agency are also central to Chapter 7. Here, attention is given to the global circulation and local consumption of youth-oriented media. While recognition must be given to the way processes of conglomeration and internationalisation have delivered vast power to global media corporations, it is argued that crude notions of 'cultural imperialism' are unable to capture the complex nature of international media flows, nor the variety of ways 'youth media' have been 're-embedded' in local contexts. Instead, attention is given to the way forms of 'teenage' culture originally developed in the West have been reconfigured and integrated within a wide array of local youth cultures and identities. These themes are continued in Chapter 8, which examines in more detail the way contemporary youth cultures and their associated media are forged through processes of interconnection and transformation. Particular attention is given to the local 'inflection' of global media, with young audiences in different locales appropriating and giving new meanings to globally-circulating cultural forms and media texts. The chapter also discusses the 'hybridised' character of contemporary youth culture and media, and considers the way media forms geared to young audiences may offer fertile spaces for the configuration of multiple and dynamic identities.

Chapter 9 examines the impact of new media and communication technologies on young people's social and cultural lives. From an analysis of the distinctive features of the 'new' media, the chapter goes on to explore the significance of 'digitisation' in the youth market and its possible consequences for young people's patterns of media consumption. Attention is also given to popular representations of young people's use of new technology, and the way these portrayals are constituent in the long history of concern about the media's impact on youth. Finishing with a survey of the ways young people have engaged with 'new' media, the chapter argues that the rise of digital media and communications technologies may have helped redefine experiences of space and time but, in terms of everyday cultural experience, they have supplemented rather than replaced 'old' media forms and have been integrated within youth's existing cultures and social relationships.

The book ends with an overview of recent directions taken in the disciplines of media and cultural studies and their implications for the analysis of youth, media and culture. Particular attention is given to the notion of 'circuits of culture' and the way the meanings of media texts and cultural artefacts – Diesel's 55DSL fashion line, for example[6] – are generated through an intersection of processes of production, identity formation, representation, consumption and regulation. If young people's relationship with the media is to be adequately understood, it is argued, attention must be devoted to each of these processes and the ways they interact with the other aspects of the cultural circuit. As Douglas Kellner has cogently emphasised, 'in order to grasp fully the nature and effects of media culture, one needs to develop methods to analyse the full range of its meanings and effects' (Kellner, 1997: 109). In these terms, issues of political economy, textuality and audience reception are not antithetical, but can be constructively combined in a 'transdisciplinary' and 'multiperspectival' analysis of youth and its relationship with the media.

# 2

# THE 'FAB PHENOMENON'

## The rise of the commercial youth market

Today, the teenagers pay the piper – largely because they are the most numerous group with money to spare *on this kind of thing* – and the tunes they call have their elders in a whirl. With astonishment, dismay, curiosity or even fear, the adults find themselves on the outside, looking in at a vast industry with an annual turnover of many millions which is entirely devoted to the satisfaction of caprices and whims expressed by those who, only a few years ago, were expected to be seen and not heard.

(Peter Leslie, 1965: 15)

## 'IT'S ALL ABOUT THE BENJAMINS': THE POLITICAL ECONOMY OF 'YOUTH MEDIA'

Sean 'Puffy' Combs was not best known as an incisive political economist. Owner of the hip-hop media empire, Bad Boy Records, Combs forged a reputation as a strong-arm gangsta rap impresario during the 1990s, his output lionising a ghetto life of sex, violence and lavish high-rolling. But, while Combs' 1997 single, 'It's All About the Benjamins' (referring to $100 bills), was an anthem to outrageous excess, the song's title also stands as a neat epithet for the economic imperatives central to the history of the commercial youth market, its products and associated media.

Regarding structures of economic organisation as 'ultimately the most powerful of the many levers operating in cultural production' (Murdock and Golding, 1977: 20), political economists of the media have taken patterns of ownership and control as their central objects of analysis.

Even committed political economists acknowledge, however, that economic relationships do not shape cultural life in a deterministic way. Hence, while the accent of this chapter (and the next) is on issues of production and economic control, it does not advocate a crudely 'reductionist' model of analysis that perceives media texts and their meanings as simple 'reflections' of economic relations. At the same time, however, production, representation and consumption do not exist as autonomous spheres. Instead, they are mutually constituted through an ongoing cycle of commodification. With this in mind, we begin with a consideration of the development of the modern youth market within its broader social and economic context.

This chapter outlines the economic conditions and business dynamics that have been fundamental in the development of youth-oriented media. Beginning with the early stirrings of a commercial youth culture in the late nineteenth and early twentieth centuries, the growth of the youth market is traced through its boom years of the 1950s and 1960s, to its subsequent development amid the shifting economic landscape of the 1970s, 1980s and 1990s. Throughout, emphasis is placed on the relation between the youth market and wider patterns of social, economic and political change – the history of 'youth media' being constituent in the broader transformation of production, distribution and consumption in industrialised societies. While broad commercial trends are foregrounded (for example, the emergence of youth-oriented media and marketing during the 1950s), recognition is also given to the unique characteristics of national experience (for example, the contrasting forms of 'teenage' market that appeared in post-war Britain and America) as Western economies followed different paths into the age of modern consumerism.

## 'YOUTHQUAKE': THE EARLY TREMORS

'Youthquake' is a phrase charged with connotations of deep-seated generational upheaval. Coined in the 1970s by cultural commentators such as Richard Neville (1970: 14), Kenneth Leech (1973) and Peter Lewis (1978: 118), the phrase was used to denote the seismic transformations these writers saw as occurring in young people's lives during the 1950s and 1960s. For Neville, cultural changes since the Second World War had divided the world into two generational 'armed camps' (1970: 13), while Leech maintained that the 1950s had been 'supremely the decade of the teenager', with 'commercial interests in both the textile and recording industries' promoting the development of an identifiable youth culture as an 'international phenomenon' (1973: 1). Lewis, meanwhile, was more specific, citing the year 1956 as the epicentre of an 'explosive discovery of teenage identity' (Lewis, 1978: 118). And, undoubtedly, there is justification for seeing the 1950s and 1960s as a period of profound change – both in young people's life experiences and in the social, cultural and economic significance of youth. At the same time, however, these changes were not unprecedented. Rather than representing an earth-shaking break with the past, the 'youthquake' of the 1950s and 1960s had been anticipated by much earlier tremors.

In Britain, something resembling a commercial youth market had already taken shape during the nineteenth century. The Victorian era saw the emergence of a nascent mass-entertainment industry geared to an urban working class whose disposable income and leisure time were gradually being extended. Constituent in these developments was the rise of working youngsters as a distinct consumer group, their spending power laying the basis for an embryonic youth leisure market. By 1905, for example, a commentator in Manchester observed how a nineteen-year-old, semi-skilled youth earned a pound a week in an iron foundry and, after surrendering twelve shillings to his parents for board, was free to spend the remainder on clothes, gambling and the music halls.[1] Indeed, according to historian John Springhall, the commercial music hall found 'its most noisy customers' among such youths, whose healthy income and lack of family responsibilities meant they 'were now better off than at almost any other age and could afford to go out and enjoy themselves, spending their hard-earned shillings on the halls, football matches and the early picture palaces' (Springhall, 1980: 89).

During the 1920s and 1930s the British youth market developed further. Although some youngsters experienced periods of unemployment, demand for young workers generally remained high since their labour was relatively inexpensive (compared to that of adults) at a time when many employers were cutting costs. Inter-war Britain, therefore, saw a steady increase in working youngsters' income, David Fowler estimating that youth's money wages rose by between 300 and 500 per cent between the wars. Retaining around 50 per cent (or more) of their earnings, young wage-earners 'invariably enjoyed a standard of living higher than that of the rest of the family' – this lucrative, young market increasingly attracting the attention of entrepreneurs and manufacturers (Fowler, 1995: 95, 101). For Fowler, then, a 'hard-sell youth market' began to blossom during the 1920s and 1930s as cinemas, dancehalls and magazine publishers all courted the spending power of young workers (Fowler, 1995: 170).

In the United States, too, a commercial youth market existed long before the 'youthquake' of the 1950s and 1960s. By the late nineteenth century American cities were quickly growing into bustling centres of entertainment and consumption, and (as in Britain) youth was a significant force in the transformation. Kathy Peiss (1987), for example, shows how young, working women were pivotal to the development of commercial leisure in *fin de siècle* America, young women representing a major segment of the audience for dancehalls, amusement parks and movie houses. Young men were also a notable consumer group. By the end of the century groups of young, working men – both white and African-American – were making a virtue of conspicuous consumption. Flamboyantly promenading in broad-brimmed hats, embroidered shirts and black frock-coats, these 'mashers' and 'b'hoys' (as they were known) were a distinctive feature in urban centres of commercial leisure (Swiencicki, 1998: 786). Middle-class young men were also an important consumer market, Howard Chudacoff (1999) showing how an extensive 'bachelor subculture' developed around the network of eating houses, barber shops, tobacconists, tailors, city bars, theatres and array of other commercial ventures that thrived on the patronage of affluent, young 'men about town'.

During the 1920s the US youth market, like that in Britain, underwent further growth. Generally, the 1920s saw the American economy boom, domestic product rising by nearly 40 per cent between 1922 and 1929. Amid this age of prosperity, a fully formed, commercial youth market came into view. Stanley Hollander and Richard Germain (1993), for example, show how a substantial number of marketers began to direct their efforts towards youth spending during the 1920s. 'Entrepreneurs, consultants and marketing scholars', they argue, 'expounded the significance of the youth market', while 'special youth promotion, special youth pricing, and special youth distribution [was] applied to a wide range of products such as automobiles, apparel items, personal hygiene products, typewriters, and cigarettes, and services provided by such establishments as hotels, inns, dancehalls and barber shops' (Hollander and Germain, 1993: 114, 55).

The rise of this market went hand-in-hand with the expansion of a largely middle-class 'campus culture'. The prosperity of the American middle class during the Jazz Age provided the basis for a huge expansion in higher education. Once the preserve of a small elite, colleges and universities saw a threefold increase in enrolments between 1900 and 1930, nearly 20 per cent of the college-age population attending some kind of educational institution by the end of the 1920s. Young, relatively well-to-do and free of family responsibilities, students were an attractive market for American business and attempts to court youth spending were invariably focused on the college sector (Hollander and Germain, 1993: 24–25). In turn, the products of the youth market fed back into the development of what Paula Fass identifies as 'the first modern American youth culture' – a collegiate universe that formed around student fraternities, dancehalls, cinemas, cafeterias and other campus hangouts (1978: 122).

The student culture chronicled by Fass weathered the lean years that followed the Wall Street Crash of 1929. More generally, however, American youth was hard hit by the Depression. Young people represented 27.5 per cent of those unemployed in 1930, and by 1937 16 per cent of the total youth population remained out of work. During the 1940s, however, the American youth market was revitalised by the labour demands of the wartime economy. The economic pressures of the war drew increasing numbers of young people into the US workforce, partially reversing earlier trends towards extended schooling and dependency on parents. In 1944, for example, US Census Bureau statistics showed that more than two in five young men aged between sixteen and seventeen were gainfully employed, with 35 per cent of these having left school altogether to enter full-time work (Modell, 1989: 165–166). As a consequence, greater disposable income was delivered into young hands. By 1944 American youth accounted for a spending power of around $750 million (Adams, 1994: 127), an economic muscle that not only helped crystallise notions of young people as a uniquely autonomous social group, but which also provided the basis for an additional expansion of the commercial youth industries and associated media – which, in turn, further fostered the sense of young people as a consumer group of exceptional independence and influence.

Well before the 1950s and 1960s, then, the rise of a commercial youth market had registered on the 'Richter scale' of social change. By the end of the Victorian era, on both sides of the Atlantic, manufacturers, advertisers and media industries were already tapping into young people's spending power, the trend picking up momentum during the 1920s and 1930s. Nevertheless, while youth-oriented industries and entertainments were not unique to the 1950s and 1960s, there remain grounds for seeing the mid-twentieth century as an important phase in the development of 'youth media' and the modern youth market.

## 'IT'S "TERRIF"': THE INEXORABLE RISE OF THE AMERICAN YOUTH MARKET

The 'teenager' was a creation of the 1940s. Distinct patterns of youth consumption and related industries had existed long before, but it was only in America during the 1940s that the specific concept of the 'teenager' began to coalesce. Since the 1600s it had been common to refer to an adolescent as being someone in their 'teens', yet it was only in 1941 that an article in *Popular Science* magazine featured the first published use of the word 'teenager', and the term increasingly leaked into popular usage (Hine, 1999: 8–9). The commercial media played a decisive role in the term's dissemination. The advertising and marketing industries were especially crucial in popularising the concept, marketers using the term 'teenager' to denote what they saw as a new breed of affluent, young consumer who prioritised fun, leisure and the fulfilment of personal desires. A *Business Week* feature of 1946 exemplified trade enthusiasm for this consumer group. 'Teen-Age Market: It's "Terrif"', proclaimed the journal, as it trumpeted 'the jackpot market' that had 'come into its own during the war'. Whetting commercial appetites, *Business Week* described how 'the going is high, wide and handsome with this market whose astounding responsiveness and loyalty endear it to any manufacturer's heart' (*Business Week*, 8 June 1946).

Evidence of the growing scale of the American youth market was provided by the runaway success of *Seventeen* magazine. Conceived as a publication geared to young women at college, *Seventeen* was launched in 1944. Its premier edition selling out within two days, *Seventeen*'s circulation had shot up to over a million a month by 1947 and by 1949 was touching the two-and-a-half million mark (Schrum, 1998: 139). *Seventeen*'s business strategies, moreover, were indicative of the increasingly sophisticated methods through which commercial interests were tapping into youth spending. Keen to maximise the magazine's economic potential, Helen Valentine, *Seventeen*'s first editor, hired a professional research team – Benson and Benson from Princeton – to survey her readership's buying habits. With this data at their disposal, *Seventeen*'s editorial team could tempt advertisers with valuable information on the tastes and desires of a group that was shaping up as one of the most lucrative consumer markets in post-war America.

By the 1950s the scope and scale of the American youth market seemed spectacular. The growth was partly a consequence of demographic trends, with wartime increases in the birth rate and a post-war 'baby boom' rocketing the US teen population from 10 to 15 million during the 1950s, eventually hitting a peak of 20 million by 1970. A post-war expansion of education, meanwhile, further accentuated the profile of youth as a distinct generational cohort (Modell, 1989: 225–226). The proportion of US teenagers attending high school, for example, rose from around 60 per cent in the 1930s to virtually 100 per cent during the 1960s. College and university enrolment also spiralled. In 1950 about 41 per cent of high school graduates went on to college, but by 1960 this had risen to 53 per cent, the trend giving a new lease of life to the campus culture that had surfaced between the wars.

The vital stimulus behind the growth of the commercial youth market, however, was economic. Peacetime saw a decline in full-time youth employment, but the wartime rise in youth spending was sustained by a combination of part-time work and parental allowances – some estimates suggesting that young Americans' average weekly income rose from just over $2 in 1944 to around $10 by 1958 (Macdonald, 1958: 60).[2] For some, the purchasing power of American youth had become an astonishing phenomenon, an awe-struck 1959 edition of *Life* magazine announcing the arrival of 'A New $10-Billion Power: the US Teenage Consumer'. As the magazine explained, American youth had now:

> emerged as a big-time consumer in the US economy . . . Counting only what is spent to satisfy their special teenage demands, the youngsters and their parents will shell out about $10 billion this year, a billion more than the total sales of GM [General Motors].
>
> (*Life*, 31 August 1959: 78)

Such news stories were notable for *what* they reported – the growing spending power of young people – but also significant was their representation of youth as the embodiment of vibrant and conspicuous commodity consumption.

American business was quick to grasp youth's commercial potential. Following in the footsteps of Helen Valentine and *Seventeen* magazine, a host of marketers developed strategies to zero-in on adolescents' wallets. A young entrepreneur from Chicago led the field. Nineteen-year-old Eugene Gilbert was working as a shoe store clerk in 1945 when he noticed that, despite stocking the latest styles, the shop attracted few young customers. Persuading the owner to advertise more directly to young buyers, Gilbert was struck by the sudden rise in sales and began to develop market research among his peers as a viable business proposition. By 1947 Gilbert's research organisation, Youth Marketing Co., was flourishing – with plush offices in New York and accounts with prestigious clients such as Quaker Oats, Studebaker and United Airlines. Gilbert was especially proud of his innovative style of market research. Rather than relying on 'number-crunching' and quantitative surveys, he favoured a more qualitative approach. Recognising that young people themselves were best placed to gauge the attitudes of the teenage market, Gilbert recruited an army of students to interview their friends, canvassing opinions and providing feedback on their consumer preferences. Gilbert's enterprise also neatly illustrated the way media interest in young people as a commercial market, in itself, consolidated the emergence of youth as a distinct consumer group. Indeed, Gilbert himself was celebrated as a figurehead of youth consumption. Profiled by magazines such as *Newsweek* and *Harper's*, he was hailed as a leading authority on modern youth. Pronouncements in his syndicated newspaper column – 'What Young People Think' – charted the caprices of the young, while his book *Advertising and Marketing to Young People* (1957) became a manual for those chasing adolescent cash. With missionary zeal Gilbert evangelised youth as a commercial market of unprecedented importance. As he explained to *Advertising Age* in a 1951 interview:

> Our salient discovery is that within the past decade teenagers have become a separate and distinct group within our society, enjoying a degree of autonomy and independence unmatched by previous generations.
>
> (*Advertising Age*, 26 February 1951: 1)

It was hardly surprising, then, that commercial interests scrambled to stake a claim in the teenage goldmine. The range of media and products geared to the young was legion, consumer industries interacting with and reinforcing one another as they wooed young consumers. Of the $10 billion in discretionary income wielded by American youth in 1959, *Life* estimated that 16 per cent (roughly $1.5 billion) went to the entertainment industries, the remainder being spent on everything from fashion and grooming products to cars and sporting goods (*Life*, 31 August 1959).

Exemplifying the growth of the teen market was the rise of rock 'n' roll – a genre of popular music tied much more closely than its predecessors to processes of mass marketing, media dissemination and youth demand.[3] The roots of the new music lay in black rhythm and blues (R'n'B),[4] where the phrase 'rock 'n' roll' was coined as a euphemism for sex. With African-American migration during the 1940s, the popularity of rhythm and blues had spread to northern and western cities where black radio shows regularly featured R'n'B records produced by Atlantic, Chess, Sun and a growing number of independent labels. The music was geared to a black audience, but it also picked up a significant white market as young radio listeners tuned-in to late-night shows. The crossover of R'n'B into the white youth market was further galvanised by entrepreneurs such as Alan 'Moondog' Freed, a Cleveland disc jockey whose playlists began to feature R'n'B records during the early 1950s. Moving to a bigger station in New York in 1954, Freed continued to champion the original, black R'n'B performers but, in being pitched to a mainstream youth market, the music was steadily 'whitened' and reconfigured as 'rock 'n' roll'.

In a process of 'hybridisation' that was to become a recurring feature of youth media and culture (see Chapter 8), rock 'n' roll fused (black)

**Figure 2.1** 'Thirst-y cha-cha-cha?' – Advertisement for Seven-Up, 1962

R'n'B with elements of (white) country and western music. Rock 'n' roll retained a rebellious aura, but the sexual overtones characteristic of rhythm and blues were toned down as the major labels recruited white performers to produce 'acceptable' covers of R'n'B standards. Decca, for example, enjoyed early success with 'whitened-up' interpretations of R'n'B by Bill Haley, who scored hits with 'Shake, Rattle and Roll' in 1954 and 'Rock Around the Clock' the following year. A bigger commercial triumph, however, came in 1956 with RCA Victor's signing of Elvis Presley. The singer had enjoyed small-scale success on Sam Phillips' independent Sun label but, with the backing of a major company, Elvis became a cultural phenomenon – selling over eight million records within six months and representing a $20 million industry within a year.

Yet, Presley was not just a recording artist contributing to the coffers of the music media. His meteoric cinema career ('the King' made thirty-one features), also marked Elvis as a cross-media commodity. Quickly contracted to a lucrative movie deal with MGM, Presley's prolific film appearances were indicative of Hollywood's growing interest in the youth market. As Thomas Doherty (2002) shows, a decline in adult cinema audiences during the 1950s prompted the American film industry to focus more attention on young cinemagoers and, alongside Presley's movies, Columbia Pictures also capitalised on the rock 'n' roll boom by backing Alan Freed and Bill Haley in the films *Rock Around the Clock* and *Shake Rattle and Rock!* (both 1956), while *Don't Knock the Rock* (1957) and many others quickly followed. Rather than the major studios, however, it was the independent sector that most successfully exploited teen demand. Leaders of the pack were American-International Pictures (AIP). Founded in 1954, AIP cashed-in on the youth market and the flourishing drive-in circuit, the 'teenpic' industry coming of age as the studio cranked-out a glut of quickly made, low-budget sci-fi, horror and romance features (Doherty, 2002: 29).

Young audiences were also addressed by the budding medium of television. During the 1950s teenage life was a firm feature in many American TV soap operas and family-based sitcoms. As Mary Celeste Kearney (2004) observes, shows such as *The Adventures of Ozzie and Harriet* (ABC, 1952–1966), *Father Knows Best* (CBS, 1954–1955; NBC, 1955–1958; CBS, 1958–1962) and *Leave It to Beaver* (CBS, 1957–1958; ABC, 1958–1963) all featured teenage characters who became increasingly central to storylines over the course of the 1950s. The launch of the situation comedy *The Many Loves of Dobie Gillis* (CBS, 1959–1963), meanwhile, saw the arrival of the first prime-time TV show focused on teenage characters, the series chronicling the hapless adventures of Dobie and his beatnik buddy, Maynard.

The rise of American teen TV was the result of broadcasters' attempts to pull in advertisers through developing new programme formats that would appeal to young audiences. This was especially true of the ABC network. Since its bigger, more established rivals (CBS and NBC) were best placed to exploit the mass TV audience, the younger and smaller ABC network sought to compete by courting more specialised markets – the network developing a reputation for programming aimed at youth and young families with children. During the 1950s local stations also played their part in the growth of teen TV. Shows featuring pop performers and their fans became a staple of local TV stations' afternoon and Saturday morning schedules, examples including *Teen Twirl* (WNBK-Cleveland, 1955) and *Teen Club Party* (WGN-Chicago, 1957). Most famous, however, was *American Bandstand*. Launched by WFIL-Philadelphia in 1952, the show's success ensured that in 1957 it transferred to the ABC network, where its audience figures could touch 20 million.

The delights of teenage consumption, however, were not equally available to everyone. The teen market that emerged in the US after the Second World War was pre-eminently white and middle class. A rise in African-American high school enrolment brought black and white youth together as never before,[5] while the emergence of rock 'n' roll bore witness to important processes of inter-ethnic cultural exchange. Nevertheless, as Grace Palladino has observed, embedded racism and economic inequality ensured that throughout the 1950s 'black teenagers remained invisible as far as mainstream society was concerned' (Palladino, 1996: 175–176). Generally, the growth of teenage spending was concentrated in the affluent suburbs, where the post-war prosperity of the American middle class afforded their children a life of material comfort with little financial responsibility. In 1947, for example, market research produced for *Seventeen* testified to the middle-class character of the magazine's readership – 63 per cent of readers' fathers working as company executives, professionals, or owning their own business (cited in Schrum, 1998: 139). Of course, the styles, fashions and music of American youth culture were not the exclusive province of the white middle class. Throughout the 1950s and early 1960s working-class (together with African-American and Mexican-American) youth generated their own, highly visible, styles and cultural identities that fed into (indeed, were a crucial influence upon) the wider constellation of modern youth culture. However, the 'teenage' merchandise and media churned out in the US during the 1950s and 1960s were chiefly targeted at a white, middle-class market. As sociologist Jessie Bernard observed in 1961, 'teen-age culture' was essentially the culture of a 'leisure class':

> Youngsters of lower socioeconomic classes are in the teen-age culture only in their early teens. They are more likely than children of higher socioeconomic class to enter the labor force or the armed forces or to get married soon after high school and, thus, to disappear into the adult world. This exit from the teen-age world by youngsters of lower class background means that those who remain are disproportionately from the higher socioeconomic class background.
>
> (Bernard, 1961: 2)

At home, American business eagerly chased the spending power of this young 'leisure class'. The European market, however, was viewed with scepticism. Visiting Britain in 1954, and again in 1956, Eugene Gilbert decided no potential existed for a permanent marketing office in London. Dwight Macdonald agreed. In his 1958 survey of the teen market, the cultural commentator averred that 'Teenagers in England haven't enough freedom, or enough money, to be commercially interesting' (Macdonald, 1958: 67). And, certainly, the 'teenage market' developing in Britain was quite different to that in the US. But Macdonald was a little rash in his verdict that 'the concept of the teenager hardly exists as yet in Europe' (1958: 67).

## 'READY, STEADY, GO!': THE BRITISH YOUTH MARKET TAKES OFF

Compared to the US, Britain's development as a modern consumer economy was slower, partial and more uneven (Mort, 1997). In contrast to America's wartime growth, the Second World War had brought the British economy to its knees, while the additional hardship of Britain's 'austerity years' during the late 1940s and early 1950s meant that consumer spending developed only falteringly. As a consequence, the rise of 'teenage' consumption was more hesitant in Britain than in the US. Nevertheless, the British youth market gradually came into its own. By the late 1950s and early 1960s full employment and a sustained rise in real earnings had boosted standards of living, ensuring that the British people had 'never had it so good' (as Prime Minister Harold Macmillan famously quipped in 1957). And, according to many commentators, youth were the leading beneficiaries.

The equation of 'youth' with 'affluence' became a prevalent theme in Britain during the late 1950s. Not only was youth associated with spending per se, it also assumed prominence in those indices of 'new affluence', the new mass medium of broadcast television and the rejuvenated advertising industry. Market research produced by Mark Abrams also played a key role in popularising the notion that young people, more than any other social group, had materially prospered since the war. Conducted for the London Press Exchange and widely cited in an array of official reports, books, magazines and newspaper articles, Abrams' research suggested that youngsters' real earnings had risen by 50 per cent since 1945 (roughly double the increase for adults) while youth's 'discretionary' spending had grown by as much as 100 per cent – representing an annual expenditure of around £830 million (Abrams, 1959: 9). Furthermore, Abrams maintained, this spending was concentrated in particular consumer markets (representing, for example, 44 per cent of total spending on records and 39 per cent of spending on motorcycles) which, he averred, represented the emergence of 'distinctive teenage spending for distinctive teenage ends in a distinctive teenage world' (Abrams, 1959: 10).[6]

As in America, the growth of the British youth market was indebted to several factors.[7] In Britain, like America, demographics played a part. A post-war 'baby boom' ensured a growth in the youth population, with the number of people aged under twenty growing from around three million in 1951 to just over four million in 1966 (Department of Employment, 1971: 206–207). As in the US, an expansion of education also helped bracket youth as a distinct age category, the 1944 Education Act leading to a major expansion of Britain's secondary education, while the school-leaving age was raised to fifteen in 1947. And, as in the US, the growing economic power of British youth was also crucial – though here some important differences existed between the American and British experiences.

In America during the 1950s and 1960s, 'teenage' consumption was largely a feature of middle-class suburbia. In Britain, however, the post-war youth market was understood as a more working-class phenomenon. In his survey of the 'distinctive teenage world', for example, Abrams judged that 'teenage demand' was 'typical only of working class teenagers' and was 'largely without appeal for middle class boys and girls' (Abrams, 1961: 10). The 'teenage market', Abrams insisted, was 'almost entirely working class', with 'not far short of 90 per cent of all teenage spending conditioned by working class taste and values' (Abrams, 1959: 13). Indeed, the increase in British youth's spending power was largely the outcome of shifts in working-class labour markets. After 1945 the workforce as a whole felt the impact of a decline in heavy industry, the movement of capital into lighter forms of production (especially the manufacture of consumer goods), the expansion of production-line technologies and trends towards 'de-skilling'. But these changes had particular consequences for young workers. Labour market shifts created demand for flexible, though not especially skilled, labour power and young people (because they were cheaper to employ than adults) were ideally suited to the role.[8] As a consequence, the 1950s and early 1960s saw buoyant levels of youth employment. In fact, rather than undertaking a period of relatively poorly paid training or apprenticeship, many youngsters preferred the relatively high immediate rewards offered by unskilled and semi-skilled work.

The rise of the youth market had a mixed impact on the British media. Radio, for example, reacted slowly. During the 1950s rock 'n' roll could be heard only by tuning in to the American Forces Network or Radio Luxembourg. At the BBC it was largely ignored as a consequence of 'needle time' restrictions on the broadcast of recorded music[9] and offi-cialdom's disdain for a music it deemed crassly commercial. Radio stations specifically geared to a youth audience appeared in Britain only during the early 1960s, with the rise of unlicensed, 'pirate' stations such as Radio Caroline and Radio London – the BBC finally responding in 1967 with the launch of its own Radio One.[10] In contrast, the younger medium of television responded more swiftly. Initially, pop music programmes such as *Hit Parade* (BBC, 1952), *TV Music Shop* (ITV, 1955) and *Off the Record* (BBC, 1956) were low-key in their youth appeal. By the later 1950s, however, a TV genre targeted more specifically at youth was taking shape.[11] Partly, this was a consequence of regulatory change. Under the terms of the 1954 Television Act, TV companies had been obliged to suspend broadcasting between six and seven o'clock in the evening. Known colloquially as 'the Toddlers' Truce', the pause was intended to allow parents to put their children to bed without distraction. But in 1957, at the insistence of ITV (Britain's first commer-cial channel, launched in 1955), the 'Truce' was ended. As a result, programmers were forced to look for shows that could fill the vacant slot quickly and cheaply, the urgency of demand affording sudden oppor-tunities to new production talent and programme formats – and effectively laying the way for new TV series aimed more explicitly at a youth audience.

British TV saw no teen sitcoms in the vein of *The Many Loves of Dobie Gillis*, and little US teen TV reached British schedules. But domestic pop shows such as *Six-Five Special* (BBC, 1957–1958) and *Juke Box Jury* (BBC, 1959–1967) proved popular. These series, however, still made conces-sions to an adult audience through the inclusion of variety entertainers and dinner-jacketed compères, but the launch of *Oh Boy!* (ITV, 1958–1959) – a pop show broadcast live from the Hackney Empire – heralded the rise of a quick-fire format aimed squarely at youth. The genre was further developed with the launch of ITV's pop flagship, *Ready, Steady, Go!* (1963–1966). Initially, the programme harked back to earlier traditions, with avuncular host Keith Fordyce ensuring the pop party never got out of hand. Fordyce, however, soon looked out of place. Trading on the 1960s explosion in beat music and the rise of mod subcul-ture, *Ready, Steady, Go!* increasingly revelled in teen exclusivity and Fordyce was gradually edged out in favour of his bubbly co-presenter, nineteen-year-old Cathy McGowan.

The British film industry, too, made overtures to youth. Britain had nothing to match the scale of the American 'teenpic' phenomenon, but

British filmmakers made a pitch to young cinemagoers with films featuring popular singing stars. Tommy Steele, for example, starred in *The Tommy Steele Story* (1957), while Cliff Richard featured in *Expresso Bongo* (1959), *The Young Ones* (1961), *Summer Holiday* (1963) and *Wonderful Life* (1964).[12] The British pop industry also thrived on the growth of the youth market. The initial wave of American rock 'n' rollers (Bill Haley, Chuck Berry, Little Richard, Elvis Presley) were soon joined by the home-grown talents of Adam Faith, Billy Fury, Cliff Richard, Tommy Steele and Marty Wilde. And, with the 1960s boom in beat music, British bands such as the Beatles and the Rolling Stones were soon dominating the world of pop.

The Beatles, in particular, were a spectacular media and commercial phenomenon. In 1962 the Fab Four already enjoyed moderate success, though were still only one among a motley assortment of aspiring popsters. In 1963 it all changed and, by December, Beatlemania was in full flood. With seven of their records presiding over the Top Twenty, the band headlined a Royal Variety Performance and their every appearance was besieged by hordes of screaming fans. Merchandisers raced to cash-in on the frenzy. High streets brimmed with all manner of Beatle-bounty (from collarless Beatle jackets, to plastic figurines and bubblegum cards), and in London's Bethnal Green a factory toiled round-the-clock to meet the voracious demand for 'Beatle Wigs'. The following year the band became a global commodity. In early 1964 the Beatles played their first concerts in America and were showcased on television's *Ed Sullivan Show*. At each event they were swamped by ecstatic crowds and, in 1964 alone, American stores sold an estimated $50 million worth of Beatles merchandise (Davies, 1978: 219).

## 'THE NEW GENERATION': THE SHIFTING DYNAMICS OF THE YOUTH MARKET

In both America and Britain, then, previous levels of youth consumption were thrown into the shade by the 'teenage' markets that emerged during the 1950s and 1960s. As changes in lifestyles and labour markets delivered greater economic power to the young, the media and leisure industries (serviced by a new army of advertisers and marketers) scurried to exploit the lucrative potential of youth spending.

The 'youth' market was also creeping up the age scale. Increasingly, more mature consumers – adults in their twenties, thirties and older – adopted the outlooks and interests associated with youth culture. Indeed, Ron Eyerman and Andrew Jamison argue that during the 1960s youth:

became the model and set standards for the rest of society in many spheres of culture, from the most superficial like clothing and hair-styles, to the most deeply rooted like the basic social interactions of men and women and blacks and whites.

(Eyerman and Jamison, 1998: 113)

During the 1960s the affluent and upwardly-mobile middle class, especially, were keen to embrace products and media whose 'youthful' connotations seemed to guarantee a hedonistic and independent lifestyle. Advertisers worked hard to foster this association, Thomas Frank (1997) showing how a 'creative revolution' in American advertising saw marketers habitually mobilise 'youth' as an aphorism for fun, freedom and consumer fulfilment. The trend registered across a wide range of products and advertising campaigns of the 1960s, but was probably best encapsulated by the success of the Ford Mustang. First rolling off assembly lines in 1964, the sporty Mustang was designed to be a 'youth' car – exploiting the profitable youth market, but also appealing to older consumers who sought to identify with 'youthful' themes of adventure and fun. And, indeed, the Mustang was a major hit in older markets, 16 per cent of first-year sales going to men in the 45 to 55 age bracket.

From the mid-1960s to the early 1970s, on both sides of the Atlantic, the emergence of new consumer groups ensured the continued buoyancy of the youth market. In Britain, for example, the expansion of higher education increased the market potential of middle-class youngsters. Between 1963 and 1971 the total population of students in full-time education doubled, reaching a figure of 457,000. The expansion was intended to improve working-class students' access to higher education, but the opportunities were exploited most successfully by the middle class. Compared to their working peers, students commanded relatively small disposable incomes, but the experience of studenthood offered other compensations – not least, greater amounts of leisure time and the independence of living away from the parental home – hence students were increasingly targeted by the media and consumer industries.

In the US, African-American youth became a more prominent consumer market. Although white racism and economic inequality remained entrenched, by the early 1960s the combination of civil rights activism and greater employment opportunities had improved living standards for many African-Americans, who gradually emerged as a significant consumer group. This was reflected in the realm of youth culture by the soul music boom of the 1960s. The success of Detroit's Tamla-Motown record labels was indicative. Founded by musician and producer Berry Gordy Jr in 1959, Motown broke into the commercial mainstream in 1962, scoring six top-ten hits in the *Billboard* chart. Further success followed, with fourteen hits in 1966, thirteen in 1967 and ten in 1968. Motown emerged as the most successful independent record company in the US, and by 1973 Gordy was Chairman of Motown Industries – a multi-million-dollar company that boasted record, motion picture, television and publishing divisions. Motown's output appealed to both black and white audiences, but the success of other soul labels (for example, Atlantic and Stax) was based more squarely on the African-American market, while the early 1970s saw most major record companies introduce divisions to deal specifically with black music (Negus, 1998: 369). TV executives and advertisers also began to pay more attention to black youth culture and African-American audiences. In 1970, for example, the Chicago TV station, WCIU, launched *Soul Train* as a black counterpart to *American Bandstand*, the show's success leading to its syndication the following year, while youth-oriented TV dramas such as *Room 222* (ABC, 1969–1974) and situation comedies such as *What's Happening!!* (ABC, 1976–1979) began to focus on the experiences of young African-Americans.

Throughout the 1970s and 1980s, in both Britain and America, the youth market remained a cornerstone of the media and consumer industries. From the mid-1970s, however, a combination of demographic trends and economic recession began to shake the commercial confidence that had characterised the 'jackpot' years of the 1950s and 1960s. Decreasing birth rates brought a decline in the size of teenage populations on both sides of the Atlantic as the 'baby boomers' made way for the 'baby bust' generation. In the US, for example, the proportion of the national population aged under 18 rose from 31 per cent in 1950 to 36 per cent in 1960, but then dropped to 28 per cent by 1980 (Department of Health and Human Services, 1998: 16). In Britain, too, falling birth rates were significant; the proportion of the population aged under 16 dropping from a high point of 25 per cent in 1961 to 20 per cent by 1990 (Office of National Statistics, 1999).

At the same time, the favourable economic conditions that had paved the way for the post-war explosion of youth consumption – economic growth, full employment and rising living standards – increasingly unravelled during the 1970s. Advanced capitalist economies slid into a long downturn punctuated by particularly severe recessions in the mid-1970s, the early 1980s and the early 1990s. Youth employment was a major casualty of the slump. In the US the jobless rate for teenagers hovered at around 15 per cent throughout the late 1980s (Stern *et al.*, 1995: 5), while in Britain the labour markets that had buoyed-up levels of youth employment during the 1950s and 1960s steadily contracted so that by

1986 the number of unemployed aged between 16 and 24 had reached 727,000 – nearly a third of Britain's jobless total (International Labour Office, 1988: 651). Generally, young people's routes into employment were extended and became more unpredictable. Labour market shifts saw many youngsters channelled into low-paid and part-time 'McJobs',[13] while others were displaced into a proliferation of training schemes and educational provision.[14] As Phil Cohen and Pat Ainley explained, young people entering this new economic environment found themselves pioneering:

> a life cycle paradigm which entails moving from education to part-time work interspersed with periods of education and training. Many young people find themselves moving from one scheme and training course to another without ever entering full-time, secure employment.
>
> (Cohen and Ainley, 2000: 83)

In this context, many young people faced bleak prospects. In America, for example, researchers such as Donna Gaines (1991, 1994) revealed the existence of a 'teenage wasteland' – an alienated sub-stratum of American youth who struggled with the hardships of social and economic disfranchisement. In Britain, too, large numbers of young people were excluded from consumer prosperity, Robert Macdonald (1997) arguing that increases in unemployment and homelessness during the 1990s had created a youth 'underclass' that was marginalised (both culturally and economically) from mainstream society. Equally desolate was Ian Brinkley's (1998) portrait of an 'underworked and underpaid' generation that had born the brunt of restructured labour markets, rising joblessness and cuts in welfare benefits, while Cindi Katz argued that profound shifts in the global economy had 'cut a swathe' through the everyday environments of young people all over the world – with movements of capital, the decline of manufacturing economies and the transformation of labour markets combining to shatter the social and economic certainties that young people had once taken for granted (Katz, 1998: 130).

During the 1980s and early 1990s the rise of youth unemployment, coupled with the decline in the youth populations of most Western countries, prompted pessimism about the youth market's commercial potential. Reflecting on American marketing trends, for example, Hollander and Germain observed that 'emphasis on the youth market declined somewhat' during the 1980s with 'fewer marketing research and advertising agencies claim[ing] to specialize in the youth market during that decade than was true during the 1960s' (Hollander and Germain,

1993: 110). In Britain, too, many commentators were uncertain about the youth market's future. Fiona Stewart, for example, speculated that the 1990s might see 'the commercial and cultural centre of gravity . . . shift up the age spectrum to the middle age group', with the consequence that '"young people" will no longer be the drivers of change that they have been perceived to be over the past thirty years' (Stewart, 1992: 207, 225). And, indeed, the 1980s and 1990s saw many consumer and media industries direct attention towards older market segments, in particular 'empty nesters' and the 'thirty-something' generation.

Reports of the youth market's death, however, were greatly exaggerated. Indeed, despite rising levels of youth unemployment, the 1980s were a time of relative prosperity for many youngsters. In America, for example, Dennis Tootelian and Ralph Gaedeke calculated that although the teenage population had dropped by 15.5 per cent during the 1980s, their collective spending power actually increased by nearly 43 per cent, with individual consumer spending rising from $1,422 to $2,409 per capita (Tootelian and Gaedeke, 1992: 35). Those British youngsters lucky enough to be in full-time employment (or who could rely on well-heeled parents) also enjoyed a measure of affluence – and were even fêted by marketers and advertisers as the embodiment of a wider spirit of thrusting entrepreneurialism and hectic consumerism. For example, in their 1988 report, *Youth Lifestyle*, market analysts Mintel claimed to have discovered among British youth a 'new consumption and success ethic' that had been generated by 'the sustained economic growth of the enterprise culture' (Mintel, 1988: 23). In a similar vein, McCann-Erickson's international survey, *The New Generation*, identified a 'New Wave' of 'post-permissive' youngsters who exhibited 'the most highly developed form of the new multi-profile consumption in our society' (McCann-Erickson Worldwide, 1989: 25).

Generally, the 1980s saw the youth market survive as a mainstay of media and consumer industries. While some youth-oriented media forms withered away, others quickly emerged to take their place. In America, for example, the drive-in movie circuit (already struggling by the 1970s) virtually disappeared during the 1980s as new competition surfaced in the form of mall and multiplex cinemas.[15] But, while the era of the classic 'teenpic' had passed away, Doherty (2002: 198) notes how the youth audience remained a key Hollywood market and spurred the rise of new 'teen' movie genres. The box office success of *Halloween* (1977) and *Friday 13th* (1978), for example, was followed by a prolific cycle of teen 'axploitation' horror movies, while *The Breakfast Club* (1985) and *St. Elmo's Fire* (1985) heralded a succession of self-absorbed 'Brat Pack' films. The success of the *Porky's* movie series (1981, 1983, 1985),

meanwhile, signposted the arrival of the teen sex comedy, a genre
sustained in films such as the *American Pie* trilogy (1999, 2001, 2003) and
the less than hilarious comedies *Road Trip: Unseen and Explicit* (2000) and
*Dude, Where's My Car?* (2000).[16] For the television industry, too, youth
remained a crucial audience. Indeed, from the moment it began broadcasting in 1986, the Fox network was candid in its intention to go after
the youth market, and across American TV the 1980s and 1990s saw the
appearance of a horde of new 'teen-oriented' dramas and soap operas,
such as *21 Jump Street* (Fox, 1987–1990), *Beverley Hills 90210* (Fox,
1990–2000) and *Dawson's Creek* (WB, 1998–2003).[17]

The 1980s also saw the emergence of new media formats to compete
against, and ultimately eclipse, older systems. Launched by Sony in 1982,
for example, the Compact Disc (CD) quickly developed as an internationally accepted standard, ushering in the age of digital audio technology
and ultimately shunting vinyl records into specialised markets. The
launch of MTV in 1981, meanwhile, not only initiated cable and satellite TV programming aimed at youth, but also provided the impetus for
the rise of music videos as an important adjunct to the record industry.

Despite the recessions of the 1980s and early 1990s, then, youth continued to be a lucrative and influential consumer market. By the beginning of the new millennium, moreover, demographic shifts and economic
trends seemed to signal a return to the 'jackpot' days of the 1950s
and 1960s. Although the long-term decline in birth rates continued, the
youth populations of both Britain and America were set to grow during
the early twenty-first century as the 'echo' of the 'baby boom' worked
its way through each country's demographic profile. In Britain, projec-
tions suggested that by 2010 the teenage population would stand at
5.6 million, or 800,000 (16 per cent) more than in 1992 (Gunter and
Farnham, 1998: 5). For market research gurus this represented exciting
vistas of commercial opportunity. In 1999, for example, Market
Assessment International (MAI) hailed the arrival of 'Millennium Youth'
or the 'M-Generation'. According to MAI's research, the first teenagers
to come of age in the new century were 'richer than any previous generation – if measured in terms of possession of consumer durables and personal disposal income', with 80 per cent of Britain's 11- to 16-year-olds
owning their own television and 83 per cent possessing their own bank
account (MAI, 1999: 4).

In the US, developments seemed even more dramatic. During the late
1990s social and market researchers began talking of a new 'baby
boomlet' (Finard, 1998: 6) and the possibility of a fresh 'youthquake'
(COTS, 1997), as the children of the original 'baby boom' generation
matured and the number of American teenagers steadily grew. By 2000

the US teenage population stood at 31.6 million, nearly 6 per cent higher than the 'baby boomer' peak of 29.9 million in 1976 (US Census Bureau, 2001). Even more than their British cousins, American marketers were energised at the prospect of this 'Teen Dream for Investors' (*Business Week*, 15 July 2002). A PBS TV special aired in February 2001, for example, spotlighted the army of market analysts and advertisers eagerly chasing 'the hottest consumer demographic in America' – the 'largest generation of teenagers ever' who 'last year . . . spent more than $100 billion themselves and pushed their parents to spend another $50 billion on top of that'.[18] The following year, meanwhile, commercial enthusiasm reached fever pitch. In a widely publicised report, youth market analysts Teenage Research Unlimited (TRU) announced that since 1996 teen spending in the US had climbed from $122 billion to $172 billion a year, TRU estimating that between 1998 and 2001 the discretionary spending of the average American teen had increased from $78 to more than $104 a week (TRU, 2002a).

The recessions and industrial restructuring of the 1970s, 1980s and early 1990s, then, undermined the economic conditions that had been the basis of the boom in teenage consumption during the 1950s and 1960s. Nevertheless, in both the US and Europe the youth market continued to represent a lucrative and influential business sector. The late 1990s, in fact, saw a combination of economic, demographic and cultural trends come together to re-energise youth-oriented media and marketing, with 'youthful' tastes and values coming to define desirable consumer lifestyles. Indeed, the next chapter shows how 'youth media' have been central to recent changes in the organisation and operation of media and consumer business – in particular, trends towards industry conglomeration, synergy and internationalisation, and the increasing 'segmentation' of consumer markets and media audiences.

# BRAVE NEW WORLD

## 'Youth media', business conglomeration and post-Fordism

> The word 'teenage' was coined as a marketing term in the Fifties, so it's pretty much in its dotage by now. You can tell as much by looking at the age of the practitioners. A generation of cultural entrepreneurs gets rich on staying forever young – think of Matthew Freud, marrying his fortune with the Murdoch dynasty and still wearing his leather trousers, or Jamie Palumbo, flogging off parts of the Ministry of Sound to a venture capital group.
>
> (Rachel Newsome, 2001)

## 'YOUTH MEDIA' AND THE CHANGING BUSINESS LANDSCAPE

Acclaimed as the 'CEO of Hip-Hop' by *Business Week* in 2003, Russell Simmons represents one of America's most illustrious media magnates (*Business Week*, 27 October 2003). Growing up in New York, as a student Simmons had spent his spare time promoting parties and club shows around Harlem and Queens. During the early 1980s he honed his entre-preneurial skills managing his brother's popular rap trio, Run DMC, and in 1984 he joined Rick Rubin (a record producer and punk rock fan) in co-founding Def Jam records, a label whose impressive roster of rap artists – including Public Enemy, L.L. Cool J and the Beastie Boys – helped take hip-hop to the centre of American (and subsequently global) popular culture. Following Rubin's acrimonious departure in 1988, Simmons became head of Def Jam and began transforming the company into a multi-sector business empire. By 2003 Simmons was heading Rush

Communications, a vast corporation that encompassed a footwear company, an advertising agency, a luxury watch company and clothing lines that alone grossed around $400 million a year (*Ebony*, July 2003).

Simmons' huge business successes were indicative of the way the media and cultural industries had become increasingly central to the operation of capitalist economies. They also exemplified the way the youth market and its associated industries had, by the end of the twentieth century, become influential aspects of economic and cultural life. But Simmons career and the development of his companies also illustrated broader trends in the organisation and operation of modern media enterprise. The variety of Simmons' interlocked business interests, for example, was typical of trends towards commercial diversification. In 1985 Simmons had already branched out of the music industry into film production with the release of *Krush Groove* (a fictionalised account of Def Jam's founding). In 1988 he followed up with *Tougher Than Leather* (a vehicle for Run DMC), and in 1995 with the hip-hop documentary *The Show* and actor Eddie Murphy's comedy hit, *The Nutty Professor*. Further box-office success came with the release of *Gridlock'd* and *How to Be a Player* (both 1997). The early 1990s also saw Simmons extend his reach into TV production with the groundbreaking HBO series, *Russell Simmons' Def Comedy Jam* (1992–1998) – a forum for black stand-up comedians to perform uncensored routines for a wider audience – while in 1992 he established the fashionable sportswear label, Phat Farm ('classic American flava with a twist'). Meanwhile, 1996 saw the launch of Simmons' hip-hop lifestyle magazine, *One World* (which, in turn, spawned a syndicated TV show), and in 2003 he was even moving into the beverage market with the launch of Defcon3 – a high-energy soft drink.

Simmons attention to crafting his brands' image – especially the development of his Def Jam and Phat Farm labels – also exemplified broader trends towards the 'aestheticisation' of media products and consumer goods, as companies worked increasingly hard to invest their products with cultural values that would appeal to particular groups of buyers. The rise of vast business conglomerates was also embodied in the growth of Rush Communications, the multi-faceted corporation that administered Simmons' sprawling business network. Although he remained head of Rush, in 1999 Simmons sold his share of Def Jam to the Universal Music Group for a reported $100 million dollars in a move that, again, exemplified shifts towards conglomeration and a concentration of ownership within the modern media.

This chapter explores the role of youth culture and the youth market within these broad trends in the organisation and operation of media and consumer industries. It begins with a survey of shifts towards business conglomeration and internationalisation, and the ways these have registered in the field of 'youth media'. Developments in marketing practice and advertising are also explored, with attention given to the 'post-Fordist' targeting of more differentiated youth audiences and consumer groups. The chapter concludes with a consideration of recent trends towards the 'aestheticisation' of economic activity, and a discussion of the way media and consumer industries have increasingly drawn on 'youthful' tastes and values in an effort to associate their products with particular kinds of consumer lifestyle.

## CONGLOMERATION, INTERNATIONALISATION AND SYNERGY IN THE YOUTH MARKET

During the 1980s and 1990s developments in the youth market and its related industries were constituent in wider processes of economic change. To a large part, these developments stemmed from an intensification of international business competition. By the late 1960s the emergence of a new, more volatile world market was already detectable. During the 1970s, however, the trend became more pronounced as a consequence of saturated Western markets, increased competition from Japan and newly industrialised nations (such as Taiwan, Korea and Singapore), and the rise in international oil prices. In response to these pressures, business sought to adapt and realign. According to authors such as David Hesmondhalgh (2002), the more competitive and less predictable market environment encouraged companies to secure their economic survival by adopting strategies of horizontal integration (buying-up rivals who operated in the same industrial sector), vertical integration (taking control of companies involved at different stages of production and circulation), internationalisation (buying or partnering companies abroad) and multi-sector integration (buying into related industries to ensure a cross-promotion of products) (Hesmondhalgh, 2002: 20).[1] At the same time, these strategies were spurred-on by the 'free market' policies that were the hallmark of governments elected in both Britain and America (and many other advanced capitalist nations) during the 1980s and 1990s. By the end of the twentieth century, therefore, a combination of intensified economic competition and market deregulation had led to the emergence of huge, multi-interest business conglomerates whose corporate strategies straddled national boundaries in an increasingly interconnected (but unevenly developed) world economy.

Processes of internationalisation and integration were not unique to the media and consumer industries of the 1980s and 1990s. In the youth market, for example, the international success of Elvis Presley during the 1950s and the worldwide grip of 'Beatlemania' during the 1960s were early signposts of the emergence of 'global' media phenomena. Mary Celeste Kearney (2005), meanwhile, has shown that practices of cross-media promotion – or synergy – existed in America long before the 1980s. During the 1950s, Kearney argues, youth-oriented TV shows such as *A Date with Judy* (ABC, 1951–1953) and *Meet Corliss Archer* (CBS, 1951–1952; syndicated 1954–1955), developed from earlier radio series and subsequently appeared across a profusion of media formats (the two TV series being joined by a plethora of stage plays, books, magazines and films). During the 1980s and 1990s, however, trends towards interna-tionalisation and cross-promotion were significantly accelerated by a succession of company mergers and acquisitions. These processes of busi-ness integration and conglomeration were clearly evident in the youth market and its associated industries, with the production and circulation of media geared to young audiences increasingly dominated by a coterie of massive corporations – AOL Time Warner, Viacom, Disney, News Corporation, Vivendi Universal, Sony and Bertelsmann AG.

The biggest of these 'magnificent seven' was AOL Time Warner. Forged in January 2001 through a $165 billion mega-merger between AOL and Time Warner, this media powerhouse controlled an array of internet, telephone and TV platforms, as well as a host of publishing and sports interests. For example, alongside the AOL internet service provider and TV networks such as HBO, TNT and the Cartoon Network, the media Goliath owned publishing concerns such as DC Comics and *MAD* magazine, as well as a roster of record companies that included not only industry majors such as Warner Bros., but also more specialised (formerly independent) labels such as Rhino, Sub Pop and Tommy Boy. Another American-based media giant was Viacom. Formed in May 2000 through a merger agreement between Viacom and the CBS Corporation, its international media interests embraced TV networks such as MTV and VH1, around 180 radio stations, Paramount Pictures, the Blockbuster video rental chain and the *Star Trek* franchise. Disney also emerged as a global media conglomerate, with revenues that topped $25 billion in 2000 – around 27 per cent of which was derived from its theme parks and resorts, 24 per cent from studio entertainment and a further 17 per cent from a media empire that included the Disney Channel and the ABC television network.

Rupert Murdoch also emerged as a media Titan. By the end of 2000 the Australian mogul's News Corporation had assets totalling $38 billion. With holdings throughout North America, Europe, Australia, Latin America and Asia, Murdoch's media stable included such well-known names as Twentieth Century Fox, the Fox TV network, British Sky Broadcasting and newspapers such as (in the US) the *New York Post* and (in Britain) *The Times* and *The Sun*. Vivendi Universal was also huge. Created in December 2000 through an international merger of Vivendi, Canal+ and The Seagram Company Ltd, the union combined Vivendi's communications assets with Canal+'s broadcast capacity and Seagram's film, TV and music interests. With the giant Universal Music Group as one of its subsidiaries, Vivendi Universal effectively became the leading music company in the world through its control of labels such as MCA, Polygram, Island/Def Jam, Motown, Decca and Geffen.

Another key player in the music industry was Sony. The Sony Corporation began life in 1946 as Tokyo Telecommunications Engineering but, alongside its valuable non-media assets (most obviously its electronics division), Sony also developed into a major media concern. By the end of the 1990s Sony had colossal holdings in the markets for both media 'hardware' and 'software', the Corporation gaining control of film companies such as Columbia and TriStar Pictures, an array of cable TV channels, together with record labels such as Columbia and Epic. The other leading media conglomerate to emerge during the 1980s and 1990s was Bertelsmann AG. A German-based corporation whose interests extended to more than 600 companies in 53 countries, Bertelsmann's sales figures topped $13 billion in 1999. In November 2000, moreover, Bertelsmann made headline news after agreeing to lend $50 million to the internet provider Napster for the design of technology that would force customers to pay for the download of music files. Bertelsmann's aim was to expand its media empire ever-further, using Napster's file-sharing technology as a platform through which users could ultimately download films, books, TV programmes and a wealth of other media products. In 2003, meanwhile, in response to sliding music sales, Bertelsmann and Sony announced plans to merge their music divisions. The proposed alliance would establish Sony BMG (to be equally owned by Sony and Bertelsmann), a company that would control 25.2 per cent of the global market for recorded music – marginally smaller than the 25.9 per cent share commanded by Vivendi Universal.

Alongside this conglomeration of business interests, media industries have also increasingly operated on a transnational basis. Major political events in the late twentieth century (for example, the break-up of the Soviet Union and trends towards deregulation in the world economy) had a major impact on the strategic thinking of media corporations. The prospect of new market opportunities in eastern Europe, China, southern Africa and Latin America prompted many businesses to adopt a 'global' strategy in their ventures, re-mapping the world in terms of a series of regional market blocs. The history of MTV, with its firm youth audience, is exemplary. From the mid-1980s MTV rapidly expanded its overseas operations, beginning broadcasting to Western Europe in 1987 and moving into Eastern Europe with the launch of a service in Hungary in 1988. Further expansion followed during the early 1990s as MTV established networks in Japan, Latin America and Australia, so that by 1991 (MTV's tenth anniversary), the station could claim to be broadcasting in 41 countries and reaching 204 million homes (Levinson, 1995).

During the 1980s and 1990s trends towards media cross-promotion (or synergy) also became more pronounced as corporations sought to increase efficiency across their holdings by developing comprehensive systems of transmedia exploitation. Again, MTV serves as a good example. Owned by the vertically-integrated media empire Viacom, MTV was part of a wider corporate entity that included the film studio Paramount, the Blockbuster video rental chain and a bulging portfolio of other media holdings. Effectively, then, much of the entertainment 'news' and features delivered by MTV – for example, a Justin Timberlake video or a TV 'special' on Britney Spears' movie, *Crossroads* (2002) – served as a way of promoting other Viacom products. Rupert Murdoch's News Corporation exploited its TV series *The X-Files* (1993–2002) in a similar fashion. A show that generated a major cult following among young audiences, *The X-Files* was not only produced by the media giant, it was also aired on its Fox TV network and endlessly repeated on Fox's 22 affiliated stations and FX cable network. A welter of *X-Files* books and merchandise, meanwhile, further milked the product. Indeed, the late twentieth century saw merchandise 'tie-ins' emerge as a hugely profitable example of media synergy. By the late 1990s, for example, many feature films were generating four times more profit from related merchandising and licensing than from their domestic box office earnings.

'Branding' also emerged as an important dimension to the operation of the media and consumer industries. During the 1980s and 1990s corporations increasingly viewed brand names as strategic economic assets. In the youth market, especially, a brand's image was increasingly seen as an important economic property, with the symbolic associations of a brand name or logo – for example, the Nike 'swoosh' or the Stüssy 'signature' – allowing products to be linked with distinct values and identities. Fashion companies were in the forefront of this trend towards a more systematic exploitation of brand image, Paul Smith (1997) showing how the clothing company Tommy Hilfiger developed a particularly methodical and aggressive approach in the licensing of its brand name.

Trends towards conglomeration, global promotion, synergy and branding were not confined to the biggest media empires. The same strategies were also adopted by nominally 'independent', players in the youth market. The history of Ministry of Sound, Britain's leading dance club, is illustrative. The brainchild of James Palumbo (the son of Lord Palumbo, a property tycoon), the south London nightclub was opened in a disused bus depot in 1991. The club was transformed into a major money-spinner after the 1994 Criminal Justice Act tightened the control of outdoor dance events and pushed many smaller rave organisers out of business (see Chapter 5). By the end of the decade Ministry of Sound had developed into a 'superclub', with an annual turnover in excess of £100 million and impressive interests across the record, magazine and fashion industries. For instance, after releasing its first album in 1993, by 2001 Ministry of Sound had become not only the UK's largest independent record label (with album sales topping the 15 million mark), but also a powerful global business that boasted offices in London, Berlin, Sydney and New York. Additional product synergy was provided through expansion into other business sectors. *Ministry*, a dance music magazine with a readership of 300,000, was launched in 1998,[2] while the Ministry of Sound logo was emblazoned across merchandise ranging from puffa jackets and beach towels to DJ headphones and disposable cameras. Ministry's radio show, meanwhile, was syndicated in 38 different countries by the end of 2001 and the club's touring division (with annual club tours of Australia, Europe and America) provided further global reach. Ministry also established lucrative club residencies in Ibiza, Ayia Napa and Benidorm, and in 2001 moved into the organisation of large-scale events with a New Year's Eve party at London's Millennium Dome that attracted 18,000 people.[3] In 2001 Ministry was even mooting the idea of an airborne nightclub in Australia, with events staged in modified airliners. The same year also saw moves towards merger and conglomeration, as 3i (Europe's largest venture capital group with media holdings across three continents) bought a 24 per cent stake in Ministry for close to £24 million – a 3i spokesman announcing:

> This is another significant investment for 3i's Media team. Ministry of Sound is a high quality and fast growing business . . . With our support, we hope they will develop into a globally recognised media brand. We are pleased to be a part of their exciting future.[4]
>
> (LongAcre, 2001)

American 'independents' also adopted business strategies akin to the major corporations. Hip-hop magazine *The Source*, for example, began life in 1988 as a crudely photocopied news-sheet published by Harvard business student David Mays and his friends. Ten years later it had not only grown into a glossy monthly with a circulation of over 400,000 but had spawned The Source Enterprises Inc. – a multi-media business worth around $100 million, with interests spread across publishing, radio and TV, a horde of hip-hop compilation CDs and an internet site dedicated to hip-hop music, culture and politics. Bad Boy Entertainment adopted similar commercial strategies. Founded by Sean 'Puffy' Combs in 1993, by the end of the 1990s the rap record label had a turnover in excess of $100 million, and Combs had become an *über*-celebrity who presided over a multi-sector corporation that included a movie production company, two restaurants and the Sean John clothing line.

During the 1980s and 1990s, therefore, developments in youth-oriented media and related industries exemplified broader shifts towards business conglomeration, internationalisation, synergy and branding. Some commentators, however, were deeply critical of these trends. According to some observers, moves towards global business conglomeration were accompanied by a deeply exploitative international division of labour. During the 1990s this critique was articulated by a broadly-based (though often quite young) anti-globalisation movement that sought to challenge the grip of the transnational corporations. In November 1999, for example, a conference of the World Trade Organisation in Seattle was confronted by 50,000 demonstrators, while 2001 saw further protests at the World Economic Forum in Salzburg and the G-8 Summit in Genoa. The anti-globalisation movement found an unofficial spokeswoman in the figure of Canadian journalist, Naomi Klein. In her best-selling book, *No Logo* (2000), Klein launched a broadside against the power of multinational companies. According to Klein, processes of merger and synergy had allowed huge corporations to seize the reins of the global economy, with business conglomerates able to manipulate world markets to their own advantage. Klein was particularly critical of what she saw as the growing cultural ubiquity of advertising and marketing. For Klein, the phenomenon of corporate branding was especially insidious, the symbolic connotations of brand names and logos becoming more important than the actual products they adorned. With the expansion of large brands, Klein claimed, consumer choice had narrowed, as smaller companies struggled to compete against the aggressive business strategies of the multinationals. Moreover, in an era where image had become nearly everything, Klein portrayed consumers as being transformed into brand-obsessed zombies, or 'walking, talking, life-sized Tommy [Hilfiger] dolls, mummified in fully branded Tommy worlds' (Klein, 2000: 28).

As we shall see in Chapter 6, Klein's depiction of consumers as a mass of manipulated dupes is deeply problematic. But her account of the

**Figure 3.1** Sean 'Puffy' Combs at the 2001 MTV Movie Awards
Courtesy of Pictorial Press

inequalities of the global economy and the exploitative character of the international division of labour has more merit. In 2003, for example, the leaders of a workers' rights group in Honduras claimed that the employees of a company supplying the Sean John fashion label worked 11- to 12-hour shifts and were paid around 24 cents for sewing a single $50 Sean John sweatshirt.[5] Even at the hippest end of the youth market, then, global business networks and their systems of subcontracting have often been profoundly unequal and exploitative.

## BUY, BUY, BABY: MARKET SEGMENTATION AND 'YOUTH MEDIA'

Recent developments in the youth-oriented media and consumer industries can also be seen as constituent in other important shifts in patterns of business organisation and operation. According to some theorists, for example, since the late 1960s modern capitalist economies have undergone a fundamental transformation – moving from a 'Fordist' era of mass production for mass consumer markets, into a new, 'post-Fordist' epoch of flexible production for a profusion of differentiated market segments.[6] In contrast to the mass production of standardised goods characteristic of Fordist enterprise, post-Fordist business practice is characterised by the deployment of sophisticated technology in more flexible forms of manufacture and distribution, with the production of small batches of goods geared to a plurality of market segments. Style, image and marketing practice are also seen as playing a more important role in post-Fordist economic life, as businesses strive to invest their products with values and meanings that will appeal to buyers associated with specific 'lifestyles' and market 'niches' (Murray, 1989: 43).

According to Stanley Hollander and Richard Germain (1993), these kinds of development have been evidenced especially clearly in the field of youth marketing. For Hollander and Germain, contemporary appeals to an array of 'niche' groups of young consumers are a marked contrast to the approach taken during the 1950s, when products were pitched to a more homogenous youth market:

> True, the products, services, and marketing appeals that were being aimed at youth [during the 1950s] were differentiated from those designed for younger and older groups. But whether we look at apparel or popular music or some other youth-oriented category of offerings, we see things that were intended for *masses* of youths.
>
> (Hollander and Germain, 1993: 107)

In some ways, however, the production of 'teenage' media and consumer goods during the 1950s could, in itself, be seen as a pioneering move away from concepts of a monolithic 'mass' market. In this respect, the practice of interpellating youth as a discrete consumer group, associated with particular tastes and interests, could be seen as an early form of 'post-Fordist' marketing strategy. Nevertheless, while 'niche' segmentation may have first emerged in the youth market of the 1950s and 1960s, 30 years later its significance was extended by a combination of technological development and business deregulation. In both Britain and America, for example, the introduction of cable and satellite delivery systems, combined with a relaxation of controls on media ownership, allowed moves towards 'narrowcasting' – a style of programming that eschewed appeals to mass audiences in favour of smaller, more nuanced audience groups. As a consequence, the 1980s and 1990s saw a proliferation of cable and satellite TV stations targeted at particular sections of the youth audience. In Britain, for example, the menu of choices stretched from the interactive smorgasbord available on The Box ('Smash Hits You Control'), to the remorseless helpings of heavy rock served up on Kerrang! ('Life Is Loud 24/7'). Music Choice, meanwhile, tempted viewers with a selection of over 30 specialised options (from 'Hard Rock' to 'Chillout Gold'), while MTV's eight specially devoted channels included the R'n'B and urban music channel MTV Base ('Check out the booty shakin', bumpin' and grindin' that went down at the hardest beach party ever'), and MTV Dance ('Droppin' in some bangin' tunes to get you in the party mood'). With the introduction of digital technology, moreover, further segmentation within the youth audience seemed set to follow. In Britain, for example, 2002 saw the BBC extend its digital radio service through the launch of 1Xtra – a digital station whose mix of hip-hop and UK garage made it 'the home of new black music'.[7]

Similar moves towards market segmentation were also evident in the magazine industry. Titles geared to young readerships that identified with specific music genres or interests were nothing new, but the 1980s and 1990s saw the rise of titles whose seamless flow of glossy features and advertisements was pitched to distinctive lifestyles and tastes. American news-stands, for example, saw the appearance of titles such as Thrasher ('Skate and Destroy', launched in 1981) and Big Cheese ('Hardcore Lifestyle', 1996), magazines focused on the skateboard and alternative music scenes. In Britain, meanwhile, the 1980s saw the arrival of slick style-Bibles such as The Face and i-D (both launched in 1980), followed in the 1990s by a new generation of irreverent style magazines geared to fashion-conscious club-goers – a roster of titles that included

*Dazed and Confused* (launched in 1990) and Swinstead Publishing's stablemates *Jockey Slut* ('Disco Pogo for Punks in Pumps', 1993) and *Sleazenation* (1996).

Quickly developing into internationally distributed style magazines, the success of *Jockey Slut* and *Sleazenation* allowed Swinstead (an up-and-coming publishing independent) to expand and diversify. Transforming itself into a 'one-stop youth solutions company', Swinstead's services grew to include brand consultancy, distribution, events management, contract publishing and online assistance to firms wanting to tap into the youth market. Swinstead's success was also shared by many other relatively small, independent media companies during the 1980s and 1990s. Indeed, as Hesmondhalgh (2002: 60) has observed, alongside the growth of vast business conglomerates, the period also saw a proliferation of smaller 'independents'. Partly, this was indebted to ideological factors, governments' commitment to the free market finding its corollary in a rhetoric that encouraged entrepreneurial endeavour. But probably more important were technological developments that freed many production processes from dependence on large workforces, big plants and expensive machinery. Changes in patterns of business organisation were also crucial. Facing a more competitive economic environment, many large firms took advantage of new technologies to reduce labour costs, but they also responded by subcontracting many of the functions of the main business to an army of smaller organisations. The aim was to create a solid business 'core' that outsourced work to a range of smaller media and manufacturing firms whose flexibility allowed them to respond quickly to changes in taste and demand – but who could be easily 'jettisoned' by the core if changing market conditions required.[8]

According to some accounts, the rise of this 'post-Fordist' business environment has had a positive impact in the realm of 'youth media'. In their account of the British dance music scene of the late 1990s, for example, Richard Smith and Tim Maughan (1998) argue that the greater availability of recording technology laid the way for the emergence of a host of independent 'micro-labels' associated with the wide spectrum of dance music genres and sub-genres. Smith and Maughan see the rise of these 'micro-labels' as a democratisation of the recording industry, their success marking the emergence of 'a fluid and decentralized economy; an economy which in its structure and operation is so different from the dominant music corporations that it is effectively a different form, a post-Fordist rather than the Fordist "rock" structure' (Smith and Maughan, 1998: 211).

Certainly, the modern youth market includes an impressive array of 'grass-roots' enterprises – record labels, magazines, fashion companies and websites – that have developed in association with not only British dance music, but also a diverse universe of hip-hop, 'indie' rock and punk scenes worldwide. Whether this 'post-Fordist' universe of youth media represents a new era of creative freedom for young entrepreneurs, however, is moot. Hesmondhalgh, for example, has observed that many 'post-Fordist' media industries have been characterised by poor terms and conditions of work (2002: 70–71), while Angela McRobbie's (1998) study of the British fashion industry pointed to acute tensions between the artistic aspirations of young designers and a business whose ruthlessly commercial working practices militated against the expression of 'creative individuality'. More generally, McRobbie (2002) argued, the late 1990s had seen the 'independent' creative industries increasingly governed by 'fiercely neo-liberal' business practices that stood in marked contrast to the aura of freedom and creativity that surrounded 'independent' cultural producers:

> In this new and so-called independent sector . . . there is less and less time in the long hours culture to pursue 'independent work'. The recent attempts by the large corporations to innovate in this sector means that the independents are, in effect, dependent sub-contracted suppliers. And where such contracts are to be had, in a context of increasing competition, it is hard to imagine that there is time and space for private reading never mind wider critical debate.
>
> (McRobbie, 2002: 523)

In these terms, then, any suggestion that the growth of 'independent' businesses in the youth market has represented a move outside (or in opposition to) conglomerate control is questionable. For Smith and Maughan, the rise of dance music 'micro-labels' during the 1990s had pointed to 'the possibility of a mass of music production, that is no longer controlled and dominated by the majors' (1998: 224). But many authors have noted the long tradition in which small, independent companies have pioneered new musical genres and talent, only to be 'co-opted' by large corporations through processes of amalgamation, joint venture or buy-out. Such a narrative of 'incorporation', for example has been identified in the history of R'n'B (Gillett, 1983), rock 'n' roll (Chapple and Garofalo, 1977) and punk rock (Laing, 1985). It was quite possible, then, that the most successful dance 'micro-labels' would ultimately lose their autonomy through being absorbed into the major companies.

Moreover, as Simon Frith (1983) has observed, the very term 'independent' is something of a misnomer in the recording industry.

Rather than existing in an autonomous market sphere, 'independent' record companies effectively act as 'talent scouts' for the major labels, developing new acts which the more powerful companies then buy-up and exploit. Indeed, Keith Negus argues that, instead of a binary opposition existing between 'independents' and majors, it is better to see these distinctions in terms of a 'web of major and minor companies', with the majors 'split into semi-autonomous working groups and label divisions, and minor companies connected to these by complex patterns of ownership, investment, licensing, formal and informal and sometimes deliberately obscured relationships' (Negus, 1992: 180). Tricia Rose highlighted exactly this kind of relationship in the development of American rap music during the 1980s. Rather than competing against the smaller (more street-savvy) labels for new rap acts, Rose argued, the major labels developed a new commercial strategy in which they bought-up the independents and integrated them within their systems of production and distribution (Rose, 1994a: 6–7). Instead of being an autonomous creative force, then, 'independent' media businesses can be seen as a 'development division' for the larger corporations. More flexible and dynamic than the majors, independent companies are able to develop and 'road test' new products and genres – the bigger corporations subsequently picking up the most successful ideas and exploiting them more systematically. According to Hesmondhalgh the 1980s and 1990s saw a growing prevalence of these 'interdependent webs', with the major and 'independent' media sectors increasingly drawn together in complex networks of licensing, franchising and distribution (Hesmondhalgh, 2002: 151–152).

## GETTING CLOSE TO THE CUSTOMER: GENERATION X, COOLHUNTERS AND MARKETING 'GUERRILLAS'

Alongside moves towards flexible production and market segmentation, promotional culture also became a crucial aspect of economic life during the late twentieth century. According to Sean Nixon (1997) the 1980s and 1990s saw an increased 'aestheticisation' of consumer industries as advertising, design and marketing became more central to the selling of goods and services. As manufacturers increasingly targeted specific market segments, Nixon argues, they relied more heavily on 'cultural intermediaries' – design, marketing and advertising practitioners – to 'articulate production with consumption', imbuing products with values and meanings that would prompt consumers to identify more closely with a particular product or brand (Nixon, 1997: 181).

Market analysts emerged as especially important cultural intermediaries. As businesses sought economic advantage by 'getting close to the customer', market researchers and forecasting agencies were increasingly relied upon to monitor subtle shifts in consumers' attitudes. Justin Wyatt, for example, has shown that while market research always had a place in Hollywood's economic strategies, from the late 1970s studios' marketing departments wielded greater power and prestige (Wyatt, 1994: 155). Parallel changes have been identified by Negus in the recording industry, with a move away from 'inspired guess work, hunches and intuition' towards the wide-ranging use of advanced quantitative and qualitative methods of market research (Negus, 1999: 53). The growing importance of this research was especially evident in the youth market, where ever-more sophisticated methods of analysis were deployed to monitor the attitudes and behaviour of young consumers, allowing products and brands to be pitched in just the right way to win their allegiance.

The techniques of marketing pioneered by Eugene Gilbert in the 1950s (see Chapter 2) were an early move in this direction. With his young army of market researchers reporting on their peers' tastes, Gilbert's attention to consumers' feelings was a foretaste of the emphasis on attitudinal research that became commonplace in marketing practice during the 1960s and 1970s.[9] Indeed, during the 1980s and 1990s such approaches were still central to the work of youth market analysts such as Teenage Research Unlimited (TRU). Founded in 1982, TRU emerged as one of America's foremost market research agencies specialising in youth demand. With a client base of more than 150 major companies (including brand names such as Adidas, Gap, Nike, Tommy Hilfiger and Coca-Cola), TRU boasted that its combination of quantitative and qualitative research was 'at the forefront of . . . new teen-specific research methods and techniques', its twice yearly 'TRU Teenage Marketing and Lifestyle Study' cutting to 'the essence of what being teen means. From the meaning of "cool" to the truths about brand loyalty and age aspiration, it shows . . . the world of teens – in vivid color and exciting detail' (TRU, 2002b).[10]

During the 1990s, however, many businesses saw the 'world of teens' as an especially challenging market. From the title of Douglas Coupland's (1991) tale of quirky and anomic youngsters,[11] the term 'Generation X' was integrated into marketing discourse to denote a new cohort of young consumers whose media-savvy and cynical outlook seemed to contrast with the idealism and relative naivety of the earlier 'Baby Boomers'. In America, for example, Karen Ritchie (1995: 11) warned advertisers that they would 'have to learn new methods to cope with the changing markets'. 'Media, marketing, and advertising were simpler sciences when Boomers were young', Ritchie counselled (1995: 64). 'Xers', in contrast, had already developed 'a healthy scepticism about advertising and a love/hate relationship with the media' (1995: 87):

> Generation X learned to handle television like a team of lawyers handle a hostile witness – we did not raise a stupid generation here. The ground rules were established early: Generation X would take from the media what they needed and what they found entertaining, but they would never accept information from the media at face value. They would learn to be critical. They would learn to recognise hype, 'weasel words,' and exaggeration. And, like all good lawyers, they would always seek to control the communication.
>
> (Ritchie, 1995: 114)

In Britain, too, commentators spoke of a new 'Generation X', characterised by a wary suspicion of advertising and the media. For example, drawing on qualitative data produced for the independent research organisation, Demos, David Cannon depicted a generation of young people who were 'highly individualistic' and had 'sophisticated knowledge of consumer products' (Cannon, 1994: 2). Having grown up in an age of uncertainty and rapid developments in media technology, Cannon explained, Generation X had become suspicious, fiercely independent and were 'highly aware and critical of appearances' (1994: 10).

By the end of the 1990s, the original Generation Xers were well on their way to adulthood. Taking their place, however, was a cohort seen by marketers as equally media literate and advertising-wary. Dubbed 'Generation Y' for their propensity to question everything, this group were presented by marketers in both Britain and America as a consumer market that was potentially lucrative, but uniquely elusive (*Business Week*, 15 February 1999). In August 2000, for example, more than 200 representatives of British advertising agencies met at Marketing Youth Perspective Five, a conference held to consider strategies for targeting these young consumers. While the potential profitability of the youth market was emphasised, many delegates stressed the challenge of selling to a generation who were exceptionally media-savvy and suspicious of advertising. As one speaker explained:

> They are turning the guns on the big brands and asking fundamental questions of them. They value themselves by experiences, not labels, and don't want to be walking billboards.
>
> (cited in *The Guardian*, 5 October 2000)

Of course, advertisers and market analysts had a vested interest in depicting the youth market as treacherous waters – as a sea of capricious consumers, where businesses would flounder without employing the navigational skills of accomplished specialists. According to some researchers, however, the marketing patter exaggerated young people's degree of media literacy. John Thorup's (1998) study of the reception of advertising for Diesel jeans in Denmark, for example, found that many of the campaigns' subtle ironies were lost on young audiences whose reading strategies were 'not nearly as modern and media conscious' as the advertisers assumed (Thorup, 1998: 53). In 2002 similar conclusions were reached in research commissioned by Guardian Newspapers, Channel Four and several advertising firms. 'Previous generations were suspicious of advertising', explained Stuart Amron, author of the research, 'they might have liked ads, but they wouldn't necessarily buy the product. But this generation has been consuming since they were born. They don't see any reason to be suspicious' (*The Guardian*, 11 February 2002).

Nevertheless, in a cut-throat economic environment, businesses deployed increasingly sophisticated research in their efforts to 'get close' to the youth market. MTV was in the forefront of the trends. The station's methods of audience research were already extensive, but during the 1990s they were supplemented by the addition of 'Ethnography Studies' — with MTV researchers visiting teenagers at home to videotape wide-ranging discussions about the youngsters' attitudes, tastes and lifestyles. A new throng of youth-oriented forecasting agencies also appeared. Writing in *New Yorker* in 1997, Malcolm Gladwell coined the term 'coolhunters' to describe a new wave of marketing consultants who specialised in keeping their finger on the pulse of the youth market, using a mixture of quantitative surveys, qualitative interviews and clued-up intuition to link-up big business with young people's attitudes and tastes. Established in the late 1990s, for example, Dee Dee Gordon and Sharon Lee's Look-Look agency claimed to be 'a bridge that connects youth culture to the professional who wants to understand it'. In a strategy redolent of the methods pioneered by Eugene Gilbert in the 1950s, the agency used its 'global network of 10,000+ youth correspondents, respondents and photojournalists' to report on their own lives and culture, Look-Look claiming this gave 'a powerful collective voice to youth . . . allow[ing] them to speak honestly about topics important to them' (Look-Look, 2002).

In a similar vein, the founders of the Sputnik agency presented themselves as the thrusting Young Turks of American market research. By drawing on their 'network of young correspondents across the country', Sputnik boasted they were uniquely placed to 'get to the streets, the neighborhoods, the clubs, the basements and the playgrounds, and talk to the street cultures' (Lopiano-Misdom and de Luca, 1998: 10). By mining their rich seam of qualitative data, Sputnik claimed they could get 'inside the minds and souls of this largest growing consumer group', offering business an unparalleled opportunity 'to turn to the progressive trendsetters, to get close, to understand what they are doing culturally and socially by tracking the shifts, where they are going or what they will be doing next' (Lopiano-Misdom and de Luca, 1998: 8). In Britain, too, business relied on more sophisticated methods of market research to monitor shifts in young people's tastes and lifestyles. The 1990s, for example, saw the market research agency BMRB develop its twice-yearly Youth Target Group Index survey, assessing shifts in the youth market through the collection of data from a 3,000-strong sample of 7- to 19-year-olds. Britain also had its own 'coolhunting' experts, the late 1990s seeing the launch of numerous specialised youth market consultancies, the roster including such firms as Murmur, Sorting Office, Captain Crikey and Blowfish 24.

In addition to new forms of consumer research, the appeal to specific market segments also led to innovations in advertising practice. In the youth market, for example, the late 1990s saw the rise of 'guerilla marketing'. Eschewing high gloss and hard sell, marketers began to associate products with qualities of 'rebellious' individualism through the use of playful irony and 'subversive' forms of promotion – 'guerilla' marketing campaigns using techniques of stencilling, stickering and flyposting, as well as engineering outrageous PR stunts aimed at causing a stir. Diesel's 55DSL campaign of 2002 (see Chapter 1) was a case in point, though many other brands also adopted 'guerilla' tactics to cultivate an offbeat aura intended to connect with young consumers. In 2002, for example, the instant (and somewhat unappetising) snack, Pot Noodle, launched its own 'guerilla' marketing strategy. With humorous references to sex shops and sordid trysts, Pot Noodle bragged it was 'the slag of all snacks' in a series of TV advertisements whose risqué irony was designed to appeal to young audiences.[12] In a similar vein, the same year saw London brand consultancy, Headlight Vision, encourage businesses to add 'criminal kudos' to their products:

Look at ways of recreating the spirit or thrill of the illicit. Criminal references can be an effective way of enhancing brand edge. Explore pirate radio stations, illegal parties and drinking dens to understand the appeal of the illicit. Look for the reasons why they are attractive and investigate potential link-ups and avenues for covert marketing.

(cited in *Sunday Times*, 14 April 2002)

As the producers of 'youth media' increasingly sought to associate their goods with particular attitudes and identities, therefore, the work of coolhunters, marketing 'guerillas' and other cultural intermediaries became increasingly important. This trend was constituent in a more general 'aestheticisation' of economic activity during the late twentieth century, as the line between the 'cultural' and the 'economic' became increasingly blurred. Culture, as Stuart Hall explained, 'ceased to be, if it ever was, a decorative addendum to the "hard world" of production and things, the icing on the cake of the material world . . . Through design technology and styling, "aesthetics" . . . penetrated the world of modern production' (Hall, 1988: 28).[13] In these terms, rather than being secondary to the 'real' business of heavy industry and manufacturing, cultural production became an economic mainstay. This was especially true in Britain, where a long economic downturn and a chronic lack of investment had eroded the country's manufacturing base. In its place, governments increasingly sought to develop Britain's media and culture industries. The election of Tony Blair's ('New') Labour administration in 1997, for example, was quickly followed by the launch of the Creative Industries Task Force (CITF), established as a forum where government ministers could work with leading figures from the media and the arts to map out how the economic potential of Britain's creative industries could be maximised.[14] And, as we shall see in Chapter 5, the youth market was given a prominent place in these attempts to forge Britain's modernised cultural economy.

## FOREVER YOUNG: CONSUMPTION, LIFESTYLE AND 'GREYING YOUTH'

With the growing 'aestheticisation' of consumer goods, the youth market expanded well beyond its 'generational base'. An embrace of youth-oriented media and products by older consumers was already discernable during the 1960s (see Chapter 2), but during the 1990s the trend became more pronounced, so that a large amount of 'youth media' was neither aimed at, nor consumed by, especially 'young' audiences. In 2001, for example, American marketers were showing interest in the 'graying hip hop generation' – adults in their thirties and forties, who had grown up during the 1980s listening to rap artists such as Run DMC and (having established families, homes and careers) were beginning to 'rediscover' the genre (DiversityInc, 2001). 'Puffy' Combs, meanwhile, rebranded himself as 'P Diddy' as his Bad Boy hip-hop empire began supplementing its original 'gangsta' appeal with a pitch towards an older audience of black professionals. Other media industries, too, began to target 'greying' youth markets. For example, pop-oriented cable and satellite TV stations such as VH1 (launched by MTV in 1985) were slanted to older viewers, while music magazines such as *Q* (launched in 1986) and *Mojo* (1993) laid an emphasis on 'mature' journalism and retrospective features. The rise of the CD as the predominant format for popular music also depended heavily on older consumers. The success of the CD during the 1980s and 1990s was largely indebted to the whole-sale reissue of artists' back catalogues on CD format, much of which was targeted at older buyers who had originally bought the vinyl product during their youth.

The rise of a 'greying youth' market, however, was not simply an exercise in nostalgia. During the 1980s and 1990s many media and enter-tainment industries that had traditionally focused on youth demand began to broaden their appeal, embracing a market of older consumers who seemed to have retained their 'youthful' attitudes and patterns of con-sumption. In Britain, for example, marketers coined the term 'middle youth' to denote consumers aged from their late twenties to early for-ties who resisted the trappings of encroaching middle age, favouring instead the tastes and lifestyles (pop music, clubbing, fashion, drugs) that were once the preserve of the young (McCann, 1997).[15]

In some respects, then, concepts of 'youth' had become detached from a specific generational group. Instead, 'youthfulness' had become associated with particular mindsets and aesthetic tastes. In Britain, for example, Simon Frith argued that since the 1980s, rather than being targeted at a particular demographic cohort, 'youth TV' was aimed at an audience with a 'particular type of *viewing behaviour*' (Frith, 1993: 75). As Frith explained, programmers increasingly worked with a model in which 'youth' became 'a category constructed by TV itself, with no other referent: those people of whatever age or circumstance who watched "youth" programmes became . . . *the future of television*' (Frith, 1993: 75). In her analysis of the development of British 'youth television' during the 1990s, Karen Lury concurred. For Lury, much 'youth' programming of the decade was not aimed at young people as such, but at an audience who shared an ironic and irreverent sensibility – shows such as *The Word* (C4, 1990–1995), *Eurotrash* (C4, 1993 to present) *TFI Friday* (C4, 1996–2000) and the *Big Breakfast* (C4, 1992–2002) using elements of self-reflexivity, parody and bad taste to appeal to 'not a group of indi-viduals defined by age, but an audience who share [particular] tastes and ambitions' (Lury, 2001: 30).

In America, Kearney (2004) found comparable trends. In the US, she argued, the 1990s had seen 'youth' come to represent a distinct 'attitude and lifestyle' as manufacturers, retailers and advertisers deployed notions of 'youthfulness' to appeal to:

> not just teenagers, but also pre-teens, who are encouraged by the market to buy commodities produced for older consumers, as well as many adults, who, despite their age, are encouraged by the market to think, act, look, and, most importantly, shop as if they were young.
>
> (Kearney, 2004)

The shift, Kearney argued, was especially detectable in the TV industry. From the 1980s, she observed, the growth of cable and satellite stations increasingly fragmented traditional, mass TV audiences. As a consequence, networks began developing new programming strategies to target audience segments that were small, but potentially very profitable. This move to 'narrowcasting', Kearney argued, was characterised not by appeals to particular demographic groups, but by efforts to attract 'a coalition of viewers' who shared a similar cultural sensibility or lifestyle (Kearney, 2004). In these terms, then, the growing profusion of specialised cable and satellite music channels was part of a general shift away from 'generational broadcasting' and towards 'lifestyle narrowcasting'.

The growth of a 'middle youth' market for media and entertainment formerly targeted at younger consumers was the outcome of a combination of factors. According to Andrew Calcutt (1998), the appropriation of 'youthful' lifestyles by older age groups can be traced to the 1960s counterculture and its refusal to accept the norms associated with 'maturity' and 'adulthood'. According to Cohen and Ainley (2000), however, processes of economic restructuring have also been an important influence. As we saw in Chapter 2, changes in patterns of employment during the 1980s and 1990s meant that young people's transition into adult labour markets was extended and became less predictable. But, Cohen and Ainley argued, these changes also impacted upon older age groups. The new instability of employment markets, they suggested, undermined traditional 'linear' career paths, so that 'images of youth and adulthood have become blurred and confused' (Cohen and Ainley, 2000: 81). As a consequence, 'the idea (or ideal) of adult status as a completed state of psychological identity and/or "vocational maturity"' has been increasingly replaced 'with the notion of continuous and provisional development or becoming' (ibid.). In these terms, traditional 'life stages' have been destabilised by processes of economic transformation, with increasing numbers of people postponing or rejecting (or unable to obtain) full-time, permanent employment and turning instead to temporary jobs and/or extended periods of education. Trends towards later marriage and the deferment of children, meanwhile, have further 'uncoupled' traditional 'life phases'. As Kearney has suggested, 'adolescence is no longer a life stage associated with only those in their teenage years, [but] has become instead an identity that describes a much broader group of individuals' (Kearney, 2004).

Rather than interpreting these developments as a general extension of youth culture's generational boundaries, however, it might be better to see the 'greying youth' market as a facet of new modes of adulthood and lifestyle developing among specific social groups. Here, the work of Pierre Bourdieu is illuminating. In *Distinction* (1984), his study of changes in the fabric of bourgeois culture in modern France, Bourdieu argued that after 1945 there began to emerge a new form of capitalist economy in which power and profits were increasingly dependent not simply on the production of goods, but also on the continual regeneration of consumer desires (Bourdieu, 1984: 310). Associated with this new economic order was the emergence of new middle-class groups who championed the cause of commodity consumption and judged people 'by their capacity for consumption, their "standard of living" [and] their life-style, as much as by their capacity for production' (Bourdieu, 1984: 310). Lacking the economic, cultural or social capital that distinguished the traditional petite bourgeoisie, this new class faction established its own distinctive status by colonising new occupations based on the production and dissemination of symbolic goods and services – fields such as the media, advertising, journalism, fashion and so on. This new petite bourgeoisie, moreover, marked out their status and identity through the promotion of 'new model lifestyles'. Above all else, Bourdieu argued, the new class faction conceived of themselves as connoisseurs in 'the art of living', breaking away from the traditional bourgeois 'morality of duty' (with its ideals of probity, reserve and restraint) and embracing instead a new 'morality of pleasure as a duty', in which it became 'a failure, a threat to self-esteem, not to "have fun"' (Bourdieu, 1984: 367).

The rise of the 'greying youth' market in both Europe and the US, then, could be seen as a facet of this new 'ethic of fun' – notions of 'youthful' hedonism coming to define the expressive, consumption-oriented lifestyles of an ascendant faction of the middle class.[16] In the next chapter we look more closely at the changing connotations of 'youth', assessing the ways that media representations of young people and their 'youthful' lifestyles have been related to wider patterns of social, economic and political change.

# 4

# GENERATION AND DEGENERATION IN THE MEDIA
## Representations, responses and 'effects'

The young ones
Darling, we're the young ones
And the young ones
Shouldn't be afraid
To give love
While the flame is strong
'Cos we may not be the young ones very long.
(Cliff Richard, 'The Young Ones'
(Columbia Records, 1962))

## THE YOUNG ONES: MEDIA REPRESENTATIONS OF YOUTH

The 1961 British pop musical, *The Young Ones*, is an exercise in zestful sparkle. A light-hearted romp, the film is a sprightly tale of swinging adolescence in west London. Facing the demolition of their favourite youth club by a money-grabbing tycoon, chirpy youngsters launch a fund-raising drive to save their hangout. Needless to say, a happy ending ensues, all concerned joining together in an all-singing, all-dancing grand finale. Essentially a vehicle for rising pop star Cliff Richard, *The Young Ones* was hardly a cinematic masterpiece. Nonetheless, the film is significant in several respects.

Most obviously, the release of *The Young Ones* was illustrative of the growing importance of the youth market during the 1950s and 1960s. As we saw in Chapter 2, the production of pop-oriented films like *The*

*Young Ones* was one among countless attempts to tap into youth's growing spending power. But *The Young Ones* is also significant for the particular way it represents young people. The film gives a positive, pulsating spin to its images of youth. The 'young ones' of the title, for example, come from a wide variety of social backgrounds, but all are depicted as sharing the same lifestyle of vivacious fun. Nowhere is this clearer than in the film's opening sequence, where a diverse range of youngsters are pulled together in a celebration of teenage good times. *The Young Ones* opens as a Friday afternoon draws to its weary end. Across London a legion of youngsters from all walks of life – a builder, a shop girl, a ballet dancer, a delivery boy and even a young, bowler-hatted accountant – race home, all eager for an evening of music and fun at their favourite club. The sequence is, effectively, a celebration of a classless 'culture of youth', *The Young Ones* portraying a teenage world in which social divisions have been effaced by youngsters' common commitment to an ethos of leisure and pleasure.

In this way *The Young Ones* exemplifies the 'ideological' dimensions to media images of youth. The media do not simply 'reflect' reality. Instead, they actively explain and interpret, deploying visual codes and textual techniques to suggest specific ways of making sense of the world. Media representations of youth, then, are not a straightforward 'reflection' of young people's cultures and lifestyles. Instead, they offer a particular interpretation of youth, constructing images of young people that are infused by a wealth of social meanings. These meanings, moreover, are often related to much wider discourses. Media representations of youth are frequently an avenue through which broader social issues are explored, made sense of and interpreted. The images of classless, dynamic youth that were at the heart of *The Young Ones*, for example, were constituent in a much wider set of ideological discourses circulating in Britain during the early 1960s – discourses that configured British society as marching into a new era of modernity and consensus.

Media images of youth, then, often condense much wider themes and issues, representations of young people functioning as a kind of 'metaphorical vehicle' that encapsulates more general hopes and fears about trends in cultural life. It is, perhaps, almost inevitable that conceptions of 'youth' and 'generation' feature in attempts to make sense of social change. But many British authors (for example, Smith *et al.*, 1975; Clarke *et al.*, 1976; Davis, 1990) point to the way youth's metaphorical capacity has been powerfully extended at moments of profound transformation – for instance, the twilight years of the nineteenth century or the period of social and economic realignment that followed the Second World War. In America, too, theorists have highlighted the important symbolic dimensions to the 'youth question'. As Joe Austin and Michael Willard explain, 'public debates surrounding "youth" are an important forum where new understandings about the past, present, and future of public life are encoded, articulated and contested', so that 'youth' functions as 'a metaphor for perceived social change and its projected consequences' (Austin and Willard, 1998: 1). Indeed, Neil Campbell has argued that discourses of 'youth' have been especially central within American cultural life, the United States viewing itself as 'a mythic nation of youthfulness formed out of the Old World "parent" culture and creating itself anew' (Campbell, 2004: 2).

Media representations of youth, moreover, have been characterised by a recurring duality. This Janus-like quality has seen young people both celebrated as the exciting precursor to a prosperous future and, almost simultaneously, vilified as the most deplorable evidence of cultural bankruptcy. These contrasting images – termed 'youth-as-fun' and 'youth-as-trouble' by Dick Hebdige (1988b: 19) – are often distorted and exaggerated stereotypes that bear tenuous relation to the life experiences of young people themselves. But, historically, they have wielded significant connotative power and have often served as key motifs around which dominant interpretations of social change have been constructed. This chapter, then, explores the way media representations of youth have figured in debates about more general social issues and broader patterns of cultural change – debates in which young people have been *both* lauded as the shape of wonderful things to come *and* reviled as the incarnation of malevolent forces menacing established ways of life.

The chapter begins by exploring the way young people have often been (mis)represented as the vulnerable victims of pernicious media 'effects' – with the 'influence' of film and TV on young people's behaviour often cited as the most glaring evidence of the popular media's negative social impact. The chapter also shows how contemporary concerns about the media's 'effects' on youth are constituent in a longer history of anxiety, with a succession of 'media panics' blaming commercial entertainment for social problems whose causes lie in much more complex social, economic and political issues. The role of media institutions *themselves* in the construction of these concerns is also considered, with an account of the notion of 'moral panic' in which the media are conceived as playing an active role in the escalation of social problems through their distortion of real or imagined episodes of deviance. But media representations of youth have never been entirely negative. Indeed, at certain historical moments, media images of 'youth as fun' have overshadowed the more fearful depictions of 'youth as trouble'. This chapter concludes, therefore, with an account of the way media configurations of 'the teenager' during the early 1960s served to promote visions of liberating consumerism and national renewal in both Britain and the United States.

## NATURAL BORN KILLERS?: MEDIA 'EFFECTS' AND YOUNG AUDIENCES

A stark contrast to the upbeat optimism of *The Young Ones* was the tragedy that unfolded at Columbine High School in Colorado on 20th April 1999. Armed with an arsenal of pistols, shotguns and pipebombs, eighteen-year-old Eric Harris and seventeen-year-old Dylan Klebold went on a deadly rampage through classrooms and corridors, killing twelve of their fellow students and a teacher, before turning the weapons on themselves. In Britain, the murder of two-year-old James Bulger in 1993 was equally appalling. Abducted from a shopping centre in Merseyside, Bulger was beaten to death by two ten-year-olds, Robert Thompson and Jon Venables. Both events were horrific, made all the more shocking by the youth of the killers. But the Columbine massacre and the Bulger murder also shared other things in common. In their aftermath, both events were configured in media coverage and public discussion as the embodiment of a general moral malaise that had registered its direst consequences among the young. Moreover, in both cases, popular entertainment was erroneously cited as a factor that had directly influenced the killers' behaviour.

In the Bulger case, there was speculation that Thompson and Venables had been influenced by the violent content of horror videos – in particular *Child's Play 3*, a film depicting a malevolent doll's spree of murder and cruelty.[1] Such was the concern that in 1994 the British government introduced greater restrictions on the availability of violent videos, strengthening controls that had already been made some of the toughest in Europe by the 1984 Video Recordings Act (itself introduced in response to earlier anxieties about the possible link between 'video nasties' – as they were dubbed – and juvenile crime).[2] In the wake of the Columbine carnage, attention also focused on the possible role of popular entertainment. The press quickly conjectured that the 'goth' subculture might be a factor in the killings, since Harris and Klebold had been members of a loose group of friends who supposedly shared a taste for 'goth' music and style. As a consequence, *The New York Post* ran a feature entitled 'Telltale Signs Your Kids Might Be Ready to Explode' alongside a picture of Adolf Hitler and photographs of teenagers in 'goth' make-up. Rock musician Marilyn Manson was also singled out for criticism, many commentators citing the dark imagery of Manson's songs and performance as an influence on the Columbine killers.[3] Computer games were also blamed. Harris and Klebold had been keen on games such as *Doom* and *Final Fantasy VII*, and the games' violent content was cited as contributing to the murders. In 2001 relatives of the Columbine victims even filed a $5 billion lawsuit against 25 computer companies (including Sony and Nintendo), claiming the firms' products had triggered the killings.

There was, however, scant evidence to support the alleged links between popular entertainment and these high-profile murders. The police officer who led the Bulger investigation later stated that neither of the killers had been interested in 'violent' videos, nor had they seen *Child's Play 3*. Notions that rock music and computer games had been a factor in the Columbine murders were also without foundation. It subsequently emerged that neither Harris nor Klebold had been fans of Marilyn Manson, while in 2002 a court dismissed the Columbine relatives' lawsuit, a judge ruling that the computer games firms had no case to answer.

Notions of a causal relationship between 'violent' media content and aggressive behaviour by young people, however, remain entrenched. The popular press are especially virulent in their regular attacks on the 'corrupting' influences of 'violent' or 'pornographic' entertainment. In Britain, for example, amid the furore that surrounded the Bulger murder in 1993, the tabloid newspaper *The Sun* organised a public burning of copies of *Child's Play 3* and urged its readers: 'For the Sake of ALL Our Kids: BURN YOUR VIDEO NASTY' (26 November 1993). In America similar critiques have also won a wide audience. For instance, Michael Medved's account of popular entertainment's malignant impact on American social life, *Hollywood Versus America* (1992), became a bestseller and was serialised in several newspapers. In the US particular anxiety has surrounded Oliver Stone's film *Natural Born Killers*, which has been held responsible for several 'copycat' crimes since its release in 1994. The concerns seemed to be born out in March 1999 when the Supreme Court ruled in favour of Patsy-Ann Byers's lawsuit for negligence against Stone and Time-Warner Entertainment (the film's distributors). Byers had been shot and paralysed by two young adults who embarked on a cross-country crime spree in 1995 after taking LSD and watching a video of *Natural Born Killers* several times. According to Byers's petition, Stone and Time-Warner 'knew or should have known that the film would cause and inspire people . . . to commit crimes such as the shooting of Patsy Ann Byers'. However, while the Court initially decided in favour of Byers, the lawsuit was dismissed in 2001 after a ruling that there was no evidence to show that Stone or Time-Warner had intended to incite violence. Nevertheless, while Byers's lawsuit was unsuccessful, media coverage of the case made *Natural Born Killers* notorious and several other murders by young people were presented as 'copycat' crimes inspired by the film.[4]

Social scientific research has often been cited as evidence of the detrimental impact of popular entertainment on young audiences. In America during the 1920s, research financed by the Payne Fund marked one of the first systematic attempts to analyse the media's effects on audiences. Assessing the cinema's impact on young people, the Payne research team were quite reserved in their findings, arguing that films' effects on social behaviour were fairly limited – perhaps influencing things such as fashion preference, but registering little impact on morality or beliefs. These qualified findings, however, were twisted by moral crusaders to support notions of the cinema's malicious effects on the young. Later social scientific research was also used as ammunition by moral campaigners. In America during the 1960s, for example, laboratory-based psychological studies by Albert Bandura (1973) and Leonard Berkowitz (1962) seemed to point unequivocally to a causal link between media depictions of violence and aggressive behaviour by young people. In Britain, meanwhile, a similar 'cause and effect' relationship seemed to have been uncovered in James Halloran's (1970) collection of research studies. Longitudinal research, tracing the impact of media representations of violence on young people over a long period of time, also seemed to point to a link between media 'violence' and audience aggression. William Belson's (1978) study of 1,565 London boys was one of the best known, Belson concluding that boys exposed to high levels of TV violence in their childhood went on to commit 49 per cent more acts of serious violence than those who had been exposed to much less.

Belson's study exuded clear-eyed, scientific confidence, though critics have highlighted important weaknesses in his research methodology. Indeed, other pieces of longitudinal research have produced very different findings. In one of the largest studies of its kind, for example, Ronald J. Milavsky and his associates surveyed 3,200 young people over a three-year period, and concluded from their work that watching acts of violence on television had relatively little influence on youngsters' behaviour (Milavsky *et al.*, 1982). Important criticisms can also be levelled at the psychological experiments carried out by Bandura and Berkowitz. The artificiality of their laboratory-based research has been especially highlighted.[5] Far removed from 'real-life' social conditions, critics argue, the findings of such studies become virtually meaningless. 'Effects' research, moreover, gives little attention to the social meanings that surround both media texts and social behaviour. Most obviously, scant regard is given to the meaning of media 'violence'. Few researchers offer definitions of 'violence' beyond 'acts of hurting or harming', so they largely ignore the extent to which different *kinds* of violence set in different contexts (for example, 'violence' depicted in a cartoon; presented in a news report; or featured in a horror movie) might be interpreted and understood by audiences in very different ways. As David Buckingham explains, 'effects' research invariably gives little regard to the social process through which meanings are produced and circulated:

> Meaning is seen to be inherent in the 'message', and to be transmitted directly into the mind and thence the behaviour of the viewer. As a result, it becomes unnecessary to investigate what viewers themselves define as violent, or the different ways in which they make sense of what they watch.
> (Buckingham, 1993a: 7)

Generally, quantitatively-based research is ill-suited to uncovering the way people make sense of media texts and give meaning to their social behaviour. Rather than employing quantitative methodologies in a bid to 'discover' laws of media 'cause and effect', many authors have argued that a better approach is to use qualitative research methods (for example, ethnography, interviews and focus groups) to explore the various meanings and interpretations different audiences give to the media. Adopting such strategies, researchers such as Buckingham (1993b, 1996) and Bob Hodge and David Tripp (1986) found that even very young audiences were 'literate' and discriminating media consumers.[6] In these terms, rather than being passive recipients of media messages, young people can be understood as actively constructing meanings around media texts, making informed judgements about genre and representation.

Nevertheless, notions of the media exercising a harmful influence on young audiences have continued to secure significant support. Most famously, Elizabeth Newsom's study, *Video Violence and the Protection of Children* (1994), seemed to be a watershed in the long debates about the media's effects on youth, her report claiming to demonstrate conclusively that 'violent' media caused young people to behave violently. Commissioned by the British government in the wake of the Bulger murder and widely publicised, Newsom's study claimed to be based on considerable empirical evidence and to draw on a wealth of scholarly expertise. On close inspection, however, Newsom's study proved less than convincing. In systematic (though much less publicised) critiques, Martin Barker (1997) and Guy Cumberbatch (2002) both showed Newsom's work to be largely speculation based on an uncritical survey of assorted press stories, while none of the twenty-five media 'experts' she cited had actually published academic work in the field. This is not to say that the media have no impact whatsoever on their audiences, but evidence regarding the media's negative 'effects' on young people remains (at best) inconclusive, while the relationships between media texts and their consumers are much more complex and multifaceted than simple 'cause-and-effect' models would have us believe.[7]

## 'NIGHTMARES OF DEPRAVITY': YOUTH AND 'MEDIA PANIC'

The spotlight that the Bulger and Columbine murders cast on the supposedly 'corrupting' influence of popular entertainment was part of a long history of anxiety surrounding young people and popular culture. As John Springhall (1998) shows, since the nineteenth century wave after wave of scares have cited commercial entertainment as a corrupting influence on the young. During the Victorian era, for example, British moral crusaders linked an apparent rise in juvenile crime to the popularity of sensationalist 'penny gaff' theatres and 'penny dreadful' novels. In America, lurid 'dime' and 'half-dime' novels attracted similar criticisms from campaigners such as Anthony Comstock and were targeted in the Federal Anti-Obscenity (or 'Comstock') Law of 1873 which suppressed the circulation of popular fiction and allowed for the arrest of publishers of 'pernicious literature'.[8] During the 1920s and 1930s gangster films were a focus of similar controversy. Hollywood was accused of delivering impressionable youth into a career of crime through depicting mobsters as glamorous and exciting, and in both America and Europe many gangster movies were either censored or banned outright.

In the US, concerns about the 'corruption' of youth by popular entertainment reached a crescendo in the 1950s. In 1953 concerns about rising levels of juvenile crime prompted the appointment of a Senate Subcommittee to investigate the causes of delinquency. Headed by Tennessee Senator, Esteves Kefauver, the Subcommittee considered the role of various factors, though the possible influence of the media was a recurring preoccupation. Testimony was heard from a parade of moral campaigners, including Frederic Wertham, whose 1954 study – *Seduction of the Innocent* – had presented popular 'horror' and 'crime' comics as a font of juvenile depravity. The Subcommittee's findings, however, were inconclusive. Scrutinising the comics industry, followed by television and Hollywood, the Kefauver hearings found little evidence of a clear link between the media and juvenile crime. Nevertheless, while the clamour for federal censorship was resisted, the Subcommittee demanded that the media exercise stricter self-supervision and the call was generally acceded to. Hence comic publishers adopted a strict, self-regulatory Comics Code in 1954 that proscribed any content dealing with 'shocking' or 'sensational' subjects. In Britain similar concerns also surfaced and led to the passage of the Children and Young Persons (Harmful Publications) Act in 1955, which effectively outlawed the import and reproduction of all American 'horror' and 'crime' comics.[9]

In view of this long catalogue of complaint, it becomes difficult to substantiate claims that new media forms like 'video nasties' or computer games present a uniquely threatening danger to young minds. Instead, popular entertainment has served as a useful 'whipping boy', a scapegoat that politicians and moral crusaders have conveniently blamed for problems whose origins are rooted in more complex social and economic issues. As Buckingham explains:

> the media routinely serve . . . as an easy scapegoat, which may actively prevent a more considered, and more honest, appraisal of the issues. To blame the media provides a convenient means of displacing the concern away from questions which are much harder to examine, and which we may actively wish to avoid.
>
> (Buckingham, 1993a: 5–6)

Campaigns against popular entertainment should also be understood as part of a wider set of power relations. According to Springhall, recurring concerns about the 'debasing' influence of comics, rock music and computer games represent an attempt to define and police a hierarchy of taste in which middle-class cultural preferences are validated and zealously promulgated – while those of less powerful groups are denigrated and suppressed (Springhall, 1998: 139). For Springhall, issues of social stability are also at stake, with concerns about 'media influence' embodying dominant groups' fears of autonomous, working-class youth subcultures over which they have little control (Springhall, 1998: 35).

Issues of 'race' have also been prominent in anxieties about 'media influence'. In America during the 1980s and 1990s, for example, concerns about the 'corrupting' influence of popular entertainment were given their fullest voice in campaigns against rap music. Rap, for instance, was a key target in the crusade launched by the Parents Music Resource Center (PMRC). Founded in 1985 by Tipper Gore (wife of Democrat Senator and Presidential candidate, Al Gore) and Susan Baker (wife of Treasury Secretary, James Baker), the PMRC canvassed against forms of popular music it deemed 'explicit' or 'obscene'. It urged record companies to 'reassess' the contracts of those performers it found objectionable and lobbied for the introduction of a ratings system that could review and regulate pop music content. Keen to avoid federal intervention, record companies agreed to voluntary regulation, 1990 seeing the introduction of 'Parental Advisory' warning labels (sometimes referred to derisively as 'Tipper Stickers') for albums with 'explicit' lyrical content. The PMRC campaigned against a variety of music genres, but African-American rap musicians attracted particular criticism. The late 1980s also saw a spate of attempts by state authorities to suppress forms of rap music they deemed offensive. The rap group 2 Live Crew became a particular cause célèbre. Released in 1989, 2 Live Crew's album, *As Nasty As They Wanna Be*, was roundly condemned by the PMRC for its lewd content and profanity, while a Florida court ruled the record to be obscene and in 1990 the group were arrested on stage for singing profane lyrics.[10]

Further controversy surrounded the rise of 'gangsta' rap during the late 1980s and 1990s. The songs of 'gangsta' rappers such as Schoolly D, Ice-T, NWA, Snoop Doggy Dogg and Tupac Shakur were uncompromising in their graphic descriptions of life in the tough neighbourhoods of New York and Los Angeles – and a storm of criticism condemned the artists' misogyny (women were routinely referred to as 'bitches' and 'hos') and their histrionic celebration of guns, violence and hatred of the police. In 1992 particular notoriety surrounded Body Count (a rap/heavy metal band fronted by gangsta rap star Ice-T) and 'Cop Killer', a song included on the group's debut Warner Brothers album.[11] To some, the lyrics of the song were unacceptably inflammatory ('I got my twelve gauge sawed off / I got my headlights turned off / I'm 'bout to bust some shots off / I'm 'bout to dust some cops off'). Outraged by the song, the Dallas Police Association and the Combined Law Enforcement Association of Texas launched a campaign to force Warner to withdraw the album and, within a week, they were joined by police organisations across the US. Objections to the song were not simply on grounds of taste (though these were prominent). Adopting a crude media 'effects' model, some critics argued that the song could actually *cause* crime and violence. As Paul Taylor, President of the Fraternal Order of Police, explained:

> People who ride around all night and use crack cocaine and listen to rap music that talks about killing cops – it's bound to pump them up. No matter what anybody tells you, this kind of music is dangerous.
>
> (cited in Shank, 1996: 129)

Over the next month the campaign against Ice-T's band grew. Vice President Dan Quayle branded 'Cop Killer' 'obscene', President George

Bush (Snr) publicly denounced any record company that would release such a product and, at a Time-Warner shareholders' meeting, the actor (and right-wing activist) Charlton Heston stood up, read out lyrics from Body Count's song 'KKK Bitch' to an astonished audience, and demanded that the company take action. As a consequence, stores across the US pulled Body Count's album from their shelves, and 'Cop Killer' was ultimately deleted from the record.[12]

The ferocity of the attack on Body Count and 'Cop Killer' is best explained by the episode's historical context. The controversy came in the wake of the 1992 Los Angeles riots, sparked by the acquittal of white police officers charged with the brutal beating of African-American, Rodney King ('Cop Killer' was, in some senses, an angry reaction to the case). Against this backdrop, the crusade against 'Cop Killer' could be interpreted as a reactionary political response to the racial and economic tensions that lay behind the Los Angeles disturbances – the campaign functioning as a scapegoating exercise in which urban crime and violence could be conveniently blamed on African-American music and culture. Indeed, these themes remained prominent in conservative political discourse throughout the 1990s. Senator Bob Dole gave them particularly strong expression. In 1995, with his eyes on running for the Presidency, Dole launched a vitriolic denunciation of the American entertainment industry, accusing popular films, music and television of flooding the country with 'nightmares of depravity'. 'We must hold Hollywood and the entire entertainment industry accountable for putting profit ahead of common decency', asserted Dole, and the following day William Bennett (a former Education Secretary and drug czar) sent letters to Time-Warner board members asking the company to stop distributing rap albums with 'offensive' lyrics (Time, 12 June 1995). Feeling the heat, Time-Warner sold its share of rap label Interscope Records to MCA for $200 million.

Of course, there may be much to criticise in the attitudes espoused in many gangsta rap songs, especially their celebration of violence, misogyny and homophobia. But, in the rhetoric of arch-conservatives like Dole, gangsta rappers were scapegoated for social problems that stemmed from more deep-rooted causes – not least, structured inequalities of status, power and opportunity. Campaigns such as that against 'Cop Killer' were also fuelled by white, middle-class angst that their own children would become 'contaminated' by ghetto culture. Such anxieties have punctuated the history of American youth culture since the 1950s, when the popularity of rock 'n' roll prompted fears that white, middle-class youngsters were falling under the spell of lower-class and black cultural values.[13] During the 1980s and 1990s similar concerns arose in relation to gangsta rap. Indeed, significantly, those rap artists most often targeted by moral crusaders were those achieving mainstream success, their appeal reaching out from black subculture to reach youngsters in the affluent, white suburbs. Body Count, for example, enjoyed particularly strong sales in white markets through their fusion of (black) rap lyricism with (white) heavy metal.

The 1990s also saw sections of the black middle class rally alongside the pro-censorship lobby. Most obviously, C. Delores Tucker (head of the National Congress of Black Women) emerged as a 'professional testifier', touring America to sermonise against the 'evils' of gangsta rap. Echoing white, middle-class distaste for the 'repulsive' culture of an urban underclass, Tucker's simplistic rhetoric was also a replay of the most inane media 'effects' theories. 'You can't listen to all that language and filth', she blithely pontificated, 'without it affecting you' (cited in Springhall, 1998: 150).

Alongside issues of social class and 'race', notions of generational 'difference' have also figured in the recurring anxieties about the social impact of popular entertainment. From 'penny dreadfuls' to computer games, the appearance of new media forms has invariably been accompanied by adult concerns regarding their influence on the young, fears that have often prompted campaigns to regulate or ban young people's access to the new medium. Kirsten Drotner (1992) has coined the term 'media panic' to denote these successive episodes of alarm. According to Drotner, these fears about the social impact of media innovation have consistently focused on the young because, since the mid-nineteenth century, youth have been pioneers of new popular media – to the extent that many commercial entertainments have been 'fundamentally, if not exclusively, media for the young' (Drotner, 1992: 56). As trailblazers of new media forms, Drotner explains, the young command a degree of technical competence and cultural independence that poses (or is seen to pose) a threat to hierarchies of taste and to the balance of social power. In response, 'media panics' and their associated censorship campaigns attempt to re-establish the generational status quo, restoring traditional values and reinstating structures of cultural authority. For Drotner, then, 'media panics' represent a 'tacit or explicit means of social regulation' that serves to reinforce cultural norms and reassert generational power relations (Drotner, 1992: 57). So, in these terms, 'media panics' tell us very little about the actual object of concern. Instead, these episodes of alarm are a product of wider struggles over taste and cultural autonomy, with fears about the corrupting 'effects' of popular entertainment representing a 'discourse of power whose stakes are the right to define cultural norms and social qualifications' (Drotner, 1992: 50).

# 'MANIFESTATIONS OF YOUTHFUL RUFFIANISM': MORAL PANICS AND THE NEGATIVE STEREOTYPING OF YOUTH

Social concern has not only surrounded the possible influence of popular entertainment on the young. The behaviour and morality of young people *themselves* has also prompted regular unease. Here, the media have often been instrumental in orchestrating anxiety. Through a 'negative stereotyping' of youth, the media have constructed a succession of fearful images that have functioned as a symbolic embodiment of wider controversies – the media presenting youth crime, violence and sexual licence as woeful indices of broader patterns of social decline.

For example, we have already seen how 1950s America was gripped by the perception that juvenile crime was spiralling out of control. The appointment of an investigative Senate Subcommittee in 1953 seemed to confirm fears that the problem was escalating and concerns were further fuelled by a tide of media exposés in magazines, newspapers and news-reels that depicted a form of delinquency frighteningly new in its extent and severity.[14] The perception seemed borne out by a relentless rise in crime statistics, yet James Gilbert has shown that this 'juvenile crime wave' was, in fact, largely a statistical phenomenon produced by new strategies of law enforcement and changes in the collation of crime data (Gilbert, 1986: 66–70). Rather than being a response to a genuine erup-tion of adolescent vice, Gilbert suggests, the alarm surrounding juvenile delinquency during the 1950s served as a symbolic focus for broader anxieties in a period of rapid and disorienting change – the concerns about youth crime articulating 'a vaguely formulated but gnawing sense of social disintegration' (Gilbert, 1986: 77).

Similar concerns also registered in Britain. Like America, Britain saw an increase in official indices of juvenile crime after the Second World War and media anxiety helped popularise notions of an unprecedented wave of delinquency. As in America, however, closer inspection suggests this 'explosion' of youth crime was largely a statistical phenomenon, the outcome of a formalisation of policing practice.[15] Again, the concerns about youth crime can be seen as a symbolic vehicle for a broader sense of unease at a time of profound social upheaval. These anxieties were also constituent in what Geoffrey Pearson has seen as 'a long and connected history of fearful complaint and controversy' in which 'each succeeding generation has understood itself to be standing on the brink of some rad-ical discontinuity with the past, and in which the rising generation has been repeatedly seen as the harbinger of a dreadful future' (Pearson, 1984: 102). According to Pearson, the successive anxieties surrounding frighteningly 'new' waves of delinquency have not addressed genuine leaps in the level of juvenile crime, but have served as a medium that condenses wider apprehensions about the nature of social change and the state of the nation.

In this 'history of fearful complaint and controversy', the media have often presented youth's subcultural styles as a telltale index of cultural decline. In Britain during the early 1950s, for example, media anxieties about a 'new' form of vicious delinquency crystallised around the figure of the Teddy boy. The Ted's style of long, drape jackets and drainpipe trousers was sometimes interpreted as an adaptation of Edwardian fashion (hence the sobriquet 'Teddy' boy), but it was really a variant of the American-influenced styles that had become popular among many working-class youngsters in Britain during the 1940s – a trend inspired by the iconography of the Chicago gangster and the zoot-suit styles imported with the arrival of GIs during the war. First identified by the media in the working-class neighbourhoods of south London in 1954, the Teddy boy was soon being presented as a violent delinquent stalking streets and dancehalls all over the country. The negative imagery surrounding the Ted was further compounded in the sensational press coverage of cinema 'riots' that followed screenings of *The Blackboard Jungle* (1955), *Rock Around the Clock* (1956) and other films with rock 'n' roll associations. As Paul Rock and Stanley Cohen (1970: 310) have observed, these disturbances were small in scale but attracted a welter of overwrought publicity that painted the Teddy boy as an uncontrollable social menace.

A similar picture emerged in media responses to a spate of urban disorders in Nottingham and Notting Hill in 1958. Dubbed 'race riots' by the press, the incidents were actually a series of racist street attacks by white mobs. Media coverage and political responses, however, ignored issues of racism. Instead, the events were presented as the consequence of an 'alien' presence in British cities and tighter immigration controls were suggested as the logical remedy. But the tacit racism of this analysis was also accompanied by a rhetoric of concern about youth and delinquency. Drawing attention to the numbers of Teddy boys involved in the disorders, *The Times* speculated that the events could be partly explained as 'the latest manifestation of that youthful ruffianism, long endemic in both areas, which has variously expressed itself in raids on post offices, the wrecking of cinemas and cafés, and gang clashes and stabbings' (*The Times*, 3 September 1958). By exploiting the familiar themes of violence and criminality that had sedimented around the Teddy boy, therefore, the media effectively drew a veil over the institutional dimensions to racism and discrimination and, instead, a small group of working-class youngsters became 'a scapegoat for respectable British society to cover up its own failures and prejudices in dealing with its immigrant population' (Rock and Cohen, 1970: 314).

Media coverage of the Teddy boy, however, was not simply an exercise in scapegoating. Rock and Cohen (1970) argued that the sensationalised press stories also gave greater form and substance to the Ted as a distinct subcultural identity. Here, Rock and Cohen were influenced by the social transaction theories developed in American sociology – in particular Howard Becker's (1963) arguments that 'deviance' is a socially constructed category applied to the actions of certain individuals, who then come to identify with the negative labels attached to them by the media and agencies of social control. In a similar fashion, Rock and Cohen argued, the sensationalist media reports of the 1950s introduced the Teddy boy not only to the public, but also to himself:

> He learned that, because he wore Edwardian suits, he must be a certain type of person. His suit led to differential treatment. He could not pretend that he was a member of 'normal' society because people did not treat him as one. He was rejected from more and more public places; in some areas only the cafés and the streets were open to him. He thus became even more conspicuous and menacing. Above all, he learned that he shared common enemies and common allies with those who dressed like him.
>
> (Rock and Cohen, 1970: 302)

By the early 1960s the drape-suit and brothel-creeper shoes of the Teddy boy had been largely displaced by the chic, Italian-inspired styles associated with the mod subculture. Media responses to mod style, however, often reproduced the fearful, overwrought treatment given to the earlier Teds. Like the Teds before them, the mods' appearance was often presented by the media as a symbol of national decline – an approach that reached a peak in press responses to the 'battles' between the mods and their leather-clad, motorcycle-riding rivals, the rockers, at British seaside resorts during 1964. In his landmark study of the events, Stanley Cohen further developed the ideas he had formulated in relation to the Teddy boy. In *Folk Devils and Moral Panics*, originally published in 1972, Cohen argued that the total amount of violence that took place during 1964's seaside 'invasions' was actually very small, and received little coverage in the local press. But, in the absence of other newsworthy material, reporters from national newspapers seized upon the relatively innocuous events and created headlines and feature articles suggesting there had been a wholesale breakdown of public order. Cohen termed this kind of overblown media alarm a 'moral panic' in which:

A condition, episode, person or group of persons emerges to become defined as a threat to societal values and interests; its nature presented in a stylised and stereotypical fashion by the mass media, the moral barricades are manned by editors, bishops, politicians and other right-thinking people; socially accredited experts pronounce their diagnoses and solutions; ways of coping are evolved or (more often) resorted to; the condition then disappears, submerges or deteriorates and becomes more visible.

(Cohen, 2002: 1)

Cohen's ideas have been hugely influential. Drotner's (1992) notion of 'media panic', for example, was obviously indebted to Cohen's analysis – though, whereas Drotner's research concentrated on the history of social anxieties surrounding the 'effects' of media innovations on young audiences, Cohen's analysis focused on the role played by media institutions *themselves* in creating social concerns and amplifying cultural behaviour.

Cohen's concept of 'moral panic' denoted processes through which the media contribute to the escalation of social problems by distorting the activities of real or imagined deviant groups – or 'folk devils'. In terms of the 1960s mods and rockers, for example, Cohen argued that these youth groups were initially ill-defined, with little enmity existing between them. The polarisation of the two camps, he contended, developed only as a consequence of the sensationalist news stories, with young people coming to identify with the 'folk devil' images of mods and rockers conjured-up by the press. The melodramatic reporting also influenced the agencies of social control. Sensitised by the early press stories, Cohen argued, the police subsequently reacted strongly to the slightest hint of trouble and, as a consequence, arrest rates soared and magistrates (also affected by the process of sensitisation) imposed harsher penalties.[16] Media attention and exaggerated press reports, therefore, fanned the sparks of an initially trivial incident, creating a self-perpetuating 'amplification spiral' which steadily escalated the social significance of the events.[17]

Cohen's case-study focused specifically on media representations of the 1960s 'battles' between mods and rockers, but his arguments could easily be applied to the subsequent procession of spectacular youth groups. From the skinheads of the late 1960s, through the punks of the 1970s, to the 'New Age travellers' and 'acid-house ravers' of the late 1980s and early 1990s, British youth styles have invariably been subject to processes of stigmatisation in the media which, paradoxically, has worked to popularise and lend substance to youth groups that were initially small-scale and vaguely defined. In America, too, the concept of moral panic could be constructively applied to the media's representation of various youth groups, from the Hells Angels motorcycle gangs of the 1960s, through to the gangsta rappers of the 1980s and 1990s.[18]

Young women have generally been marginal to episodes of moral panic related to violence and public order. Alarm associated with the mods and rockers' lawlessness, the punks' outrageousness or the aggression of gangsta rap has largely (though not exclusively) focused on the behaviour of young men. In contrast, girls have figured more visibly in moral panics related to sexual behaviour and 'permissiveness'. In America during the 1940s, for example, the press ran lurid stories about the criminality of (male) delinquent street gangs, but unease also cohered around 'Victory-' or 'V-girls' – young women whose 'free and easy' liaisons with servicemen were interpreted by the media as evidence of a breakdown in national morality. In Britain, meanwhile, the post-war period has been punctuated by anxieties regarding perceived rises in the number of teenage pregnancies. Typical was the *Daily Mirror*'s shrill account of 'the startling truth about teenage sex' in 1991, the newspaper ominously announcing that Britain was 'in the grip of a teenage pregnancy crisis' (*Daily Mirror*, 24 November 1991). In 1996, meanwhile, concern over the explicit discussion of sex in young women's magazines such as *J17*, *Sugar* and *Bliss* prompted Peter Luff, Conservative MP for Worcestershire, to propose the Periodicals (Protection of Children) Bill – with the aim of tightening legal controls over the sexual content of magazines aimed at young readers. The Bill itself was ultimately withdrawn, though only after magazine publishers had agreed to a voluntary code of conduct.

The concept of moral panic has been a useful tool in the analysis of media representations of youth culture and juvenile crime. Indeed, the term has even filtered into popular discourse, with politicians, journalists and even police officers drawing on the concept in perennial debates about deviance and delinquency. A number of criticisms, however, have been made of the way notions of moral panic have been applied. Springhall, for example, has voiced reservations about attempts to 'debunk' sensational crime stories by stressing historical precedent along the lines of 'there's nothing really new about all this'. Such responses, he argues, risk sliding into academic condescension if they show insufficient regard for people's genuinely felt sense of concern about levels of crime (Springhall, 1998: 8). Similarly, Ian Taylor (1981) has warned that a simple dismissal of crime and violence as a spurious 'moral panic' not only devalues 'ordinary' people's genuine experiences and perceptions of these phenomena, but also creates a political vacuum open to exploitation by the reactionary 'law and order' lobby.

Moreover, while Cohen's study gave close attention to the media's role in the construction of social phenomena, it gave little consideration to the meanings held by the social actors involved. As Cohen himself conceded, his focus on the media's role in the seaside 'battles' of the 1960s meant the mods and rockers themselves were seen only 'through the eyes of the societal reaction' and tended to appear as 'disembodied objects, Rorschach blots on to which reactions are projected' (Cohen, 2002: 15). The meanings and attitudes of the 'folk devils' themselves, therefore, were left relatively unexplored. Additionally, Marxist theorists argued that, while Cohen's model of moral panics was useful, it fell short of placing social phenomena within their broader historical and political context. In their own account of the 1970s moral panic surrounding street crime, therefore, Stuart Hall and his associates took pains to place events within a more 'panoramic' political framework – *Policing the Crisis* (1978) relating the flurry of media concern about 'mugging' to broad shifts within the British state and attempts to orchestrate consent for a political order increasingly willing to rule through force and compulsion rather than consensus (see Chapter 5).

## 'SEIZED BY CHANGE, LIBERATED BY AFFLUENCE': TEENAGE CONSUMPTION AND THE POSITIVE STEREOTYPING OF YOUTH

The media and politicians alike have made recurring use of themes and images of 'youth' as a vehicle for comment on broader patterns of social change. Often, 'moral panics' about juvenile crime and youth subcultures have configured young people as the deplorable nadir of society's descent into moral turpitude. Popular representations of youth, however, have never been exclusively negative. Alongside the moral panics and malevolent stereotypes, there have always co-existed more positive media constructions in which youth has been presented as the vibrant vanguard of a prosperous future. Indeed, at certain historical moments, media images of 'youth as fun' have eclipsed the darker, more apprehensive iconography of 'youth as trouble'. During the early 1960s, for example, youth was habitually constructed as the sharp-end of a new, dynamic consumer culture that promised soon to be within everyone's grasp. *The Young Ones* (1961) was not alone in its representation of the young generation as upbeat, exciting and refreshingly fun. Throughout media and political discourse (in both America and Britain) the early 1960s saw young people – or, more specifically, 'teenagers' – frequently presented in glowing terms, as an energetic and uplifting alternative to the dead hand of tradition.

In America, the Kefauver Subcommittee's investigation into the causes of juvenile crime lumbered into the 1960s. By this time, however, the intensity of the delinquency panic was dissipating. Criticisms of media 'influence' continued, and rates of juvenile crime were still rising, but by the end of the 1950s more positive images of youth were coming to the fore as young people were portrayed (celebrated even) as an invigorating and inspiring social force. Ideals of 'youth', for example, were powerfully mobilised by John F. Kennedy in both his public persona and in his optimistic vision of America's 'New Frontier'.[19] But commercial interests were also central to this upbeat 're-branding' of youth. As James Gilbert has argued, the rise of more positive social responses to young people during the late 1950s and early 1960s was 'derived from a further extension of the market economy in American cultural life' (1986: 214). With the growing profitability of the teen market, the media and consumer industries fêted young people as never before and 'youth' became enshrined as the signifier of a newly prosperous age of freedom and fun.

Above all, it was the concept of the 'teenager' that embodied this positive, uplifting iconography of youth. Constructed as the epitome of prosperous modernity, the 'teenager' became symbolic of wider changes in patterns of American life. As we shall see in Chapter 6, in some quarters 'teenage' culture was treated with contempt, derided as the worst example of commercial massification. More widely, however, the late 1950s and early 1960s saw the teenager cast in radiant terms. Here, youth was constructed as the epitome of an America in which the sheer pace of economic growth seemed set to engender a new era of consumer abundance and social harmony. Taken as the quintessence of an exciting social transformation, 'teenagers' were configured as the vanguard of a new consumer culture – a social group distinguished not simply by their youth, but by a particular style of conspicuous, leisure-oriented consumption.[20]

As Chapter 2 demonstrated, the leisure-oriented consumption that was the hallmark of American 'teenage' lifestyle during the 1960s was, in reality, relatively specific to the white, middle class. In media and advertising rhetoric, however, the 'teenager' was promoted as an essentially classless avatar of pleasure and universal abundance. Here, Kirse May (2002) argues, images of Californian youth culture were in the forefront. During the early 1960s, the Golden State – home to surfing, hot rods and pop groups such as the Beach Boys – set the pace for America's

'New Frontier' in teenage leisure, pleasure and good living. As media images of monstrous delinquents slipped into the backround, therefore, they were superseded by archetypes of 'well-behaved, well-meaning, middle-class teenagers' as films, TV series and pop records all 'packaged California's kids as a beautiful and wholesome generation living it up on the coast' (May, 2002: 119).

In Britain, too, the early 1960s saw the media project a positive imagery of youth, with newspapers and magazines popularising notions of young people as a vibrant contrast to the tired conventions of the past. Leading the field was the *Daily Mirror*, where the theme of 'youth' (along with an explicit appeal to a young readership) became a feature of the newspaper's attempts not only to boost its market share, but also to offer a meaningful response to the pace of social change.[21] In 1961, for instance, a television advertising campaign announced that 'the *Daily Mirror* believes in young people'. Alongside film of jitterbugging teens, the advert's voice-over pronounced, 'They look fine to us, these citizens of tomorrow. . . . The *Daily Mirror* backs the young because the young are *alive*'. As in America, then, the media deployed images of youth as a shorthand signifier for flourishing modernity. And, again, themes of a dawning age of affluence and progress were condensed in the concept of the 'teenager'. The term 'teenager' did not simply denote a generational age group, but signified a new brand of liberated, classless and unashamedly hedonistic consumption. As Peter Laurie contended in his taxonomy of *The Teenage Revolution*, published in 1965:

> The distinctive fact about teenagers' behaviour is economic: they spend a lot of money on clothes, records, concerts, make-up, magazines: all things that give immediate pleasure and little lasting use.
>
> (Laurie, 1965: 9)

Consumer pleasure in an age of swinging modernity, then, was the central theme in configurations of the 1960s 'teenager'. It was hardly surprising, therefore, that politicians of the period sought to capitalise on the dynamic aura of youth. Touring America in 1964, for example, the Beatles had been wined-and-dined by the British Ambassador and on return to Britain they were acclaimed by Sir Alec Douglas Home, the Conservative Prime Minister, as 'our best exports' and 'a useful contribution to the balance of payments'. The Labour opposition were indignant, Harold Wilson (leader of the Party) protesting that the Conservatives were 'trying to make the Beatles their Secret Weapon' (Davies, 1978: 222). Yet Wilson, himself, was not above exploiting the Fab Four's kudos and in 1964 jumped at the chance to present the

**Figure 4.1** The Beatles show off their MBE awards in 1965
Courtesy of Pictorial Press

band with Variety Club awards (the Beatles, with characteristic humour, greeting Wilson as 'Mr. Dobson'). In 1965 the Labour leader played a more illustrious gambit, investing the Beatles as Members of the Order of the British Empire. A calculated appropriation of the imagery of youth, the award exemplified Wilson's vision of a rejuvenated and vigorously modern 'New Britain'.

Even the mod subculture could be embraced in the 1960s celebration of youth. Indeed, at the same time as they were reviled as the *bête noire* of the affluent society, the mods were also hailed as stylish consumers *par excellence*. Superficially clean-cut and well-dressed, mods were often treated as the pacesetters of 1960s élan, the press eagerly charting changes in the minutiae of their fashion and music. Even in 1964, at the height of the moral panic about the mods' seaside 'invasions', the *Sunday Times Magazine* featured a sumptuous nine-page photospread spotlighting the mods' sartorial flair (Halton, 1964). The association drawn between youth and liberated modernity reached its apex in the mid-1960s. The image of 'Swinging London' – with its throbbing nightclubs and fashionable boutiques – encapsulated ideas of Britain entering an exciting age of consumer freedom. It was an image that also caught on abroad. In America, British cultural exports such as Beatlemania, mod style and Mary Quant's chic fashion designs accrued connotations of exciting 'difference', *Time* magazine's 1966 cover story on 'London: The Swinging City' capturing this sense of Britain as the font of youthful dynamism. 'Youth is the word and the deed in London', *Time* enthused, 'seized by change, liberated by affluence . . . everything new, uninhibited and kinky is blooming at the top of London life' (*Time*, 15 April 1966).

By the end of the 1960s, however, the positive configurations of young people and social change were running out of steam. In America, the economy was faltering by the mid-1960s and liberal optimism gradually crumbled in the face of racial violence, urban disorder and the quagmire of the Vietnam War. Against this backdrop, the iconography of youthful high spirits began to give way to more negative representations of youth – with students and countercultural radicals attracting particular media venom. In Britain, too, economic downturn and a resurgence of political conflict were accompanied by more abrasive representations of youth. For example, the skinhead subculture, which first surfaced in Britain during the late 1960s, was unequivocally condemned in the media. Whereas the smoothly tailored appearance of the mods allowed them to be integrated relatively easily within discourses of prosperous modernity, the skinheads' defiantly proletarian posture (work boots, braces, prison 'crop' hairstyle) ensured the media invariably presented them as public enemy number one. As in America, media hostility also extended to elements of the counterculture. However, whereas working-class subcultures such as the skinheads were stigmatised as delinquent *symptoms* of social decline, the overtly political elements within the counterculture were vilified as an even more subversive threat – and were cast as an active *cause* of social instability and cultural decline.[22]

The 1960s counterculture, however, was never a homogeneous movement. Rather, it was a network of loosely affiliated groups, with a disparate membership drawn from a variety of social backgrounds. Responses from the media were also diverse. While political radicalism invariably prompted criticism and reproach, the counterculture's aesthetics and lifestyles often elicited fascination, sympathy, even a degree of admiration. In Britain this attitude was evident in reactions to the Rolling Stones' drugs trial of 1967. Amid a blaze of publicity, Keith

Richards and Mick Jagger were convicted and sentenced to three months' imprisonment for the possession of illegal drugs (though both walked free after an appeal). Rather than denouncing the Stones, however, significant sections of the media rallied to their defence. Famously, *The Times* published an editorial asking 'Who Breaks a Butterfly on a Wheel?' – the newspaper defending Jagger and Richards and attacking their prison sentences as unreasonably draconian (*The Times*, 1 July 1967). The media were also fascinated by the hippies' hedonistic lifestyles. In 1968, for instance, a feature series in *The Times* championed the 'fresh approach to living' developed by 'The Restless Generation' (*The Times*, 18 December 1968). Similar sentiments also featured in the American media. In 1969, for example, *Life* magazine was breathtaken by 'The Phenomenal Woodstock Happening', a multi-page photospread describing in awestruck tones how the Woodstock extravaganza was 'less a pop festival than a total experience, a phenomenon, a happening, high adventure, a near disaster and, in a small way, a struggle for survival' (*Life*, 15 September 1969).

Rather than being universally reviled, then, the 1960s counterculture could also be a source of fascination. Indeed, the libertine ethos of self-expression and 'doing your own thing' proved widely attractive at a time when cultural values were rapidly changing. As traditional ideals of restraint and respectability gave way to an emphasis on hedonism and personal consumption, the fashions, hairstyles, music and attitudes of the counterculture all percolated into mainstream social life. In fact, rather than representing the antithesis of modern consumerism, the 1960s counterculture is better seen as a developmental phase in its evolution. As Thomas Frank has suggested, the counterculture was not the nemesis of the consumer society but 'may be more accurately understood as a stage in the development of the values of the American middle class, a colorful instalment in the twentieth century drama of consumer subjectivity' (Frank, 1997: 120). For advertisers, especially, the countercultural scene offered images of 'youthful' pleasure and freedom commensurate with consumerist agendas. As one American adman affirmed in a 1968 editorial for *Merchandising Week*: 'Everywhere our mass media push psychedelia with all its clothing fads, so-called "way-out" ideas etc. Youth is getting the hard sell' (cited in Frank, 1997: 120).

Since the 1960s positive representations of youth have not disappeared, but media depictions of youth have become increasingly ambiguous and ambivalent. Of course, the stock 'youth-as-fun' and 'youth-as-trouble' images identified by Hebdige (1988b) were fairly crude 'ideal types' and, in reality, the two configurations often overlapped and co-existed. But, by the end of the century, many authors were arguing that much more blurred and open-ended media representations of youth were coming to the fore. It is, then, this recent history of the media's representation of young people that we examine in the next chapter.

# 5

# THE USUAL SUSPECTS
## Media, politics and images of youth

Hi kids! Do you like violence? (Yeah yeah yeah!)
Wanna see me stick Nine Inch Nails
Through each one of my eyelids? (Uh-huh!)
Wanna copy me and do exactly like I did? (Yeah yeah!)
Try 'cid and get fucked up worse than my life is? (Huh?)
My brain's dead weight,
I'm tryin' to get my head straight
But I can't figure out which Spice Girl I wanna impregnate.

(Eminem, 'My Name Is', *Slim Shady* LP)

(Interscope, 1999)

## 'FOUL MOUTHED YOBS': THE DEMONOLOGY OF DELINQUENT YOUTH

When Sex Pistols guitarist, Steve Jones, called television presenter Bill Grundy a 'fucking rotter' on live TV, he helped spark one of the most intense moral panics Britain had seen since the 1960s. In 1976 punk rock stalwarts the Sex Pistols (then a little-known band) had been booked onto an early evening TV chat show to discuss their first single, 'Anarchy in the UK'. However, baited by Grundy (the programme's host), the band sneered, swore and made themselves as disruptive as possible. The insults were jokey, but the humour of the episode was lost on the British press and the tabloids lambasted the Pistols as 'Foul Mouthed Yobs' (*Daily Mirror*, 2 December 1976). In the furore that followed, promoters cancelled the Sex Pistols' concerts, the band were beaten-up in the street and the BBC refused to play their records. Nevertheless, paradoxically, the reaction also lent decisive momentum to events and – as with the mods and rockers of the early 1960s – the fevered media attention gave greater definition to the emergent punk subculture and the Sex Pistols' records soared up the charts.

The moral panic that surrounded punk rock dramatised a wider sense of crisis and social polarisation that characterised Britain during the late 1970s. In the face of rising unemployment, urban disorder and fraught industrial relations, the confident post-war rhetoric of growth and social cohesion steadily crumbled and gave way to a more abrasive form of political relations. This shift found its corollary in increasingly negative social responses to subcultures like punk. Positive media representations of youth did not disappear, but there was a palpable resurgence of more negative coverage. In the wake of punk, the 1970s and 1980s saw the British media parade a whole demonology of baleful youth as indices of a perceived growth in lawlessness and cultural malaise. A seemingly endless series of anxieties saw new terrors (lager louts, New Age travellers, acid-house ravers) grafted onto older, more established themes of social decline (the collapse of family life, delinquency, urban disorder). In America, too, the 1970s and 1980s saw a spate of media anxieties about youth culture focused around such phenomena as the rise of gangsta rap and the growth of drug abuse.

This chapter begins with an exploration of this media coverage and the way in which some theorists have seen it as linked to broader shifts within political relations and the rise of more coercive forms of state apparatus. While Stanley Cohen's notion of 'moral panic' (see Chapter 4) is useful in understanding these episodes, some authors have suggested that his original model requires significant revision in order to take account of the changing nature of the contemporary media. This chapter examines and assesses these critiques of Cohen's 'moral panic' framework. The chapter goes on to explore attempts to revive more positive representations of youth culture in Britain during the 1990s, specifically focusing on the Labour Party's effort to mobilise concepts of 'youthfulness' in its vision of a dynamic and reinvigorated 'New Britain'. The chapter shows, however, that as the Labour governments of the late 1990s increasingly struggled to deliver on their election promises, they steadily retreated into more authoritarian postures that sought to engender popular support through a new crusade against crime and 'delinquent youth'. Nevertheless, the proliferation and fragmentation of the modern media has meant that representations of youth have invariably been complex and shot through with contradictions – and the chapter concludes with a discussion of the ambivalent and ambiguous sensibility characteristic of much contemporary 'youth media'.

## THE 'LAW 'N' ORDER' BANDWAGON: YOUTH, MEDIA AND THE RISE OF 'AUTHORITARIAN POPULISM'

The themes of crisis woven into the British media's response to punk rock were commensurate with the political climate of the period. According to Stuart Hall and his colleagues (Hall *et al.*, 1978; Hall and Jacques, 1983), Britain during the late 1970s and early 1980s was characterised by a sense of social tension and the rise of a more authoritarian state apparatus. For Hall and his associates, the 'consensus politics' that had distinguished the post-war era were increasingly undermined by economic decline, industrial unrest and social conflict. In place of 'consensus', they argued, a new 'control culture' began to take shape, a more coercive form of political state that reached fruition in the policies of Margaret Thatcher's Conservative governments. According to Hall, the Thatcher governments of the 1980s marked the ascendance of 'authoritarian populism' (Hall, 1983) – a New Right political programme that won electoral support by combining a doctrinaire commitment to free-market economics with an authoritarian stance on issues of law and order. Youth occupied an important position in this agenda. A flagship of the Conservatives' political strategy was a tough stand against juvenile crime, and Thatcher's governments garnered significant support through their introduction of more coercive forms of policing and a more disciplinarian system of juvenile justice. These attempts to trade on popular anxieties, moreover, were marked by distinct elements of racism, with media and political discourse casting 'black' muggers and 'inner-city rioters' as a threatening, 'alien' presence in British society (Hall *et al.*, 1978).

Elements of racism also featured in the drug scares prominent in America throughout the 1980s and 1990s. Drug abuse was undoubtedly a social problem in the US, but Craig Reinarman and Harry Levine (Levine and Reinarman, 1988; Reinarman and Levine, 1989, 1995; Reinarman and Levine (eds), 1997) have suggested that media and political responses to the issue have been a politically orchestrated attempt to engender moral panic. In an account redolent of Hall *et al.*'s (1978) analysis of the 'mugging' scare in 1970s Britain, Reinarman and Levine have argued that American concerns about 'crack' cocaine during the 1980s and 1990s were 'concocted by the press, politicians, and moral entrepreneurs to serve other agendas' (1995: 157). In some senses, then, US anxieties about 'crack' can be seen as constituent in a distinctively American version of 'authoritarian populism'. Asserting that the US crusade against drug use represents an exercise in scapegoating, Levine and Reinarman argue that the campaign has not only appealed to 'racism, bureaucratic self-interest, economics, and mongering by the media' (1988: 258), but has also 'allowed conservative politicians to be law-and-order minded; . . . [and] permitted them to give the appearance of caring about social ills without committing them to do or spend very much to help people' (1988: 255).[1]

Henry Giroux (1996, 1997), too, has been deeply critical of the US media's scapegoating of youth – especially black youth – as a cause of urban America's social problems. For Giroux, media representations of African-American youth have helped promote 'a white moral panic' (1996: 97) which has not only 'reproduce[d] racist stereotypes about blacks by portraying them as criminals and welfare cheats', but has also 'remove[d] whites from any responsibility or complicity for the violence and poverty that has become so endemic to American life' (1996: 66). Moreover, like Levine and Reinarman, Giroux sees this racist stereotyping as not simply the result of prejudice, but as part of wider political strategies. Representations of African-American youth as predatory and violent, Giroux explains, have fed into 'the increasing public outcry for tougher crime bills designed to build more prisons and legislate get-tough policies with minorities of color and class' (Giroux, 1996: 67).

The 'law 'n' order' bandwagon, however, did not entirely displace images of 'youth-as-fun'. On both sides of the Atlantic, increases in youth unemployment during the 1970s and 1980s made the image of the 'swinging teenager' an anachronism, but not all young people lost out. A fortunate minority enjoyed the high-rolling prosperity offered by a massive expansion of the business and financial sectors. Rather than the 'teenager', however, it was the young, urban professional – or 'yuppie' – that symbolised the mood of 1980s 'good times'. According to a *Newsweek* cover story, for instance, 1984 was the 'Year of the Yuppie' as economic shifts from manufacturing and distribution to financial and information services laid the way for the rise of ambitious, young business executives who seemed to exist on 'a new plane of consciousness, a state of Transcendental Acquisition' (*Newsweek*, 31 December 1984). The self-obsessed materialism of the archetypal yuppie was the cultural counterpart to the New Right's free market ideals and, in both Britain and America, the championing of youthful entrepreneurs was prominent in New Right attempts to mobilise popular support via the promise of consumer empowerment.

An authoritarian stance on law and order, however, remained a key theme of political programmes into the 1990s, and developments in youth culture regularly prompted political sabre-rattling. In Britain, for example, anxieties about the general trajectory of cultural change were projected onto youth culture in moral panics that seemed to echo the social concerns of the 1950s and 1960s. Originally coined in 1987 by satirical TV comedian Harry Enfield, the phrase 'loadsamoney' passed into public debate, used by both politicians and the media to denote what was perceived as a gaudy affluence that promoted belligerence and boorishness. In 1988 the anxieties found specific focus, a moral panic developing around incidents of drunken violence in provincial towns. The finger of blame was pointed at a 'new' generation of affluent but undisciplined youth, the media and politicians such as Douglas Hurd (the Home Secretary) coining the term 'lager louts' to describe young people 'with too much money in their pockets [and] too many pints inside them, but too little self-discipline and too little notion of the care and responsibility which they owe to others' (Hurd, cited in *The Guardian*, 10 June 1988). Itinerant hippies dubbed 'New Age travellers' were also a target for opprobrium – their unorthodox lifestyle and association with direct action politics winning them vilification in the popular media and condemnation from the authorities. The period's most intense episode of media alarm, however, arose in response to the 'acid house' phenomenon of the late 1980s.

## RAVING MAD: REAPPRAISING MORAL PANICS

Pioneered in American black and gay clubs such as Chicago's Warehouse and New York's Paradise Garage, new forms of dance music – house, garage, techno – filtered into British youth culture during the 1980s and early 1990s. Manchester's Haçienda club became a hub of northern dance culture, club nights such as Nude and Temperance introducing Chicago house and Detroit techno to British dancefloors. In London, too, DJs such as Danny Rampling, Andy Weatherall and Trevor Fung were influenced by the American club scene, but also drew inspiration from the nightlife of Ibiza. During 1987 and early 1988 the lively Balearic resort had become a centre for club culture, its DJs experimenting with house beats to produce continuous mixes of music that kept dancefloors packed throughout the night. The drug MDMA (or, as it became more commonly known, 'ecstasy' or simply 'E') had also become a feature of the Ibiza club scene, and during the late 1980s 'E' rapidly became British clubbers' recreational drug of choice. Back in Britain, the heady atmosphere of Ibiza was recreated not only in London 'acid house' clubs such as Shoom and Spectrum, but also in a circuit of one-off (often illegal) 'warehouse' parties. Initially, these impromptu events were advertised through word of mouth, but by 1988 bigger, open-air raves were being organised entrepreneurially. Arranged by professional promoters such as Sunrise, Biology and Eclipse, the so-called 'orbital raves' (staged at locations around the M25 motorway circling London) attracted crowds of thousands. Though unlicensed, these were often huge events that boasted enormous sound systems, elaborate light shows, smoke machines and sometimes even fairground rides.

At first, the popular press eagerly embraced the acid-house scene as the latest exciting dance craze. During the summer of 1988, however, as the links between acid house and ecstasy (outlawed as a class 'A' drug since 1977) became more widely known, media coverage turned hostile. Tabloid headlines reviled 'the evil Acid House cult' and news stories painted lurid pictures of 'drug-crazed kids' and 'evil drug dealers' (*The Sun*, 26 June 1989). Responding to the sensational media reports, authorities increasingly clamped down on the rave circuit. Particularly significant was the passage of the 1994 Criminal Justice and Public Order Act. More generally known as the Criminal Justice Act, it was a comprehensive piece of legislation covering a wide range of areas – from the prevention of terrorism to the control of pornography – but Part V of the Act seemed specially targeted at the acid house 'problem'. By strengthening police powers of eviction and creating the new offence of 'aggravated trespass', the Act effectively undermined rave organisers' ability to stage unlicensed outdoor events.[2]

In some respects, the furore that surrounded the acid-house scene seemed like a classic episode of moral panic. The behaviour of rave-goers was distorted in sensational press stories, the overwrought media coverage escalating events by both prompting sterner measures of policing and galvanising the development of a recognisable 'acid house' subculture. And, just as Stuart Hall and his colleagues (Hall *et al.*, 1978) situated the 1970s 'mugging' panic within broader political shifts, Andrew Hill (2002) has convincingly argued that responses to acid house were constituent in a wider political agenda. According to Hill, the acid-house scene provoked such a punitive reaction from the agencies of social control because, for the Conservative government, it represented part of a more general 'enemy within'. In Conservative political discourse of the 1980s, Hill suggests, the acid-house phenomenon – along with trade unionists and peace activists – was configured as a dangerous threat to social order and stability. But, Hill argues, acid house was conceived as *especially* problematic because many of the raves were held in the resonant setting of the English countryside – the heartland of conservative values and culture.

In other respects, however, the acid house 'moral panic' differed to the model originally developed by Stanley Cohen (see Chapter 4). According to Chas Critcher (2000, 2003), the media response to rave was more complex than that outlined in Cohen's classic formulation. Critcher pointed out that, in practice, there were actually three over-lapping panics – about raves, about ecstasy and about New Age travellers. Though often conflated in the media coverage, Critcher argued, the action taken over each was quite distinct. Ambiguity also surrounded the identity of the 'folk devils'. As Critcher observed, the rave organisers were presented as irresponsible, but seldom as inherently evil. The ravers themselves, meanwhile, tended to be constructed as hapless victims. Here, there was also a marked 'sexualisation' of concern, with girls por-trayed as especially vulnerable to the 'morally corrupting' influences of ecstasy (which itself was caricatured as a 'mind-bending sex drug'). This facet of the media response became particularly pronounced in 1995 fol-lowing the death of Leah Betts, an Essex teenager who had lapsed into a coma after taking an ecstasy tablet. While earlier ecstasy-related deaths had attracted publicity, this was nothing compared to the uproar that fol-lowed the Betts tragedy, the media mobilising her death as a potent image of corrupted innocence.[3] According to Critcher, the one group who *did* attract blame in the 'ecstasy panic' were the drug dealers – though even they remained indistinct figures in the background. Rather than being a specific 'person' or 'group', then, Critcher argued that the 'folk devil' in the acid-house panic was (in terms of Cohen's original model) a 'con-dition' or 'episode' – in this case, the rave itself. The media reaction to acid house, moreover, was more varied than the notion of 'moral panic' might imply. Critcher argued, for example, that there was a marked degree of ambiguity in many of the news stories, while coverage in the broadsheet press and broadcast media tended to be more balanced than the sensationalist accounts in the tabloids.

Some authors were even more critical of the 'moral panic' model, arguing that the acid-house episode showed Cohen's original formula-tion required radical revision. Both Angela McRobbie (1994b) and Sarah Thornton (1994, 1995), for example, argued that the classic moral panic framework operated with an excessively monolithic view of society and the media. For McRobbie and Thornton, analysis of contemporary media culture needed to take 'account of a plurality of reactions, each with their different constituencies, effectivities and modes of discourse' (McRobbie and Thornton, 1995: 564). Compared to the 1960s, for instance, the 1980s and 1990s saw a greater range of agencies and experts stepping forward to challenge the media's demonisation of youth and countering the vocality of the traditional moral crusaders (McRobbie, 1994b: 217;

McRobbie and Thornton, 1995: 566). Indeed, although groups such as the Freedom to Party Campaign were effectively a mouthpiece for the acid-house entrepreneurs, they still succeeded in mobilising opposition to anti-rave legislation – in 1990 a Freedom to Party rally in Trafalgar Square attracting a crowd of over 10,000 supporters. In America, too, there emerged new pressure groups working to challenge the media's 'folk devil' stereotypes. In June 2001, for example, the Hip-Hop Summit Action Network (HSAN) held the first of its annual meetings in New York. Partly financed by hip-hop business mogul Russell Simmons, the HSAN and its regional chapters drew together a wide constituency of rap artists, record industry executives, civil rights leaders and scholars who worked to promote the interests of hip-hop culture, countering claims from religious groups, the media and politicians that rap music incited violence and crime.

In these terms, then, the 'folk devils' themselves were better able to engage with, and contest, the media's distorted representations. McRobbie and Thornton argued that this had been partly facilitated by changes in the media itself. The proliferation and fragmentation of mass, niche and micro-media, they argued, had generated a 'multiplicity of voices, which compete and contest the meaning of the issues subject to "moral panic"' (McRobbie and Thornton, 1995: 560).[4] Stressing the diversity of media responses to the rave scene, McRobbie and Thornton argued that the 'classic' notion of moral panic not only failed to distinguish between different kinds of mainstream media, but also ignored the alternative accounts offered in the 'micro' and 'niche' media that had mushroomed within the youth cultures of the 1980s and 1990s. In response to mass media scare-mongering about the rave scene, they argued, the subcultural press (for example, magazines such as *i-D*, *The Face* and *New Musical Express*) 'tracked the tabloids' every move, re-printed whole front pages, analysed their copy and decried the *misrepresentation* of Acid House' (McRobbie and Thornton, 1995: 568). Overall, McRobbie and Thornton challenged the original moral panics model which, they argued, had conceptualised the media as (mis)representing an objective social reality to a gullible audience. In contemporary cultural life, they argued, social reality was increasingly constituted through *competing* media representations and decoded in a *variety* of ways by sophisticated audiences.

Indeed, some members of the rave scene actually greeted media condemnation with relish, since it confirmed their romantic self-image as transgressive rebels (Thornton, 1994). Commercial interests, moreover, increasingly exploited (even deliberately cultivated) episodes of moral panic as a neat marketing strategy. As McRobbie and Thornton explained:

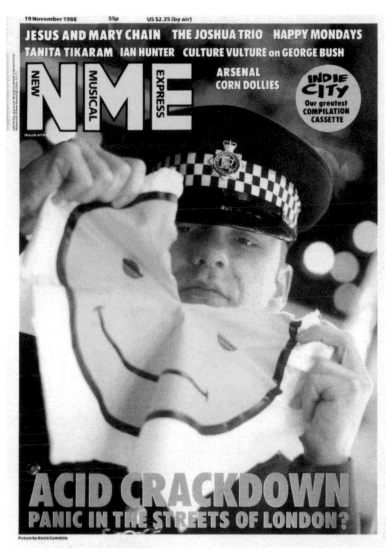

**Figure 5.1** 'Acid Crackdown' – *New Musical Express* challenges the acid house moral panic (*NME*, 19 November 1988)

> Culture industry promotions and marketing people now understand how, for certain products like records, magazines, movies and computer games, nothing could be better for sales than a bit of controversy – the threat of censorship, the suggestion of sexual scandal or subversive activity.
>
> (McRobbie and Thornton, 1995: 572)

Rather than being inherently flawed, however, Chas Critcher suggested that the moral panic framework should be revised and updated. Responding to McRobbie and Thornton's critiques, Critcher acknowledged the greater ambiguity and multiplicity of media voices in the late twentieth century, but he insisted that some voices were more powerful than others. 'When the police, the tabloid press and the governing party conjoin in the concerted campaign', Critcher observed, 'the weak power base of the alternative media is revealed' (2000: 154). Indeed, by their very nature, 'micro' and 'niche' media are targeted at a relatively narrow market. Largely preaching to the converted, 'niche' media have only limited ability to sway wider public and political opinion. For Critcher, then, the notion of moral panic remained a sound analytical concept. Account had to be given to the specific character of any one moral panic, to the contradictory nature of media coverage and to the complexity of social and political responses – but, Critcher maintained, in attempts to understand the media's construction of social reality and its active role in shaping events, the essential features of the moral panic model 'remain an indispensable account of the basic processes at work' (2000: 154).

Yet Critcher *did* detect a shift in the form of modern moral panics. Although the power of 'niche' media was relatively limited, Critcher suggested that during the 1980s and 1990s attempts to portray youth as a threatening social menace had become harder to sustain in the face of arguments to the contrary from young people themselves, their allies and expert opinion. As a consequence, he argued, the construction of youth as folk devils had been increasingly displaced by the presentation of *children* as *the victims* of folk devils. With an eye to the mounting anxieties about paedophilia during the 1990s, Critcher speculated that the army of claim-making crusaders had 'retreat[ed] to safer ground where its moral concerns are unlikely to be challenged' (Critcher, 2003: 162).

## CHAMPAGNE SUPERNOVA: THE RISE AND FALL OF 'COOL BRITANNIA'

In Britain during the late 1990s it looked as though a resurgence of more positive representations of youth was underway. In November 1996 a *Newsweek* cover story had hailed London as 'the coolest city on the planet' (*Newsweek*, 4 November 1996) and throughout 1997 'Cool Britannia' was a buzzing phrase, coined in the media to denote a rising generation of 'Britpop' bands (most obviously Blur and Oasis); a new wave of young artists, writers, filmmakers and fashion designers; and a surge of innovative style magazines and fashionable restaurants. Striving to present themselves as agents of modernity, the Labour Party scrambled to

**Figure 5.2** 'Cool Britannia' – 'London Swings Again' (*Vanity Fair*, No. 439, March 1997)

Courtesy of Pictorial Press

capitalise on the verve of the 'Cool Britannia' style renaissance. National rejuvenation, for example, became a key theme in Tony Blair's speeches both before, and immediately after, the 1997 general election – the Labour leader promising the 1996 Labour Party Conference that his government would 'make this the young country of my generation's dreams' (*The Guardian*, 4 October 1995).[5] Once in office Blair's attempts to forge a 'New Britain' also tapped into the energy of contemporary youth culture, the Prime Minister throwing champagne receptions attended by both Noel Gallagher (boisterous frontman of Oasis) and Alan McGee (founder of leading 'indie' label, Creation Records), while McGee was subsequently drafted in as a special advisor to the Creative Industries Task Force (CITF – see Chapter 3).

Blair's strategy obviously echoed Harold Wilson's attempts to co-opt the Beatles into his earlier vision of a reinvigorated 'New Britain' during the 1960s (see Chapter 4). But Blair's push for 'youth appeal' was also inspired by the razzmatazz of Bill Clinton's 1992 Presidential campaign. Presenting himself as a 'youth friendly' man of the people, Clinton had appeared on MTV to answer questions from a teenage audience (including a query on his preference for underwear – 'boxers or briefs?'),[6] had played saxophone on the *Arsenio Hall* TV show, and had admitted that as a student he had tried smoking cannabis (though strenuously denied inhaling). Blair, too, positioned himself as affable and clued-up, conversant with popular culture and at ease with 'the kids'. Like Clinton, the Labour leader usually appeared mildly embarrassed by the foibles of his student days (as an Oxford undergraduate during the early 1970s Blair had fronted a progressive rock band called Ugly Rumours).[7] But both politicians enjoyed squeezing a measure of 'hip' cachet from their fleeting brush with youthful nonconformity – and a grinning Blair was not above brandishing a guitar at the odd photo-call. Such attempts to engage with youth and popular culture often seemed clumsy, but the Conservative Party struggled even more desperately. William Hague, for example, may have been (at 36) one of the youngest-ever Tory leaders, but in 1997 his effort to update the Conservatives' image by wearing a baseball cap emblazoned with the slogan 'Hague' was a fashion *faux pas* that provoked hoots of derision.

Initially, Blair's attempts to 'rebrand' Britain as a font of creativity and entrepreneurial dynamism were reasonably successful, winning support from both the public and the pop glitterati.[8] But by the end of the 1990s the 'Cool Britannia' bubble had burst. Disillusioned with what they saw as Labour's failure to deliver on election promises to help young people and the poor, the grandees of Britpop began to round on the government. A music industry awards ceremony in February 1998 saw an early gesture of resentment when Danbert Nobacon (of the anarchist band Chumbawamba) threw a bucket of water over John Prescott, the Deputy Prime Minister, as a protest against government welfare policies. The following month saw another stinging blow, as the front page of *New Musical Express* (an influential music magazine appealing to a core readership of young(ish) males) featured a picture of a distinctly malevolent-looking Tony Blair alongside the headline 'Ever Had the Feeling You've Been Cheated?'. The accompanying editorial, entitled 'The Labour Government's War On You', damned a whole gamut of Blair's initiatives. From compulsory work programmes for unemployed youth to the imposition of university tuition fees, the magazine argued that the policies of the Labour government had been a cynical betrayal of British youth:

> *Our* music, *our* culture, *our* collective sweat of our groovy brows has been bundled up and neatly repackaged and given a cute little brand name and is being used by New Labour spin doctors to give this hideously reactionary New Labour government a cachet of radical credibility. A credibility of which it is utterly undeserving.
>
> (*New Musical Express*, 14 March 1998)

A succession of pop musicians also lined up to decry the Labour Party's 'betrayal'. In 1998 Britpop luminaries Blur joined the anti-tuition fees lobby, while Noel Gallagher was soon professing shame at having accepted an invitation to Downing Street following Blair's election. In 2000 New Labour's romance with Britpop soured further, Blur joining the Chemical Brothers and Fatboy Slim in backing Ken Livingstone's independent candidature as Mayor of London (in preference to Labour's official candidate, Frank Dobson). Alan McGee, meanwhile, angrily withdrew from the government's Creative Industries Task Force and bankrolled the short lived candidacy of maverick punk rock godfather, Malcolm McLaren.

Ignoring its critics, however, the government shifted away from the upbeat themes of 'Cool Britannia' towards a more authoritarian stance. As Shadow Home Secretary in the mid-1990s Tony Blair had already helped steer the Labour Party towards a tough stand on law and order, and by the end of the decade a new crusade against crime and delinquent youth had become a trademark of his government's attempts to win popular support. In July 2001 riots by Asian youths in Bradford, Oldham and Burnley initially met with a mixed response from both the media and the government. At first, issues of racism and social deprivation were acknowledged as an underlying cause of events, but by the end of the year attitudes had hardened. Blame increasingly shifted to the Asian communities themselves, Home Secretary David Blunkett suggesting further disturbances could be avoided through the introduction of 'citizenship classes' for young Asians, while the report of the official inquiry into the riots recommended new immigrants should be required to make a formal statement of allegiance to show 'a clear primary loyalty' to Britain (*The Guardian*, 12 December 2001). In 2002 the acquittal of two teenagers charged with the murder of ten-year-old Damilola Taylor in north Peckham prompted further authoritarian rhetoric, the popular press denouncing the case as 'a devastating indictment of Britain's amoral underclass and a judicial system that can no longer protect the law-abiding people of this country' (*Daily Mail*, 26 April 2002).

More pronounced law-and-order mongering came in 2003. After two teenage bystanders were killed in a gun battle between rival gangs at a New Year party in Birmingham, both the media and the government railed against an apparent upsurge of gang culture and gun crime in British cities. Superficially, the responses bore many of the features of a classic moral panic. Focusing on urban black youth, histrionic stories in the tabloid press painted a picture of a 'new' wave of 'gun madness' sweeping through 'Violent Britain' (*The Sun*, 6 January 2003), while the government scurried to introduce tougher laws to deal with gun crime and gang violence. Elements of 'media panic' were also prominent, with suggestions of a causal link between rap music and violence. Echoing American anxieties about the negative 'effects' of gangsta rap during the 1980s and 1990s, Culture Minister Kim Howells argued that the events in Birmingham were 'symptomatic of something very, very serious'. 'For years', Howells averred, 'I have been very worried about these hateful lyrics that these boasting macho idiot rappers come out with. . . . It has created a culture where killing is almost a fashion accessory.' Reserving his most scornful ire for London garage outfit So Solid Crew, Howells asserted that 'Idiots like the So Solid Crew are glorifying gun culture and violence . . . It is very worrying and we ought to stand up and say it' (*The Guardian*, 6 January 2003).[9] Others joined the fray, tabloid newspapers pointing not only to 'rap music's link to the scourge of gun crime', but also targeting new 'video nasty' computer games that seemed to 'glamorize violence' (*Daily Mirror*, 7 January 2003a).

Nevertheless, the debates about black youth culture and urban violence in 2003 were more complex than the classic moral panic model would suggest. Just as responses to rave culture during the 1980s and 1990s were often ambiguous and contradictory, a multiplicity of voices could be heard in the 2003 controversy. Indeed, a storm of publicity quickly followed Howells' attack on So Solid Crew, a host of commentators taking issue with the Minister's simplistic beliefs about rap music's social 'effects' and denouncing the implicit racism of his comments. Many of Howells' colleagues (most notably Dianne Abbott, MP for Hackney) were stridently critical of his stand and argued, instead, for a response that addressed more adequately the social and economic problems that were the bedrock of urban crime. Even the tabloids presented a variety of viewpoints. *The Sun* for example, waded in with a characteristically lurid and racist slant, with the headline '80% of Criminals Are On Drugs' appearing alongside a large photograph of black youngsters dressed as gun-totting 1920s mobsters.[10] But even *The Sun* acknowledged there were 'complex causes' (including poverty) to rising levels of crime (*The Sun*, 10 January 2003). Headline stories in the *Daily Mirror*, meanwhile, condemned the menace of the 'Gangsta Trap' and spotlighted 'Hip-Hop Stars' Link to Deaths' – but these existed alongside the banner headline 'Don't Let Music Take the Rap' and an interview with Trevor Nelson, a Radio One DJ, who defended rap music and criticised as scapegoating attempts to blame black youth culture for an upsurge in violent crime (*Daily Mirror*, 7 January 2003b).

Undoubtedly, then, British anxieties about rap music and violence in 2003 showed many of the classic symptoms of moral panic. Sensationalised media coverage presented growing levels of gun crime as an 'unprecedented' social problem; attempts were made to demonise black youth as 'folk devils'; simplistic notions of 'cause and effect' were used to explain the influence of popular media; and attempts were made to harvest political capital through calls for a 'law 'n' order' clampdown. At the same time, however, media responses were often more contradictory and ambiguous than a traditional moral panics framework might suggest. Kim Howells' attack on So Solid Crew, for example, was widely reported, but so too were responses from his critics and there was widespread media acknowledgement that the causes of violent crime were complex and could not be blamed simply on the music and style of urban youth. As Stanley Cohen has reflected, contemporary moral panics have seen the media become more self-reflective in their coverage, so that 'the same public and media discourse that provides the raw evidence of moral panic [also] uses the concept as first-order description, reflexive comment or criticism' (Cohen, 2002: vii).

## DAZED AND CONFUSED: DISAFFECTION, AMBIVALENCE AND IRONY IN THE SPECTACLE OF YOUTH

By the end of the 1990s, rather than being either celebratory or condemnatory, media representations of youth often seemed equivocal and ambivalent. There had always been a degree of slippage between the media stereotypes of 'youth-as-fun' and 'youth-as-trouble' identified by Hebdige (1988b), but during the 1990s it seemed as though they were giving way to a much more blurred, ambiguous and open-ended set of media representations.

There were, of course, occasions when decidedly negative connotations predominated within media representations of young people. In America, for example, a storm of publicity surrounded the arrest and conviction of five black teenagers for the brutal beating and rape of a young, middle-class (white) jogger in New York's Central Park in 1989.[11] Coining the term 'wilding' to denote the group's alleged savage rampage, the press coverage of the case reiterated a rich history of racist mythologies in which black masculinity has been constructed as violent, predatory and animalistic. The term 'wilding' was, itself, a media invention. Awaiting interrogation, some of the accused had reputedly passed the time by singing 'Wild Thing', at the time a hit for the Los Angeles rapper Tone Lōc, and police officers had misheard the lyrics as 'wilding'. Subsequently, the phrase was picked up by the press and became a staple feature of news stories about the case – the term's connotations conjuring up vivid images of 'roving bands' and feral 'wolf packs' (Baker, 1993: 49). As a consequence, Charles Acland has argued, racist discourses 'composed the lens' through which the case came to be understood, the media coverage presenting the crime as though it 'revealed something of the "nature" of the urban African-American, something different from, and ultimately feared by, white society: a crazed, violent, and sexually aggressive black mass' (Acland, 1995: 49).

For Acland, the Central Park 'wilding' case was also part of a wider discourse of 'youth in crisis' that became a familiar feature in the American media during the late 1980s and early 1990s. Invested with 'significant connotative force', Acland argued, these images served as a repository for social concern and an impetus for debate about the state of American society (1995: 19). Spectacular youth crimes were presented in the media as symbolic of wider social decay but, Acland suggested, the media also offered a more nuanced 'spectacle of wasted youth' in which adolescents were presented as alienated and anomic rather than intrinsically immoral. For example, according to Acland, films such as *River's Edge* (1986) and *Kids* (1995) depicted a 'deadended generation of apathetic and detached youths' whose lives were bleak, violent and meaningless (1995: 129). A related, though more offbeat, portrayal also featured in Richard Linklater's films *Slacker* (1991) and *Dazed and Confused* (1993). The narrative of *Slacker* proceeds through a series of accidental encounters between young characters in Austin,

Texas, the film offering a vision of youngsters leading aimless, discon-
nected lives saturated by the images and products of the mass media. Also
set in Austin, *Dazed and Confused* follows a day in the life of a group of
high-school students who are alienated from the middle-class world of
their parents and seem devoid of any goals or guiding purpose in life.
Though less visceral than *River's Edge* or *Kids*, Linklater's films shared
many of their themes, Douglas Kellner arguing they depicted a young
generation disengaged from traditional norms and values and 'discon-
nected and alienated from the mainstream culture celebrated by
television and conservative Hollywood film' (Kellner, 1995: 142–143).

From Linklater's film, the term 'slackers' passed into popular discourse to denote post-baby boom youngsters who were over-educated
for the employment available to them and who had retreated into an
apathetic lifestyle of casual jobs and trash media. The term 'Generation
X' developed similar connotations, having been introduced to the
popular vocabulary by Douglas Coupland's (1991) novel, *Generation X*.
Coupland's characters were actually relatively old (they were born in
the early to mid-1960s), but the term filtered into popular discourse
to denote youngsters in their teens and early twenties. As we saw in
Chapter 3, the phrase was picked up in the world of marketing to denote
a generation of uniquely media literate and cynical consumers. More
widely, however, the term 'Generation X' also became associated with
a youth culture characterised by its listless nihilism. Often constructed
as being lost in a 'depthless' world of media images, this construction of
youth was closely bound up with concepts of a new, 'postmodern' media
culture.

Postmodernism is a notoriously nebulous concept. Most theorists,
however, understand it as a set of cultural characteristics generated in
tandem with the profound social, economic and cultural changes of the
late twentieth century. For the proponents of postmodernism, a fundamental sea-change in contemporary life had been brought about through
the transformation of world political orders; major industrial restructuring and economic realignment; rapid developments in technology and
media; and significant shifts in family and community relationships. In
this new 'postmodern condition' (Lyotard, 1984) traditional securities
had steadily collapsed, with all overarching claims to knowledge and
'truth' being subjected to growing scepticism and doubt. Alongside this
crisis in the status of knowledge, some theorists argued, there had also
emerged a distinctive set of cultural trends and aesthetic sensibilities.
With a proliferation of media and information technologies, postmodern
theorists contended, traditional senses of time and space were transformed – so that the difference between representation and reality

collapsed and nothing remained but a surfeit of endlessly circulating images. In these terms, postmodern theorists such as Jean Baudrillard (1985) argued that an increasingly media-saturated world had brought about an 'ecstasy of communication', a condition in which boundaries between formerly discrete areas of cultural life were erased and people became immersed in a 'hyper-real' media world where the borders between the real and the imaginary were blurred and indistinct.

According to some authors, new media forms embodied this 'postmodern' emphasis on surface and inter-textuality. The rise of pop music videos in the 1980s, in particular, was hailed by some critics (Jameson, 1984; Kaplan, 1987) as emblematic of postmodern sensibilities through the way they ransacked a variety of cinematic genres and deployed a visual style that often collapsed boundaries between commercial promotion and 'high' art. Likewise, MTV was understood as a pre-eminent manifestation of postmodern aesthetics through 'its celebration of the look – its surfaces, textures, the self-as-commodity – [which] threatens to reduce everything to the image/representation/simulacrum' (Kaplan, 1987: 44).

Similar 'postmodern' traits also emerged in British television. Here, the work of TV producer Janet Street-Porter was especially influential. Constituting young people as a discrete TV audience is notoriously difficult, audiences aged from their teens to mid-twenties watching less TV than any other age group. But Street-Porter had some success, first with the magazine programme *Network 7* (Channel 4, 1987), and then as editor of youth programming at BBC2 where, in 1988, she introduced *Def II*, an early evening 'strand' of youth-oriented TV shows.[12] The success of this programming was largely indebted to Street-Porter's pioneering style of TV production. Disregarding conventional television practices, Street-Porter placed emphasis on energy and innovation. An amateurish style of presentation – inexperienced presenters, wobbly cameras, long tracking shots – was often used to create an edgy, unpredictable atmosphere, while a 'postmodern' stream of images, graphics and subtitles assumed a savvy, media-literate audience. As Street-Porter explained:

> I'm making programmes for a generation who have grown up with TV, with visual images all around them, who are very familiar with computers and video technology . . . my shows have set out to arrest audiences, to hold them, to play all sorts of tricks to keep them from turning over.
>
> (cited in Medhurst, 1988: 16)

Street-Porter's approach influenced other British broadcasters. Channel Four (established in 1982 with a remit to cater for niche audiences such as youth and to foster new and experimental programmes) responded especially quickly. The station's flagship music show, *The Tube* (1982–1987) had already won success with a quick-paced, quirky format similar to that developed by Street-Porter, and the late 1980s and 1990s saw a string of Channel Four programmes that fused this production style with a taste for playful irony, self-reflexivity, and mischievous irreverence. Music and chat show *The Word* (1990–1995) became especially notorious for its amateurish style and variety of bad taste stunts (including colostomy bags, a vomiting Santa Claus and a feature on 'Mr Powertool' – who dragged a girl on a chair across the studio floor by a rope attached to his penis). Controversy brought an end to *The Word*, but similar elements of self-reflexive irony featured in subsequent Channel Four shows, including *The Big Breakfast* (1992–2002), *Eurotrash* (1993 to present), *Don't Forget Your Toothbrush* (1994–1995), *The Girlie Show* (1996–1997) and *TFI Friday* (1996–2000). For Karen Lury (2001), these programmes were 'postmodern' not simply because they traded in inter-textual and self-reflexive styles of production, but also because their aesthetic sensibility was an ambivalent combination of 'cynicism and enchantment'. According to Lury, the shows' parodic and knowing approach acknowledged that their audiences were well-versed in media codes and conventions and had 'a deep knowledge of the inauthenticity, the over-use, and the confusing over-abundance of different experiences, products, and practices within contemporary society' (Lury, 2001: 11). But this very sense of ironic detachment, Lury suggested, allowed the programmes to draw audiences into the world of the media, so that 'although they were "not going to be taken for suckers", young people continued to invest in the pleasures and places produced by television' (2001: 1).[13]

Similar traits of irony and ambivalence also surfaced in many American 'youth' TV shows. *The Osbournes* (MTV, 2002 to present) was a particularly successful example of the *oeuvre*. A 'fly-on the-wall' TV series that documented the home life of Ozzy Osbourne (lead singer with 1970s British heavy metal band, Black Sabbath) and his eccentric family, *The Osbournes* won appeal through its affectionate depiction of the ups and downs of family life set in the surreal context of the rock singer's Los Angeles mansion. But the series was not simply an endearing portrait of an ageing celebrity and his family. *The Osbournes* was also a tongue-in-cheek pastiche of American domestic sitcoms and soap operas, with the archetypal roles of 'Mom', 'Dad' and 'teenage kids' given ironic inflection through the portrayal of the Osbournes' uniquely dysfunctional life. One episode, for example, saw Ozzy nonchalantly peeling potatoes in the family kitchen as he explained to his daughter why he had once tried to strangle her mother. The series also sent-up the absurdities of American celebrity culture through the incongruous juxtapositioning of Ozzy Osbourne's stage persona as a heavy metal 'Prince of Darkness' against his life as a world-weary father who is routinely baffled by his children's behaviour, irritated by his wife's pets and tested to exhaustion by everyday chores (Ozzy shown, for example, struggling to master a vacuum cleaner and cursing the unfathomable instructions of a video recorder).

Nevertheless, while *The Osbournes* certainly parodied traditional media archetypes and conventions, its irony was playful rather than subversive. Like the British 'youth' TV shows analysed by Lury, *The Osbournes* combined 'cynicism and enchantment' – the series representing an ironic send-up of contemporary media culture but becoming, itself, a huge media phenomenon. MTV's greatest ever coup, *The Osbournes'* US ratings peaked at 4.1 million viewers, while the cost of a 30-second advertising slot during the show soared to $117,000 (the highest ever fee for a non-sports event on a cable channel). Other MTV shows also crystallised the fusion of 'cynicism and enchantment'. *Jackass* (2001), for example, made a virtue of stupidity and achieved major success through its young daredevils' goofball stunts and grossout gags (including blindfold skate-boarding, high-speed shopping cart races and outrageous 'eat til you puke' contests). Fears that audiences would imitate the programme's masochistic exploits prompted MTV to pull the show, but in 2003 *Jackass* returned as a feature-length movie that earned over $22 million in its first weekend of release.

Taking unrepentant delight in its inane idiocy, *Jackass* shared a taste for the ironic and the lowbrow that had become a staple trait of American TV programming aimed at youth. The cartoon comedy series *Beavis and Butthead* (MTV, 1993–1996) was a trailblazer of the aesthetic.[14] Developed for MTV by animator Mike Judge, *Beavis and Butthead* chron-icled the lives of two inarticulate, mindless teens who spent most of their time watching TV and channel surfing through an endless stream of music videos (which were either 'cool' or 'sucked', according to the duo's judgement). A parody of the nadir of teenage culture, the characters were unremittingly anti-social, destructive, sexist and homophobic, with short attention spans, limited vocabulary and annoying, snickering laughs ('heh, heh, heh'). For Steven Best and Douglas Kellner, *Beavis and Butthead* was a quintessentially 'postmodern' text in that it was composed almost entirely of media references 'with its characters, style and content almost solely derivative from previous TV shows' (Best and Kellner, 1998: 78). But, more than this, Best and Kellner also saw the programme as a sophisticated satire on contemporary media culture. The show, they

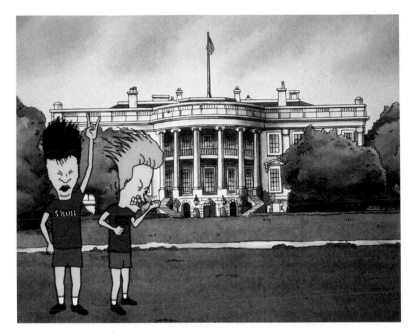

**Figure 5.3** 'Heh, heh, heh!' – *Beavis and Butthead Do America* (1996)
Courtesy of Pictorial Press

argued, was 'a complex intertextual web of cross-referencing from different quarters of advertising and the mass media world' (Best and Kellner, 1998: 87) – though in *Beavis and Butthead* this world was lampooned and parodied through the portrayal of two 'postmodern vidiots who seek scopopholic escape from everyday life, finding visceral satisfaction through subliminal immersion in the images and sounds of corporate media' (Best and Kellner, 1998: 82).

According to Best and Kellner, moreover, *Beavis and Butthead* also offered a salutary social commentary through its 'chilling glimpses into the lives of completely disaffected and alienated youth, unable to participate in the high-tech economy on the horizon' (1998: 94). For Best and Kellner, therefore, despite being 'only a cartoon', *Beavis and Butthead* was an illuminating cultural text that 'put on display youth lost in a media world, living in hyperreality . . . [with] nothing to do but to destroy things and engage in asocial behaviour' (1998: 88). This aspect of their analysis, however, tended to reproduce the media spectacle of 'wasted youth' that constructed young people as a uniquely alienated and nihilistic generation. Other authors, in contrast, were more critical of attempts to label contemporary youth as characteristically asocial and disaffected. Lawrence Grossberg (1994), for example, saw such representations as a product of an overly romantic view of the past in which the youth cultures of the baby boomer era were fondly imagined to be more radical and politically engaged than those of the present. Criticising this perspective, Grossberg argued it was an account in which contemporary youth were:

> presented as making a new generation gap, one defined against the baby boomers. Their identity crisis seems to be defined not within their experience (for within their experience they have no identity crisis) but rather within the experience of the baby boomers, who seem to have a desperate need and a total inability to identify them.
>
> (Grossberg, 1994: 53)

In the case of *Beavis and Butthead*, the show was actually a more ambivalent text than Best and Kellner recognised. While images of an aimless, disaffected and media-saturated youth culture were certainly central to the show, the series often seemed to be an impish caricature of the 'wasted youth' discourse. Indeed, in many ways *Beavis and Butthead* was actually a merciless send-up of the handwringing anxieties that surrounded notions of a 'depthless' and asocial youth culture. Through the grotesque excesses of its characters' ignorance and appalling pranks (the first episode, 'Frog Baseball', found the lads using a live frog for batting practice), *Beavis and Butthead* playfully satirised and sniggered at ('heh, heh, heh') the themes of 'wasted youth' that had become a familiar feature in the media's portrayal of young people.

By the end of the 1990s this ambivalent, profoundly ironic sensibility had become a principal convention in youth culture and style. Nowhere was this aesthetic more obvious than in the work of white rapper Eminem. Eminem (real name, Marshall Mathers) burst into the US charts in 1999 with *The Slim Shady LP* – a record that was a provocative feast of violent and twisted imagery – followed in 2000 by the equally robust *Marshall Mathers LP*, whose 1.7 million sales in the first week of release ensured a debut at number one in the US album chart. Predictably, Eminem's obscene lyrics and violent allusions were anathema to moral campaigners. Lynne Cheney (former head of the National Endowment for the Humanities, and wife of Republican Vice Presidential nominee Dick Cheney) took particular exception. Before a Senate Committee investigating the marketing of violent entertainment to children, an irate Cheney busted (as it were) some dope Eminem rhymes to illustrate her claims that 'the time has long passed when we can shrug off violence

**Figure 5.4** 'Anger Management' – Eminem (2002)

in the entertainment industry by saying it has no effect . . . It is no longer credible to suggest that young people aren't affected by music, films and video games that celebrate violence'.[15]

Indeed, taken on face value, Eminem's songs were often disturbing. In tracks such as '97 Bonnie & Clyde' (which contained lines about killing the mother of his child) Eminem appeared to be deplorably misogynistic, while the apparent homophobia of some lyrics ('And I can't wait 'til I catch all you faggots in public') was denounced by many gay rights groups. Nevertheless, large doses of irony were unmistakable in Eminem's performance. Bouncy keyboard lines and 'whiz-crunch' sound effects connoted cartoon-like comedy, while his multiple stage personas, sarcasm and blurring of truth and fiction made it difficult to distinguish his real intent from his jester-like, acerbic wit. Satire was even more pronounced in Eminem's stage act. The shows for his 2002 Anger Management tour invariably kicked off with Eminem brandishing an industrial chainsaw and wearing a hockey mask (tongue-in-cheek references to the heritage of American schlock-horror movies), and during concert performances of the song 'Role Model' a large, hypnotic spiral appeared alongside a screen that flashed the slogans 'Do What I Say', 'Take Pills', 'Have Sex' and 'Kill People'. Delighting in all that moral crusaders found shocking, liminal and 'unacceptable', the Eminem phenomenon was an ironic pageant of excess that deliberately tweaked the tail of conservative mores and satirised media archetypes of asocial youth.

It would, of course, be wrong to claim that Eminem and the media circus that surrounded him had no cultural impact whatsoever. Media representations help to organise people's understandings of the world and provide resources through which cultures are shaped and identities are forged. As Douglas Kellner argues, 'the media provide symbolic environments in which people live and strongly influence their behaviour' (1995: 151). At the same time, however, Kellner emphasises that a media text will always be a 'contested terrain in which different groups inflect its meanings in different ways' (ibid.). Crude models of 'cause-and-effect', then, do not capture the complex dialogues that take place between the media and young people. Media texts are not simple vehicles for a pre-determined 'message' that is delivered directly to the audience. Instead, they are riddled with ambiguities, inconsistencies and contradictions. Audiences, meanwhile, actively negotiate with cultural forms and media texts, occasionally appropriating (sometimes even subverting) their meanings. It is to these processes of meaning-making that we turn our attention in Chapter 6.

# 6

# ALL THE YOUNG DUDES
## Media, subculture and lifestyle

It is through the mass media that the images and desires of teen-agers are at once standardized and distorted. The printed word, the television screen, the movies and that no man's land between art and entertainment – the record industry – simultaneously extract the flashiest, most obscene and least meaningful aspects of adolescence and crystallize this titillating mixture into a commercial formula which is then beamed at teen-age America.

(Grace Hechinger and Fred Hechinger, 1962)

Revolutionary politics and oppositional art have traditionally been rooted in a transcendent critique whereby activists and artists attempt to stand outside their society in order to change it. . . . Today's youth culture proceeds from a different premise. Instead of standing outside society, it tries to work through it, exploring and exacerbating its contradictions to create unpredicatable possibilities for the future.

(George Lipsitz, 1994)

## IDOL PLEASURES: YOUTH CULTURE, MEDIA AND MEANING

In February 2002 Britain was a nation divided. Glued to the finale of ITV's 'reality' talent show, *Pop Idol*, more than 13 million TV viewers were torn between voting for boyish crooner Will Young or puppy-like cherub Gareth Gates. A huge success, the show's grand final prompted nearly nine million votes from the public, with Will narrowly pipping

Gareth to the winning post. But former choirboy Gates did not lose out. His endearing stammer and fashionably gelled hair had won the hearts of the nation, and his subsequent records twice unseated Will from the premier slot in Britain's singles chart. The format of *Pop Idol* was also a triumph. Exemplifying the global flow of media texts, *Pop Idol* was sold to TV networks in more than twenty different countries, versions of the series appearing in evening schedules from Poland and Germany to South Africa and the United States (where Texan cocktail waitress, Kelly Clarkson, scooped 58 per cent of 15.5 million votes to become the first winner of Fox TV's *American Idol*).[1] But *Pop Idol* was not a hit with everyone. Some commentators were appalled by the brazen delight the show took in the process of manufacturing a pop singer to meet recording industry expectations. Roger Daltrey (lead singer with rock band The Who) was an especially forthright critic, arguing that *Pop Idol* judge (and record industry executive) Simon Cowell was a:

> dreadful piece of crap who drags the music business down whenever he rears his ugly head . . . Pop stars today have no longevity. Rock 'n' roll is not about singing perfect notes or being a showbiz personality. It's about the anger and the angst. I hate what *Pop Idol* has done to the business.
>
> (cited in *Q*, March 2002)

Daltrey's attack can, in many ways, be seen as a bowdlerised version of a long-established critical tradition within cultural theory. From this perspective, the commercial market is equated with inane conformity and cynical exploitation. Its cultural products are viewed with disdain, condemned for lacking the qualities of authenticity and depth of meaning (or 'anger and angst' in Daltrey's terms) that are seen as the measure of 'true' artistic creativity. This chapter begins with a review of this intellectual tradition, tracing its modern development and assessing its critical contribution. As we shall see, the perspective retains influence (in both academic and popular circles), but in theoretical analysis has been steadily superseded by approaches less dismissive of commercial culture and its consumers.

In relation to young people, for example, theorists have been increasingly interested in the ways that young audiences actively engage with popular media. Rather than seeing youth as the passive victim of exploitative cultural industries, researchers have explored the pleasures young people derive from their media use and the meanings they construct around the products of the commercial market. This chapter examines the development of this approach in the study of young people's cultural practices. We will see how, during the 1970s and 1980s, there was a tendency for some theorists to interpret young people's cultural expressions (in the form of fashion, music and style) as strategies of opposition to dominant power structures. During the 1990s, however, this emphasis on 'resistance', gave way to more nuanced approaches in which the commercial media were seen as offering 'symbolic resources' that young people drew upon as they made sense of their social experiences and carved out their social identities. In these terms, then, young people's engagement with the commercial media *does* offer *some* possibilities for liberation and progressive change – though these possibilities are always constrained by the wider relations of economic and political power. Or, as David Buckingham observed (in a pithy echo of an earlier critical theorist's dictum), 'Readers do indeed make meanings, but they do so under conditions which are not of their own choosing' (Buckingham, 1993a: 14).

## SLAVES TO THE RHYTHM?: MASS CULTURE, MEDIA AND YOUTH

After 1945 the social profile of American youth was thrown into starker relief by a combination of demographic shifts, expansion of educational provision and a proliferation of the commercial youth market (see Chapter 2). Although the increased 'cultural visibility' of young people contributed to popular anxieties about juvenile crime, many social scientists responded fairly positively. During the 1940s, for example, Talcott Parsons developed the concept of 'youth culture' to denote what he saw as a distinct set of values and behaviour shared by the young. Presenting this common set of attitudes and experiences in a relatively optimistic light, Parsons stressed the positive role of youth culture as a transitionary stage between childhood and the responsibilities of adult life (Parsons, 1942, 1943). The period's most widely known study of American adolescence also depicted youth culture as relatively benign. James Coleman's *The Adolescent Society* (1961) was nervous in its survey of Illinois high-school cliques, depicting an adolescent culture increasingly divorced from the wider adult world in terms of its interests, attitudes and values. Nevertheless, Coleman was optimistic in his conclusions, arguing that prudent adult intervention could guide the peer culture towards socially beneficial goals.

More disconsolate accounts, however, also surfaced. Here, contemporary youth culture was depicted as the nadir of a general cultural malaise. While post-war affluence was widely celebrated as a benchmark of American progress and modernity, the explosion of mass consumption provoked unease among many cultural critics. During the 1950s authors from across the political spectrum reviled what they regarded as the malignant cultural fallout of the consumer boom, decrying the cynicism of manipulative marketing techniques and the rise of a shallow, debased 'mass culture'. And, for many of the mandarins of mass culture theory, the flourishing youth market was the most blatant example of the suffocating uniformity and docile banality of modern consumer culture. For example, in 1950 (the same year he lamented the 'other-directed' conformism of *The Lonely Crowd*) David Reisman condemned a pop music industry that had the power 'to mold popular taste and to eliminate free choice by consumers' (Reisman, 1950b: 361). Dwight Macdonald, too, saw the young generation as falling easy prey to the wiles of commerce. 'These days', Macdonald dolefully explained in a commentary for *New Yorker* magazine, 'merchants eye teenagers the way stockmen eye cattle' (Macdonald, 1958: 70). The most braying criticism, however, came from Grace and Fred Hechinger. In *Teen-Age Tyranny* (1962), the Hechingers launched a vitriolic attack on the mass media's 'standardized and distorted' images of teenage life (1962: 101). The Hechingers were especially dismayed by the way the whole of American culture seemed to be dancing to the tune of the commercial youth market. Americans, the Hechingers argued, were 'growing down rather than growing up', the nation standing 'in such awe of its teen-age segment that it is in danger of becoming a teen-age society, with permanently teen-age standards of thought, culture and goals' (Hechinger and Hechinger, 1962: x).

Equally despondent sentiments surfaced in post-war Britain. As was seen in Chapter 4, the rise of teenage consumption during the 1950s and early 1960s was often celebrated as the essence of prosperous modernity, but some British commentators were appalled by the growth of commercial culture. Richard Hoggart, for example, argued that a proliferation of commercial entertainment had spawned a shallow and insipid 'candy-floss world'. Looking back to his working-class boyhood, Hoggart happily validated popular culture as a meaningful field of collective experience, but in post-war cultural life he found little reason for optimism. Hoggart derided contemporary trends towards 'canned entertainment and packeted provision' that seemed, for him, to offer an 'unvaried diet of sensation without commitment' that induced 'an underlying sense of purposelessness in existence outside the limited range of a few appetites' (1957: 246). And, significantly, Hoggart singled out contemporary youth as a benchmark of this general cultural paucity. Denouncing modern youth as a 'hedonistic but passive barbarian', Hoggart poured scorn on 'the juke box boys' with their 'drape suits, picture ties and American slouch' who spent their evenings in 'harshly lighted milk bars' putting 'copper after copper into the mechanical record player' – a realm of cultural experience that, Hoggart argued, represented 'a peculiarly thin and pallid form of dissipation' (1957: 248–250).

Authors such as Reisman, Macdonald and Hoggart offered liberal critiques of a modern culture they saw as being undermined and degraded by the rise of a commercial mass market. Marxist and neo-Marxist writers developed a more radical version of this 'mass culture' thesis, attacking popular media as an oppressive apparatus serving the interests of capitalism. Writing during the 1930s and 1940s, for example, members of the Frankfurt School were deeply critical of commercial popular culture. For the Frankfurt theorists, the 'culture industry' was not only a source of profit for capitalist business, but also functioned to secure the status quo by fostering conformity, passivity and political apathy among mass audiences. Theodor Adorno produced one of the most well-known versions of this critique in his (1941) analysis of popular music. Adorno had little time for the products of the commercial music industry, arguing that they were characterised by two processes – standardisation and pseudo-individualisation. Standardisation referred to the substantial similarities between modern popular songs that, Adorno argued, were churned off a production line like any other mass-produced commodity. Pseudo-individualisation referred to the incidental differences that worked to disguise this uniformity. According to Adorno, slight variations from the norm and moments of novelty (for example, the hook-line of a chorus or a catchy musical riff) made a song attractive and gave it the semblance of originality. In contrast to the creativity and intellectual vigour of classical and avant-garde forms of music, then, Adorno saw popular songs as standardised products devoid of originality and meaning. His view of popular audiences was equally disparaging, seeing them as 'arrested at the infantile stage . . . they are childish; their primitivism is not that of the underdeveloped, but that of the forcibly retarded' (1991: 41).

The Marxist version of the 'mass culture' thesis, then, saw popular music as a bland, standardised product working in the service of capitalism. From this perspective, popular music (in common with other branches of the 'culture industry') was criticised for not only underpinning the operation of an exploitative capitalist market, but also for fostering banal conformity among its audiences. Writing in *Marxism Today* in 1973, John Boyd articulated the viewpoint succinctly. For Boyd, youth culture during the early 1970s was characterised by an 'imposed alienation'. 'Platform shoes and long skirts', Boyd warned, represented 'the antipathy of freedom', while young workers were brainwashed by that most insidious instrument of capitalist domination – the disco:

Alienation is epitomised in the discotheque – the room is darkened so that you cannot see who you are with; the 'music' is so loud that there is no possibility of conversation with others; the normal mode of 'dancing' is such that you do not touch your 'partner'; taste is dealt with by habit-forming Coca-cola; the mind is further clogged by flashing lights causing near hypnotic conditions; concentration is not required as the maximum playing time of one record is three minutes. Every sense is taken care of to ensure that not one thought, let alone a social idea, takes place.

(Boyd, 1973: 378)

Boyd's portrayal of the 1970s disco as a cunning capitalist conspiracy now seems laughable. But the elitist scorn for popular media that has been an abiding characteristic of 'mass culture' theoretical perspectives (like Boyd's) is also detectable in the work of many more recent critics. Theorists of postmodernism such as Baudrillard (1983, 1985) and Jameson (1984), for instance, viewed cultural trends in the late twentieth century with differing degrees of despair and resignation, interpreting the media-saturated age of postmodernity as marking the rise of a uniquely 'depthless' form of cultural life. A similar sense of ennui also surfaced in John Seabrook's (2001) sardonic critique of the American media. Paralleling postmodern notions of an increasing effacement of cultural boundaries, Seabrook argued that America in the late 1990s had seen a blending of highbrow and lowbrow tastes into a new sensibility he dubbed 'Nobrow'. For Seabrook, the rise of 'Nobrow' marked the triumph of a commercial culture dominated by a 'hierarchy of hotness', with aesthetic worth judged purely in terms of unit sales (Seabrook, 2001: 28). Media giants such as MTV, Seabrook argued, had 'dramatically closed the feedback loop between culture and marketing', until finally 'marketing is the culture and the culture the marketing' (Seabrook, 2001: 94, 153).

Naomi Klein's (2000) critique of the multinational 'Brand Bullies' also included more than a hint of 'mass culture' pessimism. As we saw in Chapter 3, Klein's account of the rise of international business conglomerates incisively pointed to an intensification of global economic inequality and exploitation. Her portrayal of young consumers as brand-obsessed 'walking, talking, life-sized Tommy [Hilfiger] dolls' (Klein, 2000: 28), however, echoed Adorno's view of the popular audience as 'infantile' cultural dupes and his scant regard to consumers' own cultural meanings. Klein's account of coolhunters and guerilla advertisers as 'the legal stalkers of youth culture' (2000: 72) also seemed to ascribe monolithic power to the cultural industries. According to Klein, even 'street styles' had been seamlessly absorbed into the corporate brands' relentless pursuit of global sales. 'Gathering tips from the graffiti artists of old', Klein contended, 'the superbrands have tagged everyone – including the graffiti writers themselves' (2000: 73). Alissa Quart (2003) was equally pessimistic. Taking her cues from Klein, Quart argued that the late 1990s had seen an intensification of 'the unbearable commercialization of youth' (Quart 2003: xxvi). In her scornful critique of corporate brands and coolhunters, Quart argued that young people's creativity had been crushed by the unremitting onslaught of commercial manipulation – the blurb on the back of her book ominously warning readers, 'Did you know you're being brainwashed?'.

This view of vulnerable consumers as being gripped by an irresistible (and aesthetically debased) commercial machine, however, is open to several important criticisms. Media industries, for example, are not the ruthlessly efficient capitalist operation that mass culture theorists imply. Even a mammoth investment in advertising and promotion is no guarantee of successful sales, illustrated by the glorious commercial flops that litter the history of popular entertainment. In 2001, for instance, singer Mariah Carey (the best-selling female recording artist of all time) signed to EMI Records for an estimated $80 million in one of the most expensive recording deals in history. In a neat piece of business synergy, the launch of *Glitter* (Carey's first album for her new label) was timed to coincide with the release of the pop diva's first feature film (also entitled *Glitter*) – but both album and movie bombed. Whereas Carey's previous albums had touched sales of 20 million, *Glitter* barely scraped 2 million and the following year EMI cut their losses, paying the singer $28 million to sever their contract. EMI also looked set to get their fingers burnt with Robbie Williams. In 2002 the music giant signed the singer to an unprecedented £80 million recording contract (an understandably cheerful Williams shrieking 'I'm rich beyond my wildest dreams!'). But the initial signs for the deal were less than promising. Williams' 2003 album, *Escapology*, sold well in Europe, but in the crucial American market it shifted just 21,000 copies in its first week of release, limping into the US charts at Number 43. EMI executives put a brave face on things, but Williams' disappointing stateside sales were . . . inescapable.

The music business, then, is not always the well-oiled capitalist machine described by critics such as Adorno. Moreover, the products of the 'culture industry' have not always worked to promote social stability and consensus. From rock 'n' roll to gangsta rap, popular media output has been a centre for cultural conflict and confrontation that has occasionally boiled over to embrace a more radical questioning of society's economic and political power structures (see Chapter 4).

Perhaps the biggest criticism to be made of mass culture approaches, however, relates to their elitist attitude towards popular culture. Adorno, for example, was happy to assign prestige and 'meaning' to classical and avant-garde music and its listeners, but derided popular musical forms as standardised and banal. Such a comparison, however, is unfair since it judges popular genres against classical and avant-garde ideals of 'original-ity' and 'authenticity'. As Bernard Gendron observed in his systematic (1986) appraisal of Adorno's thesis, 'standardization' is an obvious feature of many pop music genres and artists' repertoires – but recognition of similarities and connections between popular texts is often what provides their audiences with enjoyment, and so 'we might consider standardiza-tion not only as an expression of rigidity, but also as a source of pleasure' (Gendron, 1986: 29). Mass culture theorists, however, have little time for popular pleasures. Instead, the enlightened few are congratulated for their intellectual ability to resist the power of the culture industry and recognise the value of 'real' creativity, while audiences of popular texts are maligned as the passive and 'forcibly retarded' victims of the commercial machine.

Mass culture perspectives still retain influence, but within cultural and media analysis they have increasingly given way to theoretical perspec-tives that see popular audiences as more discriminating and critical in their patterns of media consumption. An early move in this direction was Stuart Hall and Paddy Whannel's argument that teenage culture was 'a contradictory mixture of the authentic and the manufactured' (1964: 276). Surveying the 'popular arts' in Britain during the early 1960s, Hall and Whannel acknowledged that the youth market represented 'a lush grazing ground for the commercial providers', but they resisted sliding into pessimistic notions of 'mass culture'. Instead, they highlighted the potential of consumers to engage actively with the products of the market, insisting that 'the use intended by the provider and the use actu-ally made by the audience never wholly coincide, and frequently conflict' (1964: 269–270). In stressing the potential of popular culture to be 'an area of self-expression for the young' (1964: 276), Hall and Whannel were influenced by the seminal ideas of Raymond Williams. Whereas traditional approaches to cultural life had established a hierarchical distinction between 'high' culture (worthy, creative, meaningful) and 'low' or 'mass' culture (worthless, commercial, banal), Williams argued that culture should instead be seen as 'a whole way of life . . . which expresses certain meanings and values not only in art and learning but also in institutions and ordinary behaviour' (1961: 57). Informed by Williams' approach, Hall and Whannel (and other researchers working in the developing discipline of cultural studies) increasingly eschewed the elitism of 'mass culture' approaches and understood the popular media as a more complex field – one in which commercial interests certainly wielded considerable power, but where audiences and consumers were also able to carve out meaningful cultures and patterns of life.

# THE KIDS ARE ALRIGHT: YOUTH, STYLE AND NOTIONS OF SUBCULTURAL 'RESISTANCE'

In Britain, Williams' notion that 'culture is ordinary' became an important theoretical influence. Most notably, Williams' ideas informed the work of the numerous authors associated with Birmingham University's Centre for Contemporary Cultural Studies (CCCS), where Stuart Hall was appointed director in 1968. Williams' emphasis on the political, economic and social context of cultural production was a key influence on the CCCS authors, and many adopted his view of media and cultural texts as being not simply the creation of individual authors, but as being forged through a series of complex relationships between authorial intent, institutional process and aesthetic form. The CCCS authors were also deeply influenced by Williams' critique of the traditional, elitist distinction between 'high' and 'low' culture. Adopting Williams' view of culture as 'a whole way of life', the CCCS authors saw popular, mass mediated texts and the ordinary concerns and practices of everyday life as every bit as relevant and meaningful as the provinces of 'high' culture or 'great art'. As CCCS author Paul Willis explained:

> Culture . . . [is] not artifice and manners, the reserve of Sunday best, rainy afternoons and concert halls. It is the very material of our daily lives, the bricks and mortar of our most commonplace understandings.
>
> (Willis, 1979: 185–186)

While the CCCS team took up Williams' notion of culture as 'a whole way of life', however, they increasingly combined this with perspectives derived from explicitly Marxist traditions. In these terms, culture was seen as being constituted through friction between competing groups, interests and 'ways of life'. Here, the CCCS authors foregrounded issues of class conflict in their arguments that societies were composed of a range of cultures ranked hierarchically in relations of dominance and subordination along a scale of 'cultural power' (Clarke et al., 1976: 11). In their various analytical projects of the 1970s, the CCCS team drew particularly heavily on the insights into politics, ideology and culture offered in the work of the Italian Marxist, Antonio Gramsci. Gramsci saw capitalist societies as being characterised by ongoing processes of class struggle and conflict but, where cruder forms of Marxist theory argued that dominant groups exerted their control simply through force and coercion, Gramsci was keener to highlight the importance of *ideological* relations in which competing class factions struggled for hegemony – or the moral, cultural, intellectual (and thereby political) leadership of society. For Gramsci, hegemony was secured not simply through the possession of economic power and coercive force but through producing a worldview; a philosophy and a moral outlook that subordinate groups were *persuaded* to accept. In these terms, hegemony had to be continually strived for and reproduced through ongoing processes of negotiation and accommodation. Crucially, however, while dominant groups were able to secure their power through this struggle, subordinate groups were *also* active social agents, and were always able to challenge and resist dominant hegemony.

For the CCCS authors, popular culture and, in particular, the way in which it was disseminated through the media, was a key location where these hegemonic relations were played out. Popular culture, they argued, was a site of political contest between dominant and subordinate interests, an arena where the rule of the powerful could be reproduced and reinforced, but also contested and challenged. The CCCS team explored these ideas in relation to a broad range of issues and debates – including the form and meaning of media texts (Hall *et al.*, 1980), the structures of working-class culture (Clarke *et al.*, 1979) and the analysis of gender relations (Women's Studies Group, 1978) – but the study of youth culture was especially central to their work. Recognising the important position of youth within patterns of post-war social, economic and political change (see Chapters 2 and 5), the CCCS authors were concerned to explore the nature of modern youth culture and its relationship with the media and other cultural industries. In what became known as 'subcultural theory', they argued that young people's subcultural styles (like those of Teddy boys, mods, skinheads and punks) were strategies of symbolic resistance to ruling-class power structures. Youth subcultures were interpreted as forms of cultural insubordination, expressions of defiant rebellion in which working-class youths appropriated the articles, artefacts and icons generated by the media and the commercial market, and symbolically reworked them to take on new, threatening and subversive meanings.

The term 'subculture' had been originally deployed as a term of theoretical analysis by the American Chicago school of sociologists during the 1920s and 1930s, and was subsequently developed in the work of sociologists such as Albert Cohen (1955) and Richard Cloward and Lloyd Ohlin (1961). These authors saw subcultures as subdivisions within the dominant culture, emerging when individuals in similar circumstances felt themselves isolated or neglected by mainstream society. Cohen (1955), for example, stressed the compensatory function of the juvenile gang, arguing that it was a subculture that offered working-class adolescents who under-achieved at school an alternative source of prestige and self-esteem by replacing the core values of the 'straight' world – sobriety, ambition, conformity – with an alternative value system that celebrated hedonism, defiance of authority and a search for deviant 'kicks'. The ideas of the Chicago school were also influential in British sociology, but during the late 1960s the ideas of the original subcultural theorists were increasingly supplemented by an attention to the social relations of capitalism. For example, authors associated with what became known as 'new criminology' (Taylor et al., 1973) argued that crime could be interpreted as a direct consequence of class conflict, an expression of the alienation and powerlessness felt by the working class as they were exploited by a capitalist society.

An emphasis on class relations also surfaced in interpretations of youth culture and young people's engagement with the media and culture industries. A seminal study in this respect was Phil Cohen's (1972) attempt to relate shifts in the form of post-war youth culture to more general transformations taking place in the ecologies of working-class neighbourhoods. Focusing on developments in London's East End, Cohen argued that post-war patterns of rehousing and redevelopment, combined with the collapse of traditional labour markets and changing patterns of consumption, had disrupted the material basis of working-class life. For Cohen, the various youth styles of the 1950s and 1960s could be understood as collective symbolic responses to this cultural dislocation. Stylistic subcultures, Cohen, argued, were attempts by working-class youth to bridge the gap between traditional patterns of working-class life and the new cultural attitudes and practices emerging in post-war Britain. By fusing together key concerns of their working-class 'parent' culture (for example, an emphasis on local identities and collective loyalties) with the new products of the developing media and culture industries (most obviously fashion and pop music), youth subcultural styles such as those of the mods and skinheads served to:

> express and resolve, albeit 'magically', the contradictions which remain hidden and unresolved in the parent culture . . . [each subculture attempts] to retrieve some of the socially cohesive elements destroyed in their parent culture and to combine these with other class fractions symbolising one or other of the options confronting it.
>
> (Cohen, 1972: 23)

Instead of dismissing youth subcultures as trivial fads concocted by the media, then, Cohen presented the styles of groups such as Teddy boys and skinheads as important purveyors of social meaning, intrinsically linked to wider patterns of cultural change. In these terms, for example, the mods of the early 1960s represented an exploration of the upwardly-mobile, consumption-oriented working-class lifestyles that began to emerge during the post-war decades. In contrast, Cohen argued, the skinhead style of the later 1960s represented a symbolic reassertion of traditional working-class values and culture.

Cohen's approach was extended further by the Birmingham CCCS. In Hall and Jefferson's *Resistance Through Rituals* (1976), the text that originally mapped out the contours of British subcultural theory, the CCCS authors saw subcultural style as a symbolic or 'magical' expression of working-class youth's social experiences. Like Cohen, the CCCS team argued that working-class youth constructed a cultural, or *sub*-cultural, response pertinent to their life experiences by fusing together elements of their 'parent' culture (for example, working-class argot, neighbourhood ties and particular notions of masculinity and femininity) with elements derived from other cultural sources – in particular, the products of the various media and consumer industries. Crucially, however, the CCCS introduced a neo-Marxist, 'Gramscian' account of young people as locked into class-based struggles and conflicts. Whereas Cohen had seen subcultural style as an 'ideological *solution*' to contradictions assailing the parent culture, the CCCS were more forthright – interpreting youth subcultures as symbolic (or 'ritualistic') strategies of *resistance* to ruling-class power structures.

According to the CCCS theorists, it was also possible to differentiate fairly precisely between *sub*cultural groups of working-class youth and the *counter*cultures of their middle-class peers (Clarke *et al.*, 1976: 60–61). For the CCCS team, subcultures (Teddy boys, mods, skinheads, etc.) generally reproduced traditional working-class values and behaviours and tended to be leisure-oriented, fairly temporary, episodes in young people's lives. Countercultures (beats, hippies, etc.), in contrast, placed more emphasis on individual experience, while the stark polarity between work and leisure characteristic of working-class subcultures was much less pronounced in the bohemian and non-conformist world of the counterculture. More fundamentally, the CCCS authors argued that working-class subcultures represented a revolt against the status quo from 'below', while the middle-class countercultures were a more politically-conscious attack from 'within' (Clarke *et al.*, 1976: 62–63).[2]

In contrast to the mass culture theorists' view of young consumers as the manipulated dupes of the commercial market, therefore, the CCCS saw young people as active and rebellious in their use of cultural artefacts and media texts. Creatively engaging with the media and culture industries, youth subcultures were seen as appropriating commercial products and investing them with meanings that offered a symbolic challenge to dominant power structures. The effect of this approach was to turn subcultural styles into texts, the CCCS deploying strategies of semiotic analysis in their attempts to 'read' the subversive meanings they saw as ingrained in the skinhead's boots and braces or the punk's bondage trousers and spiky hairstyle. Here, two concepts (both derived from the work of French anthropologist, Claude Lévi-Strauss) emerged as especially important – bricolage and homology.

Bricolage referred to the way the meanings of particular objects and media texts were transformed as they were adopted and recontextualised by subcultural groups. According to Dick Hebdige, for example, the 1960s mods appropriated the motor scooter ('a formerly ultra-respectable means of transport') and transformed it into 'a weapon and a symbol of solidarity' (Hebdige, 1976: 93). Homology denoted the way disparate stylistic elements – music, clothes and leisure activities – coalesced to form a coherent symbolic expression of a subcultural group's identity. Using the example of biker culture, for instance, Paul Willis identified a 'homological' relationship between the physical qualities of the motorcycle and the subcultural ethos of the biker gang – the 'solidity, responsiveness, inevitableness [sic.], the strength the motorcycle' corresponding with 'the concrete, secure nature of the bikeboys' world' (Willis, 1978: 53). Developing this approach, Dick Hebdige emerged as the high priest of style analysis. In *Subculture: The Meaning of Style* (1979), his classic study of late 1970s punk rock, he presented subcultural style as akin to 'semiotic guerrilla warfare' (1979: 105), an exercise in sartorial defiance that, Hebdige claimed, transformed the 'naturalized' meanings of everyday cultural artefacts and media texts into something alien, spectacular and threatening.

As the CCCS authors admitted, however, there were inevitable limits to subcultural 'resistance'. No pop record, haircut or pair of trousers (no matter how spectacular) could deliver a knockout blow to capitalism. Confined to limited realms of social life – most obviously leisure and media consumption – subcultural 'resistance' was always partial and tangential and, as Hebdige himself put it, 'no amount of stylistic incantation can alter the oppressive mode in which the commodities used in subculture have been produced' (1979: 130).

The ideas of the CCCS theorists were a major influence in the analysis of youth culture and its relation to the media and cultural industries.[3] For some, however, their heavy attention to the 'hidden messages inscribed in code on the glossy surfaces of style' (Hebdige, 1979: 18) was problematic. According to Hebdige, style could be analysed as an autonomous text, with 'resistance' taking place at a level independent of the consciousness of subcultural members – Hebdige even conceding that it was 'highly unlikely' that members of any subcultures would recognise themselves in his account (Hebdige, 1979: 139). Others, however, were critical of this lack of attention to the actual intentions behind young people's use of media texts and cultural artefacts. 'It seems to me', Stanley Cohen conjectured, 'that somewhere along the line, symbolic language implies a knowing subject, a subject at least dimly aware of what the symbols are supposed to mean' (2002: lvii–lviii).[4] In relying on an 'aesthetics which may work for art, but not equally well for life', Cohen warned, subcultural theory risked 'getting lost in the forest of symbols' (Cohen, 2002: lx).[5] Admittedly, a section of *Resistance Through Rituals* (1976) had been devoted to 'ethnography' but, even here, there was only a limited attempt to understand and represent the meanings young people *themselves* gave to their subcultural styles and patterns of media consumption.[6]

The CCCS theorists' focus on issues of social class also provoked criticism. In some respects, this aspect of their work could be applauded. Amid the post-war political rhetoric that had presented the pace of economic growth as steadily ameliorating class inequalities, there had been a tendency for some commentators to understand teenage culture as a relatively homogeneous phenomenon, defined purely in terms of generational age. The CCCS work, in contrast, underscored the enduring importance of structural inequality and social class as crucial factors in the mediation of young people's life experiences. At times, however, the CCCS privileging of class relations as the fundamental motor within youth culture was problematic. The polarity constructed between working-class subcultures and middle-class countercultures, for example, over-simplified the complex social make-up of many youth cultural phenomena. According to Peter Clecak, for instance, the 1960s counterculture was composed of diverse movements and ideas that allowed people from a variety of social backgrounds 'to find symbolic shapes for their social and spiritual discontents and hopes' (Clecak, 1983: 18). In relation to 1970s punk rock, meanwhile, Gary Clarke pointed to the contradictions between Hebdige's emphasis on punk's 'working-class creativity' and the movement's origins among the art-school avant-garde (Clarke, 1990: 86). And, more recently, Sheryl Garratt, highlighted the social heterogeneity of the late 1980s acid-house scene, arguing that there was a degree of truth to the often-repeated cliché that 'bankers were dancing next to barrow boys' (Garratt, 1998: 160).

The CCCS model was also criticised for allowing social class to overshadow other systems of power relations. Angela McRobbie (1981), for example, was quick to draw attention to the gendered assumptions that underlay much of the canon of subcultural theory. McRobbie was, herself, affiliated with the Birmingham group, but she was critical of the way some of her colleagues' work rendered the category of 'youth' as unproblematically masculine.[7] Indeed, the studies produced by many subcultural theorists seemed to marginalise young women, concentrating almost exclusively on male experience and sometimes failing to deal critically with the aggressively sexist worldviews of some of the subcultural groups they examined.[8] In contrast, rather than seeing girls' experience as a mere footnote to male subcultures, feminist researchers argued that young women's cultural activities and media usage were qualitatively different to those of men. As Angela McRobbie and Jenny Garber explained, the crucial question was not 'the absence or presence of girls in male subcultures, but the complementary ways in which young girls interact among themselves and with each other to form a distinctive culture of their own' (1976: 219).

## FROM BEDROOM CULTURE TO GRRRL POWER: FEMININITY, YOUTH CULTURE AND THE MEDIA

Compared to young men, girls' access to media texts and consumer goods has often been more economically and socially constrained.[9] In both Britain and the US, for example, young women's disposable income has generally been less than that of their male peers, while (especially for working-class girls) child-care and domestic responsibilities have meant leisure time has often been structured around the family and the private sphere of the home (McRobbie, 1978). This home-centredness of young women's culture has also been accentuated by the greater parental regulation of girls' leisure time.[10] As a result, the 1970s and 1980s saw some theorists suggest that girls' cultural spaces were chiefly concentrated within the private realm of the home – the bedroom, especially, cited as a key site 'where girls meet, listen to music and teach each other make up skills, practice their dancing, compare sexual notes, criticize each other's clothes and gossip' (Frith, 1978: 64).

This concept of 'bedroom culture' highlighted some of the unique dimensions to young women's patterns of media consumption, but its focus on the domestic realm tended to underestimate girls' role as an active and visible media audience. In contrast, the 1990s saw feminist researchers give greater attention to young women's 'public' life and their role as 'active producers of culture' (Kearney, 1998a: 286). According to some theorists, for example, pop fandom not only offered young women opportunities for friendship and communal solidarity, but also represented an avenue through which they participated in symbolic – and very public – displays of collective power. Recalling her time as a fan of 1970s pop band the Bay City Rollers, for instance, Sheryl Garratt emphasised how her screams at the group's concerts came not from meaningless hysteria, but from 'defiance, celebration, and excitement . . . It was us against the world and, for a while at least, we were winning' (Garratt, 1984: 142–145). And, in a similar vein, Barbara Ehrenreich and her colleagues interpreted 1960s Beatlemania as 'the first and most dramatic uprising of *women's* sexual revolution' (Ehrenreich *et al.*, 1987: 11).

A number of feminist theorists also highlighted young women's active role in the pageant of post-war youth style. With reference to the 1960s US beat scene, for instance, McRobbie highlighted the way many young women adopted secondhand clothes to make 'a strong sexual challenge to the spick and span gingham-clad domesticity of the moment' (1989: 34). During the late 1970s, the iconoclastic postures of punk rock also provided a fertile space for the politicisation of sexuality and female identity. Brash female artists like the Slits and Siouxsie Sioux enacted transgressive forms of femininity in their unconventional styles and assertive stage personae, and subsequently the punk subculture has been drawn upon by many young women 'to resist the prescriptions of femininity, [and] to carve out a space where they can define their own sense of self' (Leblanc, 1999: 219–220). The 'Riot Grrrl' phenomenon of the 1990s (an offshoot of American punk), too, has been championed by many commentators as a powerful and rebellious example of young women's cultural agency.[11] Spearheaded by all-female rock bands such as Bikini Kill and Bratmobile, the Riot Grrrl movement first emerged in 1991 as a heterogeneous, but self-consciously feminist, engagement with politics and culture – with many of the bands' songs confronting subjects such as misogyny and physical abuse. The Riot Grrrl movement also adopted punk's 'do-it-yourself' ethos. Deliberately eschewing the mainstream media, a multitude of 'grassroots' fanzines (for example, *Girl Germs*, *GirlFrenzy* and *Bitch Nation*) and internet websites formed a Riot Grrrl network for the sharing of ideas, information, and reviews.[12]

Some theorists also saw the dance-music scene that took shape during the late 1980s and 1990s as a site for the expression of feminine identities whose energy and independence challenged traditional models of feminine passivity. According to Kristian Russell, an Ecstasy-induced absorption in dance music, combined with the threat of HIV and AIDS, lead many young clubbers to reject 'the dated 70s notion of the disco as a meat market' (1993: 98).[13] In this context, McRobbie (1994a) argued, there emerged new, more liberating, codes of femininity in which the suffocating ideals of romance were eclipsed by an emphasis on auto-nomous pleasure. This view of contemporary club culture as a site for 'changing modes of femininity' was supported by the research of Maria Pini (1997, 2001). Whereas Sarah Thornton's earlier account had depicted club culture as 'dominated by the lads' (1995: 25), Pini saw the modern club circuit as an arena of feminine independence and pleasure. Pini conceded that women were relatively marginal to the production of dance music and the organisation of club events, but she argued that club-going itself offered women the 'possibility for . . . adventure, exploration and discovery' through the opportunities it offered for 'taking drugs, going "mental" and dancing through the night without sexual harassment' (2001: 13, 34).[14] The sense of autonomy Pini's interviewees derived from club-going was underscored by the development of what McRobbie (1994a: 169) identified as 'hypersexual' modes of femininity within the club scene. Several of the women Pini interviewed, for exam-ple, stressed the pleasure they took in cultivating a particularly 'sexu-alised' appearance, emphasising that this enactment of sexuality did not represent a 'sexual invitation', but was geared to *their own* enjoy-ment. 'Emptied of its traditional signifiers', Pini explained, the '"hyper-sexualised" performance of femininity became 'very much an end in itself' (2001: 121).[15]

During the late 1980s and 1990s an emphasis on autonomous, 'hyper-sexual' performance was also prominent in many constructions of femininity within the popular media. Many theorists, for example, inter-preted the erotic music videos and stage-shows of the singer Madonna as disrupting traditional concepts of femininity, Madonna's spirited appropriation of an array of seductive guises seeming to undermine notions of the 'feminine' as something that was fixed and inherently passive. E. Ann Kaplan, for instance, argued that Madonna's style of performance highlighted the way femininity was a 'masquerade', the singer adopting 'one mask after another to expose the fact that there is no "essential" self and therefore no essential feminine but only cultural constructions' (1993: 160).[16]

Other pop performers also seemed to challenge traditional notions of femininity as passive and submissive. The late 1990s, for example, saw all-girl fivesome, the Spice Girls, leap to the heights of pop stardom as their 1996 single, 'Wannabe', topped the singles charts of 27 countries. Recruited, modelled and marketed by a team of producers and record company moguls, in many respects the Spice Girls were a conventional product of the pop industry. Under their feisty slogan 'Girl Power', how-ever, the Spice Girls' image recast many of the qualities conventionally associated with femininity. Combining a brash cheek with fun-fuelled

**Figure 6.1** 'Girl Power' – The Spice Girls (1996)
Courtesy of Pictorial Press

energy and confident sexuality, they elaborated a version of feminine identity that (in some respects at least) transgressed traditional gender norms and conventions, Sheila Whitely arguing that the Spice Girls offered 'a challenge to the dominance of lad culture . . . [and] introduced the language of independence to a willing audience of pre- and teenage girls' (2000: 215).

The strident, self-assured image articulated by the Spice Girls can be seen as part of a wider transformation in popular cultural texts geared to young women. Surveying the media landscape of the late 1990s, for example, McRobbie identified a shift away from representations of 'lady-like' sweetness and innocence in favour of constructions of teen femininity predicated on 'sex, having fun and enjoying a sense of freedom' (McRobbie, 1999a: 129). British TV shows such as *God's Gift* (ITV, 1995–1997), *Pyjama Party* (ITV, 1996) and *The Girlie Show* (Channel 4, 1996–1997), for example, were not especially popular but were still significant for the way they relished turning the tables on men by 'subjecting male victims from the audience to the same kind of scrutiny and lascivious comment as has been the norm for women' (McRobbie, 1999b: 51). In the American media, too, many feminist commentators perceived the rise of rebellious and autonomous constructions of young femininity. The Warner TV show *Buffy the Vampire Slayer* (1997–2003), in particular, won many feminist plaudits for its representation of a femininity that was intelligent, confident and powerful. The lead character, a combination of chirpy high-school minx and occult demon-stalker, was celebrated as a 'transgressive woman warrior' (Early, 2001) – an embodiment of 'strength, power and assertiveness' (Owen, 1999: 25) who often destabilised gendered power structures by being 'a supremely confident kicker of evil butt' (Katz, 1998: 35).

It was, though, the field of girls' magazines that seemed to register some of the most striking changes in the media's address and representation of young women. During the late 1970s research by McRobbie on *Jackie* had painted a fairly bleak picture of popular magazines aimed at adolescent girls. Originally launched by the D.C. Thomson publishing group in 1964, during the 1970s *Jackie* had become one of Britain's best-selling girls' magazines, with a content that mixed pop music features, advice columns and romantic cartoon strips. McRobbie, however, was deeply critical of *Jackie*'s agenda. Arguing that the magazine reinforced traditional sex-role stereotyping, McRobbie was especially scathing of *Jackie*'s fixation with romance that, she argued, represented 'an ideological bloc of mammoth proportions, one which imprisons [girls] in a claustrophobic world of jealousy and competitiveness' (McRobbie, 1982: 265). Subsequently, however, McRobbie revised her view, distancing herself from perspectives that saw girls' magazines as simply a breeding ground for monolithic and oppressive ideologies of female passivity that were absorbed relatively unproblematically by young readers. Partly, McRobbie's shift in approach was a response to research that suggested readers engaged with girls' magazines in a much more complex way than she had initially assumed. Elizabeth Frazer (1987), for example, found from her interviews with teenage readers of *Jackie* that, rather than being vulnerable 'victims' of the text's ideologies of romance, they often read the magazine critically – even laughing at the romantic stories' lack of realism. The magazine's 'effect' on its audience, therefore, could not be deduced simply from an analysis of its textual content.

Martin Barker, moreover, suggested that the text, itself, was often more complex and contradictory than McRobbie's original analysis had allowed for. Rather than being underpinned by a uniform and unvarying 'code of romance', Barker argued, *Jackie* was 'composed of elements relating differently to girls, which might change at different paces and therefore show at times signs of tension and ambivalence' (Barker, 1989: 164). Here, Barker also highlighted important changes that had taken place in the format and style of *Jackie*. During the 1960s, he argued, *Jackie*'s central tenets had stressed 'self-sacrifice, trusting your man even when it conflicts with your own desires, and reorganising your emotions and wishes according to his needs' (1989: 165). By the end of the 1970s, however, this conservatism was on the wane. Instead, Barker detected 'a creeping freedom' in *Jackie*'s stories, with 'a real decline in confidence in romance's possibilities' (1989: 177, 178). And, by the 1980s, the romantic stories were disappearing altogether as the magazine upped its attention to pop music and fashion.

Reformulating her original analysis, McRobbie also gave close attention to the changing face of British girls' magazines. Change, McRobbie argued, was clearly evident in the pages of *Jackie* during the 1980s. A shift from cartoon to photo-strip stories, she suggested, had been accompanied by a 'new realism' in the narratives, with idealised images of romance giving way to a focus on the problems and difficulties of relationships (McRobbie, 1991: 148). This shift was also emphasised by developments in the magazine's advice columns and problem pages, where a strongly moralistic tone had made way for a more supportive and informative approach. Features on fashion and pop music, meanwhile, had become more central to the magazine, the romantic stories slipping into the background. This decline of romantic content was even more evident in a 'new wave' of glossy, high colour British girls' magazines that came to the fore during the late 1980s and 1990s. For McRobbie, titles such as *Just Seventeen* (originally launched in 1983 and revamped as *J17* in 1996), *Mizz* (1985), *More!* (1988), *Sugar* (1994) and *Bliss* (1995) '[broke] decisively with the conventions of feminine behaviour' by appealing to a 'new kind of (typically heterosexual) girl' for whom 'frank information, advice and knowledge about sex is a prerequisite for her adventures' (1999b: 50–51).[17] In America, too, a new outlook began to surface in young women's magazines. Launched in 1988, for example, *Sassy* magazine eschewed cloying romance in favour of an agenda that combined features on pop and fashion with risqué cheek and a candid approach to sexuality – a winning formula that saw the magazine's circulation rise by 60 per cent (from 250,000 to 400,000) within six months of its debut. *CosmoGirl!* was also a hit. Debuting in 1999 (and successfully launched in British edition in 2001), *CosmoGirl!* was modelled as a 'little sister' to *Cosmopolitan*, the successful women's title. *CosmoGirl!* lacked *Sassy*'s chutzpah, but its world of fun, fashion, and sexual candour matched the energetic outlook developed in British titles such as *J17* and *More!*.

The trend for girls' magazines to give more candid treatment to sexual topics, however, attracted a variety of critics. On the one hand, conservative anxieties about readers being 'corrupted' by the magazines' coverage of sex prompted attempts to regulate their content more strictly (see Chapter 4). In America, for example, *Sassy*'s frank attitude to sexual issues prompted the fundamentalist religious Right to orchestrate an advertising boycott of the magazine and, sold off by its publishers in 1994, *Sassy*'s wings were ultimately clipped by its new owners. On the other hand, however, some feminist critics also rebuked the new teen magazines' sexual politics. In Britain, for example, Stevi Jackson (1996) observed that titles such as *Just Seventeen* were 'relentlessly heterosexual' in their approach to sex and, while the magazines routinely celebrated heterosexuality, lesbian sexuality was virtually ignored. McRobbie, however, countered this criticism. Although lesbianism was not discussed regularly or in great detail in *Just Seventeen*, McRobbie (1999b) detected a gradual growth in the magazine's coverage. Moreover, while she acknowledged that there were limits to the kind of sexuality that was permissible within the pages of girls' magazines, McRobbie maintained that titles such as *Just Seventeen* clearly evidenced the impact of feminism. Both the girls who read the magazines and the female journalists who wrote them were, according to McRobbie, aware of (and influenced by) feminist ideas. And, while she conceded that this was a 'narrow and restricted' form of feminism that privileged the interests of white, First World women, McRobbie maintained that this still represented a significant development – ensuring that contemporary girls' magazines were characterised by 'a self-confidence and openness to the world rather than a retreat from it' (1999b: 46–47).

Irony, according to McRobbie, was a crucial ingredient in the more 'open' schema of girls' magazines during the 1980s and 1990s. Titles such as *J17* and *More!*, she argued, had borrowed from the sensationalist pitch of downmarket tabloids to develop an exaggerated, over-the-top house-style in their headlines and features ('Get Your Pecs Out For the Girls!', 'Long Distance Passion: Can He Keep It Up?'). This tongue-in-cheek attitude, McRobbie argued, signalled a 'licensed silliness' that offered a new, more open-ended construction of 'ironic femininity' in which readers were allowed 'to participate in all the conventional gender stereotypical rituals without finding themselves trapped into traditional gender-subordinate positions' (McRobbie, 1999b: 53). Moreover, in place of the romance that had once been the staple component of teenage girls' magazines, McRobbie detected a new accent on pop music, celebrities and entertainment. This shift of focus was partly inspired by a renaissance in British pop magazines initiated by the launch of *Smash Hits* in 1978.[18] The sparky visual style pioneered by *Smash Hits* was duplicated in the new generation of girls' magazines, their layout increasingly characterised by an abundance of facts and information snippets set in a high colour, glossy format, with written text and narrative giving way to a bright collage of images and features – a trend McRobbie saw

No. 254. NOVEMBER 16th. 1968    THURSDAYS    SIXPENCE.

# Jackie

For tender love stories that
leave you with the nicest feeling...

...and all the gen about
pop stars you find nowhere else

**Figure 6.2** The changing face of the British girls' magazine: (a) 'For tender love stories that leave you with the nicest feeling . . .' (*Jackie,* 16 November 1968)

as a microcosm of the postmodern 'ecstasy of communication' and its associated design aesthetics (McRobbie, 1991: 144).

McRobbie also highlighted a more pronounced consumerist agenda in the magazines' diet of pop, fashion and beauty features. Here, she argued, there were undeniable elements of regulation, with conventional ideals of beauty and femininity reproduced and reinforced. But, at the same

Inside the image:

LOVE QUIZ: DATE HIM OR DUMP HIM?

COSMO *girl!*

BONUS!
FREE
SIZZLING
CENTREFOLD
see p72

NEW LOOK
£1.55

All Your
**Sex**
Worries
Busted

**HOT
ASTRO
EXTRA**
Find your summer soulmate
(so accurate it's freaky!)

True life special
"Left for
dead by
joyriders"

Found! Your
**perfect**
holiday boyfriend

**Justin**
"What I really
want in a
girlfriend"

Your
**5 biggest
fears**
and how to
face them

**Fuzz off!**
Hair removal
made easy

**263 surfbabe
sexy looks!**
Acid brights, must-have minis, purse-friendly
prints, flipflops, plus tons of beauty booty

06›

9 771472 368028

cosmogirl.co.uk JUNE 2003

**Figure 6.2 contd** (b) '263 Surfbabe Sexy Looks!' (*Cosmo Girl!* (UK edn), June 2003)

time, there were also spaces where more autonomous, assertive models of femininity appeared. For instance, McRobbie argued that beauty products articulated 'a symbolic space in the transition from childhood dependence to teenage independence', while the hard-sell of the fashion and beauty features was balanced by an emphasis on self-satisfaction and self-image in which the reader was encouraged to exercise personal choice over her image and 'to play an active role in developing a personal style' (1991: 177, 166). Moreover, McRobbie suggested, young women had the ability to navigate their own way through the magazines' fragmented, fluid format. Growing-up in a multi-media universe, McRobbie argued, readers possessed a level of textual competency that allowed them to 'slot in and out of a range of media modes simultaneously' (1991: 143), deploying an active and engaged form of reading practice that belied any sense of the audience being helpless 'victims' of the text. Indeed, Mary Jane Kehily's (1999) ethnographic research supported this view of young readers as active and discriminating. Based on students at a British secondary school, Kehily's study suggested that girls engaged with teen magazines in a discerning and productive fashion. Friendship groups, Kehily found, often read and talked about the magazines among themselves, the texts functioning as both a source of humour and as a cultural resource for discussing issues of sexuality. In these terms, Kehily argued, girls' collective reading of teen magazines offered 'an opportunity for dialogue where femininities can be endlessly produced, defined and enhanced' (1999: 85).[19]

## TRIBAL GATHERINGS: NEO-TRIBES, POST-SUBCULTURALISTS AND THE COMMERCIAL MEDIATION OF STYLE

The 1990s saw wide-ranging debate about both the nature of youth subcultures and the character of their relationship to the media and other commercial industries. For some theorists, the proliferation of media and consumer culture during the late twentieth century had brought more fluid and dynamic forms of subcultural style. According to Ted Polhemus (1994, 1996, 1997), for example, the rise of a media-saturated world had seen distinctive subcultural boundaries eclipsed by an ever-changing plurality of identities in a new, postmodern 'supermarket of style' (Polhemus, 1997).

Andy Bennett (1999a, 2000), too, saw the idea of distinctively-bounded subcultures as an anachronism. Instead of 'subculture', Bennett suggested, the concept of 'neo-tribes' was better able to capture the dynamic, pluralistic relationship between young people and the contemporary media. Originating in the work of Michael Maffesoli (1996), the concept of the neo-tribe denoted the way individuals expressed collective identity through distinctive rituals and consumption practices. According to Maffesoli, these 'neo-tribal' groups were not formed according to 'traditional' structural determinants (for example, class, gender or religion), but through diverse, dynamic and often ephemeral consumption patterns – the fluid boundaries of 'neo-tribes' allowing members to wander through multiple group attachments, so that collective identity was 'less a question of belonging to a gang, a family or a community, than of switching from one group to another' (Maffesoli, 1996: 76). Drawing on these ideas, Bennett argued that young people's consumption of popular music was no longer determined by conformity to rigid subcultural genres, but by changing individual repertoires of taste. 'Shifting through various types of music, artists and sounds,' Bennett argued, 'consumers characteristically choose songs and instrumental pieces which appeal to them with the effect that the stylistic boundaries existing between the latter become rather less important than the meaning which the chosen body of music as a whole assumes for the listener.' (Bennett, 1999a: 610)

Developments within dance music and club culture during the 1990s seemed to exemplify notions of a pervasive fragmentation and fluidity within young people's patterns of media consumption. From the outset, the rave scene of the late 1980s was composed of a plethora of interlocking musical styles, and subsequent years saw a further proliferation of subgenres – from speed garage and deep house to gabba and Goan trance. This plurality and mutability in dance music and club culture was highlighted in the work of authors affiliated to the Manchester Institute of Popular Culture. Drawn together by Steve Redhead (Redhead, 1990, 1993; Redhead et al., 1997), these studies were diverse in their focus, though many pointed to the way (post)modern club cultures seemed to defy attempts at uncovering a concrete sense of 'meaning' behind their styles and appeared, instead, to be 'free-floating' sets of images that were not locked into any specific historical moment or location.[20]

These accounts, however, tended to exaggerate the degree to which earlier 'subcultural' formations (Teddy boys, mods and punks, for example) were discretely formed and clearly delineated. Throughout the 1950s, 1960s and 1970s young people's tastes and patterns of media consumption were always characterised by a degree of heterogeneity and 'fluidity' – with many youngsters making only partial and transient 'subcultural' attachments as they wandered across a range of identities and affiliations. Moreover, even amid the hectic pluralism of the postmodern 'supermarket of style', it was possible to identify (at least some) relatively distinctive and clearly bounded subcultural groups. David Muggleton, for example, judged that style-based subcultures were not a phenomenon of the past, but continued to exist as 'a liminal sensibility that manifests itself as an expression of freedom from structure, control and restraint' (Muggleton, 2000: 158). Initially, Muggleton had speculated that clearly-demarcated subcultural styles had dissolved in a new era of the 'post-subculturalist' – a uniquely capricious 'fashion tourist' who revelled in 'moving quickly and freely from one style to another' in a sartorial world where 'there is no authenticity, no reason for ideological commitment, merely a stylistic game to be played' (1997: 198). Subsequent fieldwork, however, prompted Muggleton to modify his thesis. In his interviews with youngsters who identified themselves as punks, goths and skinheads Muggleton found little evidence of the class-based 'semiotic guerrilla warfare' outlined by the CCCS authors during the 1970s, but nor did his findings support 'the more excessive postmodern claims':

> Informants did not rapidly discard a whole series of discrete styles. Nor did they regard themselves as an ironic parody, celebrating their own lack of authenticity and the superficiality of an image-saturated culture. On the contrary, attitudes were held to be more important than style, while appearance transformation was anchored in a gradually evolving sense of self. Subcultural sensibilities were, in other words, informed by a combination of a modernist depth model of reality and a postmodern emphasis on hybridity and diversity.
>
> (Muggleton, 2000: 158)

For Muggleton, then, distinct subcultural identities had not melted into a postmodern melange of 'depthless' styles. But nor did subcultural style amount to a class-based strategy of 'resistance'. Instead, for their adherents, subcultures represented 'collective expressions and celebrations of individualism' (Muggleton, 2000: 79). Regardless of their social background, Muggleton argued, subcultural members saw their tastes in style and media as a bohemian-like expression of '*freedom* – freedom from rules, structures, controls and from the predictability of conventional lifestyles' (Muggleton, 2000: 167). Paul Hodkinson's (2002) study of British goths also challenged claims that distinctive subcultural styles had fallen by the postmodern wayside. Hodkinson acknowledged that, amid the frenetic media flows of contemporary culture, stylistic boundaries had become less clear-cut, but he insisted that a sense of group belonging and collective identity remained an important force in some young people's lives (Hodkinson, 2002: 18). His participant observation of goth clubs, conventions and concerts, for instance, uncovered 'a set of tastes and norms which [had] a significant degree of consistency', with many goths feeling 'there was some sort of link between their style and certain general qualities they shared with other goths, including individuality, creativity, open-mindedness and commitment' (2002: 35, 62).

Significantly, Hodkinson also stressed the way 'commerce and media specifically constructed and facilitated the goth scene' (2002: 109). This attention to the role of the commercial media in the formation of subcultural phenomena starkly contrasted to the theories elaborated by the CCCS authors during the 1970s. The CCCS team had configured the media and cultural industries primarily in negative terms. Focusing their analysis on what they saw as the creative '"moment" of originality in the formation of style' (Clarke and Jefferson, 1976: 148), intervention by commercial business was equated with the 'neutralisation' of an authentic subculture – market intercession seen as returning once meaningful and 'oppositional' subcultural styles to the fold of bland consumerism. Hebdige was especially pessimistic, arguing that 'processes of production, packaging and publicity . . . must inevitably lead to the defusion of the subculture's subversive power' (Hebdige, 1979: 95). In these terms, then, there existed a cycle of 'incorporation' in which meaningful styles generated at 'street level' by authentic subcultures were subsequently exploited and recuperated by parasitic media industries. An influential perspective, these notions of commercial incorporation were given a new inflection in accounts of postmodern culture. Steven Connor, for example, contended that in the twilight of the twentieth century the cycle of 'innovation' and 'incorporation' within youth style had speeded up 'to the point where authentic "originality" and commercial "exploitation" are hard to distinguish' (Connor, 1989: 185).[21]

Rather than processes of 'recuperation' having undergone postmodern 'acceleration', however, other theorists have suggested that youth subcultures have *always* been entwined with the institutions of the market in an *ongoing* relationship of exchange. Indeed, this symbiotic relationship between subcultures and market institutions was a theme that featured in Stanley Cohen's early studies. As we saw in Chapter 4, Rock and Cohen's (1970) analysis of the 1950s Teddy boy phenomenon highlighted the way that media coverage gave form and substance to the Teds' subculture, while Cohen's subsequent (2002) study of the 1960s mods and rockers also underlined the role of media coverage in giving shape and definition to subcultural formations that were initially vague and indistinct. Thornton's (1995) analysis of the development of the 1980s acid-house scene also emphasised the way subcultures were locked into a symbiotic relationship with the media and other commercial interests. Like Cohen, Thornton argued that the representational power of the media was crucial in shaping a subculture's identity and its members' sense of themselves. 'Subcultures', Thornton maintained:

do not germinate from a seed and grow by force of their own energy into mysterious 'movements' only to be belatedly digested by the media. Rather, media, and other cultural industries are there and effective right from the start.

(Thornton, 1995: 117)

In contrast to Cohen, however, Thornton distinguished between different forms of media that fed into the development of a subculture. Like Cohen, Thornton recognised the role of the mass media (for example, tabloid newspapers and TV news coverage) in processes of moral panic, labelling and amplification. But Thornton also identified more specialist media that had played a key role in the construction of club culture. First, Thornton identified 'niche' media – most obviously music and style magazines – whose features and stories had constructed a coherent subculture out of what was initially 'little more than an imported type of music with drug associations' (Thornton, 1995: 158). Secondly, she pointed to even more small-scale, specialist 'micro' media – most notably flyers and fanzines – that had distributed practical information about music and events associated with the developing subcultural scene. Through performing these distinct roles, Thornton argued, mass-, niche- and micro-media had together shaped the meaning and organisation of club culture. As she explained:

> Youth subcultures are not organic, unmediated social formations, nor are they autonomous grassroots cultures which only meet the media upon recuperative 'selling out' or 'moral panic'. On the contrary, the media do not just represent but participate in the assembly, demarcation and development of music cultures.
>
> (Thornton, 1995: 160)

Thornton was careful to emphasise, however, that in highlighting the critical role of the media in the development of club culture she was not casting subcultural members as the dupes of media manipulation. 'Clubbers and ravers' she stressed, were 'active and creative participants in the formation of club cultures' (Thornton, 1995: 161). Although 'authentic' subcultures were, in essence, media constructions, Thornton argued they remained powerful sources of meaning and self-identity for their participants. Here, Thornton borrowed from Pierre Bourdieu's notion of 'cultural capital'. For Bourdieu (1984) 'cultural capital' denoted the forms of knowledge, cultural artefacts and modes of behaviour that bestowed prestige and social advantage on those social groups that possessed them. Adapting the concept, Thornton argued that '*sub*cultural capital' represented the knowledge, tastes and artefacts that conferred status in the eyes of subcultural members. 'Just as books and paintings display cultural capital in the family home', Thornton explained:

> so subcultural capital is objectified in the form of fashionable haircuts and
> well assembled record collections ... Just as cultural capital is personified
> in 'good' manners, so subcultural capital is embodied in the form of being
> 'in the know', using (but not over-using) current slang and looking as if you
> were born to perform the current dance styles.
>
> (Thornton, 1995: 11–12)

Subcultural capital, moreover, was invoked not only within the subculture's internal hierarchies of status, but also as a means by which members collectively distinguished themselves from outsiders. Thornton's
'hardcore clubbers', for example, conceived of themselves as existing
outside an 'unhip and unsophisticated' mainstream crowd who they 'denigrated for having indiscriminate music tastes, lacking individuality and
being amateurs in the art of clubbing' (Thornton, 1995: 99). In a similar fashion, Hodkinson's goths drew upon their subcultural capital to
define and strengthen their sense of collective identity. 'In contrast to
notions of the mainstream as dominated by commercial interests and a
mass narrow-minded culture', Hodkinson argued, 'goths tended to
regard their own subculture as encapsulating authentic artistic expression
by musicians, and the exercise of equally instinctive discriminating tastes
in music and clothing by a diverse and open-minded set of individual fans'
(2002: 78).

## ALL-CONSUMING PASSIONS: YOUTH AS 'CREATIVE' CONSUMERS

Theoretical distinctions between 'meaningful' youth subcultures and
'incorporated' media fabrications have always been difficult to sustain.
As Simon Frith has observed, attempts to elaborate a clear-cut divide
between the 'subcultural' and the 'mainstream' have invariably lead to
a 'false-freezing of the world into deviants and the rest' (1978: 53). This
problem was especially evident in the accounts offered by the CCCS
authors during the 1970s. In reality relatively few youngsters ever
entered the 'authentic' subcultural scenes described by the CCCS team.
As the CCCS theorists, themselves, conceded, 'the great majority of
working class youth never enters a tight or coherent sub culture at all'
(Clarke et al., 1976: 16). Indeed, rather than making a wholehearted
commitment to a subcultural lifestyle, most youngsters tended to adopt
only a limited range of subcultural trappings or media-hyped insignia
(perhaps wearing a 'mod' tie or buying a 'punk' record). As Steve
Redhead wryly observed, '"Authentic" subcultures were produced by
subcultural theories, not the other way around' (1990: 25).

Rather than focusing on spectacular subcultural styles, the late 1980s and early 1990s saw many theorists switch their attention to young people's everyday practices of media consumption. In *Common Culture* (1990), for example, Paul Willis drew together ethnographic studies of a wide range of young people's cultural activities – from fashion and music, to art and sport. Conducted in Wolverhampton and several other British cities by leading figures within British media and cultural studies,[22] the research highlighted the ways young people were involved in creative cultural production across a range of media, including fanzines, fashion and music.[23] Rather than conceiving 'creativity' simply in terms of economic production and exchange, however, Willis gave attention to more general dimensions of identity formation, in which 'young people are all the time expressing or attempting to express something about their actual or potential cultural significance' (1990: 1). Invoking Raymond Williams' notion of culture as 'a whole way of life', Willis sought to reveal the elements of agency in young people's day-to-day cultural activities and practices of media consumption.

Seeing commodities as cultural catalysts rather than as ends in themselves, Willis used the term 'grounded aesthetics' to denote the ways young people manipulated the goods and resources made available by the media and other commercial industries, youngsters re-articulating products' meanings in the creation of their own cultures and forms of self-representation. For Willis, then, meanings were not intrinsic to cultural artefacts but were generated through people's acts of consumption. From this perspective, young people did not consume commercial goods and media texts uncritically, but actively appropriated the products available in the market, recontextualising and transforming their meanings – often in ways that challenged or subverted dominant systems of power relations. As Willis put it:

> human consumption does not simply repeat the relations of production –
> and whatever cynical motives lie behind them. Interpretation, symbolic
> action and creativity are part of consumption. They're involved in the whole
> realm of necessary symbolic work. The work is at least as important as what-
> ever might originally be encoded in commodities and can often produce their
> opposites. Indeed some aspects of 'profanity' in commercial artefacts may
> be liberating and progressive, introducing the possibility of the new and the
> socially dynamic.
>
> (Willis, 1990: 21)

For Willis, then, young people's acts of commodity consumption and media use were not passive and indiscriminate, but were active practices of 'symbolic creativity'. Drawing illustrative examples from a range of rich ethnographic studies, Willis argued that a variety of cultural activities and media forms (TV soap operas and advertisements, cinema-going, teen magazines, pop music, fashion and hairstyles) were used by young people as raw materials for creative expression, youth's patterns of consumption representing 'a kind of self creation – of identities, of space, of cultural forms – with its own kind of cultural empowerment' (Willis, 1990: 82). According to Willis, therefore, media industries might invite young audiences to understand and make sense of their products in specific ways, but they had no control over the way young people often appropriated, reinterpreted and even subverted a text's meanings. The home-taping, re-recording and mixing of music, for example, were interpreted by Willis as acts of creative consumption that involved 'the exercise of critical, discriminating choices and uses which disrupt the taste categories and "ideal" modes of consumption promoted by the leisure industry and break up its superimposed definitions of musical meaning' (1990: 60). Fashion, according to Willis, offered equally creative and disruptive opportunities. Young people, he argued 'don't just buy passively or uncritically', instead they 'make their own sense of what is commercially available, make their own aesthetic judgements, and sometimes reject the normative definitions and categories of "fashion" promoted by the clothing industry' (Willis, 1990: 85).

Willis's account of young people's consumer practices as creative and discriminating stood in stark contrast to both the image of bovine consumer passivity presented by mass culture theorists (such as Macdonald and Adorno) and the notion of young people as vulnerable 'victims' that underpinned much media 'effects' research (see Chapter 4). Willis's emphasis on the 'symbolic creativity' of everyday culture, moreover, also challenged the distinction theorists such as Hebdige had made between a meaningful 'subculture' and an incorporated 'mainstream'. Echoing Hall and Whannel's earlier account of the popular media as 'an area of self-expression for the young' (1964: 276), Willis argued that the 'meaning of style' lay not so much in the 'semiotic guerrilla warfare' of a coterie of subcultural shock troops, as in the pleasures ordinary youngsters took in the creation of identity through the 'grounded aesthetics' of everyday life.

The approach Willis took in *Common Culture* was constituent in broader shifts within media and cultural studies during the 1980s and early 1990s. The emphasis Willis and his associates placed on concrete fieldwork was indicative of a more general 'ethnographic turn' within media and cultural studies – researchers increasingly moving away from theoretical approaches that privileged the 'power' of the text, and instead giving greater attention to people's own understandings of their cultural practices and media use.[24] Willis's accent on the creative dimensions to media consumption was also part of a wider attention given to audiences as 'active' participants in the processes of meaning-making. Rather than seeing audiences as helpless puppets that danced to the tune of media producers, researchers increasingly focused on the way people engaged actively with texts, their diverse responses influenced by factors of class, gender, sexual and ethnic identity, and the wider cultural contexts in which audiences encountered the media.

Attention to the 'creativity' of media audiences became an especially strong theme in the study of fans and their cultural practices. Fans and fan groups (both significant aspects of youth culture) have been popularly regarded as rather sad creatures, invariably pathologised as socially dysfunctional outsiders or maligned as irrational obsessives. But during the 1990s several theorists drew attention to the ways fans engaged actively and meaningfully with the objects of their fascination. As Henry Jenkins explained, actor William Shatner once joked that fans of his sci-fi TV series *Star Trek* should 'Get a life' – but what escaped Shatner was the fact that the fans had *already* created a 'life' for themselves in a complex and diverse subculture that drew its resources from commercial industries, but reworked them to serve alternative interests (Jenkins, 1992: 10). Rejecting stereotypes of fans as mindless consumers and social misfits, Jenkins argued that they were actually skilled manipulators of media texts. Fans, Jenkins contended, used the materials made available by the commercial market to construct their own culture, often in ways that challenged producers' attempts to regulate textual meanings.

Here, Jenkins drew on Michel de Certeau's (1984) concept of 'textual poaching'. For de Certeau, 'textual poaching' denoted the way subordinate groups subverted the meanings of dominant cultural forms, subaltern and oppressed social groups fashioning a habitable cultural environment for themselves from the resources made available by the socially dominant forms of cultural production and distribution. According to Jenkins, fans were 'textual poachers' *par excellence*. Offering an ethnographic account of fan cultures based around TV shows such as *Star Trek*, *Blake's 7*, *The Professionals* and *Beauty and the Beast*, Jenkins showed how fans used the programmes as the basis for their own stories, songs, videos and social exchanges in a rich and creative cultural network. Distinguishing fans from the general audience, Jenkins emphasised the distinctive interpretations and alternative identities generated in the texts that fans produced for themselves (for example, fanzines and fan fiction), fandom representing 'a participatory culture which transforms the experience of media consumption into the production of new texts, indeed of a new culture and a new community' (Jenkins, 1992: 46).

John Fiske was also impressed by the cultural creativity of media fans. Like Jenkins, Fiske saw fans as artfully appropriating cultural forms made available in the commercial market. Fiske contended that *all* popular audiences were (to some extent) creative in the ways they consumed and made sense of media texts, but he argued that fans took this creativity one step further by actually engaging in some form of textual production themselves (for example, organising clubs and events, writing their own fanzines and stories, or amassing splendid collections of artefacts and ephemera). According to Fiske, fan cultures operated their own systems of production and distribution, forming a 'shadow cultural economy' that lay outside the 'official' media industries and offered fans 'opportunities to make meanings of their social identities and social experiences that are self-interested and functional' (Fiske, 1992: 35). At times, Fiske conceded, this process remained at the level of a compensatory fantasy life, but at others it was translated into 'empowered social behaviour' that could 'enhance the fan's power over, and participation in, the original, industrial text' (Fiske, 1992: 43).

Fiske saw fans as especially creative media consumers, but he insisted that fandom should be seen as a heightened form of processes of active consumption that were characteristic of popular audiences more generally. For Fiske, the fan was an 'excessive reader' who differed from the 'ordinary' reader in degree rather than kind (Fiske, 1992: 46). According to Fiske, then, 'ordinary' media consumption was also a field for creativity and the active construction of cultural meanings. Like Willis, Fiske (1989a, 1989b) saw social actors as activating their own values and interests through their patterns of consumption, people creatively using the products of the market machine to engineer their own cultural spaces and identities. According to Fiske, a commercial commodity was not 'a completed object to be accepted passively', but 'a resource to be used' (1989a: 10–11) and every act of consumption was 'an act of cultural production, for consumption is always the production of meaning' (1989a: 35). Inevitably, Fiske argued, commercial cultural forms served the economic interests of dominant social groups and had 'lines of force within them that are hegemonic and work in favour of the status quo' (1989b: 2). But, while commodities made an economic profit for their producers and distributors, Fiske maintained that they could only succeed in the marketplace if they contained resources from which subordinate groups could produce their own cultural meanings.

Fiske, moreover, insisted that these meanings were an exciting realm of potential transgression and cultural 'resistance'. Drawing (like

Jenkins) on the ideas of de Certeau, Fiske saw popular culture as characterised by a series of 'guerrilla raids' in which subordinate groups plundered from the cultural raw materials provided by the commercial market, making them answerable to their own interests and implicitly challenging and defying dominant power structures. Fiske pointed, for example, to the way some teenage girls achieved a sense of self-empowerment through adopting the 'look' of Madonna, the singer's style providing them with a way of taking control of their own sexual identities (Fiske, 1989b: 100). Young, urban Aborigines in Australia, meanwhile, took great delight in watching vintage Westerns, evading the films' white, colonialist ideologies and instead 'ally[ing] themselves with the Indians, cheer[ing] them on as they attack the wagon train or home-stead, killing the white men and carrying off the white women' (Fiske, 1989a: 25). In a similar vein, Fiske cited shopping malls, video arcades, TV game shows and an array of other popular culture and media phenomena as sites for 'semiotic resistance that not only refuses the dominant meanings but constructs oppositional ones that serve the interests of the subordinate' (1989b: 10).

For some critics, however, Fiske's claims for the 'transgressive' possi-bilities of popular culture were overly celebratory. In many respects, for example, the 'shadow cultural economy' of fandom can be seen as under-pinned by systems of power relations and processes of inclusion and exclusion akin to those operating within 'official' media industries. As Matt Hills observed, fan culture is not simply a community but *also a social hierarchy* where fans share a common interest while also competing over fan knowledge, access to the object of fandom, and status' (Hills, 2002: 46). More generally, other authors detected in Fiske's work a problematic over-eagerness to equate 'active' consumption with cul-tural 'resistance'. Jim McGuigan (1992) offered an especially scathing critique, giving short shrift to ideas that, in his assessment, amounted to little more than an 'uncritical endorsement of popular taste and pleasure' (McGuigan, 1992: 6). While he was happy to accept that people were active agents in the formation of their own culture, McGuigan insisted that Fiske's arguments represented a 'cultural populism' that gave inadequate regard to the historical and economic conditions under which these processes took place. McGuigan was less critical of the research Willis had collected in *Common Culture* (1992), though he still insisted that many of the accounts of 'grounded aesthetics' lacked sufficient attention to issues of institutional power and socio-economic relations (McGuigan, 1992: 114–122).

Other theorists also argued that the attention accorded to active media audiences and creative consumers had sometimes lost sight of issues of economic power and control. Political economists such as Graham Murdock (1997) and Nicholas Garnham (1998), for example, argued that cultural theorists' interest in audience meanings and consumer practices had sometimes 'exaggerated the freedoms of consumption in daily life' (Garnham, 1998: 603) and required a more thorough engagement with 'the ways that these grounded processes are structured by wider economic and ideological formations' (Murdock, 1997: 63). In an attempt to address such criticisms, research in the field of youth culture sought to retain recognition of young people's capacity as active agents in the authorship of their culture, but with a greater awareness that these processes took place within (and often constrained by) a wider field of economic and political power. Steven Miles, for example, characterised the relationship between youth culture and the commercial market as 'mutually exploitative' – young people appropriating, transforming and recontextualising the meanings of media texts, though always within boundaries set by commercial interests. As Miles elaborated:

> The proposition that young people actively engage with the mass media and to a degree forge it in their own image is a sound one, but is only ever partially realized. Ultimately, the parameters within which young people are able to do so, are set down for them by a mass media that is inevitably constructed first and foremost on the need to sell magazines, programmes and what is essentially a consumerist way of life. Young people are therefore liberated and constrained by the mass media at one and the same time – it provides them with the canvass, but the only oils they can use to paint that canvass are consumerist ones.
>
> (Miles, 2000: 85)

An appreciation of the power of market institutions, however, does not necessarily entail sliding back into notions of commercial Svengalis leading passive and undiscriminating young consumers by the nose. Acknowledgement can still be given to the way young people's 'attachments to goods and to the "social life of things" can be productive of new social identities' (McRobbie, 1999c: 37). With this in mind, a number of theorists found the concept of 'lifestyle' an illuminating way of addressing the relationship between young people's cultures and the products of the media and consumer industries.

## A WORLD OF DISTINCTION: YOUTH, MEDIA AND LIFESTYLE

When considering youth in relation to the concept of 'lifestyle', it is important to remember that the term has a more specialised meaning than simply the common sense formulation of a 'style of life'. By the early 1960s, the term 'lifestyle' was already a fixture in the lexicon of market researchers,[25] and during the 1980s and 1990s it was increasingly used by advertisers and marketers to categorise the distinctive tastes and consumption practices of specific market segments (see Chapter 3). As an analytical concept, however, the notion of 'lifestyle' was originally developed during the early twentieth century in the work of Max Weber (1978), who argued that social stratification depended not solely on patterns of economic relation, but also on the degree of 'status' attached to the patterns of living and cultural preferences of different social groups. In *Distinction* (1984), Pierre Bourdieu also developed the concept, using it to denote patterns of taste and consumption used by social groups to distinguish themselves as distinct class formations, his ideas influencing many analyses of consumer culture and niche-marketing during the 1980s and 1990s.[26] During the 1990s these notions of lifestyle also surfaced in the study of youth culture and the formation of young people's identities, the concept being deployed to rethink the relationship between young people's position in the social structure and their patterns of taste in media and popular culture.

Early moves in this direction were made by two Swedish youth studies. Surveying young people's attitudes to entertainment during the 1980s and 1990s, Bo Reimer found that choices and tastes were affected by factors such as 'class, gender, education, income and civil status', but none of these appeared to be as significant as a common lifestyle oriented around leisure, entertainment and media consumption which existed 'almost independent of socio-economic background' (Reimer, 1995: 135). Like Reimer, Thomas Johansson and Frederik Miegel (1992) also acknowledged the influence of structural factors on youth's cultural orientations, though argued that their fieldwork suggested young people's lifestyles were the outcome of a wider spectrum of individually held values, attitudes and actions (1992: 103). As Johansson and Miegel explained:

> It is probably true that in modern society the individual has gained greater freedom to choose and create his or her own specific lifestyle. This is not to say, however, that structure and position no longer play a significant role in the making of lifestyle . . . in modern society neither structure, position, nor the individual, is the sole determinant of lifestyles. Modern lifestyles are the result of a complex interplay between phenomena at all three of these levels.
>
> (Johansson and Miegel, 1992: 37–38)

In Britain, the work of Steven Miles and his associates (Miles, 2000, 2002; Miles et al., 1998; Anderson and Miles, 1999) also drew on the concept of lifestyle to make sense of young people's relationship with the media and the commercial market. According to Miles et al. (1998), young people used their practices of consumption to develop a lifestyle in which they felt they 'fitted in' with a wider peer group, whilst simultaneously giving them a sense of unique individuality in a world characterised by instability, flux and change. Here, Miles et al. were influenced by a wider body of theoretical work that saw uncertainty and 'risk' as features increasingly endemic to life in contemporary western societies. Most notably, Ulrich Beck (1992) argued that the West was undergoing an epochal transformation, with the certainties of industrial modernity giving way to a new, less predictable era.[27] In this increasingly dangerous world, Beck suggested, people had been confronted by the pervasive risks generated by the processes of modernisation – these risks operating not only at a global level (for instance, the threat of nuclear war or environmental disaster), but also throughout everyday personal life. Beck acknowledged that these hazards were unequally spread among social groups (their distribution arranged in a fashion similar to the inequalities of a class society), but he argued that class ties had steadily weakened and people increasingly had to rely on themselves as they negotiated the challenges and dangers of day-to-day living. In this context, Beck maintained, individualised lifestyles had come to the fore, people steering their own way through different life options and making their own sets of identifications and allegiances.

Like many commentators,[28] Miles and his colleagues saw the rise of the 'risk society' as registering a particularly significant impact on the young. Youth, Miles et al. argued, faced a world in which their life experiences – in terms of family structure, educational opportunities and routes to employment – seemed to be becoming increasingly tenuous. In response, young people sought a sense of stability through constructing an identity based on the symbolic values of the products they consumed. 'Consumer goods', Miles et al. concluded from their empirical fieldwork, 'appear to provide the only viable resource by which constructive and arguably creative, conceptions of self can be established' (Miles, Dallas and Burr, 1998: 93). In this way, the media were seen as a key resource that young people drew upon as they sought to construct an autonomous (yet securely anchored) identity:

> The media provide young people with a common focus for the construction
> of their identities whether through the latest Nike advertising campaign or

via Jennifer Aniston's latest hairstyle; the media provide a template upon which young people can construct meanings around what is 'cool' and what is not. The point here is that what has developed is a symbiotic relationship between young people's 'needs' and a media-driven market intent on perpetuating those 'needs'.

(Anderson and Miles, 1999: 110)

This, then, was a configuration of youth's cultural agency very different to the notions of subcultural 'resistance' generated by the CCCS team in the 1970s, and far removed from the acts of everyday consumer 'rebellion' outlined by Fiske in the late 1980s. For Miles and his associates, young people were undoubtedly an active force in the creation of their own lifestyles, but these had more to do with the assertion of an individual sense of self than with any attempt at symbolic 'opposition'. 'Consumption', Miles observed, 'can be used in all sorts of ways and, as such, young people's patterns of consumption can just as easily buttress the status quo as rebel against it' (Miles, 2002: 138).[29]

Notions of lifestyle also drew attention to the role of space and locality in the way young people inscribed meanings in the products of the media and consumer industries. Youth's construction of symbolic meanings around commodities has always been informed by local allegiances and sensibilities – but in a world of dynamic population movement, new communications technologies and multinational media conglomerates, young people's identities also draw on a wealth of global cultural connections. These relations between the media, globalisation and young people's cultural identities are explored in more depth in the following chapter.

# 7

# ROCKIN' ALL OVER THE WORLD

## Globalisation and 'youth media'

This American invasion differs . . . from the export of ideas and modes of life which has always characterized international societies in the broad front of its attack and in the forces of mass communication upon which it is able to call. Only rarely are these instruments of mass communication used to aid the international exchange of ideas and modes of thought. Their main purpose is to promote a commercialism which is concerned primarily to shape people to the pattern most conforming to the requirements of salesmanship.

(Francis Blond, 1962: 35)

The globalizing of youth as an idea, as a style and as a commercial product is both an example of cultural colonization of countries where 'teenagers' did not previously exist, but also encourages new configurations of ethnicity, meaning and belonging in an increasingly disembedded world.

(Claire Wallace and Sijka Kovatcheva, 1998: 184)

## 'SHAKIN' ALL OVER': 'TRANSGLOBAL' YOUTH CULTURE

The sleepy resort of Calella might seem an unlikely backdrop to events that crystallised many contemporary trends in global youth culture. But in May 2003 the Spanish seaside town was host to the Wipeout Weekend, an event billed as 'Three days and nights of Surf-Beat-R&B-Garage and R&R a-go-go'. Attracting several thousand fans from as far afield as the US and Japan, the shindig was a punk-*esque* festival of early-1960s-style rock 'n' roll, the event featuring surf and garage bands from throughout Europe (including Cosmonauti from Italy, The Bambi Molesters from Croatia and, from England, the Surfin' Lungs and lo-fi rock 'n' roll guru Billy Childish). In itself, the Wipeout Weekend was relatively insignificant. Outside the ranks of the 1960s garage/surf rock fraternity, the event passed virtually unnoticed. Nevertheless, in its organisation, style and audience appeal, the Spanish festival served as a neat illustration of wider trends in the form and content of contemporary youth culture.

Primarily in their late teens and early twenties, the festival audience was generally composed of young, rock 'n' roll party animals. There was, however, also an older contingent. In their thirties and forties, this group were still up for a good time, though tended to hover around the quieter sidelines rather than braving the mayhem of the mosh pit. The presence of this small but significant troop of 'greying youth' was suggestive of the way many older adults have remained enthusiastic devotees of 'youth' media and culture. As seen in Chapter 3, the media forms and leisure practices traditionally associated with youth culture have been increasingly detached from a specific generational group, so that an event like the Wipeout Weekend could appeal to an audience who defined themselves in terms of their lifestyle and cultural sensibilities rather than their age group.

The retro flair of the Wipeout festival (manifest in its hi-octane rock 'n' roll, and the abundance of greasy quiffs and deftly sculpted sideburns) also pointed to wider trends. A vogue for 'retro' was pronounced in youth media and culture throughout the 1980s and 1990s. In Britain, for example, advertising campaigns such as that for Levi's 501 jeans in 1986 gently parodied 1950s youth style, while a revival of mod élan in the late 1990s coincided with the rise of 'Britpop' guitar bands (such as Blur and Oasis) who consciously toyed with the iconography of 1960s pop culture.

For postmodern theorists such as Fredric Jameson, this kind of recycling of the stylistic past was indicative of a paralysing cultural malaise. In the late twentieth century, Jameson argued, original cultural production had given way to a new world of pastiche, a world where cultural innovation was no longer possible and people had 'nowhere to turn but to the past' and a retreat into the 'complacent play of historical allusion' (Jameson, 1984: 65, 1988: 105). But John Storey (2001) has taken issue with Jameson's postmodern pessimism. For Storey, Jameson's account could be compared to the elitist assumptions made by mass culture theorists such as Theodor Adorno (see Chapter 6), Jameson failing to grasp the new meanings actively generated through processes of cultural recycling. Rather than being a random, and uniquely 'postmodern', cannibalisation of the past, Storey suggested, the re-animation of historical style was part of a tradition of appropriation, bricolage and intertextuality that has *always* characterised popular culture (Storey, 2001: 246). Moreover, Storey argued, trends towards retro-styling and historical allusion did not represent a depthless 'imitation of dead styles' (Jameson, 1984: 65), but were practices of active cultural enterprise in which media forms of the past were commandeered and mobilised in meaningful ways in the lived cultures of the present (Storey, 2001: 247). From this perspective, then, processes of cultural (re-)creativity might be exemplified by the retro panache of the Spanish Wipeout crowd – their fusion of punk's semiotic mischief with rock 'n' roll's robust hedonism producing a reconfiguration of 1960s Teen Americana that was part glorification and part ironic send-up.

The transnational character of the Wipeout Weekend's bands and audience also highlighted the capacity of youth style and music cultures to flow across geographic boundaries, finding resonance in diverse contexts and locales. Until relatively recently, issues of locality were seldom prominent in analyses of the relationship between media and youth culture. The Birmingham CCCS theorists of the 1970s, for example, gave little attention to regional variations in the structure and meanings of subcultural style, one contemporary critic commenting that their approach seemed 'completely absorbed with Britain south of Hemel Hempstead' (Davies, 1976: 15).[1] During the 1990s, however, greater attention was given to the role of locality in young people's lives. Exploring the global circulation of media and commodities and their consumption by young people around the world, researchers found that the predominant flow of media texts and cultural forms was from West to East and North to South. Many authors, however, have resisted seeing this as a simple process of domination and homogenisation. Instead, they have drawn attention to the way local audiences have often appropriated 'transglobal' media forms, inscribing them with new collective meanings and integrating them within their own, localised, cultures and identities. In the case of the Wipeout weekenders, for example, it could be argued that they did not simply *reproduce* American rock 'n' roll, but *reworked* it to create a new cultural hybrid.

This chapter surveys the various ways we might understand the global circulation and local consumption of youth-oriented media. Beginning with a review of the competing notions of 'globalisation', the chapter shows how notions of a 'globalised' youth culture sometimes overlook the international inequalities of wealth and power that continue to determine the life experiences of young people throughout the world. Nevertheless, while global inequalities of media access and control have to be acknowledged, it is argued that concepts of a one-way 'cultural imperialism' oversimplify the transnational flow of 'youth media'. The chapter highlights both the increasingly elaborate syncopation of international (rather than exclusively Western or American) media interests, and the way in which 'global' media forms have invariably been adapted and reconfigured for local markets. Moreover, rather than being overwhelmed by a homogenised global (or 'Americanised') youth culture, it is argued that local audiences actively reconfigure 'global' commodities, images and texts – young people around the world creatively 're-embedding' globally-circulated media forms within local contexts and cultures.

## GLOBALISATION AND YOUTH CULTURE: TOWARDS A 'GLOBAL VILLAGE' OF YOUTH?

Since the 1980s the concept of globalisation has registered an intellectual impact across a range of academic disciplines. There exist a wide variety of accounts of the nature and significance of processes of globalisation, but generally the term is used to denote trends that have seen political, economic and social activities become increasingly worldwide in scope. Central to notions of globalisation is the argument that the late twentieth century saw the firm boundaries of nations increasingly bypassed by new forms of 'global' economic and political relations, with the result that individual lives and local communities have become more deeply affected by economic and cultural forces that operate worldwide. Contemporary theories of globalisation are often very abstract, but generally they suggest that global changes have affected not only people's social relations and networks, but also their experiences of time and space. According to Anthony Giddens (1990), for example, globalisation has been marked by trends towards greater 'time-space distanciation', with a greater stretching of connections across the globe dissolving fixed links between 'time' and 'place' so that long-distance relationships can be experienced as close, even when the parties seldom (if ever) occupy the same space at the same time. Distanciation, Giddens argued, has also set in motion a process of 'disembedding', with social relationships increasingly lifted out from their local contexts and restructured across global spans of time and space – the intensification of worldwide social relations linking distant locations in such a way that local events are shaped by phenomena occurring many miles away and vice-versa.

A different interpretation of globalisation was offered by David Harvey (1989). Like Giddens, Harvey's analysis highlighted transformations in the planes of time and space, but Harvey explained globalisation as a process of 'time-space compression' – with the dimensions of time and space squeezed together, so that the world has come to seem both smaller and faster-moving. Despite their differences, however, both Giddens and Harvey saw globalisation as a stretching of relations across the world. For both, global contacts had been deepened, or intensified, so that people's local lives and experiences had become increasingly interpenetrated by globalising forces. Yet, whereas Harvey saw globalisation as the outcome of recent shifts in the organisation of capitalism, Giddens argued that it was a continuation of trends set in motion by the processes of modernity that first took shape in eighteenth-century Europe.[2] For Giddens, moreover, globalisation was a contradictory and uneven process. On one hand, he argued, globalisation 'pulled away' from 'local' communities – supra-national political organisations, for example, assuming some of the powers and capacities of nation-states. But, at the same time, Giddens observed that processes of globalisation could also give a renewed importance to local identities and institutions, with an upsurge in nationalist movements (from Scotland to Serbia) pointing to the profound contradictions in the character and effects of globalisation during the 1980s and 1990s.

Of course, supra-national institutions and social movements have hardly been unique to the late twentieth century. Over many centuries, for example, the Catholic Church bound people together across national boundaries through shared beliefs and rituals, while the development of the telegraph in mid-nineteenth-century America helped fuse together widely divergent geographic regions into federal unity. But, while globalising tendencies can be identified in earlier periods, during the late twentieth century the processes were given added impetus by a combination of factors. Developments in communications technology clearly played an important role. During the 1960s Marshall McLuhan had already highlighted the emergence of what he termed the 'global village', as developments in electronic and satellite communications seemed to draw the world together into a united media community (McLuhan, 1964). Subsequent advances in the fields of telecommunications and information technology (especially the growth of digital and fibre optic technologies, and their convergence) further increased the speed and scope of global communication and, as a consequence, contributed to a proliferation of transnational commerce.

Nevertheless, while technological developments have certainly been an important factor in the intensification of processes of globalisation, it is important to recognise that these have been constituent in a much wider nexus of social, economic and political change. Since the late 1960s the emergence of a new, more volatile world market saw accelerated turnover in production and consumption, and a surge of cross-border trade in an increasingly interconnected global economy (see Chapter 3). During the 1980s and 1990s the rise of this transnational marketplace was accommodated by a political climate that favoured a liberalisation of economic controls and market deregulation. In Europe and North America, especially, governments' moves towards a 'free market' economy facilitated the increase in international trade and the growth of global business enterprise. During the 1990s a drive for lower costs and higher profits prompted a particularly hectic phase of business concentration, conglomeration and integration, with the emergence of transnational corporations whose brand-names and advertising campaigns straddled the globe (see Chapter 3).

According to some commentators, the rise of international communications, media and marketing may have brought into being a new, McLuhan-esque 'global village' of youth – with groups of young people around the world sharing common attitudes, tastes and sensibilities. In one of the most comprehensive European studies of teenagers ever undertaken, for example, the market research agencies Euroquest and BMRB International claimed to have demonstrated that 'it is possible to take a "global" approach to youth, at least within Europe' (Ford and Phillips, 1999: 144). Based on some 10,000 interviews with 11- to 19-year-olds in Germany, France, Italy and Britain, the study surveyed attitudes to media and consumer products, identifying a typology of six key groups who seemed to transcend national boundaries. The two youngest clusters were termed the Dreamers and the Big Babies. The former were outgoing, enthusiastic users of media and technology, and were full of optimism for their future. The latter were more insecure, tending to shelter within their families and school life. Slightly older were the Good Kids, a group who were conscientious and responsible, and who got on happily with their parents and peers. More free-spirited were the Independents, whose lifestyles were based on entertainment, fun, friends and fashion, while the Searchers felt a greater sense of conflict with their families and the world in general, and were keen to explore new horizons of experience. Last were the somewhat shambolic No Hopers. Apathetic and unenthusiastic, this group were awkward with friends and family alike, and had little interest in the future, preferring simply to sit back and wait to see what happened. According to the market researchers, all six of these clusters watched TV, read magazines, went to the cinema, listened to the radio and so on – but each group possessed a distinct profile of media use and discriminated in characteristic ways between different genres, titles and frequency of consumption. Pan-European marketing strategies, the researchers concluded, were therefore a clear possibility since 'groups of young people of different nationalities can be identified who are more similar to each other in terms of their attitudes and behaviour than they are to their compatriots' (Ford and Phillips, 1999: 149).

Academics also detected the rise of a 'global' youth culture. The growth of the world wide web, MTV and transnational brands was viewed by Jo Langham Brown and her associates, for example, as providing a common menu of media and entertainment for young consumers across the world:

> The commercial media have promoted the emergence of a global community of young people free from the values and preferences of any particular social and geographical location and embedded in the ethic of consumerism, preoccupied, it seems, by celebrities, fashion and the demands of ad-oriented lifestyle.
>
> (Langham Brown, Ralph and Lees, 1999: xi)

Claire Wallace and Sijka Kovatcheva (1998) also identified 'globalising' trends within contemporary youth culture. The growth of capitalist consumer markets and global media, they argued, had given youth styles a cultural purchase throughout the world, leading to 'the globalizing of youth as an idea, as a style and as a commercial product' (Wallace and Kovatcheva, 1998: 184). But, whereas market researchers such as Euroquest and BMRB had been keen to emphasise the potential of youth as a commercial market *sans frontières*, Wallace and Kovatcheva drew attention to the distinct forms of inequality and difference that still pervaded young people's social and economic experiences. Though they acknowledged common trends in European youth culture and style, Wallace and Kovatcheva argued that factors such as social class, gender, sexuality, ethnicity and 'race' all remained forces crucial in determining young people's life chances and cultural orientations – dimensions of discrimination and disadvantage ensuring that divisions and diversity remained pronounced features of European youth culture (Wallace and Kovatcheva, 1998: 19–26). Rather than being equal participants in any 'global' youth culture, then, young people around the world remain starkly divided in terms of their wealth, power and life chances.

## WORKING FOR THE YANKEE DOLLAR: CULTURAL IMPERIALISM, AMERICANISATION AND 'YOUTH MEDIA'

Generally, the world remains profoundly divided in the fields of media and communication. Disparities of wealth and power continue to exist not only between different social groups within nations, but between different countries and global regions. Indeed, for some theorists, the spread of transnational media and the 'globalisation' of culture have worked to reinforce (even extend) these disparities. During the late 1960s and 1970s the concept of 'cultural imperialism' emerged to denote the way some commentators saw the trans-global flow of the media as driven by the economic and political interests of powerful, capitalist countries – especially the United States. The work of Herbert Schiller was particularly influential. In *Mass Communication and American Empire* (1969) Schiller argued that American capitalism was consolidating its position of global domination through its export of media texts. According to Schiller, American films and TV series functioned as vehicles for the promulgation of capitalist values in developing nations, thereby strengthening America's position as a world power and generating markets for US businesses and advertisers. Rather than engendering a cosmopolitan and heterogeneous 'global village', therefore, Schiller saw the proliferation of transnational media as a strategy of neo-colonialist exploitation and ideological manipulation.

Mass culture theorists were also critical of what they saw as the homogenisation and debasement of cultural life that followed the spread of US media. As Dick Hebdige (1988c) has shown, America – the home of monopoly capitalism and commodity consumerism – came to epitomise processes of cultural decline in the intellectual anxieties of many European writers during the 1950s and 1960s.[3] From this perspective, indigenous cultures and the communities that sustained them were being eroded by a crude and tawdry commercialism emanating from America. As Chapter 6 demonstrated, representations of youth were frequently to the fore in these fears of a levelling-down – or 'Americanisation' – of cultural life. In Britain, for example, Richard Hoggart's scornful critique of the 'spiritual dry rot' of post-war popular culture zeroed-in on the 'juke-box boys' who, Hoggart argued, were 'living to a large extent in a myth-world compounded of a few simple elements which they take to be those of American life' (1957: 248). Similar concerns also surfaced in other countries. For example, according to the British features magazine, *Picture Post*, the Russian press of the 1950s had highlighted the problem of the *Bikiniarz* – youngsters who adopted American styles of dress in a rebellion against the disciplines of the school and the workplace (Bardens, 1954). *The Times*, meanwhile, reported Japanese concerns about *Tayozoku* youths, who affronted orthodox cultural values by sporting 'a sort of shaggy crew-cut, sunglasses, aloha shirts, [and] stovepipe trousers' and prompted social concern by 'drinking whisky, brawling, rough-housing and love-making with equally youthful and abandoned young women' (*The Times*, 12 September 1956).

The accelerated pace of globalising trends during the 1980s and 1990s gave added impetus to concerns about the impact of 'Americanisation' and the growth of cultural homogenisation. The increasingly global reach of Western television, film and music was seen by some theorists as spawning a Westernised commercial culture that steam-rollered over indigenous 'folk' cultures, values and ways of life. Rather than a politically-motivated strategy of American foreign policy, however, it was transnational business corporations that were seen as the principal agents of cultural homogenisation. According to Robert McChesney (1999), for example, the rise of new communication technologies and the deregulation of national media industries during the 1990s laid the way for the rise of a global media market dominated by a handful of towering conglomerates. In this highly concentrated and advertising-saturated media system, McChesney argued, news coverage was constrained, cultural expression was suffocated and democracy smothered by media empires driven solely by their hunger for profit. As we saw in Chapter 3, Naomi Klein (2000) was equally critical of the growing power of global business conglomerates. According to Klein, the corporate giants were even calling the shots in the subcultures of urban youth. The grip of big business, Klein argued, had blunted the radical edge of youth subcultures, global corporations such as Nike and Hilfiger fostering their cachet as hip lifestyle brands by appropriating the style, attitude and imagery of subcultural youth. 'The indie skateboarders', Klein observed:

> all have Vans sneaker contracts, road hockey is fodder for beer commercials, inner-city redevelopment projects are sponsored by Wells Fargo, and the free festivals have all been banned, replaced with the annual Tribal Gathering . . . where the organizers regularly confiscate bottled water that has not been purchased on the premises.
>
> (Klein, 2000: 65)

As Chapter 3 argued, there exists much validity to notions of global corporations dominating contemporary media systems. The 1980s and 1990s saw marked trends towards the conglomeration of global media corporations, so that by the end of the twentieth century a handful of multinational companies accounted for a considerable slice of the world's media output. The global scale of advertising and marketing, moreover, ensured that Western products – and, with them, Western cultures and lifestyles – were diffused to all corners of the world. The worldwide availability of Western film, music and TV, for example, allowed the styles and consumption practices of teenage America to circulate globally, with Western configurations of 'youthfulness' taking root in regions that hitherto had little experience of a commercial youth market

(Wallace and Kovatcheva, 1998: 153). Nevertheless, while inequalities of power and control have to be acknowledged, notions of a linear and unilateral 'cultural imperialism' (or, for that matter, 'Americanisation') oversimplify and distort the flows of media production, distribution and consumption. Indeed, researchers have increasingly drawn attention to the complex and multi-faceted nature of trans-global media flows – and, in the field of 'youth media', the complexity of these processes has been especially evident.

## 'THINK GLOBALLY, ACT LOCALLY': 'GLOCALISATION' AND 'YOUTH MEDIA'

Even during the 1950s and early 1960s, international media flows were more complex than allowed for by crude models of 'cultural imperialism'. The explosion of Beatlemania as an international phenomenon in 1964, for example, is at odds with simple concepts of American domination of popular media. Admittedly, the British pop 'invasion' of the US during the early 1960s could be seen, in some respects, as a by-product of 'Americanisation' – with the British media remaking and re-marketing music genres that had initially been imported from the States. In Britain, however, these genres had been appropriated, re-interpreted and synthesised with local cultural elements, so that the end-product was recognisable as a distinctly 'British' (even specifically Liverpudlian) cultural form that fed back into the development of popular music and youth style in America.[4] Throughout the mid-1960s, in fact, British style exerted a strong influence on American popular culture. The miniskirt and Mary Quant's chic designs, for example, were British exports that had a significant impact on the development of women's fashion in the US. British men's fashion also made a big impression. In its survey of the swinging London scene, for example, *Time* magazine had been impressed by 'the new, way-out fashion in young men's clothes' (*Time*, 15 April 1966), and autumn 1966 saw a flurry of media excitement around the arrival of British 'Mod' style in American fashion ranges.[5] 'The Mod Shirts Are Here' proclaimed the advertising campaign for Jayson's '<u>authentic</u> Mod look from England', while the 'London Look that gets admiring glances every time' was the by-line for the new 'Carnaby Cut' trousers introduced by Key Man Slacks (manufactured, somewhat incongruously, in El Paso).

Concepts of a one-way 'cultural imperialism', meanwhile, have been further undermined by changing patterns of media production and distribution which, since the 1970s, have seen developing nations emerge as major players in the media environment, with Western media control

# THE MOD SHIRTS ARE HERE

Mod ties and Mod sweaters too! That master Mod, Harvey of Carnaby Street, is behind it all. He's bringing the authentic Mod look from England exclusively to Jayson's new Tiles collection. There are shirts in bright, bold patterns and colors, with collar styles that'll really grab you. There are great new ties coordinated with the shirts. And there are turtleneck sweaters to top off the modern look of Mod. How's that for stirring up a revolution!

Tiles<sup>T.M.</sup> Collection by Harvey of Carnaby Street, designed exclusively for Jayson. Harvey, captain of the Mod crew, wears a pink, high roll button down shirt, about $9. The cranberry shirt has a rounded point collar, about $7. The navy shirt has a high roll, spear point collar, about $7. The striped high turtleneck in 100% virgin worsted wool is about $25. The solid color sweater in 100% Shetland wool is about $11. Ties about $3 to $5. Prices slightly higher in the West. Jayson®, Inc., 390 Fifth Ave., N. Y. 10018. **Jayson**

**Figure 7.1** 'Mod Shirts' arrive in America – advertisement for Jayson's menswear (1966)

increasingly cross-cut by an elaborate syncopation of non-Western communication systems and business interests. The American share of the global market for popular music, for example, shifted during the 1990s as the relatively low cost of making and distributing recordings (compared to films and TV programmes) made it possible for a wide range of national music industries to prosper. In some instances indigenous output came to overshadow American products. Luciana Mendonca (2002), for example, has shown how sales of American pop music in Brazil declined significantly during the 1990s, while Brazilian music came to constitute around 80 per cent of recordings broadcast on the country's radio.

'Global' media genres, moreover, have often been adapted and reconfigured for local markets. According to Roland Robertson (1995) this blending of the global with the local – or 'glocalisation' – does not lead to cultural homogenisation, but to a situation in which cultural forms that originated in the West are tailored to local audiences and conditions. During the 1990s, for example, MTV's operations were underpinned by a 'think globally, act locally' philosophy in which each of the company's international TV stations (MTV Asia, Australia, Brazil, Europe, Latin America and Russia) adhered to an overall style of programming, but configured this around local tastes and musical talent. In itself, for example, MTV Asia comprised three regional channels – MTV Mandarin, MTV Southeast Asia and MTV India. Launched in 1995, the Chinese-language station MTV Mandarin broadcast to viewers in China, Hong Kong, Taiwan and Singapore, with 60 per cent of its playlist consisting of Mandarin music videos. MTV Southeast Asia was also launched in 1995 and was available throughout Asia, offering a mix of music from Indonesia, Malaysia and Thailand. In 1996 MTV Southeast Asia was split into a third channel, MTV India. Available in India, Pakistan, Bangladesh and Sri Lanka, 70 per cent of MTV India's programming was made up of Indian pop music and films, with the balance made up of international music videos. In 2000, meanwhile, the MTV stable expanded further, with the launch of MTV Japan – a 24-hour, Japanese-language station with programming largely composed of Japanese material. MTV Korea followed in 2001 and, again, featured original, locally-produced content as its mainstay.

Processes of globalisation, then, are more complex than a simple drive towards a homogenisation that reflects only the interests and ideals of an all-conquering Western (or American) culture. Instead, Arjun Appadurai (1996) has argued that globalisation is better seen as an aggregation of flows composed of media, technology, ideologies and ethnicities that move in many different directions. Appadurai's model, then, moves away from accounts that see globalisation as a coherent, unitary process, in which a few capitalist corporations possess overpowering strength in the fields of media and communications. Instead, Appadurai has argued that globalisation is better seen as a network of cultural flows that have no clearly defined centre or periphery. Appadurai's account still acknowledges the crucial role played by large corporations in the production and circulation of cultural texts, but suggests that important attention should be accorded to the precise character of the production (and consumption) of media in specific local contexts. Indeed, a sophisticated analysis of the global production and consumption of cultural texts demands careful attention to the way patterns of media interpretation and use are invariably diverse. Audience-based research (for example, that conducted on different national audiences for TV soap operas by Tamar Liebes and Elihu Katz (1990), and Daniel Miller (1992)) has suggested a relative openness to the meanings of transnational media that allows for a range of divergent – in some respects even 'resistant' – readings by indigenous audiences. In these terms, therefore, rather than uncritically buying into a Westernised cultural diet of burgers, blue jeans and Bon Jovi albums, young consumers around the world can be seen as actively engaging with commercial commodities – creatively 're-embedding' them within local cultures and contexts.

## FROM CATFORD TO KATHMANDU: GLOBAL MEDIA AND 'RE-EMBEDDED' YOUTH CULTURE

Local institutions and identities, then, have not necessarily been subsumed by a homogenised global (or 'Americanised') culture. Authors such as Giddens and Robertson highlight the way political, economic and socio-cultural forces have worked to intensify tendencies towards *both* globalisation *and* localisation – sometimes in parallel, sometimes in opposition. 'Indigenous' and 'alternative' media, for example, may exist as powerful counterweights to the influence of 'globalised' or 'Americanised' cultural products. Local and regional audiences, moreover, often reconfigure the meanings of 'global' commodities, images and texts, authors such as James Lull (1995) and John Thompson (1995) highlighting the way local audiences appropriate and inscribe new meaning into global media forms, reworking them to take on fresh cultural significance. As Thompson explains, the way media products are understood and used 'is always a localized phenomenon':

> it always involves specific individuals who are situated in particular socio-historical contexts, and who draw on the resources available to them in order

to make sense of media messages and incorporate them into their lives. And messages are often transformed in the process of appropriation as individuals adapt them to the contexts of everyday life.

(Thompson, 1995: 174)

From this perspective, then, it is important to consider the nuanced ways that 'global' cultural texts and images are received and fitted into – or 'rembedded' in – specific local contexts. In fact, rather than being resented as an unwelcome instrument of US cultural imperialism, American goods and media have often been embraced by local audiences as positive symbols of freedom and modernity. As Steve Chibnall has observed, for many people around the world, buying Levi's jeans or Coca-Cola:

can take on the status of a personal political statement because the symbolic association of these objects with freedom, individuality and the 'American way' is underwritten in countless cinematic and televisual texts which relate product aesthetics to social attitudes, personal aspirations and nationality.

(Chibnall, 1996: 150)

Obviously, the American Dream of untrammelled freedom and boundless opportunity is a myth, and bears scant relation to the realities of life in the United States. For many audiences around the world, however, American goods and media are symbolic tokens of autonomy and emancipation. And, as Chibnall has argued, because American style has been such an emotionally-charged carrier of hope for change, it has been the perennial target of conservative criticism and control. Chibnall offered the example of Britain during the early 1950s, where popular American films, fashions and magazines were the target of conservative scorn not only because they seemed to threaten authentic folk cultures with a tide of shallow commercialism, but also because they 'carried messages of hedonism and individualism which were anathema to the centralizing state bureaucracy and its ideology of self-sacrifice and welfare collectivism' (Chibnall, 1996: 152). Indeed, it was precisely this aura of exciting, freely expressed hedonism that appealed to the popular imagination. Against the drab conventions of austerity Britain, American popular culture offered a vision of fast-paced thrills and limitless choice in a Utopia of material abundance.

This appeal was felt especially keenly, Chibnall argued, by working-class youth, for whom 'Yankee style offered a sense of worth, individuality and empowerment' (Chibnall, 1996: 155). According to Chibnall, the zoot suit was a pre-eminent example of the way cultural forms transplanted from America took on new meanings in post-war Britain. The broad, draped jackets and pegged trousers of the zoot suit had originally been sported by young Mexican American Pachucos and black hustlers in US cities during the early 1940s. Brash and flamboyant, the style offered insolent defiance to expectations that members of subordinate groups should necessarily exhibit that subordination through their appearance. The swaggering gesture was not lost on white society and, in 1943, gangs of off-duty servicemen roamed the streets of Los Angeles brutally beating zoot-suited Mexican-Americans in a series of racist attacks that spread throughout California.[6] By the end of the 1940s, however, the violence dissipated as zoot style crept into mainstream American men's fashion. But in Britain, Chibnall (1985) argued, the zoot suit retained its rebellious connotations.

Imported with the arrival of GIs during the war, the zoot suit was adopted by British 'spivs' – flashy petty villains who wheeled-and-dealed in the wartime black market. By the late 1940s, however, the style had become more firmly equated with working-class youth culture. For example, commenting on the crowd at a London dancehall in 1949, an observer drew attention to young men he termed 'the "Dago" or "Spiv" type', who were 'dressed in their own, or rather the American singular style – i.e. cut back collar with large knotted tie; "Boston Slash Back" hair cut; and a "house coat" style of jacket' (Willcock, 1949: 49). In contexts such as this, Chibnall argued, the original, 'racial' significance of the zoot suit was lost.[7] Filtered through indigenous conceptions of style, he argued, 'the impenetrable argot and defiant machismo of the Pachuco and Harlem hipsters were cut away and replaced with the familiar rhyming slang and quick-witted banter of the artful dodger, the rascally opportunist' (Chibnall, 1985: 66). According to Chibnall, the zoot style took particular root among the brasher youths of London's East End, where it gradually evolved into the distinctive image of the 1950s Teddy boy. For these youngsters, the 'blasphemous mixture of orthodox British dandyism and Yank style' was an assertion of hedonistic freedom and autonomy and, among both working-class youth and officialdom, was recognised as 'a symptom of a fundamental disrespect for the old class modes and manners – a disrespect born of a romance with an alien culture' (Chibnall, 1985: 74, 69).

Behind the 'iron curtain', too, American style was borrowed and 're-embedded' within the fabric of post-war youth culture. In 1950s Russia, for example, the *stilagi* were a topic of hot controversy. Groups of relatively well-to-do urban youngsters, the *stilagi* showed little interest in official forms of Soviet culture and instead adopted Western forms of music and fashion, developing their own distinctive image – *stil'* –

a (re)interpretation of American rock 'n' roll styles. Reviled as ideologically subversive and unacceptably bourgeois by the Soviet establishment, the *stilagi* faced concerted opposition from the press and state institutions. Brigades of *Kosmosol* (the official Soviet youth movement) were formed to campaign against the influence of *stil'* and, in the cities of Sverdlovsk and Ul'ianovsk, *Kosmosol* patrols were reported to have cut both the trousers and hair of local *stilagi* (Pilkington, 1994: 226). The impact of the Western counterculture of the 1960s and early 1970s was also felt in the Soviet Union. The authorities continued to take a tough line against young people who embraced Western popular culture, but significant interest in Western pop music and youth style continued, developing into a more politicised form of dissent after the Soviet crushing of Czechoslovak reformism in 1968. In this context, Western cultural idioms were a source of ideas and inspiration but, as Paul Easton (1989) has shown, these fed into the emergence of a distinctly Russian rock scene, with bands singing in Russian and addressing issues that were particular to Soviet society and the experiences of Russian youth. More recently, Hilary Pilkington (2002) has shown that, while Western media are pervasive within the lives of young people in post-Soviet Russia, Russian youth have a 'pick and mix' attitude towards Western cultural commodities – with their receptiveness to Western media forms existing alongside a careful guarding of local identities.

Similar cultural dynamics also played out in Mexico. As in Europe, in 1950s Mexico conservative opinion condemned American rock 'n' roll and US youth style as harbingers of cultural decline and social disorder. Eric Zolov (1999: 27) has described how, in Mexican public debate, rock 'n' roll (and later rock music) became associated with notions of *desmadre* – a slang term denoting a condition of social chaos that springs from the literal 'unmothering' of a person or situation. By the end of the 1950s legislation had been introduced to restrict the content and distribution of 'offensive' mass culture, while the promotion of a sanitised, Spanish-language version of rock 'n' roll sought to contain the influence of the more raucous import. The popularity of Western rock 'n' roll, however, was unabated. Zolov shows, moreover, that the challenge posed by rock 'n' roll to the authoritarian structures of Mexican society was amplified by the arrival of more explicitly rebellious forms of rock during the 1960s. During the late 1960s a significant section of urban Mexican youth were attracted to the music and values of the Western counterculture, prompting official concern that such an interest undermined indigenous culture and 'reinforced subservience to foreign values' (Zolov 1999: 111). And, undoubtedly, the Mexican hippie movement – or *jipitecas* – did draw on aspects of American popular culture. But, Zolov argues,

American texts did not simply bulldoze their way across Mexican cultural life. Instead, elements of the US counterculture were combined with local cultural forms in a configuration that 'allowed youth to invent new ways of *being* Mexican, ways that ran counter to the dominant ideology of state-sponsored nationalism' (ibid.). Rather than seeing rock music as a tool of Western imperialism, Zolov suggests, Mexican youth were attracted by its avant-garde associations and its ties to student movements elsewhere in the world. 'Re-embedded' within the political radicalism of Mexico's developing student movement, therefore, Western rock music became a vehicle for dissent in the struggle against the country's authoritarian government.

In a similar fashion, Western punk rock was embraced by sections of Mexican youth during the 1980s. Mexico City, for example, saw the emergence of *los chavos banda*, lumpenproletariat punks who were championed by the radical Left as a voice of angry protest from the barrios. This history of Mexican youth's creative engagement with Western popular culture, Zolov argues, served as a salutary example of broader patterns of cultural relations. The 'globalisation' of popular media, he suggests, was not simply a question of the monolithic reconstruction of local cultural identities to the benefit of multinational capital. Instead, Zolov sees the history of Mexican youth culture as exemplifying Appadurai's notion of complex global media 'flows', with a plurality of nuanced generational and national identities being generated from 'the ongoing, patterned dispersion of people, media images, technology, finance capital, and ideology that interrupts the delineated coherency supposedly fixed by national boundaries' (Zolov, 1999: 14).

The development of *raï* music in Algeria stands as another example of a creative fusion between Western media and indigenous popular culture. Originally an Algerian acoustic folk music, *raï* was transformed during the 1980s as local popular songs and rhythms were increasingly mixed with Western instruments (electric guitars, synthesisers and drum machines), American disco and Europop. As a consequence, Marc Schade-Poulsen has observed, modern *raï* was a synthesis of traditional folk music and Western pop that expressed the 'ambivalent or fundamental duality in the identity of Algerian youth' (Schade-Poulsen, 1995: 85). According to Schade-Poulsen, *raï* music's popularity lay in the way its fusion of different musical idioms addressed Algerian youth's own attempts to negotiate the tensions between their interest in Western lifestyles and their commitment to traditional institutions of family and religious life.

In many places throughout the world, the 1980s and 1990s saw Western 'youth media' creatively 're-embedded' in local youth cultures.

Karl Taro Greenfield, for example, presented a compelling portrait of Japan's *bosozoko*, or speed tribes – the bikers, punks and other subterranean clans of Tokyo's urban sprawl who were 'as accustomed to hamburgers as *onigiri* (rice balls), to Guns N' Roses as *ikebana* (flower arranging), and are often more adept at folding a bindle of cocaine or heroin than creasing an origami crane' (Greenfield, 1994: xiv).[8] Mark Liechty (1995), meanwhile, has shown how the proliferation of the mass media during the 1980s and 1990s guaranteed that the local experiences of young people almost anywhere in the world would be permeated by the flow of transnational 'youth media'. Focusing on the experience of Nepali youth, Liechty described how young people's identities were formed and re-formed at the intersection of local culture and global media. The advent of a commercial youth market in Kathmandu during the late 1980s, Liechty argued, was accompanied by a new use of the English word 'teenager' to denote a phenomenon hitherto unknown in Nepal – youth identities formed around the consumption of fashion, pop music, film, video and other media commodities. While Liechty acknowledged that this shift was largely business-driven, motivated by a commercial quest for markets and profit, he also emphasised the way young people in Kathmandu actively drew on 'global' media products as cultural resources, integrating them within their own, localised, cultures and identities that were a response to the experience of growing up in a developing nation:

> From the young men who appropriate certain items of 'ethnic Nepali' clothing (produced for the tourist trade) as part of their own uniforms as modern youth . . . to the local rock band whose members recorded an all-original Nepali language album in the style of the Beatles, examples abound of new forms of youth expression that are clearly 'youthful' and modern. . . . Within and between these peer groups, styles and behaviours take on meanings that are locally determined, even if they are often deployed in commercially mediated images, ideas, practices and other consumer goods. Young people as groups of peers assemble the components of a youth identity with which they seek to mark off the new cultural space in which modernity has deposited them.
>
> (Liechty, 1995: 192)

At the same time, however, Liechty recognised the marked inequalities of power and control that operated in this landscape of global-local youth culture. Nepali youth, he observed, were haunted by a sense of global 'exclusion'. Many youngsters in Kathmandu, Liechty found, felt themselves to be voyeurs on an exciting youth scene happening elsewhere in the world. Measuring their lives against the visions of glamorous consumption depicted in Western rock videos, films and glossy magazines, Nepali youth were left with an acute sense of 'self-peripheralisation', the mass media offering them alluring glimpses of a lush, modern future 'like animals receiving a lesson in evolution and power in some cultural "wildlife safari park"' (Liechty, 1995: 186). This experience, however, might not be unique to youth in the developing world. In the West, too, the mythologies of 'youthful' freedom and independent hedonism that pervade the popular media may seem painfully ironic against the unemployment, poverty and lack of opportunity faced by many young people, from the south Bronx to Salford.

According to Liechty, inequalities of socio-economic power also pervaded Nepali youth's experience of 'global' media cultures. The wonderland of 'teenage' consumption, Liechty observed, was largely available only to middle-class Nepali youngsters and, even for them, choices often occurred within the commercial market's '"ready-made" structures of the imagination, for few have the resources, confidence and cultural authority to construct their own alternative, non-mediated visions of valued, modern and Nepali selves' (Liechty, 1995: 186). In these terms, then, there may well be myriad ways in which global patterns of commodity exchange are reconfigured locally and, in turn, are projected back into a 'global ecumene' (Hannerz, 1989). Yet the global circulation of goods, capital and ideas remains uneven – with the tone and content of 'global' media disproportionately dominated by North America, Europe and a handful of transnational media conglomerates.

Nevertheless, this recognition should not detract from the capacity of local youth cultures to borrow from, reconfigure and creatively 're-embed' internationally circulated media, images and icons. Modern youth cultures are not formed in isolation, but through complex processes of connection, interface and interrelation. As Doreen Massey observed in her account of Mayan youth culture in Yucatán (Mexico), local youngsters' interest in computer games and Western music ensured that their culture was '*a product of interaction*':

> It is certainly not a closed, local, culture, but neither is it an undifferentiatedly global one. And such interactions could be exemplified in a million ways. The spatial openness of youth cultures in many if not all parts of the world is clear. . . . The youngest generations of diaspora societies wrestle constantly to find an enabling interlocking of the different 'cultures' in which they find themselves: it is a struggle indeed to build another, different – 'hybrid' – culture.

(Massey, 1998: 122)

Even the transnational 'brand bullies' condemned by Naomi Klein (2000) can be symbolic resources, open to being 're-embedded' in ways radically different to their original functions and meanings. For young people throughout the world, brands can play an important role in the formation of subcultures and the expression of collective (though often contested) values and identities. Indeed, despite companies' efforts to define brand identity and image, local consumers sometimes actualise the meanings of brands in ways startlingly different to those intended by manufacturers. In Los Angeles, for example, lines of popular sports clothing have frequently been appropriated as the 'colours' of local street gangs – the sports brand British Knights, for example, was adopted by the LA Crips (for whom the brand's 'B' and 'K' initials took on the more ominous meaning of 'Blood Killers'), while the Columbia Knights brand was taken up by the Crips' rivals, the Bloods (the 'C' and 'K' initials used to signify 'Crip Killer'). In England, meanwhile, the late 1990s saw Stone Island (an Italian line of designer menswear) adopted by style-conscious soccer hooligans as a badge that combined classy élan with uncompromising 'attitude'.

While recognition must be given to the way processes of globalisation and conglomeration have delivered enormous power to capitalist corporations, therefore, account must also be taken of the way young people reconfigure the meanings of cultural forms and media texts, integrating them within local cultures and identities. The next chapter explores further the dynamic interplay between global media and young people's local identities, with particular consideration given to the forces of hybridity, interconnection and fragmentation that have come to characterise contemporary youth culture.

# 8

# 'INSURGENCY ACROSS ALL BORDERS'

## Hybridity, identity and 'youth media'

[I]n black popular culture, strictly speaking, ethnographically speaking, there are no pure forms at all. Always these forms are the product of partial synchronization, of engagement across cultural boundaries, of the confluence of more than one cultural tradition, of the negotiations of dominant and subordinate positions, of the subaltern strategies of recoding and transcoding, of critical signification, of signifying. Always these forms are impure, to some degree hybridised from a vernacular base.

(Stuart Hall, 1992c: 28)

## MUTINY: 'YOUTH MEDIA' AND GLOBAL/ LOCAL CULTURAL IDENTITIES

Co-founded in 1997 by filmmaker and music producer Vivek Bald (aka DJ Siraiki) and DJ Rekha Malhotra (a London-born, New York-raised daughter of Indian immigrants), the Manhattan nightclub, Mutiny, exemplified the dynamic interconnections central to contemporary youth culture. Under the slogan 'Musical Insurgency Across All Borders', for six years Mutiny was an international hub of the south Asian electronica music scene. Bringing together artists from different parts of the south Asian diaspora, the club was host to a roster of British Asian musicians and DJs, including Talvin Singh, Choque Hosein (frontman of Black Star Liner), Asian Dub Foundation, Cornershop, FuñDâMental and State of Bengal. Mutiny also boasted its own, musically diverse and innovative, crew of resident DJs – Siraiki, Rekha, Navdeep, Anju and Zakhm (aka Atul Ohri). Working at the cutting edge of electronic dance music, they effaced boundaries of ethnicity and musical style – mixing the fierce, heavy beats of drum 'n' bass with the rapid-fire breakbeats of hip-hop and the soaring strings and vocals of Indian classical, folk and film music.

Mutiny embodied the way contemporary youth cultures and their associated media are forged through processes of interconnection, transformation and translation. This chapter explores these practices of production and reproduction. Modern youth cultures, it is argued, are not located in an 'essential' ethnicity or culture, but are a fluid amalgam of local and global identities. Formed through continuous exchange and fusion, they are constituent in a wider diasporic experience that is defined 'not by essence or purity, but by the recognition of a necessary heterogeneity and diversity; by a conception of "identity" which lives with and through, not despite, difference; by *hybridity*' (Hall, 1990: 235).

The chapter begins by exploring the way popular music has been used by young people to establish a sense of localised identity. Using the example of rap and hip-hop, it is argued that genres of popular music become 'glocalised', given new inflections and meanings as they are appropriated by youngsters in different locales around the world. The chapter goes on to examine the distinctly 'hybridised' character of contemporary youth culture and media. While the globalisation of 'youth media' (via international marketing, satellite TV, the internet, etc.) has been an important factor in the promotion of cultural dialogue and fusion, equally crucial have been patterns of population movement and 'diaspora' – with new cultural forms and identities shaped at the juncture of different peoples' histories and experiences. Using the example of British Asian youth culture and its relationship with global and local media forms, the chapter shows how young people's identities operate across diverse cultural sites and are formed through the intersection of multiple subjectivities. The chapter concludes by considering the 'fluid' and open-ended nature of contemporary cultural identities and examines the way media forms geared to young audiences may offer fertile spaces for the configuration of multiple and dynamic genders, ethnicities and sexualities.

## BOYZ N THE HOOD: YOUTH, LOCALITY AND HIP-HOP

Just as 'globalisation' is a varied and contested concept (see Chapter 7) so, too, are notions of the 'local'. Often, theories of 'globalising' processes have left the spatial definition of the 'local' relatively hazy. In some instances, the term 'local' has been used to refer to distinctly *national* (rather than international or 'global') media forms and cultural phenomena. On other occasions, the term has been used to denote more specific urban or rural locations. Despite their differences, however, each of these formulations has conceived the local as a relatively 'fixed' physical space. In contrast, more recent theoretical approaches have understood the local as a contested territory, one crossed by a variety of different identities and meanings. Doreen Massey, for example, has shown how 'place' is not a bounded entity, but is connected to much wider social processes and experiences. Using the example of Kilburn High Street in London, for example, Massey (1993) demonstrated how patterns of migration by a variety of ethnic groups had seen Kilburn become a hub of innumerable cultural flows. Each ethnic group that had settled in the area had introduced aspects of their own cultural identity to the district's everyday life, so that 'while Kilburn may have a character of its own, it is absolutely not a seamless, coherent identity, a single sense of place which everyone shares. It could hardly be less so' (Massey, 1993: 65). In these terms, the increasing movement of people between countries had introduced new cultural forms and identities into the fabric of local environments – though the meaning of urban spaces was always contested, since each group defined and marked out the locality in terms of their own cultures and collective identities.

Drawing on Massey's ideas, Andy Bennett (2000: 63) has argued that popular music has represented a particularly important avenue through which young people have sought to establish a sense of localised identity. According to Bennett, for example, by turning disused factories into dance music venues and city squares into meeting places for skateboaders and breakdancers, groups of young people have appropriated and reworked local spaces to construct urban narratives 'that enable them to view the local in particular ways and apply their own solutions to the particular problems or shortcomings that they identify with their surroundings' (Bennett, 2000: 66–67). Bennett, however, resisted seeing these processes as generating distinctive *subcultural* identities. Instead, he argued that music and style are used in diverse ways by groups of youngsters in different contexts, so that 'the same music and style will often produce not one but a variety of responses on the part of young people to the particular local circumstances in which they find themselves, each response being underpinned by a common set of base knowledges relating to the local but using this knowledge in different ways and to different ends' (Bennett, 2000: 67). The development of rap music and hip-hop culture exemplifies these processes.

The antecedents of rap lie in improvised vernacular poetry that has long been a central feature to the oral traditions of African-American culture.[1] The more direct precursors to contemporary rap, however, were politicised, black American poets such as Gil Scott Heron, Amiri Baraka and the Last Poets who, during the late 1960s and early 1970s, experimented with a fusion of music and poetic verse. During the mid-1970s rap was further developed in New York's south Bronx, where Jamaican émigré DJ Kool Herc introduced American dancefloors to the Jamaican practice of 'toasting' – improvised and syncopated wordplay laid over dub versions of records – while artists such as Afrika Bambaataa and Grandmaster Flash exploited technological developments in mixing, dubbing and sampling as they cut-up and reassembled fragments of music, lyrics and soundbites in an eclectic rhythmic soundscape.[2] In 1979 the success of the Sugarhill Gang's single, 'Rapper's Delight', brought rap wider commercial attention and during the 1980s artists such as Run DMC, Eric B. & Rakim, Boogie Down Productions and Public Enemy established rap as an integral aspect of the American music industry.

Cultural theorists such as Jeffrey Decker (1994), Michael Dyson (1996) and Russell Potter (1995) have highlighted the political dimensions to rap music, seeing it as an idiom that articulates both an expressive critique of the history of US race relations and a meaningful response to the experience of inner-city life in modern America.[3] Tricia Rose, too, drew attention to the way rap and the associated culture of hip-hop (graffiti, dance, style) gave 'voice to the tensions and contradictions in the urban public landscape' and attempted 'to seize the shifting urban terrain, to make it work on behalf of the dispossessed' (Rose, 1994b: 72). But Rose also emphasised the importance of locality (the 'hood') and collective identities (crews and posses) in rap and hip-hop, arguing that hip-hop culture was effectively a symbolic reappropriation of urban space:

> Rappers' emphasis on posses and neighborhoods has brought the ghetto back into the public consciousness. It satisfies poor young black people's profound need to have their territories acknowledged, recognized, and celebrated. These are the street corners and neighborhoods that usually serve as lurid backdrops for street crimes on the nightly news. Few local people are given an opportunity to speak, and their points of view are always contained by expert testimony. In rap videos, young mostly male residents speak for themselves and for the community, they speak when and how they wish about subjects of their own choosing. These local turf scenes are not isolated voices; they are voices from a variety of social margins that are in dialogue with one another.
>
> (Rose, 1994a: 11)

The plurality of voices alluded to by Rose points to the way rap has been an idiom for the expression of a wide diversity of cultural identities and local allegiances. The Mexican-American and Latino communities, for example, were involved in hip-hop culture since its inception,[4] while the late 1980s and 1990s saw artists such as Cypress Hill, Kid Frost and South Park Mexican fuse hip-hop beats with Latino styles and idioms. Transformation and translation also took place during the 1980s as rap and hip-hop took root on the West Coast, with the rise of Los Angeles 'gangsta' rappers such as Ice-T and NWA (Niggas With Attitude) who rewrote the hip-hop agenda in visceral anthems to LA gang life that deliberately obscured the line between fantasy and reality (see Chapter 4). The commercial success of artists such as Ice-T and NWA, combined with the box-office pull of films that chronicled the violent world of LA street gangs (for example, *Colors* (1988), *Boyz N the Hood* (1991) and *Menace II Society* (1993)), ensured that the focus of American hip-hop moved west during the 1990s. The decade saw NWA rappers Ice Cube and Dr Dre develop lucrative solo careers, though these were eclipsed by the phenomenal worldwide success of Dre's protégé – Snoop Doggy Dogg. In 1993 *Doggystyle*, Snoop's debut album, sold four million copies, ensuring that the artist's record company – the Los Angeles-based Death Row Records – became the most successful rap label of the 1990s.[5] Co-founded in 1992 by Dr Dre and the redoubtable Marion 'Suge' Knight, Death Row enjoyed continued success through the 1990s with artists such as Tha Dogg Pound and Tupac Shakur. By the end of the decade, however, the label was embroiled in a violent feud with Bad Boy Records – Sean 'Puffy' Combs' East Coast hip-hop empire.

From its beginnings hip-hop always had a competitive edge. The earliest struggles were between competing sound systems, such as those operated by Kool Herc and Afrika Bambaataa, whose rivalry was descended from the established Jamaican soundclash culture that émigrés such as Herc brought with them to New York. During the 1980s swaggering postures became a hip-hop trademark as rappers bragged about their own talent and disparaged their rivals with cartoonish hyperbole. But the 1990s saw rivalries intensified by the passionate local loyalties of East and West Coast hip-hop factions, and by the bitter commercial rivalry between Suge Knight's Death Row Records (in the West) and 'Puffy' Combs' Bad Boy label (in the East). The mid-1990s saw an escalation of the sniping between the two camps. In 1994 Tupac Shakur (a leading Death Row rapper) was robbed and shot several times; Shakur blamed Combs and Biggie Smalls (aka Notorious B.I.G. – Bad Boy's biggest star) for the attack. Eight months later, Suge Knight publicly mocked Combs at an awards party and, when a Death Row employee was murdered in Atlanta, Knight blamed Combs for the hit. Then, in

1996, Shakur was fatally wounded by gunmen as he left a boxing match in Las Vegas; and six months later Biggie Smalls was shot dead in his car leaving a party in LA – the murders widely seen as tit-for-tat killings in the East Coast versus West Coast rap rivalry.[6]

The 'rap wars' of the mid-1990s were indebted to egotistical machismo and fierce commercial competition. They were, however, given particular intensity by the strength of local allegiances, hip-hop culture emerging as a powerful focus of local identities. Certainly, many hip-hop rivalries have been played out for promotional effect. Feuds have been a source of cheap publicity for rappers such as Jay-Z, Nas, Snoop Doggy Dog, Eminem, Jermaine Dupri and 50 Cent, all of whom advanced their careers through battles of insult disseminated by their record companies and sensationalised in magazines such as *Vibe* and *The Source*.[7] Nevertheless, while rap is a commodity that has been manufactured and marketed by calculating commercial interests, this should not detract from its ability to articulate meaningful cultural identities for a range of local audiences, not only in America but also around the world.

During the 1980s and 1990s rap became a worldwide cultural force, Bennett arguing that it functioned as a resource for young people in a variety of global locations as they formulated local identities in responses to their particular social and economic circumstances. Focusing on two local examples, Bennett (1999b, 2000) has shown how the globally established culture of hip-hop was appropriated and adapted in different ways by young people in different geographic locales. In Frankfurt am Main in Germany, Bennett argued, hip-hop was used by Turkish and Moroccan youth as a medium to challenge racism. In contrast, in Newcastle (in north-east England), local hip-hoppers embraced rap as a more exciting alternative to what they saw as a 'narrow-minded' local youth scene. These different local (re)articulations of hip-hop culture, Bennett suggested, provided an 'especially animated' example of Robertson's (1995) concept of *glocalisation* (the reconfiguration of global media forms in local contexts – see Chapter 7). Rather than being unified and consensual, however, Bennett emphasised that the various global translations of hip-hop were always 'fraught with tensions and contradictions as young people attempt to reconcile issues of musical and stylistic authenticity with those of locality, identity and everyday life' (Bennett, 2000: 138).

Bennett stressed that *all* forms of popular music could be subject to processes of 'glocalisation' – all musical genres having potential to be taken up and reworked by local audiences. But he argued that certain characteristics of hip-hop made it an idiom especially suited as a form of local expression. The commercial packaging of hip-hop as a global commodity, Bennett argued, had facilitated its easy access by young people in many different parts of the world (Bennett, 2000: 137), but he also highlighted the distinctive 'hands on' nature of the genre which meant that audiences and performers became essentially interchangeable. Thus, while hip-hop existed as a huge commercial industry, it could still retain 'a strong identification with the street and with the ethos of grass roots expression' (Bennett, 1999b: 86).

Other authors supported Bennett's account of the 'glocalisation' of hip-hop. Tony Mitchell's (1996, 2003) research on hip-hop in Europe and Oceania, in particular, testified to the wide-ranging uses of rap and hip-hop style across the world, with French[8] and Italian hip-hop functioning as a vehicle of protest against racism and police harassment, while in New Zealand Maori rap groups campaigned for the rights of indigenous peoples around the world (Mitchell, 1996: 40, 244–250). In Sweden, meanwhile, Erling Bjurström (1997) found that hip-hop was used by youths from minority ethnic groups as a form of collective resistance against the racism of white skinheads, while Ian Condry's (1999, 2002) studies of hip-hop culture in Japan showed how Japanese hip-hoppers used their preferences in music and style to mark themselves out from the cultural 'mainstream'.

## DIASPORA, HYBRIDITY AND 'SYNCRETIC' YOUTH CULTURE

The international reach of hip-hop and its diverse local (re)articulations exemplifies the dynamic interplay between global media and young people's local cultures and identities. These relationships were also clearly demonstrated in Adam Briggs and Paul Cobley's (1999) study of black British youth style. Briggs and Cobley's research showed how young rap fans in London regarded America as the 'mothership' of hip-hop culture, but consciously synthesised US hip-hop with cultural forms that were distinctively African-Caribbean and black British. The youngsters interviewed by Briggs and Cobley imported and (re)embedded (rather than simply duplicated) aspects of American hip-hop, filtering ideas and information from a multiplicity of media and integrating them with 'other oral sources, often based on personal experience or second-hand (or third-hand or fourth-hand) tales from travels in the global diaspora' (Briggs and Cobley, 1999: 340–341).

For many of Briggs and Cobley's respondents, these processes of interconnection were exemplified by jungle, a form of music that was a creative 'thief' in the way it plundered from a variety of sources and styles (ibid.: 343). Jungle (or breakbeat/drum 'n' bass) first emerged during the mid-1990s as a pre-eminently black dance music spearheaded by DJs such as Fabio and Grooverider, and was subsequently popularised by performers such as Goldie – a former graffiti artist who became the face of jungle through the success of his debut album, *Timeless*, in 1995. Rattling along at 160 beats per minute, jungle was dominated by a thumping reggae bassline, but was also characterised by its fusion of ragga, hip-hop, hard-core and house musical styles – an eclectic mix of sound that laid the way for the development of an urban dance music scene that was distinctly 'hybridised' in the way it drew together diverse elements of African-Caribbean, American and British media and culture.

Modern youth cultures, therefore, are not formed in isolation, but through interconnection, fusion and amalgamation. The proliferation of global communication networks and media flows has been crucial in facilitating these processes, but patterns of population movement and settlement have also played an important role. Many theorists have used the concept of 'diaspora' (from the Greek phrase meaning 'to disperse') to analyse the cultural impact of population dispersion and travel across borders. According to Avtar Brah, in the process of diasporic movement new forms of cultural identity are generated that 'are at once local and global', being composed of 'networks of trans-national identifications encompassing "imagined" and "encountered" communities' (Brah, 1996: 196). Such cultures are not tied down to particular places, but are better conceptualised in terms of motion and contingency. Or, as Paul Gilroy has put it, they are a matter of *routes* rather than *roots* – patterns of movement and diffusion that involve the formation of 'creolized, syncretized, hybridized and chronically impure cultural forms' (Gilroy, 1997: 335). Moreover, Gilroy emphasised the issues of power and conflict that have been central to the development of these 'diasporic identities', arguing that they are generated through 'forced dispersal and reluctant scattering', so that:

> diaspora identity is focused less on the equalising, proto-democratic force of common territory and more on the social dynamics of remembrance and commemoration defined by a strong sense of the dangers involved in forgetting the location of origin and the process of dispersal.
>
> (Gilroy, 1997: 318)

A member of the Centre for Contemporary Studies at the University of Birmingham during the 1970s (see Chapter 6), Gilroy's early work represented a multi-layered analysis of the complex struggles around 'race', class and nation in contemporary Britain.[9] His later work gave particular attention to black 'expressive culture' and its relation to processes of diaspora and political struggle, Gilroy arguing that black culture and experience could only be understood in terms of its trans-atlantic connections. Gilroy eschewed notions of a pan-global, homogeneous black identity, but he also resisted notions of distinctly British, American or West Indian black culture. Instead, he introduced the concept of the 'Black Atlantic' to denote the history of intercultural connections linking globally dispersed black peoples (Gilroy, 1993a). For Gilroy, a series of forced and voluntary migrations (including the slave trade, but also the free movement of people and cultural forms back and forth across the Atlantic) had spread black people across the globe, but they remained linked by a long history of cultural connection and exchange – so that no one part of the Black Atlantic could be understood without considering its relation to the others. This process of cultural dialogue, Gilroy argued, produced a plurality of hybrid identities and cultural forms within and between the various locales of the black diaspora. Hip-hop culture and rap music, Gilroy suggested, were pre-eminent examples:

> Rap is a hybrid form rooted in the syncretic social relations of the South Bronx where Jamaican sound-system culture, transplanted during the 1970s, put down new roots and in conjunction with specific technological innovations, set in train a process that was to transform black America's sense of itself and a large proportion of the popular music industry as well.
> (Gilroy, 1993b: 125)

In some respects, Gilroy's account of rap's hybrid character was anticipated by Dick Hebdige's earlier (1987) historical survey of Caribbean music. Tracing the development of Caribbean music from calypso and ska, through reggae and Jamaican club culture, to New York rap and hip-hop, Hebdige emphasised the dynamism of these musical forms, their histories and associated cultural identities. Instead of attempting to trace the roots of these genres to their historical source, Hebdige argued that the 'roots' themselves were in a constant state of flux and change. 'The roots', Hebdige explained, 'don't stay in one place. They change shape. They change colour and they grow' (Hebdige, 1987: 10). Hence, Hebdige drew attention to the way Caribbean music had developed through ongoing processes of fusion and interconnection, a 'splicing together' of sounds and identities that addressed communities stretching from Africa to western Europe and the United States.

The term 'hybridity' has often been coined to denote these processes of cultural cross-fertilisation, though many authors have seen its use as problematic, given the term's history within racist discourses of colonialism. Instead, the 1990s saw the notion of 'synergy' – with its more positive and energetic connotations – often preferred as a concept to denote the processes through which new cultural forms and identities are constituted at the intersection of different places, histories and experiences. According to theorists such as Gilroy and Stuart Hall, attention to this 'syncretic' criss-crossing of cultural discourses opened up new ways of theorising ethnicity and identity – an approach that moved away from notions of ethnic identities as essential and fixed, and instead conceived them as constructed, multiple and dynamic.

Both Hall and Gilroy used the term 'diasporic culture' to explore the complex intercultural exchanges and transnational linkages through which ethnic identities are translated and transmitted, and in which 'new ethnicities' are made and remade (Gilroy, 1993a; Hall, 1992a). Gilroy, for example, highlighted musical genres such as bhangra as a space of intercultural dialogue where 'new ethnicities' have taken shape. According to Gilroy, through its fusion of Punjabi and Bengali folk music with hip-hop, soul and house, bhangra could be seen as 'the opening up of a self-consciously post-colonial space in which the affirmation of difference points forward to a more pluralistic conception of nationality' (Gilroy, 1993b: 62).

Other researchers have also explored the configuration of 'new ethnicities' in contemporary youth culture. Les Back (1996), for example, drew on extensive ethnographic research to analyse how new ethnic identities had taken shape within the syncretic forms of music and cultural expression that emerged in urban Britain during the 1990s. Jungle/drum 'n' bass, Back argued, stood as a pre-eminent example of a cultural sphere where 'the aesthetics of the nation [were] recomposed, resulting in more inclusive translocal notions of what it means to reside within UK boundaries' (1996: 233). In his survey of these processes, Back also underlined the importance of the Asian[10] diaspora (a theme somewhat sidelined in Gilroy's analysis). For Back, the coming together of Asian and African diasporic cultures in Britain represented an important intersection in the creation and articulation of new, syncretic identities, Back observing that in the development of new, 'translocal' forms of popular music:

> This process takes on further transnational nuances when South Asian lexical and cultural elements are introduced into these syncretic processes. The modes of expression that are produced possess a kind of triple consciousness that is simultaneously the child of Africa, Asia and Europe.[11]
>
> (Back, 1996: 185)

# BRIMFUL OF ASIA: 'TRANSCULTURAL' IDENTITIES AND BRITISH ASIAN YOUTH

This kind of 'multiple consciousness' has been highlighted by many studies of young British Asians' 'homegrown' cultural identities and media use. Indeed, a significant body of work has pointed to the way British Asian youngsters have negotiated within and between not only differences of age, gender and class; but also the discourses of 'Britishness' and 'Asianness'. While British-born Asians were once characterised as being caught 'between two cultures' (Watson, 1977), during the 1990s a number of writers showed how second and third generation British Asians had actually configured *their own* 'transcultural' identities.

In her continuing research on Asian youth in Southall (in south London), Marie Gillespie found that youngsters used the array of international media forms available to them (British TV soaps, videos of Indian films and so on) as a forum to evaluate and experiment with a variety of different cultural identities. In some respects, Gillespie argued, Southall youth's media consumption prompted discussion around issues common to most young people (fashion, friends and family, growing up, dating and so on). In other respects, however, she found that the diversity of international media consumed by Southall youngsters encouraged distinctly 'cross-cultural, comparative analyses of media representations' (Gillespie, 2000: 165). This, she argued, heightened their already well-developed consciousness of distinctive social worlds, languages and cultural spheres. In these terms, Gillespie suggested, Southall youth's media usage was an arena for their ongoing practices of identity creation and negotiation (Gillespie, 2000: 165, 166).[12] Similar findings were also produced by Chris Barker's (1999) study of young British Asian girls' everyday discussion of TV soaps. British Asian girls, Barker found, were well aware of the way their identities were informed by a variety of cultural discourses, using their engagement with TV soaps as a way of enunciating themselves as Asian, while at the same time reworking the meanings of 'Asianness' to encompass their own British-Asian syncretic culture.[13]

These processes of cross-cultural identity formation were compellingly explored by filmmaker Gurinder Chadha in the movies *Bhaji on the Beach* (1993) and *Bend It Like Beckham* (2002). Both films achieved a high measure of mainstream success, but they also won marked appeal among young, second and third generation British Asians whose negotiation of generational, gendered and ethnic identities were central themes in Chadha's films.[14] Young British Asians also represented a significant audience for Hindi cinema. Widely available in a multitude of urban video and DVD rental stores, as well as on satellite television networks such as Zee TV and B4U TV, 'Bollywood' movies won a dedicated fan base among many young British Asians who, journalist Tabasam Haseen found, relished the films' stylish representations of Asian culture:

> Although the three-hour plush musicals do have a unique appeal, there is a more telling reason as to why they are so popular among British-born Asian youth. As one Bollywood fan recently told me: 'In English films, Asians are portrayed as weak and pathetic. In Bollywood movies Asians are cool, sexy and stylish'.
>
> (Haseen, 2002)

Forms of popular music such as bhangra have also been highlighted as an important arena in which young British Asians have negotiated their identities. Like Gilroy, many authors have seen bhangra as a genre of music shaped by processes of migration and diaspora. The music took its name and origins from a form of Punjabi folk music played on traditional drums such as the *dholak* or *dholki*, but during the mid-1980s bhangra was reconfigured by young Asians living in Britain. Increasingly, the traditional bhangra beats were fused with a variety of Western dance styles (including disco, house and rap) to produce a musical form 'at least as quintessentially "British" as it is "Asian"' (Huq, 1996: 62–63). Blending elements of bhangra with ragga (dubbed 'bhangramuffin' by the pop press), the Birmingham-born singer Apache Indian took Asian dance music to mainstream commercial success during the early 1990s with a string of hit singles (including 1993's 'Arranged Marriage' and 1995's 'Boomshackalak') and critically acclaimed albums such as *No Reservations* (1992). Alongside Apache, the Midlands-based producer/performer Bally Sagoo also attracted significant attention. Interweaving Bollywood film scores with pulsating Western basslines, Bally Sagoo sold over 100,000 copies of six albums during the early 1990s, signing to Sony Records in 1994 in a deal reputedly worth £1.2 million, and scoring Britain's first Indian language Top Twenty hit with 'Dil Cheez' in 1997.[15]

The 1990s saw a surge of press interest in Asian bands, musicians and club culture, as music journalists hailed the rise of 'Asian Kool' (Morris, 1993). But, as Rehan Hyder (2004) has observed, the idea of a unified Asian music scene was tenuous. 'Asian Kool' actually embraced a wide diversity of bands who incorporated elements of 'Asian' music in their performance in very different ways. Though acknowledging a degree of 'slippage' between them, Hyder identified two broad genres – Asian dance music and an 'indie guitar' scene. For Hyder, Asian dance music incorporated a diverse range of musical genres (including hip-hop, house and techno), with artists such as FuñDâMental, Panjabi MC, Asian Dub Foundation and Hustlers HC fusing typically Asian sounds and samples with influences drawn from Black America, Europe and contemporary Britain. FuñDâMental, for example, used samples of a variety of Asian instruments, blending them with hip-hop beats and radically political raps in tracks such as their 1993 single, 'Wrath of the Blackman'.[16] In contrast, Hyder saw 'indie guitar' bands such as the Voodoo Queens and Cornershop as less explicit in their political stance. Their engagement with 'Asian' music was also distinctive, Cornershop merging instruments such as the *sitar* and *dholki* into a guitar-oriented mix that drew influence from the punk traditions of the late 1970s, and from 1980s 'indie' bands such as The Smiths and The Jesus and Mary Chain. 'Asian Kool', then, covered a wide variety of musical styles and forms of cultural expression, Hyder arguing that these represented differently nuanced articulations of a dynamic and multi-faceted British Asian identity.

The various contributors to Sanjay Sharma *et al.*'s (1996) anthology, *Dis-Orienting Rhythms*, took a similar view, arguing that the new Asian dance music of the 1990s could be read as 'a cultural form that narrates diasporas, dynamically affirming, transforming and mutating both imagined and material linkages' (Sharma *et al.*, 1996: 9). Indeed, for this group of authors, the category 'British Asian' was unable to convey the dynamism and diversity of these various, sliding subjectivities. Instead, Raminder Kaur and Virinder Kalra suggested 'Br-Asian' as a more open-ended term, better able to denote 'the complex subject positions of migrants and their offspring settled in Britain' (Kaur and Kalra, 1996: 219).

The authors in *Dis-Orienting Rhythms* were at pains to emphasise the heterogeneity of 'Br-Asian' youth and their expressive cultures. Yet some critics detected in their work tendencies towards overgeneralisation. Bennett, for example, took issue with Sharma's claim that musical forms such as bhangra suggested 'a means for Asian youth to assert their "Asianness" and locate themselves firmly in their contemporary urban surroundings' (Sharma, 1996: 35–36). Such interpretations of bhangra's cultural significance for young Asians in Britain, Bennett argued, tended to 'gloss over the true complexity of the relationship that exists between the music and its audience' (Bennett, 2000: 106). Drawing on his own ethnographic study of bhangra in Newcastle, Bennett questioned the notion that the music spoke a 'common language' to its audiences. Instead, he argued that the meanings and uses of bhangra were locally inflected. According to Bennett, the cultural responses of young Asians towards bhangra varied depending on regional demographics and local arrangements governing the music's production and consumption. In the case of Newcastle, for example, Bennett found that the comparative novelty of bhangra events, combined with the relative 'whiteness' of the local population, meant that bhangra became a site for the promotion of what was considered to be 'traditional' Asian life:

> Local bhangra events permit such articulations of tradition by allowing young Asians to dress in the traditional clothes of their parent cultures, the wearing of such clothes being blocked at other times by the predominantly white nature of the local environment and the fear of young Asians of appearing to be *out of place*.
>
> (Bennett: 2000: 110)

Hyder also saw the arguments made in *Dis-Orienting Rhythms* as occasionally too sweeping. He was especially sceptical about Sharma *et al.*'s grander claims regarding the dimension of political radicalism within Asian popular music and style. Certainly, Hyder agreed, there was an uncompromising political punch to many of the songs produced by artists such as FuñDâMental and Asian Dub Foundation. Moreover, Hyder argued, the success of Asian bands during the 1990s had exploded popular stereotypes of Asians as being 'trapped' in their parents' cultural world, 'bound by the strict conventions of the "community" and more likely to be doing school work or toiling in the local corner shop than playing or enjoying pop music' (Hyder, 2004). But, Hyder suggested, the authors of *Dis-Orienting Rhythms* had focused too exclusively on the political agendas of a handful of bands. Authors such as Sharma, Hyder argued, had based their conclusions almost entirely on their own (possibly somewhat subjective) readings of the lyrics of songs by bands such as FuñDâMental and Hustlers HC and, as a consequence, may have obscured the complex multiplicity of identities and articulations at play in the music cultures of young Asians. In contrast, Hyder argued that his own interviews with Asian bands and musicians indicated that, while most took a broadly anti-racist political stand, this was not necessarily an explicit feature of their music and the artists shared no common or clear-cut political agenda.

Nevertheless, *Dis-Orienting Rhythms* was still a significant intervention in the analysis of youth culture, media and identity. During the 1970s and the early 1980s issues of 'race' and ethnicity had been relatively peripheral in many analyses of British youth culture. And, while authors such as Hebdige and Gilroy subsequently gave attention to African Caribbean music and style, the lives and culture of south Asian youth went relatively unexplored. In many respects, therefore, Sharma *et al.*'s discussion of Asian dance music was a crucial contribution to the study of youth culture in contemporary Britain. Their attention to the plurality of negotiated and dynamic 'Br-Asian' identities, moreover, highlighted the way processes of social, economic and cultural globalisation had brought a widening of potential identities and subjectivities for young people. Syncretic youth cultures still had a strong link with their place of 'origin' and its cultural traditions, though they had also become 'translated' by their new cultural context – exemplified by the way Cornershop celebrated the veteran Hindi film songstress Asha Bhosle in their 1998 indie guitar hit, 'Brimful of Asha'. As Homi Bhabha (1990) has argued, therefore, many people have learned to inhabit (at least) two cultural identities, negotiating and translating between them to form a 'third space' which:

> displaces the histories that constitute it, and sets up new structures of authority, new political initiatives, which are inadequately understood through received wisdom. The process of cultural hybridity gives rise to something different, something new and unrecognisable, a new area of meaning and representation.
>
> (Bhabha, 1990: 211)

By the end of the 1990s, British Asian youth was gradually being recognised by commercial media and consumer industries as an important market segment. Indicative was the appearance of specialised 'coolhunting' agencies such as Br-Asian Media Consulting, who assured clients of their ability 'to target the British Asian youth and middle youth audiences, a market with high disposable income, and proven keen interest in music, fashion, film, sport and general lifestyle issues' (Br-Asian Media Consulting, 2004). There was, however, also a significant minority of British Asian youth who rejected the appeal of the commercial media and consumer industries. Instead (in response to cultural racism and exclusion), these youngsters sought either to 're-identify' with their cultures of origin or asserted a trenchant form of religious orthodoxy. In his (1998) study of young British Asians in Bradford, for example, Yunas Samad found that Islam had emerged as a powerful point of cultural identification for many youngsters of Pakistani origin. Yet, rather than being coterminous with a resurgence of religious 'fundamentalism', Samad argued that British Asian youngsters' identification with Islam was, itself, a syncretic cultural form, created through a process of cultural exchange as young people negotiated their local, generational and gendered identities:

> Rather than a defence of tradition, Muslim identification, which is being articulated by the youth, is hybrid in character. This identification blends popular

culture and Pakistaniness in a novel manner, producing new identification.
. . . In what sense is the diasporic identity of these young people transnational? Only as much as they are using Islamic rhetoric, metaphors and
symbols for the purpose of constructing identification. The intersection of
Islam, a global ideology, with the locale provides a resource, which is then
imaginatively deployed – not the other way around whereby a trans-national
ideology is gaining a foothold in Bradford. Increasing influence of Islam
among young people is more to do with debates in the locale.

(Samad, 1998: 437)

Instead of being pure, fixed or 'authentic', then, *all* young people's
subject positions have come to operate across, and within, multiple
cultural sites – their identities constituted by the intersection of criss-
crossing discourses of age, ethnicity, gender, class, sexuality and so on.
Syncretic cultural identities, however, are not necessarily a uniquely
contemporary phenomenon. The open-ended, dynamic and 'hybridised'
cultural forms and identities that many theorists have seen as a trait of
the late twentieth century were, perhaps, anticipated by tendencies long
a feature of youth culture and style. Indeed, with its fusion of black
R 'n' B and white country and Western music, and with its history of
being rearticulated and re-embedded across an infinite range of cultural
contexts and configurations, it might be possible to see rock 'n' roll as
the 'grand daddy' of syncretic youth culture.

## 'SHAKE YOUR THANG': YOUTH, MEDIA AND THE 'FLUIDITY' OF CULTURAL IDENTITY

For some theorists, the fluidity and open-ended nature of cultural identities in the late twentieth century was indicative of a general 'crisis
of identity' (Hall, 1992b). From this perspective, globalisation and
processes of social and economic change had eroded many established
allegiances and commitments – not only those formed around ethnicity,
but also those surrounding notions of gender, sexuality, class and generation. This perception of old sureties as being increasingly undermined
and fragmented was informed by post-structuralist critiques of the
assumptions that had characterised Western thought and philosophy
since the Enlightenment. Post-structuralism is a broad and diverse
church, though its advocates share a general rejection of the totalising,
essentialist and foundationalist concepts associated with Enlightenment
epistemologies. In contrast to the Enlightenment's veneration of 'truth',
rationality and progress, post-structuralist theorists have emphasised the

inherently unstable nature of the social order, arguing that claims to order and 'truth' have been related to systems of power in which some voices have been given authority and status while others have been silenced and marginalised. Moreover, rejecting the Enlightenment view of 'the Individual' as a unified and coherent essence, post-structuralist theorists have seen people as composed of manifold identities that are discursively created (and continuously re-created) through cultural meanings and practices.

From this perspective, the social, economic and political dislocations of the late twentieth century may have brought a 'decentring' (Hall, 1987) of identity. With the de-stabilisation of traditional assumptions and securities, potentially liberating spaces may have opened up for the artic-ulation of identities once confined to the periphery of cultural systems – and theorists of ethnicity, gender, and sexuality have all been keen to explore the multiple subjectivities that may have sprouted through the fissures and disjunctions of late modern societies. Perhaps, though, it is the sphere of youth culture that most readily exemplifies this 'decen-tring' of identity. Indeed, with their unstable fusion of fragmented identities and cultural reference points, modern youth cultures have always encompassed fluid and dynamic subjectivities. Rather than being fixed and coherent, youth cultures have invariably been mutable and transient, youngsters often cruising across a range of cultural affiliations, constantly forming and reforming their identities according to social context.

Media forms geared to young audiences have also offered a fertile space for the configuration of a variety of genders, ethnicities and sexu-alities – some of which may have challenged notions of identity as being stable and unchanging. In this respect, Judith Butler's concept of gender as a 'performance' has been especially influential. Rather than conceiving gender as a stable identity or an 'agency from which various acts follow', Butler argued that gender was better understood as 'an identity tenu-ously constituted in time, instituted in an exterior space through a *stylized repetition of acts*' (Butler, 1990: 140). Drawing on the ideas of French critical theorist Michel Foucault, Butler saw gender as a historically dynamic 'corporeal style' that was fabricated and sustained through a set of performative acts and 'a ritualized repetition of conventions' (Butler, 1995: 31). Many theorists have drawn upon Butler's ideas to explore constructions of gender and sexuality in popular culture. For example, according to E. Ann Kaplan (1993) (and many other theorists), the singer Madonna undermined essentialist notions of femininity through adopting a series of 'performative' masquerades in her videos and stage shows (see Chapter 6). According to Butler (1991), 'drag' performance also had subversive potential in the way it spotlighted the disjunction between anatomical sex and gendered identity. Hence 'gender-bending' artists, from Boy George to Marilyn Manson, might be seen as subverting traditional notions of gender and sexuality through their deliberate blurring of masculine and feminine conventions. Female artists such as Annie Lennox and k.d. lang might equally be seen as usurping gender conventions, their adoption of a variety of masculine, androgynous and (occasionally) lesbian guises pointing to the 'performative' character of gender.

Female rappers might also be seen as negotiating multiple identities and social boundaries. Nancy Guevara (1996) has documented how women were involved in the development of rap since its emergence during the 1970s, though were often marginalised in the genre's male-dominated culture. During the 1980s and 1990s swaggering machismo remained a prevalent theme in hip-hop, and the songs of artists such as 2 Live Crew and NWA were often excruciatingly misogynistic. At the same time, however, a new wave of confident and independent female rappers also came to the fore. Artists like M.C. Lyte, Queen Latifah, Yo-Yo and Salt 'n' Pepa developed reputations for raps that were biting critiques of masculine manipulation and abuse of women. Moreover, as Tricia Rose explained, while these raps told stories of men taking advantage of women, they were not 'mournful ballads about the trials and tribulations of being a heterosexual woman' – instead, they were 'caustic, witty and aggressive warnings directed at men and at other women who might be seduced by them in the future' (Rose, 1994a: 155).

Independence and confidence were also watchwords in the career of Missy 'Misdemeanor' Elliott. Rising from a neighbourhood singing group, Sista, in the early 1990s, Elliott carved out a niche as a pioneering hip-hop/R 'n' B writer and producer, as well as a groundbreaking performer with innovative and influential albums such as *Supa Dupa Fly* (1997) and the multi-platinum selling *Miss E . . . So Addictive* (1999). In Britain, the success of north London rapper, Ms. Dynamite (Niomi McLean-Daley) was also significant. Working with garage producers Sticky, Ms. Dynamite provided the vocals to the 2001 hit single, 'Booo!' and was hailed as one of the most talented artists to emerge from the burgeoning UK garage scene. Signed to the major label Polydor in 2002, her solo single 'It Takes More' was an infectious blend of hip-hop and reggae, but the song also foregrounded Ms. Dynamite's self-assured and politically-conscious attitude through its stand against the violent postures often taken in the UK garage scene. The lyrics to tracks such as 'Put Him Out', meanwhile, were a confident challenge to misogyny and sexual exploitation:

Don't need him if he makes u sacrifice
Ur freedom get him out of ur life . . .
I understand u love him and ur down
But that don't mean u gotta b his clown

Other female rappers, however, have adopted a different form of 'performative' femininity. Artists like Lil' Kim and Foxy Brown (and also Salt 'n' Pepa), for example, crafted an image distinguished by its blatant sexuality. Rather than simply catering to an objectifying male gaze, however, Rose argued that these artists' public displays of physical sexual freedom challenged male notions of female sexuality and pleasure. According to Rose, for instance, Salt 'n' Pepa's rap 'Shake Your Thang' (with lyrics and video that focused on the pair's sexual dancing and the responses it elicited) was a 'verbal and visual display of black women's sexual resistance', that drew its power from Salt 'n' Pepa's irreverence toward the morally based sexual constrictions placed on them as women' (Rose, 1994a: 166–167). Beverly Skeggs offered a similar assessment. For black women, Skeggs argued, 'sexuality is one of the few cultural resources that they can use for the construction of embodied self worth' (Skeggs, 1993: 310). According to Skeggs, therefore, female rappers invested the explicit sexual language of rap with new meanings that celebrated female sexuality and autonomy, female rappers effectively turning themselves from sexual objects into sexual subjects.[17]

While analyses of the fabrication of gender have often focused on the 'performance' of femininity, it is only relatively recently that the social construction of masculinity has attracted similar attention. In Britain, attention to the heterogeneity and variability of constructions of masculinity came to the fore during the 1990s. Much of this analysis focused on the figure of the narcissistic and self-conscious 'new man' and the array of new, glossy lifestyle magazines (for example, *Arena*, launched in 1986) with which he was associated. Authors such as Frank Mort (1988, 1996) and Sean Nixon (1996) mapped out what they interpreted as a new relationship between young men and the traditionally 'feminine' areas of commodity consumption. These developments, they argued, had generated a promotional culture whose visual codes worked to 'rupture traditional icons of masculinity', thus making space for a plurality of more provisional masculine identities (Mort, 1988: 194). In these terms, the growing interface between masculinity and consumer practice could be seen in a relatively positive light. In particular, the more overtly sexualised visual codes of the 'new man' were interpreted as a 'loosening of the binary opposition between gay and straight-identified men', thereby extending 'the space available within the representational regimes of

**Figure 8.1** Missy Elliott at the 2003 US Soul Train Awards
Courtesy of Pictorial Press

popular consumption for an ambivalent masculine identity' (Nixon, 1996: 202).

This perspective, however, was qualified by Tim Edwards. The attention Mort and Nixon gave to archetypes of masculine consumerism of the 1980s and 1990s, Edwards suggested, tended to elide the much longer history of men's active and overt practices of commodity consumption (Edwards, 1997: 92). For Edwards, moreover, rather than being necessarily progressive, models of masculinity premised on consumption could also veer towards aspirationalism and conservative individualism – models of masculine consumerism being 'as equally personally destructive and socially divisive as they are individually expressive and democratically utopian' (Edwards, 1997: 2). Indeed, more recent trends in men's magazine publishing seemed to question the degree to which traditional constructions of masculinity had been profoundly ruptured.

In 1994 the launch of *Loaded*, a key moment in the recent history of British masculinity and its 'youthful' identities, pointed to a new wave of 'lad's mags' that celebrated a world of boisterous male camaraderie. Billing itself as the magazine 'For Men Who Should Know Better', *Loaded* deliberately presented itself as a challenge to the feminist-friendly, sensitive narcissism of the 'new man'. Promoting an incarnation of young masculinity popularly known as the 'new lad', *Loaded* and a succession of competitors (for example, *FHM* and *Maxim*[18]) seemed to mark a return to traditional masculine values of sexism and macho braggadocio, perhaps representing an attempt to reassert the power of masculinity deemed lost through the concessions made to feminism by the 'new man'. 'New lad' magazines such as *Loaded*, however, also placed considerable emphasis on hedonistic good times (drinking, sport, holidays) and tongue-in-cheek humour. Arguably, this emphasis on irony and 'knowingness' served as a gloss to legitimate the magazines' misogyny and homophobia. Alternatively, however, these magazines' dimensions of self-conscious reflexivity might suggest a profound ambivalence about traditional masculine archetypes. In these terms, rather than attempting to shore-up traditional gender identities and power structures, 'new lad' magazines such as *Loaded* and *Maxim* could be interpreted as a manifestation of the contradictory, ambiguous and fragmented forms of masculine identity that circulate in contemporary culture.[19]

More generally, it could be argued that youth cultures have *always* been sites of ambiguous, fluid and fragmented masculine identities. Indeed, the history of British (and probably also American) youth style could be written as a narrative of shifting, multi-faceted configurations of gender and sexuality. Interaction and exchange between gay and straight identities has been an especially pronounced feature of these processes.[20] The flamboyant 'Edwardian' look of the 1950s Teddy boy, for example, had been anticipated by the appearance of similar styles within the gay underground during the late 1940s. Elements of cross-fertilisation were also evident in the mod and gay subcultures of the early 1960s, the mod 'look' first cohering as an identifiable style within the gay clubs of London's West End. Murray Healy (1996), meanwhile, has given a perceptive account of skinhead style as a meeting-ground between gay and straight masculine identities. And during the early 1970s mod narcissism was further amplified in the glam rock cult that (again) plundered from the wardrobe of gay subcultural style. Glam rockers of the 1970s, such as The Sweet and Slade, were traditional masculine rock bands who drew on camp and androgynous imagery for their shock value – but others, most notably David Bowie, used their stage personae to explore a variety of gendered and sexualised identities.

In America, too, theorists drew attention to the heterogeneity of masculine identities that were constructed within popular culture. Robert Wasler (1993), for example, highlighted the way a wide variety of masculine archetypes were 'enacted' by leading heavy metal bands of the 1980s. Guns N' Roses, for instance, embodied a free-wheeling, non-conformist machismo, Bon Jovi were constructed as romantic heroes, while Poison adopted a style that was more androgynous and 'glam' – though all, in their different ways, represented a spectacle of heterosexual masculine power.[21] Indie rock bands like Nirvana and the Lemonheads, in contrast, constructed forms of male heterosexuality that laid an emphasis on male angst and vulnerability. Gangsta rap, meanwhile, became notorious for its aggressive misogyny and sexual bluster.

The sexism of gangsta rap has attracted understandable criticism. For instance, Tricia Rose, who otherwise applauded rap's ability to provide transcripts of cultural resistance, was deeply critical of the sexual politics of rappers who crafted 'elaborate and creative stories about the abuse and domination of young black women' (Rose, 1994a: 15). At the same time, however, Rose voiced deep suspicions of conservative outrage regarding rap's misogyny, suggesting that the music had become 'a scapegoat that diverts attention away from the more entrenched problem of redefining the terms of heterosexual masculinity' (Rose, 1994a: 16). Rose also recognised that these tales of sexual domination might serve to provide a sense of self-worth to young African-Americans who otherwise had little access to social status.[22] Indeed, the outrageous sexism of rappers such as Ice-T, Snoop Doggy Dogg, and 50 Cent might be interpreted as a hi-jacking of racist discourse. Just as

LA rappers NWA (and African-American street culture more generally) appropriated the pejorative term 'nigger' and reconfigured it as a form of positive self-identification, the sexism of gangsta rappers might be understood as an inversion of racist myths of the predatory 'black buck', rappers commandeering the stereotype and investing it with a sense of black authority and power – albeit in a deplorably misogynistic and homophobic way.

Like gender and 'race', 'whiteness' is also a cultural construct, though has seldom been treated as such. As Richard Dyer (1997) has argued, the power and authority of white culture has afforded 'whiteness' a quality of virtual invisibility, with images and representations of white culture naturalising themselves as a norm from which all others diverge. In reality, however, 'white' (like any other 'racial' category) has been historically fabricated, Dyer arguing that 'whiteness' has often been associated with the 'mind over body' qualities of 'tightness, . . . self control [and] self-consciousness' (Dyer, 1997: 6). But, like any other identity, 'whiteness' has also been dynamic and multi-faceted, often drawing on 'Other' cultures as a source of exciting 'difference'. Black subcultures, for example, have been a perennial influence on the styles of white youth, the two engaging in an ongoing process of aesthetic dialogue. Indeed, for Dick Hebdige, the prominence of 'race' as an organising principle within British youth culture meant that the development of modern youth styles could be read as 'a phantom history of race relations since the War' (Hebdige, 1979: 45). Mods and skinheads of the 1960s, for example, obliquely reproduced what they saw as the effortless cool of the West Indian rude boy, while 1970s punks often lionised Rastafarians as 'authentic' and rebellious outsiders.[23]

In American youth culture, too, a similar history of black/white exchange can be traced, from the jazz clubs of the roaring 1920s, through to the 1950s rock 'n' roll boom and the beats' veneration of black hustlers – Norman Mailer providing the classic exposition of beat reverence for black street style in his (1961) essay, 'The White Negro'. White hipsters, Mailer argued, had 'absorbed the existentialist synopses of the Negro' and had come to represent 'a new breed of adventurers, urban adventurers who drifted out at night looking for action with a black man's code to fit their facts' (Mailer, 1961: 273). The same could also be said of white fans of contemporary gangsta rap. Indeed, gangsta rappers' displays of curl-lipped aggression may not be aimed so much at their peers on the street as they are at white, middle-class 'suburban homeboys' who are thrilled by images of a threatening African-American machismo. As Jerry Heller (the white, middle-aged, manager who helped steer NWA to commercial success) wryly observed:

Obviously inner-city kids aren't buying the volume of rap records that sell.
So when you're talking about those kind of albums . . . those have captured
middle-class white America.

(cited in Fernando, 1995: 99)

The (white) romanticisation of gangsta rap as an 'authentic' voice of
street rebellion is problematic. Such a starry-eyed view obviously over-
looks the important role played by commercial forces (managers, record
companies, promoters) in shaping and marketing gangsta rap as an
expressive form. But the stereotyping of 'Other' cultures as an incarnation of 'authentic' dissent can also be seen as implicitly racist in its
essentialist assumptions. Since the eighteenth century, colonial stereotypes of the murderous black primitive have been paralleled by the
romantic (and equally racist) myth of the 'Noble Savage' as an embodiment of spiritual freedom and exhilarating 'difference'. And this highly
selective mythologising of 'exciting' Others is a theme that has run
through the history of Western youth culture.[24] In the late 1960s, for
example, Tom Wolfe coined the phrase 'radical chic' to denote the countercultural avant-garde's attempts to garner a rebellious cachet through
flirting with black radical movements such as the Black Panthers (Wolfe:
1970). In a similar vein, the term 'ghetto chic' might be applied to
contemporary white, middle-class attempts to identify with what is
fondly imagined to be the raw and vital 'authenticity' of gangsta rap.

The same criticisms might also be levelled at white appropriations of
Asian style and culture. In its penchant for 'ethnic' kaftans and 'eastern
mysticism', for example, the late 1960s counterculture can be seen as
invoking an essentialist stylisation of 'Otherness'. Equally, the British
media's fascination with 'Asian Kool' in the late 1990s often smacked of
an opportunist exploitation of 'exotic' difference. John Hutnyk (2000),
for example, has singled out (white) indie pop band Kula Shaker's appropriation of 'ethnic Indian' sounds and style as representing the latest
instalment in a history of 'trinketisation' that has repackaged (and trivi-
alised) south Asian culture as a totem of spiritual karma. At the same
time, however, Karla and Hutnyk (1998) acknowledged that the popularity of Asian music in Britain during the late 1990s had opened up,
more prominently than ever before, a public sphere for Asian artists
playing 'hybrid' music. Simply because artists such as Kula Shaker had
cynically cashed-in on 'ethnic' style, they argued, that should not detract
from the strategic significance of celebrating the visibility of Asian culture
in the centre of metropolitan life.

Exploitation and essentialist stereotyping, then, have clearly been
pronounced features of white youth culture's engagement with 'Others''

style. But, at the same time, more positive dimensions have also existed to this contorted and contradictory relationship. Simon Jones's (1988) account of the dialogue between black and white youth cultures in Birmingham during the 1980s, for example, emphasised the degree of alliance that could develop between local black and white youngsters. In certain parts of the city, Jones argued, the growth of social ties between black and white communities had meant that residents developed a common identification with 'the shared spaces and cross-cutting loyalties of street, pub and neighborhood' (1988: 128). Especially close links had developed among the young, Jones finding that local white youths had adopted many aspects of black music and style. In this way, he suggested, African-Caribbean youth culture had acquired localised meaning as a symbol of community that included both black and white youngsters. More generally, Jones asserted, black music had consistently supplied white British youth with raw material for their own distinctive forms of cultural expression. Highlighting the particular historical importance of Jamaican reggae, Jones emphasised the way the music had resonated with the lives of white youth, providing them with an avenue through which they could address their own social experiences:

> The reggae tradition has acted as a catalyst and inspiration to a whole generation of young whites, providing them with a vehicle through which to signify their own struggles for cultural and political power, and to express oppositional meanings, whether in relation to the dominant culture or to mainstream rock and pop cultures.
>
> (Jones, 1988: 232)

The same might also be said of white youth's embrace of rap and hip-hop. Here, David Roedigger has underscored the potentially radical processes of 'racial' exchange in his (1998) taxonomy of the epithet 'wigger'. An abbreviation of the phrase 'white nigger', the term 'wigger' initially existed as a white-on-white slur, but during the 1980s and 1990s developed meanings that were more complex and contradictory. The original, derogatory connotations of the word persisted, but it was also used in new ways, Roedigger arguing that 'wigger' (or 'wigga') was adopted by African-American youths as a phrase for deriding the deemed inauthenticity of white youths who affected hip-hop style. But, according to Roedigger, the phrase could also be used approvingly by white hip-hoppers who proudly asserted that they '"wished they were black"' (Roedigger, 1998: 361). Roedigger acknowledged the naivety and romantic essentialism that underlay such sentiments, but he also speculated that the fact that white rap fans were listening to explicit critiques of 'white' society might have a radicalising impact on their processes of identity formation. Drawing on the ideas of criminologist Zaid Ansari, Roedigger suggested that the popularity of hip-hop among white youth, together with the widespread veneration of Malcolm X by white as well as African-American youth, raised the possibility of white youngsters 'becoming X' – that is, losing the quality in whiteness that 'keeps them accepting oppression, including their own oppression' (Ansari, cited in Roedigger, 1998: 363).[25]

This kind of fracturing and reconfiguring of identity positions is indicative of the multiple, contradictory allegiances that circulate in the realm of contemporary youth culture. It might also be seen as symptomatic of a much wider condition of identity 'dislocation', perhaps exemplifying Hall's (1992b) notion of a generalised 'crisis of identity' in which the frameworks that once gave individuals a stable anchorage in the cultural world have been ruptured by the profound social, economic and political upheavals of the late twentieth century. As a consequence of these disruptions, Hall argued, the autonomous and self-sufficient identity of the Enlightenment – 'the Individual' – had increasingly given way to a new universe of subjectivities that produced 'a variety of possibilities and new positions of identification, . . . making identities more positional, more political, more plural and diverse; less fixed, unified or trans-historical' (Hall, 1992b: 309). In these terms, the flux and fluidity that characterise young people's processes of identity formation might neatly epitomise the wider diversity of dynamic subject positions that Hall sees as a distinctive feature of late modern societies.

For some theorists, the development of new communications technologies further intensified this fragmentation of the traditional cultural landscapes of class, gender, sexuality, ethnicity, 'race', and nationality. The nebulous, ever-changing nature of the internet, in particular, has been seen as accelerating the breakdown of boundaries between established social categories. The following chapter explores these possible developments and assesses their specific relevance to the lives of young people.

# 9

# TOTALLY WIRED
## Youth and new media

The internet has become the primary communication tool for teens, surpassing even the telephone among some groups, according to a study by AOL. The national survey of more than 6,700 teens and parents of teens was conducted by AOL subsidiary Digital Market Services, Inc. It found that 81 per cent of teens between the ages of 12 to 17 use the internet to e-mail friends or relatives while 70 per cent use it for instant messaging to send instant text messages both from one's computer and via wireless devices. Among older teens (18 to 19 years), these statistics jump to 91 per cent for e-mail and 83 per cent for instant messaging.

(Michael Pastore, 2002)

## SLAYERS IN CYBERSPACE: NEW MEDIA AND YOUTH CULTURES OF PRODUCTION AND CONSUMPTION

In May 2000 a rag-tag band of young rebels were limbering-up for battle. They were poorly resourced and ill-equipped, but were intent on inflicting a punishing blow against their considerably bigger, more powerful foe – Twentieth Century Fox. A few months earlier, lawyers representing the media giant had sent out stern letters to operators of unofficial websites dedicated to Fox's demon-stalking TV series, *Buffy the Vampire Slayer*. In a threatening tone, the letters warned that legal action would follow unless the fans immediately removed from their sites all copyrighted material (whether it be logos, transcripts, video and sound clips, or any kind of picture).[1] Effectively an attempt to close-down the unofficial websites, the studio's heavy-handed intervention outraged many young *Buffy* fans. A particularly infuriated faction sprang into action. One high-school freshman (identifying herself only as 'Jade') organised a widely publicised National Blackout Day that saw unoffical fan sites across the world cease activity for 24 hours to draw attention to Fox's overbearing attitude. At the same time, a 17-year-old from Los Angeles (who administered a *Buffy* fan site and worked under the pseudonymn 'Solo84') formed the 'Buffy Bringers' – a group of incensed fans who launched an angry letter-writing campaign designed to deter advertisers from sinking money into Fox until the studio had backed-down. To many people, these internet '*Buffy* wars' might seem a relatively trivial spat between an overwrought TV studio and an errant group of young viewers. The events, however, crytallised many issues surrounding cultural production, circulation, control and consumption in the fast-changing landscape of the new media.

The profusion of *Buffy* internet sites (both official and unofficial) was indicative of the way developments in communication technologies created a wealth of new media outlets during the 1990s. Alongside these new outlets, extensive intertextual tapestries also emerged, with narratives and ideas flowing across a multiplicity of different media channels. In some respects at least, this rise of an integrated and interactive multimedia universe stood as a good example of Jean Baudrillard's (1985) notion of a dawning age of postmodern 'hyperreality' – with borders between formerly separate areas of cultural life increasingly effaced in a media-saturated world where distinctions between the real and the imaginary became increasingly hazy.

New uncertainties also accompanied the rise of new media systems and technologies. Technological developments posed a particular challenge to the conventional means through which producers and state agencies maintained control of cultural forms. Media companies became especially nervous of the way new technologies might provide consumers with greater ability to mould and modify the media experience, and many businesses scurried to protect their financial investments. Hence the speed and aggression with which Twentieth Century Fox fired-off 'Cease and Desist' (or 'C and D') letters to unofficial *Buffy* websites – the company seeing them as a threat to its intellectual property. Indeed, for many commentators, the emergence of new media technologies had encouraged more active modes of media consumption. The unofficial *Buffy* websites, for example, might be seen as the creations of a young audience segment that was not only critically aware and discriminating, but which also sought to take control of the text, actively shaping and reconfiguring it around their own cultural agenda.

New media developments may also have impacted upon cultural allegiances and identities. Offering instant communication across the world, new media technologies may have accelerated the dissolution of barriers of time and space, redefining notions of the 'global' and the 'local' and offering possibilities for the development of new communities based on affinities of interest, politics or any form of cultural identity (exemplified by the global interconnections of online *Buffy* fandom). According to some theorists, the new potential for cultural production and participation in cyberspace might also have fed into a wider 'decentring' of identity in contemporary society, with individuals able to articulate an ever-widening range of diverse identities and selves – evidenced, perhaps, in the way many online *Buffy* fans took pleasure in configuring themselves as valiant confederates of the fictional vampire-slayer.

In popular discourse youth is often presented as being at the cutting edge of these developments. As Julian Sefton-Green argues, young people and new technology are often yoked together in discussions about the nature of contemporary social change since both concepts embody 'similar teleological assumptions about growth, progression and development' (Sefton-Green, 1998: 2). This chapter considers the array of debates surrounding the relationship between young people and recent innovations in media and communications technology. It begins with a consideration of the distinctive features of 'new' media, their impact on the youth market and on young people's patterns of media consumption. Attention then switches to popular representations of the relationship between young people and new media, with an analysis of the way these motifs are constituent in a long history of debate about youth and its relation to patterns of social change. The chapter concludes with a survey of the various ways young people have used new media, and have integrated new technologies within their everyday lives and cultures.

## 'TECHNO, TECHNO, TECHNO . . .': THE DIGITAL REVOLUTION AND THE WORLD OF NEW MEDIA

The phrase 'new media' denotes a wide variety of recent developments in the fields of media and communications. It encompasses not only new forms of media delivery, but also new convergencies between media technologies and new ways in which people use, and interact with, media texts. Fundamental to these trends has been the growing significance of digital technology in the production, storage and transmission of images, text, sound and data. Compared to earlier, analogue systems (where information is represented by continuously changing signals), digital technology encodes data in binary form. This affords a higher quality of reproduction and allows for easier, faster and more reliable usage. The introduction of CDs in 1982 was an early step in the march towards 'digitisation', the advantages of digital technology allowing the rapid ascent of the CD as the dominant platform for recorded music. The spread of digitisation was given further impetus by developments in computer technology. By the mid-1980s computers could already convert relatively complex data (for example, graphics and music) into a digital format – but, for the most part, these developments took place in separate production contexts such as video editing and software design. During the early 1990s the growth of the internet, and particularly the world wide web, provided the crucial stimulus that brought together these different digital applications. The web's growth was exponential. In 1993, two years after its launch, there were 130 web servers worldwide, but by 1995 the figure had leapt to 23,500. The meteoric rise of the web further accelerated the shift from analogue to digital formats and was the decisive force that drew together the range of sophisticated digital technologies.

The history of media and communication has been punctuated by important technological innovations and these have always had significant social and economic consequences. Digitisation, however, is seen by many commentators as representing an especially dramatic moment of technologically-driven change. And, certainly, the media in the 'digital age' possess features that seem to set them apart from their predecessors. Compared to analogue technology, for example, digital formats allow a much greater compression of data, making it possible for broadcast systems to carry many more times the volume of information. Digital technology, therefore, has facilitated a shift to 'narrowcasting', with producers able to tailor media content to specific niche (even individualised) market segments. As we saw in Chapter 3, this trend has been exemplified by the proliferation of cable and satellite TV channels and digitial radio stations targeted at particular sections of the youth market.

Greater dimensions of interactivity are also possible with digital technology. Digitally-based websites, games, DVDs and TV services all allow for new, innovative ways for audiences to participate in, perhaps even take control of, the processes of media consumption. In itself, the character of the web is distinctly interactive, users creating their own 'trails' through cyberspace as they click through an infinite matrix of hypertext links. Computer games, with a strong appeal to the youth market, also offer a strong sense of interactivity. The first video games of the 1970s such as Atari's *Pong* (launched in 1975) and Midway's *Space Invaders* (1978) were relatively crude, but their interactive interface seemed dazzlingly exciting compared to the relative passivity of watching television.[2] The development of games played from a first-person perspective further heightened the immersive experience of computer gaming. The release of id Software's *Wolfenstein 3-D* and *Doom*, in 1992 and 1993 respectively, inaugurated the 'first person shooter' – games where the players adopt the first person perspective of combatants moving through an arena of three-dimensional carnage. Hugely successful, 'first person shooters' propelled the phenomenal growth of video and computer gaming, with the world market for leisure software tripling in value between 1995 and 2002, to reach a figure of nearly $17 billion.

Also significant is the degree of media convergence made possible by digital technology. Whereas analogue media relied on a variety of non-compatible formats, the use of digital code by 'new' media means they share a common form of data storage and distribution. This enables text, images and sound to be easily combined in one service, and allows for greater compatability between different delivery 'platforms' (for example, computers, CDs, DVDs and so on). This greater convergence between media formats has also brought increasing overlap and interdependence between media products. As Chapter 3 demonstrated, media 'tie-ins'and cross-promotions are nothing new, but the convergence of digital media forms has allowed a much greater degree of media intertextuality and marketing synergy. Films such as the *Mortal Kombat* (1995, 1997) and *Tomb Raider* series (2001, 2003), for example, were modelled after successful computer games, while *Tomb Raider* heroine Lara Croft became a cultural icon of the late 1990s, her pneumatic figure circulating across a multititude of media products. Websites, meanwhile, now exist not simply to promote popular movies, TV programmes, games and recording artists, but often serve as important adjuncts to the 'original' text. The convergence of digital, satellite and cable technology, moreover, has transformed systems of media distribution, allowing producers to escape the geographical, cultural and regulatory boundaries that formerly governed media circulation and reception. In these terms, Marshall McLuhan's notion of the 'global village' may have become a reality, Brian McNair arguing that the rise of 'new media' technologies has engendered 'the most radical dissolution of the barriers of time and space which have constrained human communication since we left the savannas and learnt to use language' (McNair, 2002: 188).

Room exists, however, to qualify some of the more grandiose and celebratory claims made for the impact of new media technology. The 'new' media, for example, have supplemented rather than swept away older formats. Significant continuities exist between 'old' and 'new', with 'new' media systems relying on existing technologies such as established TV services and telephone lines, while most 'new' media platforms have depended on the repackaging of older material (the success of CD sales, for instance, relying on the re-issue of artists' back catalogues). McLuhan's vision of the global media 'village', meanwhile, may still be a long way off since the world remains starkly divided between the 'media rich' and the 'media poor'. In 2002, for example, over 53 per cent of the US population had access to the internet, while in Britain the figure stood at around 40 per cent. But this compared to barely 8 per cent of the population of Brazil, 1.5 per cent of the population of India and under 1 per cent of the whole of Africa (International Telecommunications Union, 2003).

Technological innovations, moreover, have not emerged in a vacuum. Rather than being a force that exists independent of society, technological development is always deeply embedded in a wider nexus of social, economic and political relations. In these terms, the proliferation of 'new' media systems can be seen (at least partly) as a consequence of political and industrial pressures for the liberalisation of economic markets during the 1980s and 1990s. As many countries loosened the regulation of their media structures, large business corporations scrambled to take advantage of the new business opportunities, moves which relied upon the exploitation of (and, in turn, stimulated the further development of) new media formats and quicker, more efficient forms of trans-global communication.

As the new media and communications technologies initially took shape, optimistic pundits such as Nicholas Negroponte (co-founder of the influential Media Lab at the Massachusetts Institute of Technology) argued that they held out the promise of a more decentralised and democratic business environment. For Negroponte, the relative cheapness, greater accessibility and ease of operation of digital technologies would undermine the grip of huge companies, leading instead to the emergence of 'new players, new economic models and a likely cottage industry of information and entertainment providers' (Negroponte, 1995: 18). However, the collapse of media empires and proliferation of grassroots activity envisioned by Negroponte has yet to be realised. Digitised media may have given consumers more choice (in terms of an expanded set of available options), but the playing-field remains dominated by the major business corporations who have deployed the full power of the new technologies in their attempts to exploit and control lucrative global markets. Contrary to Negroponte's vision, then, the media big boys have retained their grip on the world of information and commercial entertainment through licensing and copyright restrictions, strategic alliances and takeovers – the 2001 mega-merger between communications giant

Time-Warner and internet provider AOL showing how a growing convergence of media formats had, in turn, spurred greater moves towards business conglomeration.

The major corporations have also sought to neutralise any potential threat new media technologies might pose to their structures of cultural control and their ability to channel profits. Indicative of this resolve were the (aforementioned) internet '*Buffy* wars' and other campaigns mounted against unofficial online fandom. Also illustrative was the Napster saga of 1999–2000. Based on a form of file-sharing software, Napster was launched as an online music-swapping service in May 1999, its users able to locate and trade thousands of songs stored as MP3 files (a recording format launched in 1997 and able to compress digital recordings without sacrificing sound quality). Within six months, however, the Napster corporation was being sued for copyright infringement by the Recording Industry Association of America (RIAA).[3] The case went badly for Napster and by 2002 the company had been driven into near bankruptcy. As the campaign against illegal downloads continued, the 'legitimate' market for online music proliferated. The expansion was spurred-on by the launch of Apple Computers' personal digital music player, the iPod, in 2001 and Apple's online music store, iTunes – launched in the United States in 2003 and selling more than 70 million downloads in its first year of business.

At the same time, however, the power of the major corporations has not been invincible. While Napster was soon emasculated, other file-sharing and peer to peer (P2P) services – such as Bearshare.com, Gnutella and Freenet – quickly took its place.[4] And, despite the best efforts of media corporations like Fox and Viacom, a legion of unofficial fan websites continue to thrive, while the 'Buffy Bringers' have broadened their remit to become an international pressure group working to defend online fan culture.[5]

In the digital age consumers are not the helpless victims of big corporations, but the new communications technologies have certainly allowed the major media producers to monitor, segment and target markets much more effectively. A dramatic leap forward in consumer surveillance, the new technologies allow companies to amass a wealth of sophisticated sales data through the analysis of interactive media usage. As Michael Dawson and John Bellamy Foster have observed:

> The interactive nature of the information superhighway offers the possibility of detailed information on each potential buyer . . . Nowadays the focus is on 'hypertargeting' in which the market segment is frequently an individual household or even an individual.
>
> (Dawson and Foster, 1996: 57)

Using digital and internet technology, a wealth of detailed information can be recorded about consumer tastes and transactions. This allows for increasingly specific targeting by product developers and advertisers. Even the data itself can be a valuable commodity, able to be sold on to other interested agencies – and the continued spending power of young people makes the youth market an especially attractive online prize.

## THE 'NET GENERATION': NEW MEDIA AND THE YOUTH MARKET

New media and communications technologies have come to play an increasingly significant role in young people's lives. According to empirical data collected by Sonia Livingstone and Moira Bovill in 1999, for example, nearly all British households with children and teenagers had a television and video recorder, two-thirds had a TV-linked games machine and nearly half had cable or satellite television. Of the newer media, meanwhile, over half these households had a personal computer, while four in ten had multiple television channels, and a rapidly growing minority had internet access (Livingstone, 2002: 37). Moreover, as Livingstone emphasised, these figures were swiftly increasing. Indeed, by 2000 statistics produced by the market researchers National Opinion Poll showed a pronounced growth in the ownership of new media technology. According to their data, the proportion of British households where children and teenagers had access to a computer had grown to 70 per cent, access to a mobile phone had risen to 77 per cent and access to the internet had increased to 36 per cent (with 75 per cent of 7–16-year-olds having used the internet in one location or other by 2001) (cited in Livingstone, 2002: 38). American figures were equally high, a study produced by the Kaiser Family Foundation in 1999 showing that 69 per cent of US households possessed a computer, with 7 per cent of American children able to access the internet from their bedroom (Rideout et al., 1999: 10–14).

Young people's growing access to new communications technology has made a big impression on marketing interests. In 2000, for example, market research by Nickelodeon Online/Harris Interactive KidPulse suggested that online spending by American 18- to 24-year-olds was four times greater than that among older age groups (Pastore, 2000). The following year, market analysts Datamonitor urged marketers to take advantage of the more than 65 million youngsters aged between five and seventeen who had internet access at home and wielded, it estimated, a collective spending power of $60 billion (Pastore, 2001). While the rate of young people's access to the internet varied from country to country,

Datamonitor calculated that by 2005 74 per cent of the youth population in Western Europe and North America would have regular access to the web, representing an auspicious market for those advertisers able to exploit the advantages of internet technology. Generic, teen-oriented websites, Datamonitor warned, were unable to appeal to young consumers with sufficient force or precision. Instead, narrowcasting was suggested as a much more effective way of pursuing youth spending, the agency advising marketers to seek out websites designed around the specific characteristics of their target audience.

Nevertheless, *some* generic teen sites have enjoyed significant success. During the late 1990s attempts to cash-in on the elusive 'Generation Y' market (for whom computers and the internet were second nature) saw the launch of numerous commercial websites in the US. Some, such as Delias.Com, were little more than web-based shopping catalogues for teens. But others blended their e-commerce with attempts to build a sense of online community. Bolt, for example, emulated the friendly sociability of a teen magazine. Boasting over 800,000 members, Bolt kicked-off its home page with a profile of its 'Member of the Day', and offered subscribers chatrooms, quizzes, polls, horoscopes and a rolling feed of headlines to hot 'Gen-Y' stories ('Student Suspended for Blue Hair' and other burning issues of the moment). Bolt promoted itself as a communications platform that enabled young adults 'to interact in a relevant, member-created environment', though to advertisers it also pushed its potential as a gateway to the 15- to 24-year-old market. Through its 'relationship with and access to millions of teens', Bolt advised its potential clients, the company could 'generate data and behavior analyses that result in tremendous CRM (Customer Relationship Management) capabilities and targeted messaging opportunities'. In a similar fashion, Alloy Online promoted itself as a 'Teen Community Site', embedding its advertising and sales content in pages of advice columns ('How do I get rid of hickeys?'), sports coverage and music. In 2003 even Microsoft were developing new ways to cash-in on the online 'Gen-Y' market, the computing colossus launching a specialised NetGen division – a team of recent college graduates whose brief was to develop software products geared to the interests of the 'Net Generation' (teens and young adults who had grown up with the internet and felt at ease with online media).

'Generation Y', however, were not the only group of new media consumers to be targeted by 'youth' marketers. As Chapter 3 argued, during the late twentieth century qualities of 'youthfulness' became increasingly detached from a specific demographic category and instead became associated with particular mindsets and consumer lifestyles. This was especially evident in the spheres of media and entertainment, where many industries that had traditionally focused on youth demand began to direct their sales drive to consumers who were older (and more afflu-ent), yet who seemed to retain a 'youthful' interest in leisure, style, and hedonistic patterns of consumption. Trends in the sales of computer and video games were one of the clearest examples of the rise of this 'grey-ing youth' market. According to Games Investor (a British consultancy firm specialising in the games industry), the mid-1990s saw a clear shift in the games market. After 1995, Games Investor argued, the average age of players of computer and video games rose significantly. In the UK, buyers of games for personal computers were the oldest, with magazine surveys suggesting the average age of players was between 27 and 31 years old (similar surveys in the US suggested American computer gamers were slightly older, at between 32 and 36 years old). The mar-ket for video console games was younger, but in Britain the average age of the PlayStation gamer still stood at around 25 to 30 years old, while the average Nintendo buyer was between 18 and 25 (Games Investor, 2003). The trend towards older consumers was the outcome of several factors. Partly, it was due to many first generation (1980s) teenage gamers remaining active players as they grew to adulthood. Increased cost also began to put games platforms and software out of the reach of many younger consumers. But also important was a conscious shift in marketing focus, with games companies increasingly targeting an older 'youth' market. A landmark of the shift was the launch of Sony's 32-bit PlayStation in 1995. With advertising pitched towards club culture and hip 'twenty-somethings', the PlayStation developed a userbase much older than that of previous games consoles and pointed the way towards the future development of the video and computer games industry.

Marketing excitement, moreover, disguises the way many young people have been left out of the 'digital revolution'. In America, for example, a survey published by the Kaiser Family Foundation in 2001 pointed to marked patterns of inequality in young people's access to, and use of, the internet. According to the study, while 90 per cent of teens and young adults (aged 15 to 24) had experience of going online, import-ant disparities existed between different ethnic and socio-economic groups. For example, the research found that while just 6 per cent of white youth had never been online, this compared to 13 per cent of African-American youth and one in four Hispanic youngsters. And, while 93 per cent of upper- and upper-middle-class youths had been online, this compared to only 85 per cent of their working-class peers (Rideout, 2001: 15–17).

Research conducted in Britain by Keri Facer and Ruth Furlong (2001) also challenged pervasive images of a young generation who were the confident citizens of a technologically saturated society. In a study based on young people in southwest England and south Wales, Facer and Furlong drew attention to the large number of young people who either actively disassociated themselves from computer use or struggled to gain access and expertise. According to their findings, financial or cultural issues within particular families sometimes determined whether children had home access to a computer. Broadly, however, Facer and Furlong found that disparities between young people's access to computers reproduced existing inequalities along lines of gender, ethnicity and socio-economic class.

Even more significantly, Facer and Furlong's research suggested that many young people did not share wider society's high regard for new technologies. 'Far from being seen as the key to successful participation in the "real world"', they found that certain peer groups 'argued that computer use, quite simply was not relevant to their day-to-day activities' (Facer and Furlong, 2001: 466). In some cases young people were even developing entrenched positions against new technologies, identifying themselves as 'non-computer users' and proudly wearing the claim as an important element of their identity (ibid.). In sum, Facer and Furlong concluded, the numbers of young people who shunned computers, or who struggled to gain skills in their use, meant that the prevalent image of young people as technologically proficient 'cyberkids' needed to be radically rethought.

## INVASION OF THE CYBERKIDS: REPRESENTATIONS OF YOUTH AND NEW MEDIA

Popular notions of a new, technologically dexterous generation of 'cyberkids' reproduce the symbolic dimensions that have long characterised representations of youth. As was seen in Chapter 4, media images of young people and public debates about youth culture have invariably condensed wider themes and issues, concepts of 'youth' encapsulating perceptions of more general shifts in cultural life and their consequences. The conflation of youth and technological progress makes for an especially potent symbolic combination. Representations of youth and technology both have the capacity to serve as motifs of social change, so the synthesis of the two creates a particularly powerful narrative of society's potential for both improvement and deterioration. As Julian Sefton-Green has observed:

The concept of an 'audio-visual generation' (or what seems to be called, at the moment 'cyberkids') seems to have become a shorthand way of labelling these hopes and fears, and it clearly illustrates how each category seems to have become a way of talking about the other.

(Sefton-Green, 1998: 2)

Media images of the hi-tech 'cyberkid' have reproduced the duality central to the history of popular representations of youth. In the concept of the 'cyberkid' the contrasting stereotypes that Hebdige (1988b: 19) termed 'youth-as-fun' and 'youth-as-trouble' have frequently been reiterated. In the broadly optimistic version of the 'cyberkid' mythology, youth is cast as the spearhead of a new digital epoch that heralds an unprecedented expansion of knowledge and greater opportunities for community participation, self-expression and creativity. Pessimistic accounts, however, present new media technologies as having a pernicious impact on the young, with video games seen as triggering violence and computer-based media portrayed as promoting unfulfilling and excessively privatised lifestyles. Neither the optimistic nor the pessimistic version of the 'cyberkid' myth bears much relation to the realities of young people's engagement with new media – but both have been an influential presence in popular discourse.

Writing in *Wired* magazine in 1996, media critic Jon Katz crystallised the optimistic version of the 'cyberkid' myth in his argument that youth was 'the epicenter of the information revolution, ground zero of the digital world' (Katz, 1996). For Katz, young people were the harbingers of a new, technologically-driven era of freedom and opportunity. 'Not only is the digital world making the young more sophisticated, altering their ideas of what culture and literacy are', Katz enthused, 'it is connecting them to one another, providing them with a new sense of political self'. The young, Katz concluded, 'occupy a new kind of cultural space. They're citizens of a new order, founders of the Digital Nation' (ibid.). Katz's portrait of young people using the web to 'reach past the suffocating boundaries of social convention' echoed claims that the very nature of new communications systems offered unique horizons of cultural autonomy. Authors such as Ilana Snyder (1998), for example, have argued that the structure of the world wide web is inherently empowering to the reader. Multi-authored and composed of infinite, unbounded hypertext pathways, the web is seen as challenging the traditional, linear hierarchies of knowledge that have characterised printed texts. Other authors have been even more Utopian in their depiction of the liberatory, even revolutionary, potential of new media technologies. Former countercultural drugs guru, Timothy Leary, was especially enthusiastic. Having coined the phrase 'Turn On, Tune In and Drop Out' in the late 1960s to proselytise what he saw as the consciousness-expanding properties of LSD, Leary became fascinated with the potential of computer-mediated communications to provide equally revelational experiences. The early 1990s saw Leary eulogise the anarchy of cyber-space, arguing that it was a path to a new humanism denoted by independent thought, a questioning of authority and virtually limitless individual creativity (Leary, 1994).

Douglas Rushkoff also emerged as a leading advocate of the internet's radical possibilities. In *Cyberia: Life in the Trenches of Cyberspace* (1994), Rushkoff presented the unfolding terrain of digital information as a richly imaginative cultural landscape being tapped by a maverick 'cyberian counterculture'. A snappy, wide-eyed travelogue through the subcul-tures of cyberspace, *Cyberia* charted a surge of 'techno-utopianism' among young ravers, performance artists and writers who shared a faith in the creative and emancipatory potential of the new technologies. A more measured, though still somewhat romantic, tour was offered by Mark Dery. In *Escape Velocity: Cyberculture at the End of the Century* (1996), Dery chronicled the rise of a high-tech underground of cyberpunks, cybernauts and technopagans who used computer technology in ways that were never intended (indeed, in some instances would have been totally unimaginable) by its manufacturers. Among others, the intriguing groups profiled by Dery included New Age cyber-hippies who used the personal computer in obscure mystical rituals, would-be cyborgs who dreamt of downloading their minds into computers, and online swingers who plied for cyber-sex in a virtual boudoir. All were a far cry from the humdrum world of Microsoft spreadsheet programmes.

In the early, freebooting days of the internet, the eager idealism of authors such as Leary, Rushkoff and Dery seemed persuasive. But, in today's online world of e-commerce and exclusive web domains, claims for the inherent egalitarianism of computer-based communications are less convincing. Michael Joyce (1998), for example, has highlighted the ways the world wide web is more hierarchical than the idealists assumed – with movement through the web being constrained by the design of pages, the structure of links and the commercial principles of many search engines. John Caldwell (2002) has also seen the development of the inter-net as reviving the very forms of 'old' media commercialism that it once promised to transcend. 'With hundreds of players vying for fewer eye-balls per site', Caldwell observed, 'only the players with very deep finan-cial pockets tend to last the distance' (Caldwell, 2002: 58). Successful survival in cyberspace, therefore, demanded the traditional business economies of scale and reach. According to Caldwell, moreover, the internet may once have been 'rhizomatic in structure rather than linear or hierarchical', but media corporations had increasingly regulated its operation through subscription policies, encryption schemes and contractual alliances with major web portals (such as AOL, Lycos and Earthlink). In these terms, then, the 'Digital Nation' of the cyberkid begins to look somewhat less democratic and diverse than the excited optimists prophesised.

Scarcely more accurate, however, have been the negative representations of the relationship between youth and new media. As Chapter 4 demonstrated, wider social anxieties have frequently been projected onto youth. Coining the term 'media panic', Kirsten Drotner (1992) argued that these successive episodes of alarm often focused on the perceived consequences of technological innovation, with young people presented as being in the forefront of potentially harmful and socially destructive media developments. As each new medium has been introduced, Drotner argued, there has been a kind of historical amnesia about previous panics, with earlier media achieving social acceptance while the new form becomes a focus for a fresh wave of fearful concern. In Drotner's terms, therefore, apprehensions about the impact of new media technology on young people could be seen as the latest in a long line of 'media panics' that reflect broader political agendas and attempts to define (and impose) particular cultural standards and values.

Early concerns about young people and new media speculated that the rise of computer-based leisure was creating a generation of socially isolated couch potatoes dependent on an addictive 'fix' of cynically marketed techno entertainment. In Britain, for example, 1993 saw journalist Catherine Bennett suggest of computer games that 'after crack-cocaine they are one of the most perfect forms of capitalism ever devised' (Bennett, 1993), and in the same year the Professional Association of Teachers published an information sheet warning that computer games might discourage children from reading and writing and could promote aggression. Empirical research conducted by Livingstone and Bovill, however, has painted a very different picture. While young people valued using media alone (often in 'media rich' bedrooms appointed with an array of electronic entertainment), the researchers found that this privatisation of media consumption did 'not necessarily mean that social contacts are being replaced with social isolation' (Livingstone, 2002: 158). Instead, Livingstone explained, 'it seems that teenagers are incorporating new media into their peer networks, using both face-to-face and online communication, visiting each other's houses to talk about and play computer games just as they visited and swapped comics a generation before, using new media to supplement rather than displace existing activities' (Livingstone, 2002: 7). Far from rendering older forms of communication and entertainment obsolete, therefore, new media were adding to youth's available options, even 'to some extent prompting new, more *sophisticated*, uses for books, television, radio etc.' (Livingstone, 2002: 89).

Initially, alarm also surrounded the image of a new generation of technologically skilled but mischievous *wunderkinder* who had the ability to 'hack' into, and wreak havoc upon, the world's computer systems. An early version of the theme featured in the movie *War Games* (1983) in which a teenage techno-wizard unwittingly taps his home computer into the Pentagon's defence network, bringing the world to the brink of nuclear war. During the 1990s, however, these concerns were eclipsed by a revival of fears based on crude notions of media 'effects' – with a flurry of anxiety focusing on video games as a possible cause of violent behaviour by young people. As we saw in Chapter 4, particular alarm was sparked in America by a spate of high-school shootings such as that at Columbine in 1999. Although no evidence existed to support a causal link, the killers' interest in video games was widely blamed as a crucial influence on their actions. In the furore that followed, the ideas of David Grossman attracted widespread publicity. A former army Lieutenant Colonel and a Professor of Military Science at Arkansas State University, Grossman emerged as a leading critic of computer games following the publication of his book, *On Killing* (1995). Seeing marked parallels between the simulation training used to prepare soldiers for combat and the immersive experience of 'first person shooter' video games, Grossman concluded that games like *Doom* and *Quake* not only enhanced young people's weapons skills but also broke down the psychological barriers that prevented youngsters from killing.[6]

Views such as Grossman's attracted a great deal of media attention. But the results of social scientific research into possible links between computer games-playing and youth violence have been inconsistent and ambiguous. The overviews of video game research have been just as variable in their conclusions as the individual studies they survey. From a social-psychological perspective, for example, reviews by Craig Anderson and Brad Bushman (2001) and Eugene Provenzo (1991) argued that available research clearly demonstrated a causal relation between violent video games and aggressive behaviour among young people. Much of the research on which these conclusions were based, however, was vulnerable to the same criticisms that can be levelled at media 'effects' research more generally. Chapter 4 showed how such research tends to rely on laboratory-based experiments far removed from 'real-life' situations and relationships, while their focus on the collection of quantitative data often gives scant regard to the social process through which audiences make meanings from media texts. Indeed, studies produced by authors such as Guy Cumberbatch *et al.* (1993) and by Jessica Harris for the British Home Office (2001) found that insufficient information existed to support notions of a simple 'cause-and-effect' relationship between computer games-playing and violence. Overall, the evidence suggesting that playing computer games promotes aggression is (at very most) patchy, and the conclusions reached by Kevin Durkin in his 1995 review of the field remain pertinent. In his report produced for the Australian Broadcasting Authority, Durkin was circumspect, arguing that:

> although the research is not exhaustive and by no means conclusive, it indicates that the stronger negative claims are not supported. Computer games have not led to the development of a generation of isolated, antisocial, compulsive computer users with strong propensities for aggression.
>
> (Durkin: 1995: 71)

Other concerns, however, have also surrounded young people's use of new media. During the 1990s the difficulties in applying conventional forms of censorship to the internet prompted marked concern about the ease with which youngsters could access digital pornography. In America, a 1995 cover story in *Time* magazine demonstrated the level of anxiety. 'Cyberporn' by Philip Elmer-Dewitt purported to be the 'first survey of online erotica', and in melodramatic terms ostensibly revealed how pornography on the internet was 'popular, pervasive and surprisingly perverse' (Elmer-Dewitt, 1995). Underscoring the feature's shocking revelations, the magazine's cover depicted children as especially vulnerable to the sinister influence of internet pornography – the cover illustration depicting a young boy's face bathed in the reflected glow of a computer terminal, his eyes wide with astonishment. The story, however, prompted widespread criticism from academics and journalists who highlighted how the feature (and the research on which it drew) was riddled with conceptual, logical and methodological flaws.[7] Certainly, critics conceded, pornography was widely available on the internet, though the *Time* article had greatly exaggerated its nature and extent. Moreover, critics argued, the sensationalist journalism of the feature fuelled concerns about the negative social impact of pornography on young people when the existing evidence was inconclusive.

By the end of the decade concerns about the impact of 'cyberporn' on young people had been overshadowed by anxieties focused on the circulation of child pornography on the internet and its use by paedophiles in the abuse of children. In 2003, for example, the annual report of Britain's National Criminal Intelligence Service stated that the number of websites containing child pornography had risen by 64 per cent worldwide within a year and draft legislation in the UK proposed to make 'internet grooming' (adults' online solicitation of children with the intention of sexually abusing them) a specific criminal offence.[8] According to Chas Critcher (2003), however, British responses to the problem of paedophilia had all the hallmarks of a classic moral panic. According to Critcher, the sexual abuse of children was a genuine problem, though its magnitude remained unclear and sensationalised media representations of 'the paedophile' simply served to distort our understanding of both sexual attacks on children and those who perpetrate them (Critcher, 2003: 116–117). The role of the internet in the possible growth of child abuse remains unclear and further research is necessary. Arguments made by Critcher about the changing form of contemporary moral panics, however, seem to be supported by shifts in popular concern about the relation between young people and new media. An apparent shift in anxiety – away from the supposedly pernicious influence of video games and towards the dangers of 'internet grooming' – would seem to bear out Critcher's suggestion that the portrayal of *youth* as vulnerable to the *effects* of external influences has been increasingly displaced by the presentation of *children* as the *victims* of folk devils (2003: 162).

Media representations of the 'cyberkid' generation, then, have been loaded with powerful connotations. In popular discourse, images of technologically proficient youngsters in a media-saturated digital world have embodied both the promise of a hi-tech future and (at the same time) its potential dangers. The 'cyberkid' myth, however, bears scant relation to young people's day-to-day engagement with new media. Social research has painted a much more complex picture, suggesting young people's uses of digital media are multi-faceted and defined by the widely different social and interpersonal contexts in which they take place.

## ARE FRIENDS ELECTRIC?: NEW MEDIA, YOUTH AND COMMUNAL NETWORKS

Recent studies of young people's uses of new media have rebutted crude 'effects' paradigms that present youth as the victim of the media's irresistable (and generally harmful) influence. Also challenged, however, are the celebratory accounts of subcultural 'resistance' and consumer autonomy that featured (as we saw in Chapter 6) in many accounts of youth culture produced from the 1970s to the early 1990s. Instead, more recent research presents young people's uses of new media as varied and nuanced, shaped by an interplay of diverse social, cultural and economic forces.

Both advertisers and Utopian visionaries (such as Timothy Leary) have extolled the potential for digital technology to open up new vistas of dazzling creativity. Empirical research, however, has suggested that young people's everyday use of new technology is more prosaic. Julian Sefton-Green and David Buckingham's (1998) study of schoolchildren's home use of digital technology was especially revealing. Intially, Sefton-Green and Buckingham were intrigued when nearly 20 per cent of their sample claimed to use computers for media production of some kind – including graphics work, music production, animation and video editing. Subsequent discussions revealed, however, that the students regarded their activities as simply 'messing around'. Indeed, their actual use of the technology was generally not planned or structured, but was a 'casual, occasional or time-filling activity', with the respondents using computers 'as a way of occupying themselves when lonely or bored' (Sefton-Green and Buckingham, 1998: 74). This pattern of usage, the researchers argued, challenged notions that access to computers in itself allowed young people to become creative cultural producers. But, while their findings questioned some of the more populist claims made for 'creative consumption', Sefton-Green and Buckingham speculated that their study might point towards 'a broader, and perhaps less romantic, conception of creativity' (1998: 77). Young people's experience of digital technology, they suggested, effectively blurred the boundaries between production and consumption, so that 'what counts as a "text" – or indeed as a creative work of art – becomes subject to a wide range of definitions' (1998: 63).

Perhaps the most dramatic impact of new technologies on young people's lives has been on the way they establish, cultivate and maintain their social relationships. Here, the spectacular proliferation of mobile phones has been especially significant. In Britain, young people's ownership of mobile phones rose sharply following the introduction of prepaid 'pay-as-you-go' phones in the mid-1990s. According to the market researchers MORI, the proportion of 15- to 17-year-olds in Britain who owned a mobile phone leapt from 23 per cent in 1999 to 70 per cent in 2000. The proportion was roughly the same in Japan and was even higher in Scandinavia, though the take-up was slower in the US, where less than 50 per cent of teenagers owned a mobile.[9] The number of young American users, however, was quickly growing and their use of mobile phones outpaced all other sections of the US market in terms of number of calls placed, minutes used, text messages sent and wireless data used.

This spectacular growth of mobile phone ownership among the young was partly a consequence of parental desire to ensure the safety of (and surveillance of) their children – but the possession and use of mobiles also quickly became an important element within young people's peer culture.

Mobile phones have become a key means through which young people mediate their social relationships. For teenagers, especially, possession of a phone offers both a sense of independence and access to a network of friendship groups. Indeed, Australian-based research by Patricia Gillard and her associates has suggested that the rise of mobile phone technology may be increasing the importance of peer group relations in young people's lives. Possession of a mobile phone, they found, made it possible for young people to 'carry' their friends around with them – not only into public spaces like the school, but also into the private spaces of the home, so that for teenagers 'the combination of a private space at home and intimate talk with friends may mean that friends become more influential in their emotional development and well being' (Gillard *et al.*, 1998: 150).

SMS (Short Message Service) or 'texting' has also developed into an important medium of communication within youth peer groups. Originally conceived as a new paging system for busy professionals, the success of SMS took many in the phone industry by surprise. Whereas services such as WAP (Wireless Application Protocol, allowing phone access to the internet) were slow to take off, the more simplistic medium of 'texting' rapidly became a communications phenomenon. Youth, especially, quickly laid claim to SMS as a medium for establishing and developing peer group relations and friendships. In Britain, for example, fieldwork conducted by the Digital World Research Centre (DWRC) in 2001 found that mobile phones were *de rigeur* among teenagers and that the use of SMS was ubiquitous. The popularity of texting, however, could not be explained simply by its cheapness and ease of use. Instead, the DWRC researchers found that the exchange of text messages and the sharing of phones had evolved into a ritualised form of 'gift-giving' that worked to express and cement young people's friendships:

> For young people, the rituals of exchange, mediated through phone use, are . . . dependent on trust and reciprocity. The phone provides young people with a means of both demonstrating and testing out the trust that exists in their relationships. This is born out through meeting their obligations to reciprocate. The mutual dependence that derives from obligations, such as replying to text messages or repaying borrowed credit, binds people

> together, establishing and reinforcing the moral order of friendship and social
> intimacy. The mobile phone, then, is one of the many objects that young
> people use to perform the rituals of communion embodied in the exchange
> of the tangible.
>
> (Taylor and Harper, 2001: 18)

For young people, then, mobile phones and text messaging were a medium through which social relationships were demonstrated and maintained. The DWRC researchers found, moreover, that the constant flurries of text messaging sometimes spilled over into teenagers' home lives, so that peer culture relationships extended into even the 'private' realm of the home. Overall, mobile phones were a pervasive feature of contemporary youth culture, the DWRC study describing how phones would be 'placed on the tables to be seen, pressed and prodded during frenzied chatter, gestured with to emphasise talk, and shared between small gatherings to view the latest text messages, game scores and address book entries' (Taylor and Harper, 2001: 4). Mobile phones have also become a medium for self-expression. Of course, sleek and trendy hand-sets from Nokia, Samsung, Motorola and Sony Ericsson represent stylish status symbols but, beyond this, young people also use their phones as a means to project their sense of identity. Mobile phones represent an avenue for the creation of individuality and self-image, young people customising and personalising their phones through the addition of ringtones, graphics, games and other content related to their tastes and interests.

Business was quick to recognise the market potential of youth culture's embrace of mobile phone technology. In 2003, for example, the American firm Wildseed were one of several phone manufacturers developing products specifically targeted at the youth market. Customising its phones around popular fashion themes, Wildseed offered a range of hi-tech 'smart skins' – replaceable faceplates with computer chips that allowed teenagers to change the phone's functions as well as its appearance.[10] The economic potential of such products was enormous. In their survey *mobileYouth 2003*, for example, market researchers Wireless World Forum (W2F) estimated that in developed markets young people spent up to 13.5 per cent of their disposable income on mobile phone products. In 2003, the report estimated, the youth market would spend around €13.4 billion on mobile data services, W2F estimating that the figure would grow to over €20 billion in 2006 (youth spending on ringtones alone amounting to €2.3 billion, with Japan, Korea, USA, Germany and the UK as the five largest markets) (W2F: 2003). Moreover, W2F told its clients, the idea that mobile products for the youth market needed to privilege 'fun' was a myth. Rather than being purely based on 'fun' and 'entertainment', the report advised, the best potential for long-term growth lay in the development of products that enabled young people to engage in peer group interaction. Commerce, therefore, seemed set to capitalise on the culture of exchange that had come to surround young people's use of mobile phone technology. Early moves were the growth of 'interactive' SMS advertising campaigns and the 'text voting' systems used in TV shows such as *Big Brother* and *Pop Idol* (*American Idol* in the US). Following such successes, further commercial development in this direction seemed inevitable.

Peer group dialogue and exchange also came to characterise young people's use of the internet and the world wide web. The growth of such computer-mediated 'virtual communities' has been championed by authors such as Howard Rheingold (1994). According to Rheingold, the growth of e-mail, websites, and conferencing systems has allowed the development of online societies that offer the same kind of interaction and relationships available in 'real-life' communities. Critics such as Kevin Robins (1996), however, have justifiably questioned cyber-Utopian claims that the internet can duplicate the social relations of 'real' communities and revitalise citizen-based democracy. Nevertheless, the development of the internet has certainly offered new possibilities for cultural participation and communication that have been used, according to Chris Abbott (1998), especially effectively by young people. For Abbott, the rise of e-mail, home pages and chatrooms has vastly increased young people's opportunities to communicate with friends and like-minded people around the world.

Abbott, however, has resisted some of the more sweeping claims made by figures such as Rheingold and Sherry Turkle (1995). These theorists celebrated the liberating potential of electronic communication networks, arguing they brought a 'postmodern' blurring of distinctions between reality and simulation that dissolved the boundaries of the self and created spaces for new, experimental and multiple forms of identity. In contrast, Abbott argued that the internet promoted 'complementarity rather than alterity' (1998: 97). That is to say, for most young users, the web did not represent an 'alternative world' but a setting where they connected with their peers, swapping opinions and comparing experiences in comparative safety. This culture of online dialogue has been both facilitated and exploited by commercial interests, illustrated by the proliferation of internet chat services aimed at the youth market and the growing numbers of young people using 'real time' chat sites and instant messenger programmes.[11] Indeed, significantly, the first software developed in 2003 by NetGen (Microsoft's specialised youth division) was a communal instant messaging service. Called 'Threedegrees', it was targeted at 13-to 24-year-olds and claimed to offer the experience of 'hanging-out online' – with groups of up to ten users able to chat together, share pictures and play one another music.

Computer technology has also been central to other forms of communal network among young people. Media images of teenage hackers inflicting chaos on the world's computer systems bear little relation to reality, but authors such as Jörgen Nissen (1998) have highlighted the development of groups of youngsters (mostly young men) who pride themselves on their illicit computer skills. Around the world, Nissen argues, clusters of young hackers prove their technical prowess by outwitting computer security measures and breaking copyright protection on software – their command of new media technology representing 'a tool for young boys to cultivate and master their existence and, at least symbolically, the pressures of modernity' (Nissen, 1998: 165).

New media technologies have also allowed fan cultures to proliferate. As the conflict between Twentieth Century Fox and Buffy fans in 2000 demonstrated, alongside official websites and promotions there has also developed a profusion of unofficial fan sites and discussion forums. According to Henry Jenkins (2002), these developments further extended the active, participatory dimensions he saw as central to the experience of fandom (see Chapter 6). Jenkins' analysis of online fan culture drew on Pierre Levy's (1997) concept of 'the cosmopedia' – a new, more democratic universe of cultural production and exchange that could emerge as people more fully realised the potential of the new media environment. For Jenkins, internet fan communities represented the fullest existing examples of 'the cosmopedia'. By increasing the speed and scope of communications, Jenkins suggested, new media technologies had allowed fandom to become a much more effective platform for 'consumer activism', with fans quickly able to mobilise grassroots efforts to save cherished programmes or protest against unpopular plot developments (2002: 161).

Utopian views of online communities as a font of inclusive harmony, however, are problematic. Empirical studies, for instance, have highlighted the existence of pronounced hierarchies and processes of exclusory 'gatekeeping' within internet fan networks.[12] Fans' online 'consumer activism', moreover, hardly compares to the power wielded by the corporate giants. Indeed, Jenkins acknowledged that the media conglomerates had been quick to protect their interests (evidenced by the '*Buffy* wars' and the moves against Napster), though he argued that some media industries had also used the internet to embrace fan audiences, seeking online feedback from fans and incorporating audience-generated content into their design processes. Jenkins was optimistic about these developments, arguing they enhanced the capacity of fans to be active media consumers. In many respects, however, industry use of fans' input might simply represent a refined strategy of market research that leaves relations of power and control essentially intact.

Nevertheless, there can be little doubt that new media technologies allowed for an outpouring of cultural production by fans. Digital technologies opened new avenues for the accumulation, appropriation and rearticulation of media content by fans, with an explosion of fan websites offering a multitude of images, news, fan fiction and discussion. The wider availability of new technology also facilitated a wave of DIY subcultural creativity. Helen Cunningham (1998), for example, highlighted the way club culture deployed digital technology in a wide range of innovative ways, including the creation of music; the development of visual art for display at club events; and the production of 'niche' and 'micro' media (such as fanzines and flyers). Cunningham suggested, moreover, that as more young people gained access to tools of production such as computers and camcorders they became producers as well as consumers. In the case of the club culture underground, she argued, there had been a blurring between the worlds of the professional and the amateur, many youngsters using the new technologies to turn their subcultural involvement into a successful livelihood (Cunningham, 1998: 142).

Cunningham acknowledged that masculine dominance in the world of technology was reproduced within club culture. Nevertheless, while the use of digital media was primarily the domain of young men, she argued that women clubbers were increasingly involved in practices of cultural production using new technology (Cunningham, 1998: 145). Elsewhere, Cunningham also detected greater use of new media by young women. Playing video games, for example, was a predominantly male pursuit during the late 1970s and 1980s, but Cunningham (1995) suggested that by the early 1990s female participation in games-playing had increased. As the context of playing computer games shifted from the 'street culture' of arcades to the home, she argued, the experience of games-playing for girls was transformed, with video and computer games increasingly integrated within young women's existing 'bedroom culture'.[13] The internet, too, may have been incorporated into the cultures of many young women. Marion Leonard (1998), for example, has described how the troop of fanzines related to the riot grrrl movement (see Chapter 6) were reworked as internet 'e-zines' and discussion groups linking young women from diverse geographic locations into a global riot grrrl network.

More widely, a burgeoning number of websites and internet discussion groups have become an important element in the infrastructure of

subcultural groups. Paul Hodkinson's (2002, 2003) study of goth subculture, for example, pointed to the huge amount of online information and
resources related to 'gothdom'. The development of the internet, moreover, had provided a new avenue through which young people could
participate in the construction of their own subculture. The availability
of free web space, Hodkinson argued, had allowed goths to create a mass
of home pages and websites. More up-to-date and interactive than
fanzines, these had effectively displaced their printed counterparts as the
subculture's key 'niche' and 'micro' media. Like Chris Abbott (1998),
however, Hodkinson challenged claims that life online had dissolved the
boundaries of cultural identity. Whereas authors such as Rheingold and
Turkle had presented the internet as a space for the creation of new,
more fluid and exploratory forms of identity, Hodkinson found that
goths' internet activity was actually used to enhance their existing attach-
ment to the subculture, their use of websites and discussion groups
serving 'to concentrate their involvement in the goth scene and to reinforce the boundaries of their grouping' (Hodkinson, 2002: 176). Rather
than melting cultural identities, Hodkinson argued, online resources
and forums had facilitated the goth subculture through circulating
knowledge, constructing values and generating friendships.

The growth of the internet also enhanced 'translocal' connections
within the subcultural universe. Websites and e-mail lists increased the
global reach of subcultural identities, with group members around the
world sharing ideas, opinions, and information with one another. Web-
based communication, for example, was crucial in the transnational
growth of the garage rock 'n' roll scene discussed at the beginning
of Chapter 7 – websites and newsgroups fostering the development of
a distinct group identity and facilitating the organisation of international festivals and events such as Spain's 2003 Wipeout Weekend
(see Chapter 7). In a similar fashion Richard Kahn and Douglas Kellner
(2003) drew attention to the important role of the internet in the development and organisation of the anti-globalisation movement that
began to emerge during the late 1990s (see Chapter 3). According to
Kahn and Kellner, computer-mediated activism was central to the rise of
this movement, the growth of 'global solidarity networks' depending on
the use of internet newsgroups, websites and e-mail 'to organize mass
demonstrations and to disseminate information to the world concerning
the policies of the institutions of capitalist globalization' (Kahn and
Kellner, 2003: 306).

In this way, the development of new media technologies could be seen
as leading to a redefinition of both 'national' and 'local' identities.
Offering instant communication across geographic boundaries, the digital

era may have seen the emergence of 'globalised' cultural identities based on shared tastes, values, politics or language that supersede (or at least supplement) traditional local and national affiliations. In some senses, this was a scenario supported by Hodkinson's study of goths. The connections created by goth websites and discussion groups, he argued, contributed to the greater consistency (both nationally and transnationally) of the subculture's values and tastes and enhanced individuals' sense of the goth identity as a translocal phenomenon. Nevertheless, despite the global potential of the internet, Hodkinson found that in practice the transnational dimensions of 'gothdom' were quite limited and did not represent the advent of a global goth 'village'. According to Hodkinson, the technological possibilities for everyday international communication were used by some British goths, but for the majority use of the internet had a more local focus – most goths using newsgroups and e-mail lists to develop friendships within Britain and to enhance their day-to-day participation in the subculture's national scene (Hodkinson, 2002: 188–189).

In *some* respects, then, the rise of new media and communication technologies may have profoundly altered *some* young people's perception of the world, redefining their experience of space and time and allowing distant events, places and people to enter more often into their everyday consciousness. Nevertheless, it is possible to exaggerate the social and cultural impact of the 'new' media. New technologies have supplemented rather than replaced 'old' media forms and, instead of heralding a quantum shift into an era of innovative social practices and cultural identities, new media technologies have been integrated within existing cultural contexts and relationships. In these terms, rather than laying the basis for a qualitatively unique 'digital' youth culture, emergent media forms and technologies have been shaped by young people and incorporated into their existing cultural relationships and everyday lives.

# 10

# CONCLUSION
## Youth, media and
## 'circuits of culture'

Where is meaning produced? Our 'circuit of culture' suggests, that, in
fact, meanings are produced at several different sites and circulate
through several different processes and practices . . . In discussing the
production of culture we . . . [are] not able to avoid talking about
consumption, representation or identity . . . This suggests that meaning-
making processes operating in any one site are always partially
dependent upon the meaning-making processes and practices operating
in other sites for their effect. In other words, meaning is not simply sent
from one autonomous sphere – production, say – and received in another
autonomous sphere – consumption. Meaning-making functions less in
terms of such a 'transmission' flow model, and more like the model of
a dialogue. It is an on-going process. It rarely ends at a preordained place.
No doubt the producers of cultural goods and services wish it did and
that they could permanently establish its boundaries!

(Paul Du Gay, 1997: 10)

Despite the economic recessions and industrial restructuring of the 1980s
and 1990s, the youth market has retained its economic significance.
Certainly, the labour markets that had underpinned the explosion of
'teenage' consumption in Europe and North America during the 1950s
and 1960s have been eroded, and young people's routes into full-time
work have become more protracted and diverse. But the youth market
has remained a cornerstone of the media, consumer and entertainment
industries. In 1993, for example, the Henley Centre for Forecasting

estimated that the British rave scene was worth between £1 and £2 billion a year (Veares and Woods, 1993) and, by the end of the 1990s, Ministry of Sound alone had an annual turnover in excess of £100 million. In 2003 the business analysts Datamonitor underscored young people's continuing market importance in their report *Young Adults' Consumption Behaviour* (Datamonitor, 2003). Surveying the demographics, income and spending patterns of 14- to 24-year-olds across seven European countries, Datamonitor confirmed that entry into full-time employment was being increasingly postponed, with the total number of students set to rise from 17.3 million in 2002 to 18.1 million by 2007. Yet Datamonitor insisted that youth would still represent a propitious commercial market. While young people's spending was unlikely to increase at a spectacular rate, Datamonitor forecast that growth would remain steady. In 2002, Datamonitor estimated, teenagers aged between 14 and 17 years old wielded a total income of €9.9 billion in Western Europe, a figure likely to climb to €10.8 billion by 2007 (equivalent to an annual average growth rate of 1.7 per cent). Over the same period, Datamonitor predicted, the total income of 18- to 24-year-olds in full-time education would rise from €114.7 billion to €133.0 billion, while the combined income of those in their first year of employment would grow from €33.8 billion to €34.9 billion (Datamonitor, 2003).

The youth market, then, was set to remain a key business sector. As such, the tastes and attitudes associated with 'youth', the factors which gave rise to the youth market and the media by which that market is reached, exercised broad economic and cultural influence. In advertising, especially, the iconography of youth had become a familiar means for investing products with a hip cachet. The advertising pitch used for many new models of car, for example, was indicative of the way marketers continued to mobilise 'youth' as an avatar for heady and exciting consumer lifestyles. In Autumn 2003, for instance, the UK launch of Citroen's new C2 hatchback was heralded by an 'Urban Cool' advertising campaign that aped TV reality shows such as *Pop Idol*, challenging audiences to be 'cool enough' to turn up to promotional events at preselected nightclubs.[1] Campaigns such as that for Citroen's C2 were partly aimed at young car-buyers (testifying to the continuing economic importance of the youth market), but they also sought to appeal to older consumers who aligned themselves with 'youthful' tastes and values. Expanding beyond its 'generational base', then, the youth market had come to include groups of adults who staked out their cultural identity through expressive, hedonistic and consumption-oriented lifestyles. Effectively, 'youth culture' was no longer confined to the young, but had come to denote a particular set of consumer attitudes and outlooks. In these terms, the economic impact of the youth market *and* the social meanings surrounding concepts of 'youth' have both figured as important influences in the development of modern consumption patterns and consumer cultures. In teasing out the economic flows and cultural connections that have characterised these processes of development, it is useful to draw on the concept of 'circuits of culture'.

Originally developed in the mid-1980s by Richard Johnson, the notion of 'circuits of culture' has been used by many researchers to make sense of the way media forms circulate, and generate meaning, within cultural life. According to Johnson, the analysis of a media text and its meanings demanded attention to the way it moved through a 'circuit' consisting of three main stages – production, textuality and reception. Each stage, Johnson argued, was distinct and involved 'characteristic changes of form', but were linked together in processes of interdependence and interaction so that '(e)ach moment or aspect depends upon the others and is indispensable to the whole' (Johnson, 1997: 83). Analytic perspectives that failed to acknowledge each stage of the circuit and its relation to the others, Johnson contended, could not adequately account for the form and meaning of media texts. As an example, Johnson pointed to the theoretical approaches deployed by authors associated with the film studies journal, *Screen*. The *Screen* authors, Johnson argued, had rightly distanced themselves from economistic approaches that interpreted the meaning of films as being solely determined by the structure of the film industry. But Johnson criticised the *Screen* theorists for ignoring the influence of business organisation altogether – choosing to focus all their analysis on the text itself and 'the virtual autonomy and absolute determinacy of "signification"' (Johnson, 1997: 99). For Johnson, issues of 'textuality' were certainly important facets to media analysis, but he maintained that they should not overshadow the other stages in the cultural circuit.

Johnson himself was keen to highlight the role of production and business organisation in the development of media texts and their cultural meanings. As we saw in Chapter 6, however, during the 1980s attention to questions of institutional power tended to be eclipsed by more idealist approaches. In the field of Cultural Studies, especially, media audiences and consumers were increasingly credited with 'symbolic creativity' and an active role in the creation of meaning. The emphasis on reception and active consumption was a commendable challenge to notions of manipulated 'mass' audiences and served as a valuable corrective to the one-sidedness of purely textual analysis. But the attention lavished on audience reception, consumption and creativity often neglected issues of production and control, leading to charges of a drift to an overly celebratory form of 'cultural populism' which emphasised 'local pleasures, consumption, and the construction of hybrid identities from the material of the popular' at the expense of attention to 'economics, history and politics' (Kellner, 1997: 104).

By the late 1990s a marked dualism had developed between political economists' attention to issues of production/control and cultural theorists' emphasis on dimensions of reception/creativity. In their attempts to transcend this divide, a number of authors returned to Johnson's notion of 'circuits of culture'. Taking up from Johnson's original model, for example, Paul Du Gay (1997) argued that media texts and cultural artefacts developed their meanings through a number of mutually constitutive processes. Refining Johnson's approach, Du Gay's analysis saw meanings as being continuously re-worked through a cultural circuit that consisted of five distinct processes – production, identity formation, representation, consumption and regulation. A full analysis of a cultural phenomenon, Du Gay argued, demanded adequate attention to each aspect of this circuit. Moreover, rather than seeing the circuit as following a linear path from production to consumption, Du Gay (like Johnson before him), emphasised the connections that existed between each stage, the different parts of the circuit continually overlapping and interacting in complex and contingent ways that varied over time and between different contexts. Rather than privileging any one key factor (such as production or consumption), then, Du Gay argued that meanings were formed through the way the different elements of the cultural circuit came together in particular circumstances.

Peter Jackson and his colleagues have taken a similar approach, giving attention to 'the links between commerce and culture not just at the level of representation, through discourse analysis and textual scrutiny, but also . . . at the level of practice, from the social relations of production into the cultures of consumption that characterise our everyday lives' (Jackson et al., 2000: 2). In their analysis of the rise of 1990s 'lads mags' such as Loaded and Maxim, for example, Jackson and his associates focused on the connections between cultural formations of gender and sexuality and the commercial structures of the magazine publishing industry (Jackson et al., 2001). The 'lads mags' phenomenon, they argued, illustrated the 'leakiness' of consumption circuits and commodity chains, with focus group participants relating the commercial success of men's lifestyle magazines to a nexus of cultural transformations that included the rise of the club scene, the blurring of distinctions between 'gay' and 'straight' commercial cultures, and the links between magazine publishing and other media forms (for example, popular TV shows). Angela McRobbie has argued for a comparable analytic approach in feminist cultural studies. For

McRobbie, post-structuralist insights into issues of subjectivity and identity had made a valuable contribution to feminist analyses of culture and the media, but this had often been at the expense of giving sufficient attention to factors such as business organisation and institutional policy, and their influence on cultural life. Instead, McRobbie advocated an approach that was informed by the insights of post-structuralist theory, but which combined these with a renewed attention to the 'three Es' – 'the empirical, the ethnographic and the experiential' (McRobbie, 1997: 186).

A 'multiperspective' approach can also be productively applied to the analysis of youth culture and its relation to the media. Drawing on the ideas of authors such as Du Gay, Jackson and McRobbie, it is possible to see the commercial youth market and young people's cultural formations as co-dependent sites within an inter-linked 'cultural circuit'. Here, meanings are not generated in any one sovereign sphere (for example, production or consumption), but through the articulation of a number of processes whose interplay can (and does) lead to variable and contingent outcomes. Within this circuit, questions of political economy are undoubtedly crucial. Indeed, in any analysis of texts and artefacts (TV shows, films, popular music, fashion) associated with young people's cultures, a consideration of the nature and organisation of their systems of production is imperative. Attention to issues such as business organisation, ownership and control highlights the (rarely equal) power relationships that underpin the production and circulation of media texts and cultural goods. A focus on the realm of political economy also reveals the underlying links between patterns of economic development and political ideology. During the 1980s and 1990s, for example, the rise of transnational media giants such as MTV and worldwide style corporations such as Diesel did not take place in a political vacuum, but was indebted to the ascension of political forces that championed economic liberalisation and the deregulation of global markets. Political policies have also impacted upon the character of 'youth' as a distinct life-stage. In both America and Europe, for example, the drive towards free-market economic policies has combined with the transformation of traditional labour markets to reconfigure young people's life experiences, so that passage into the 'adult' world of full-time employment has become both prolonged and less predictable.

Issues of political economy also draw attention to the importance of technological developments within the shifting relations of production – the rise of global business conglomerates relying on (and, in turn, further stimulating) the development of new communication technologies that have allowed for quicker and more efficient international flows of information and finance. Technological developments have also had an impact on the structures of production and the cultures of business organisation. Flexible, automated electronic technologies have allowed for the development of more specialised goods and services targeted not at a monolithic mass market, but at a series of distinctive consumer groups. In the youth market, for instance, this shift towards segmentation has been marked by the rise of 'niche' magazine titles, the burgeoning number of 'narrowcast' television channels and radio stations, and the rise of fashion brands geared to particular attitudes, values and lifestyles.

With the growth of 'flexible specialisation' and market segmentation issues of meaning and representation have also become more economically significant. In their attempt to address particular markets and lifestyle groups, producers have increasingly called upon the skills of designers, advertisers and marketers. These 'cultural intermediaries' have come to occupy a pivotal economic role, their expertise in signifying practices increasingly drawn upon by manufacturers in their efforts to invest products with desirable meanings and cultural associations. Effectively, then, the growing importance of cultural intermediaries lies in their ability to connect the sites of cultural production and cultural consumption. This has been especially apparent in the youth market, where the 1980s and 1990s saw a proliferation of forecasting agencies and 'coolhunting' specialists (Teenage Research Unlimited, Look-Look, Sputnik and the rest) who sought to chart the tastes and dispositions of young people, connecting producers with the attitudes and aspirations of a lucrative – but notoriously elusive – consumer group. The increased prominence of 'coolhunters', therefore, underlines the way the 'economic' and the 'cultural' are now inseparable. Practices of production and circulation have been increasingly inscribed with cultural meanings as manufacturers strive to encode their products with values and connotations ('hip', 'cool', 'street') attractive not only to young consumers, but also (increasingly) to older market segments whose sense of identity is configured around their embrace of expressive, hedonistic and distinctively 'youthful' lifestyles.

Questions of production, then, are inseparable from issues of representation and cultural identity. But processes of consumption also play a major role in the 'cultural circuit'. An exclusive focus on producers' attempts to invest their goods and services with particular meanings reveals little about what those products actually signify for the people using them. The use and appropriation of texts by audiences and consumers is always a crucial link in the 'cultural circuit'. Cultures of consumption, moreover, 'feed back into' sites of production and representation in an ongoing cycle of commodification. In the youth market, for example, producers draw on the 'symbolic expertise' of their army of 'cultural intermediaries' (market researchers, analysts and 'cool-hunters') in their attempts to track the cultural tastes of young consumers, developing texts and products inscribed with meanings attuned as closely as possible to the attitudes, tastes and values of a lucrative and influential market segment.

As Paul Du Gay and his associates explain, then, the cultural meanings of texts and artefacts are 'constructed through a dialogue – albeit rarely an equal one in terms of power relations – between production and consumption' (Du Gay *et al.*, 1997: 103). In these terms, any attempt to understand contemporary youth cultures and their relation to the commercial media demands attention to *all* aspects of this process – with consideration given to the way meanings are produced and circulate *throughout* the mutually constitutive sites of the 'cultural circuit'. Unless adequate attention is given to all the dimensions of this circuit – production, identity formation, representation, consumption and regulation – it is impossible to grasp the full cultural meanings and significance of pop music, fashion, film, video and the full panoply of 'youth media'.

# NOTES

## 1 Introduction

1   A more detailed account of this research can be found in Roberts and Foehr (2003).
2   See also Livingstone and Bovill (1999).
3   See, for example, Rutter *et al.* (1976). A critical survey of competing theories of adolescence is provided in Coleman (1992).
4   Influenced by developments in US sociology, accounts of a homogeneous 'culture of youth' also surfaced in Britain. See, for instance, Rowntree and Rowntree (1968) and Turner (1969).
5   For a more detailed discussion of 'youth' as a socially constructed discourse see Austin and Willard (1998). Wyn and White (1997) also give attention to the relational character of 'youth' as a social category. A more detailed discussion of the evolution of modern conceptions of youth in Western Europe can be found in Mitterarurer (1992), while Chudacoff (1989) shows how the modern system of age stratification in the US emerged during the late nineteenth and early twentieth centuries as a consequence of shifts in demographics, labour markets, family organisation, education and legislation.
6   Alternatively, Du Gay *et al.* (1997) use the development of the Sony Walkman as an instructive example of the mutually constitutive processes that underpin the operation of the 'cultural circuit'.

## 2 The 'fab phenomenon'

1   C.E.B. Russell (1905) *Manchester Boys: Sketches of Manchester Lads at Work*, cited in Springhall (1980: 89).

2     See also Gilbert (1957: 21, Tables 1–6).

3     Innumerable books chronicle the development of rock 'n' roll, though Gillett (1983) provides one of the fullest accounts.

4     The term 'rhythm and blues' is now often used by record companies and media programmers to denote a fusion of soul and hip-hop. The phrase was originally coined during the late 1940s by the American music trade-paper *Billboard*, who used it as a general classification for African-American music (replacing their earlier term 'Racial Music'). From the late 1940s to the early 1960s, however, 'rhythm and blues' had a more specific meaning, denoting a pre-eminently black musical genre that fused southern (rural) blues styles with newer (urban) swing and boogie-woogie. Luminaries of the genre included Muddy Waters, B.B. King and Howlin' Wolf.

5     In the US, the percentage of African-American students finishing high school virtually doubled between the early 1940s and the late 1950s (Gilbert, 1986: 19).

6     Grounds exist for qualifying some of Abrams' claims. His definition of teenagers as 'those young people who have reached the age of fifteen but are not yet twenty-five years of age and are unmarried' (Abrams, 1961: 3) would have encompassed older, higher-earning workers, thus concealing differences of earnings and expenditure within the whole group. Moreover, his discussion of *total* expenditure and *average* earnings would, again, have disguised variations and disparities. Indeed, less widely publicised, locally-based studies – for example, those conducted by Jephcott (1967) and Smith (1966) – suggested levels of youth spending much lower than Abrams' estimates. Nevertheless, notions of 'affluent youth' had a degree of foundation, a general rise in young workers' earning power during the 1950s and 1960s affording greater levels of disposable income.

7     An extended discussion of the development of the British youth market during the 1950s can be found in Osgerby (1998: 17–29).

8     A concise overview of the impact of economic change on patterns of British youth employment is provided in Roberts (1995).

9     Since the 1930s an agreement between the BBC, the record industry and the Musicians Union had set limits on the radio broadcast of recorded music.

10    Accounts of the development of British pop radio during this period are provided in Barnard (1989: 32–49) and Hind and Mosco (1985: 7–18).

11    A chronicle of British television's early forays into the field of pop music can be found in Hill (1991).

12    The story of the British pop film is entertainingly charted in Medhurst (1995).

13    During the 1980s and 1990s the term 'McJobs' (from the McDonalds chain of hamburger restaurants) was coined to denote the growth of

employment that was often part-time or temporary and generally low-paid.

14    For more detailed accounts of these developments, see Adamski and Grootings (eds) (1989); Ashton, Maguire and Spilsbury (1990); Furlong and Cartmel (1997: 27–39); and Roberts (1995: 7, 65–66).

15    A full history of the rise and fall of American drive-in cinemas is documented in Segrave (1992).

16    Shary (2002) charts the development of various movie genres and sub-genres geared to the American teen audience during the 1980s and 1990s.

17    For an overview of the key shifts in American TV programming for young audiences during the 1990s, see Philo (2004).

18    'The Merchants of Cool', a PBS *Frontline* documentary, was originally screened on 27 February 2001.

## 3 Brave new world

1    Hesmondhalgh (2002), however, does not see these shifts as representing a fundamental 'sea-change' in the organisation of capitalism. Instead, he argues, they represent an acceleration of long-term economic trends.

2    In 2002 Ministry of Sound ceased publication of *Ministry* following a general slump in sales of dance music magazines.

3    In 2002 the club also hosted a summer dance festival for 55,000 people at Knebworth.

4    By 2002 Ministry of Sound was limbering-up for stock exchange flotation, with a view to financing an aggressive expansion into local radio – a move that pitched Ministry against established dance music radio stations such as Emap's Kiss FM. Emap was, itself, another ideal example of trends towards media conglomeration and synergy. Originally a magazine publisher, Emap stepped into the broadcasting industry with the purchase of Radio City in 1991, followed by its acquisition of Kiss FM in 1992. The late 1990s saw further diversification, Emap launching a series of websites based on its music magazine titles. By 2001 Emap's magazine profits were actually outstripped by earnings from its branded events, CD sales and radio and TV services.

5    Hip-hop mogul Sean Combs, the owner of the Sean John label, was reportedly shocked by the allegations and announced his intention to launch a full investigation.

6    Michel Aglietta (1979) was one of the first theorists to suggest that the structures of 'Fordist' capitalism were facing crisis. From the late 1960s, Aglietta argued, declines in productivity and demand prompted American industries to move into more flexible forms of production and business organisation. Subsequently, other authors

(for example, Murray (1989)) coined the term 'post-Fordism' to denote what they saw as a new economic order based on practices of flexible production and market segmentation. See Allen (1992) and Kumar (1995) for overviews of the field.

7    As part of its efforts to broaden digital TV provision, the BBC unveiled plans to launch a youth-oriented channel, BBC3, in 2001. The original proposal, however, was blocked by the government – a move widely seen as a victory for the BBC's commercial rivals, who had opposed the Corporation's digital expansion. In September 2002 BBC3 was finally given official go-ahead, but stringent preconditions meant the channel was much less 'youth-focused' than originally envisaged.

8    For more detailed discussion of 'post-Fordist' business organisation and the rise of 'flexible specialisation', see Amin (1994), Harvey (1989: 141–173) and Kumar (1995: 36–65).

9    See Brierly (1995: 36–39) and Fox (1985: 183–187).

10    Zollo (1999) provides a full account of TRU's market research strategies.

11    Coupland's title was taken from a 1970s punk rock band who, in turn, had poached their name from Hamblett and Deverson's (1964) sociological study of British youth.

12    After complaints to the Independent Television Commission, the original strapline was replaced with the more palatable slogan, 'Sounds dirty, and it is'.

13    See also Lewis (1990).

14    The economic importance of Britain's media and culture industries was confirmed by the publication of the CITF's *Creative Industries Mapping Document 2001* – an audit that estimated the country's creative industries generated £112.5 billion of revenue, accounted for £10.3 billion in exports and employed 1.3 million people. Reflecting on the figures, Chris Smith underlined the importance of the sector to Britain's economic future, the Minister of Culture, Media and Sport arguing that 'Creativity is not a luxury add-on, but an ingredient for economic success' (*The Guardian*, 14 March 2001).

15    The term 'middle youth' was first coined in a 1997 marketing campaign to launch *Red* – a British women's magazine aimed at readers aged between their late twenties and early forties.

16    This theme is explored more fully, with particular reference to developments in American cultural life, in Osgerby (2001).

## 4 Generation and degeneration in the media

1    In 1993 *Child's Play 3* was also cited in the British press as having had an influence on the murderers of Suzanne Capper. Capper, a sixteen-year-old girl, had been doused in petrol and set on fire after being held captive and tortured for six days in a house in north Manchester.

Four young people, all in their teens and twenties, were later convicted of her murder.

2    For a thoroughgoing analysis of the concerns surrounding 'video nasties' in Britain during the 1980s, see Barker (1984).

3    Wright (2000) offers a perceptive critique of the social anxieties that surrounded Marilyn Manson, his songs and performance.

4    The reports of 'copycat' violence in the US delayed the British release of *Natural Born Killers*. The film's UK video release also prompted concern in 1996, with 200 MPs (unsuccessfully) petitioning the British Board of Film Classification to rescind its decision to allow the release of the film with an '18' video certificate.

5    See, for example, Cumberbatch's (1989) meticulous appraisal.

6    In 2003 research funded by the British Broadcasting Corporation (BBC), the British Board of Film Classification (BBFC), the Broadcasting Standards Commission (BSC) and the Independent Television Commission (ITC) also concluded that young children (aged between nine and thirteen) were very 'literate' television viewers, and were 'able to distinguish between fictional violence and violence that is "real"' (Millwood Hargreave, 2003: 5).

7    Gauntlett (1995) has gone so far as to provide a requiem for crude models of media 'effects'. 'The search for direct "effects" of television on behaviour', Gauntlett announced, 'is over, every effort has been made, and they simply cannot be found' (Gauntlett, 1995: 120).

8    West (1988) provides a useful overview of the history of censorious adult reactions to American children's penchant for dime novels, rock 'n' roll and other forms of popular entertainment.

9    During the 1950s concern about the negative impact of comics on young readers was a worldwide phenomenon, with anti-comics crusades launched in at least twenty countries across four continents. Lent (1999) provides a full account of the campaigns.

10   2 Live Crew were later acquitted, while a federal appeals court overturned the ruling against *As Nasty As They Wanna Be* in 1992.

11   Shank (1996) provides an incisive analysis of the 'Cop Killer' controversy.

12   The track was eventually replaced by a spoken word message from Jello Biafra, frontman of punk band the Dead Kennedys and a renowned anti-censorship lobbyist.

13   Ogren's (1989) study of jazz during the 1920s suggests that these fears go back even further, Ogren showing how the efforts of white entertainers and fans to imitate black jazz, language and dance styles prompted considerable official alarm.

14   The extent to which the public shared these fears is debatable, though Gilbert cites Gallup poll surveys suggesting a peak of public concern in 1945, followed by a more sustained period of anxiety between 1953 and 1958 (Gilbert, 1986: 63).

15    See Pearson (1983: 213–219).

16    Grayson (1998) shows that even the British government were alarmed by the seaside 'invasions' and considered introducing more punitive legislation to deal with the mods and rockers 'problem'.

17    Paralleling Cohen's work on mods and rockers, Jock Young's (1971) study of young cannabis users also found that stigmatisation by the police and the media played an active role in constructing and reinforcing social behaviour. Indeed, Cohen (2002: xxxv) credits Young with first using the term 'moral panic', and speculates that both himself and Young may have picked up the phrase from Marshall McLuhan's *Understanding Media* (1964).

18    Goode and Nachman (1994) apply the concept of moral panic to a range of American historical phenomena – from the Prohibition movement of the 1900s to the 'war on drugs' during the 1980s.

19    For a discussion of the aura of 'youthful' idealism that surrounded the Kennedy Presidency, see Hellmann (1997: 105).

20    Further analysis can be found in Osgerby (2001: 87–119).

21    The *Daily Mirror*'s embrace of youth culture had actually begun during the late 1950s, the paper giving enthusiastic coverage of pop music and, in 1957, even sponsoring a train (the 'Rock 'n' Roll Express') to take Bill Haley to London after the American rocker arrived in Southampton for his first British tour.

22    See Clarke, Hall, Jefferson and Roberts (1976: 72).

## 5 The usual suspects

1    Reeves and Campbell (1994) also provide an incisive account of the political dimensions to the moral panics surrounding drug abuse in America during the 1980s.

2    In practice, the police and local authorities were circumspect in their implementation of the new laws, often turning a blind eye to smaller-scale events. Moreover, by the time the 1994 Act became law, the unlicensed outdoor party scene had been superseded by commercial (licensed) events and an upsurge of urban club culture.

3    In 1996 the American media found its equivalent of Leah Betts in middle-class Hillary Janean Faries, who died after drinking a soft drink 'spiked' with the drug GHB (gamma-hydroxyl-butyrate). See Critcher (2003: 61).

4    Boëthius (1995) also argued that in the late twentieth century moral panics had become more difficult to sustain. For Boëthius, the proliferation of the mass media, an increasing tolerance of diversity of taste and the collapse of distinctions between 'high' and 'low' culture had militated against the moral certainties and media histrionics that had traditionally been the foundation of moral panics.

5   Similar themes were foregrounded in *New Britain: My Vision of A Young Country*, a collection of Blair's essays and speeches published in 1997.

6   His answer was 'usually briefs'.

7   The name was taken from an album by 1960s acid rockers The Grateful Dead. Mark Ellen (music journalist and Blair's former guitarist) later recalled that, as a long-haired lead singer, the future Prime Minister had been fond of purple loon trousers and Cuban-heeled cowboy boots, and had come on stage 'giving it a bit of serious Mick Jagger, a bit of finger-wagging and punching the air' (cited in Rentoul, 2001: 39).

8   New Labour's attempt to re-imagine British national identity as though it were a commercial brand was partly masterminded by Mark Leonard and other members of the Demos think-tank. See Leonard (1997) for his vision of a Britain 're-branded' as 'an outward-looking, diverse, creative hub in an increasingly open, global economy'.

9   Howells' attack on So Solid Crew built upon earlier spates of media anxiety that had surrounded the south London rap collective. In 2001 promoters had cancelled several of the group's shows after reports of violence at concerts, while the following year more negative publicity followed as Asher D (So Solid's nineteen-year-old rapper) was sentenced to eighteen months' imprisonment for possession of an air pistol converted to fire live ammunition.

10  The group, recently convicted for a spate of car thefts and break-ins, had posed in the 1920s costumes as a joke.

11  In December 2002 the verdicts were overturned after a convicted murderer confessed to sole responsibility for the attack.

12  Running until 1994, *Def II* included current affairs programmes such as *Reportage*, music slots such as *Snub* and *Dance Energy*, and travel shows such as *The Rough Guide*.

13  Further discussion of the development of 'teen TV' during the 1990s can be found in Davis and Dickinson (2004).

14  Though successful, *Beavis and Butthead* was not the first comic portrayal of aimless youth adrift in a media-saturated world. In 1989, for example, the NBC comedy show *Saturday Night Live* featured a regular slot in which comedian Mike Myers played a dopey, rock-obsessed adolescent who ran his own ramshackle show on cable TV – the character later given fuller play in the feature films *Wayne's World* (1992) and *Wayne's World 2* (1993). Similar comic depictions of empty-headed, media-absorbed teens also appeared in the movies *Bill and Ted's Excellent Adventure* (1988) and *Bill and Ted's Bogus Journey* (1991), while Beavis and Butthead transferred to the big screen in *Beavis and Butthead Do America* (1996).

15  See Senate Committee on Commerce, Science, and Transportation, 13 September 2000: 2. www.senate.gov/~commerce/hearings/0913che.pdf.

## 6 All the young dudes

1    *Pop Idol* was not the first 'talent' show on British TV to be based
     around the grooming of young hopefuls for the pop music spotlight.
     In 2001, the earlier ITV series *Popstars* had won huge ratings and
     spawned the bubbly pop songsters Hear'Say and Liberty X. But the
     success of *Pop Idol* ensured the endurance of the programme format
     – 2002 seeing ITV launch a follow-up show, *Popstars: The Rivals*, while
     the BBC waded in with their own *Fame Academy*. Christmas 2003,
     meanwhile, saw the production of *World Idol*, a two-part global TV
     event that saw *Pop Idol* winners from eleven different countries
     compete for worldwide pop supremacy. Norwegian plumber, Kurt
     Nilsen, ultimately triumphed.

2    In seeing the counterculture as an attack by disaffected white, middle-
     class youth against the culture and ideology of its parent culture, the
     CCCS authors were not alone. Many contemporary commentators
     also interpreted the counterculture in this way. In America, for
     example, Theodore Roszak argued that the counterculture was
     composed of 'technocracy's children', so that 'The bourgeoisie,
     instead of discovering the class enemy in its factories, finds it across
     the breakfast table in the person of its own pampered children'
     (Roszak, 1969: 34). Similarly, Charles Reich argued that the coun-
     terculture was a product of 'cynicism alienation and despair in the
     best-kept homes of America' (1971: 187), while Frank Musgrove
     observed that:

> Ten years ago the young were fighting to get in; today they are often
> fighting to get out. . . . Formerly the problem of youth was associ-
> ated with privation; now it is associated with privilege. The new
> problem is far more subversive of the social order than petty theft
> and mindless vandalism. It is a principled attack on traditional social
> institutions, an adversary culture with well-heeled allies in high
> places.
>
> (Musgrove, 1974: 7–8)

3    For example, in its close attention to issues of identity and resistance,
     Brake's (1985) comparative analysis of youth culture in America,
     Britain and Canada was heavily informed by the CCCS approaches.

4    The failure of the CCCS theorists to take adequate account of the
     meanings young people *themselves* gave to their subcultural styles was
     highlighted by numerous critics. See, for example, Clarke (1990:
     87), Muggleton (2000: 11) and Widdicombe and Woofitt (1995:
     22–28).

5    During the late 1970s the dramatic stances of alienation struck by
     punk rock made it relatively easy for theorists to decode youth style
     in terms of opposition and subversion. Qualities of 'resistance',

however, were less immediately apparent in subsequent youth styles and, by the late 1980s, even Dick Hebdige appeared to have recanted his faith in the transgressive potential of subcultural style, reflecting that 'the idea of subculture-as-negation grew up alongside punk, remained inextricably linked to it and died when it died' (Hebdige, 1988a: 8).

6    In this respect a significant exception was the work of Paul Willis. In his (1977) study of working-class secondary school pupils, and his (1978) account of hippy and biker subcultures, Willis *did* devote significant attention to ethnographic fieldwork. Nevertheless, critics such as Andy Bennett (2002: 454) have pointed to an uneasy tension in his research – with Willis's ethnographic observation of subcultural actors sitting somewhat awkwardly alongside the considerable space devoted to *his own* analysis of their style and its cultural meanings.

7    See also the critique elaborated in Ward (1987).

8    McRobbie was especially critical of Willis's (1977) study of working-class lads at a secondary school. Willis, McRobbie argued, did 'not comment on the extreme cruelty of the lads' sexual double-standard or tease out in sufficient detail how images of sexual power and domination are used as a kind of last defensive resort' (McRobbie, 1978: 115).

9    See, for example, Frith (1983: 225) and Scraton (1987: 164–165).

10   See Marshall and Borrill (1984).

11   In particular, see the accounts offered by Gotlieb and Wald (1994) and Kearney (1998b).

12   Leonard (1998) examines the way fanzines and internet sites have been used to maintain the sense of a Riot Grrrl 'community'.

13   Merchant and MacDonald concurred, arguing that the displays of sexual availability and intent that had often been the *raison d'être* of conventional nightclubs had given way to 'more friendly, egalitarian forms of interchange' in modern club culture (Merchant and MacDonald, 1994: 22).

14   In this respect, Pini's observations were supported by Andy Bennett's research on club culture in Newcastle. See Bennett (2000: 93–94).

15   Fieldwork by Ben Malbon also suggested that female clubbers articulated an autonomous, 'hypersexual' mode of femininity. Like Pini's interviewees, a number of the female clubbers interviewed by Malbon described their performance of sexuality in terms of personal liberation rather than sexual invitation (Malbon, 1999: 45).

16   For further discussion of Madonna and her disruptive 'performance' of femininity, see Frank and Smith (1993), Lloyd (1993) and Schwichtenberg (1993).

17   With the rise of these new magazines, the sales of 'traditional' titles declined significantly. In its 1970s heyday, for example, *Jackie* had sold a million copies a week, but by the early 1990s circulation had fallen to barely 60,000 and the title finally folded in 1993.

18    Subsequently, the trend continued – 2002 seeing the launch of Emap's *Sneak* magazine, a British title geared to a readership of teenage girls and solely dedicated to entertainment features and coverage of showbusiness celebrities.

19    Currie's (1999) empirical research on the readers of girls' magazines reached similar conclusions. Currie, however, also suggested that the magazines provided 'frames of intelligibility' for their readers, offering them particular frameworks for making sense of the world.

20    Bennett, however, was sharply critical of this work, arguing that the grand theoretical claims made by Redhead and his associates rested on 'a series of quite poorly conceptualised semi-ethnographic studies of dance club settings' (Bennett, 2002: 457). According to Bennett, many of the contributions to Redhead's *Rave Off* (1993) were marred by their lack of critical self-reflection and their 'privileging of front-line knowledge of the house music scene over the necessity to critically engage with issues of access, field relations, and objectivity of data' (Bennett, 2002: 457). Bennett's criticisms of this work were possibly a little harsh, but his call for a 'more reflexive position in ethnographic research on youth and music' (ibid.) was well made.

21    Steve Redhead concurred, arguing that post-punk subcultures had 'been characterized by a speeding up of the time between points of "authenticity" and "manufacture"' (Redhead, 1991: 94).

22    The group included, amongst others, Simon Frith, Celia Lury, Angela McRobbie, Mica Nava, Graham Murdock, Gary Whannel and Janice Winship.

23    Numerous other ethnographic studies exist of music-making as an important arena of cultural creativity for young people. See, for example, Fornäs *et al.*'s (1995) account of three amateur rock bands in Sweden.

24    An overview of these shifts within the fields of media and cultural studies is provided in Hermes (2002).

25    The concept of lifestyle had familiar currency within American marketing circles during the early 1960s. In 1963, for example, issues of lifestyle and market segmentation were leading topics on the agenda of the Winter Conference of the American Marketing Association. See Lazer (1967).

26    According to Featherstone (1987: 55), the concept of lifestyle came into academic vogue during the 1980s as a tool in the growing analysis of consumer culture.

27    Giddens (1991) also made a significant contribution to debates about the collapse of certainty and stability in the late twentieth century. Lupton (1999) provides a thorough survey of arguments that risk has become an increasingly pervasive aspect of social and economic life.

28    See, for example, Cieslik and Pollock (2002), Davis (1999), Furlong and Cartmel (1997), and Williams *et al.* (2003).

29      Yet, as Miles *et al.* observed, since the influential work produced by
        Willis (1990), there had been relatively few examples of research
        that sought to explore the experiential aspects of youth consumption
        (though the collection of studies anthologised by Buckingham
        (1993b) was a notable exception to this). Miles *et al.* explained this
        absence as the consequence of a failure to develop innovative
        methodologies that could address the everyday impact of consump-
        tion on young people's lives. 'Despite an intuitive recognition that
        consumption plays a significant role in young people's lives', Miles
        *et al.* argued, 'research has failed to identify adequate means for
        addressing the actual *meanings* with which young consumers endow
        the goods that they purchase' (Miles, Dallas and Burr, 1998: 81).

## 7 Rockin' all over the world

1       For readers unfamiliar with British geography, Hemel Hempstead is
        an uninspiring commuter town slightly north of London.
2       In this respect, Giddens' account of globalisation can be criticised for
        offering an overly Eurocentric view of modernity. As Featherstone
        (1995) has observed, different parts of the world have become
        'modern' in a variety of different ways, requiring us to recognise a
        plurality of 'global modernities'. A useful introductory overview of
        competing interpretations of globalisation is provided in Crane
        (2002).
3       Strinati (1992) provides a thorough survey of British perceptions of,
        and responses to, processes of 'Americanisation'.
4       Acknowledging the impact of both African and British music on the
        development of American pop, Grossberg insists that 'the history of
        rock and roll in the U.S.A. has to be written as a transnational
        discourse' (Grossberg, 1987: 144).
5       Frank (1997: 190–191) charts the media feeding-frenzy that sur-
        rounded the arrival of the 'mod' look in America in 1966.
6       Similar incidents were reported from as far afield as Detroit, New
        York and Philadelphia. Full accounts of the history and significance
        of the wartime 'zoot suit riots' are provided in Cosgrove (1984),
        Escobar (1996) and Mazón (1984).
7       Though Willcock's (1949: 49) reference to 'Dago' style suggests that
        this was not entirely the case.
8       Sato (1991) offers a more rigorously sociological account of the *boso-
        zoku* phenomenon.

## 8 'Insurgency across all borders'

1       Detailed and informed histories of rap music and hip-hop culture can
        be found in George (2000), Toop (2000) and Perkins (1996).

2   This eclectic mixing of diverse cultural elements has prompted some theorists to see rap as a characteristically 'postmodern' musical form, indicative of broader contemporary trends towards the blurring and effacement of distinct cultural boundaries. See Baker (1993).

3   During the late 1980s, Boogie Down Productions and Public Enemy led the way for a brand of rap that offered hard-hitting political critique and social comment – with Chuck D, frontman of Public Enemy, arguing that rap music functioned as the 'Black man's CNN'. Artists such as Brand Nubian, X-Clan and Poor Righteous Teachers followed their lead.

4   Flores (1994) highlights the important, though often neglected, place of 'Puerto Rocks' (as Puerto Rican hip-hoppers came to be known) in the development of rap.

5   Cross (1992) provides a full account of rap and hip-hop in Los Angeles, while Ro (1998) offers a revealing portrait of the history of Death Row Records.

6   The murders prompted a Justice Department probe into accusations of robbery, assault and retaliatory executions between the two camps. Investigations continued, but six years later both murders remained unsolved. In 2002 Russell Poole, a Los Angeles Detective, sparked a new wave of interest in the cases by alleging that the notoriously volatile Suge Knight was behind both murders, his involvement covered-up by corrupt police officers. The allegations were explored by both journalist Randall Sullivan in his book *LAbyrinth* (2002), and by British filmmaker Nick Broomfield in his documentary *Biggie and Tupac* (2002).

7   Nevertheless, the murky world of hip-hop rivalry, record company competition and gangland gunplay remained a dangerous place. For example, 2003 saw two unexplained shootings at the management offices of rapper Busta Rhymes and the (unsolved) murder of Run DMC veteran, Jam Master Jay.

8   Outside North America, France has boasted one of the most prolific hip-hop cultures. French hip-hop first took root during the early 1980s, with MC Solaar emerging in the early 1990s as one of the country's foremost rap pioneers – his debut album, *Qui Sème le Vent Récolte le Tempo* (1991), becoming one of the biggest-selling rap albums outside the US. During the 1990s, however, harder-edged artists such as NTM (Nique Ta Mère) and IAM (Imperial Asiatic Men) increasingly came to the fore. For analysis of the growth of French hip-hop, see Bocquet and Adolphe (1997) and Boucher (1998).

9   See, in particular, Centre for Contemporary Cultural Studies (1982) and Gilroy (1987).

10   In Britain, the term 'Asian' is usually used to denote peoples originating from the south Asian subcontinent (primarily India, Pakistan and Bangladesh). In North America, however, the term 'Asian'

generally denotes peoples from east and southeast Asia (principally Japan, Korea and Vietnam). As yet, relatively little research has been conducted on the cultural identifications and media usage of Asian American youth, though Lee (1996), Lee and Zhou (eds) (2004) and Wei (1998) represent notable contributions.

11   While some theorists have used the concept of the crossroads to represent this conjunction of cultural 'routes', Back has argued that such a metaphor oversimplifies processes of cultural inter-action and development. Instead, he drew upon the idea of the 'rhizome' deployed in the work of the critical philosophers Gilles Deleuze and Felix Guattari. With its connotations of continuous growth and lateral roots, Back suggested, the notion of the rhizome provided a useful way of conceiving the various 'forms of cultural inter-being' (1996: 185). Following on from this, Back offered the concept of the 'intermezzo' to denote spaces where cultural sensibilities merge and new identities are generated.

12   See also Gillespie (1995).

13   Research by Dwyer also suggested that young British Muslim women actively negotiated their identities through talk about the media and youth culture, though Dwyer stressed the contextual nature of these processes, arguing that the young women's 'own reading of the media is always mediated by the ways in which they think other non-Muslims will read and understand the representations given' (Dwyer, 1998: 60).

14   Similar themes were also central to Damien O'Donnell's movie *East Is East* (1999), and to the work of authors such as Hanif Kureishi (most notably his screenplay for the film *My Beautiful Laundrette* (1985), and his novels *The Buddha of Suburbia* (1990) and *The Black Album* (1995)), and Zadie Smith – whose first novel, *White Teeth* (2000), was serialised by BBC TV in 2002.

15   After two albums, however, Bally Sagoo was dropped by Sony following disappointing sales – perhaps suggesting that the 'crossover' of Asian dance music into mainstream markets was less marked than some commentators had pronounced. See Bhattachariya (2002) and Huq (2003: 198).

16   Another notable example of such musical fusion was the genre known as 'Asian Underground' (or 'Asian Massive'), the work of a collective of British and American south Asian DJs, musicians, and producers that Talvin Singh led to fame during the mid-1990s. Singh, a classically trained tabla (an Indian percussion instrument) player, along with other artists such as Karsh Kale and State of Bengal, popularised the fusion of classical north Indian music with modern dancefloor beats (particularly drum 'n' bass), building on the work of Asian Dub Foundation and other early pioneers of the sound. Some of the most influential music from the Asian Underground was

released on the Outcaste record label, launched in 1995 alongside the success of a regular Outcaste club night in central London.

17 This practice can be seen as constituent in a tradition that has long characterised the performance of African-American female musicians. See Carby (1986). Analogies could also be made between black rappers' sexualised 'performance' of femininity and the 'hypersexual' modes of femininity identified in 1990s British club culture by Malbon (1999), McRobbie (1994a) and Pini (2001). See Chapter 4.

18 Rooted in a celebration of distinctly *British* (working-class) masculine culture, *Loaded* was unable to break into overseas markets. Its competitors, however, enjoyed greater international success. For example, *Maxim* (launched in the US in 1997) and *FHM* (launched in the US in 2000) adeptly reconfigured the *Loaded* formula for an American market and their US circulation figures skyrocketed.

19 Jackson *et al.* (2001) characterised the relationship between magazines such as *Loaded* and their readership as one of 'ambivalence and contradiction'. The 'new lad' magazines, they argued, articulated relatively open and reflexive forms of masculinity that, for some readers at least, 'opened up a space for public debate about changing masculinities in a way that [had] not previously been available in the more formal political sphere' (Jackson *et al.*, 2001: 144). For further discussion of constructions of masculinity in men's lifestyle magazines and 'lads' mags' see Benwell (2003).

20 Savage (1990) provides a perceptive overview of the influence of gay male style on the universe of British youth culture. The influence of lesbian culture has been considerably less, possibly reflecting the greater degree to which lesbians have been marginalised and disempowered within mainstream culture.

21 A similar account was offered by Denski and Sholee (1992), who drew on Butler's notion of gender as a 'masquerade' to highlight the performative character of heavy metal masculinity. Focusing on 1980s 'glam metal' bands such as Poison, Denski and Sholee argued that heavy metal culture had increasingly appropriated elements of style traditionally regarded as 'feminine', for example lipstick, mascara, scarves and jewellery, and hairstyles that were elaborately teased and moussed. But, whereas Butler saw cross-dressing as a cultural practice that disrupted notions of gender as essential and securely anchored, Denski and Sholee argued that, in glam metal, drag was simply used as a marker of outrageousness. For all its posturing and theatrics, they argued, heavy metal failed to offer a meaningful challenge to essentialist notions of gender identities and instead offered 'a thinly disguised reproduction of traditional masculine roles of power and domination presented in the context of an aggressive heterosexuality' (Denski and Sholee, 1992: 59).

22  In a similar vein, O'Donnell and Sharpe (2000) argued that the macho style favoured by many African-Caribbean youths in Britain needed to be understood in the context of slavery and post-slavery. The macho postures, they argued, were 'associated with *resistance* to and rejection of oppression and humiliation, often sexual and well as racist' (O'Donnell and Sharpe, 2000: 6).

23  Punk band The Clash, for example, were candid in the way they drew influence from the rhetoric and symbolism of African-Caribbean youth culture and (along with many other punk bands of the 1970s and 1980s) added cover versions of reggae classics to their set list. During the early 1980s The Clash were also one of the first white rock bands to draw influence from the musical styles of rap and hip-hop.

24  As Lipsitz observed, 'white' appropriations of African-American culture 'have a long and disreputable history [and] . . . their conse-quences are no less poisonous when well-intentioned . . . identifi-cation with otherness has become an essential element in the construction of 'whiteness' (Lipsitz, 1994: 53).

25  According to Connor (2003), engagement with the cultural forms of hip-hop could also be a radicalising experience for white, middle-class youths in Australia.

## 9 Totally wired

1  This was not the first time Fox had waged war against online fans of its popular television shows. Since 1997 Fox had targeted a number of unofficial fan sites for *The X-Files*, threatening legal action unless copyrighted material was removed. In 1999 Viacom had taken similar action, threatening unofficial fan sites for its *Star Trek* franchise.

2  A lucid survey of the development of videogames is provided in Newman (2004).

3  In Britain similar legal action was taken by Sony Music and the British Phonographic Industry (representing the Universal, Virgin, Polydor and EMI labels) against the EasyInternet chain of internet cafés. Seeking compensation, the plaintiffs alleged the chain had allowed its customers to make illegal downloads of copyrighted music from the internet. In January 2003 the High Court found EasyInternet guilty of copyright infringement and, rather than appealing the decision, the chain agreed to pay damages. In January 2004, meanwhile, US record companies issued 500 lawsuits against individuals who had illicitly downloaded music from online sites.

4  For an overeview of the Napster saga, together with a discussion of the future of peer-to-peer computing and online file sharing, see Merriden (2001).

5  Now known as simply 'The Bringers', their website can be found at www.bringers.org.uk/.

6    In 1999 a crusading follow-up appeared with the publication of *Stop Teaching Our Kids to Kill: A Call to Action Against TV, Movie and Video Game Violence* (Grossman and DeGaetano, 1999).

7    Elmer-Dewitt's article in *Time* was heavily indebted to research completed by an undergraduate student, Martin Rimm. Subsequently published in the *Georgetown Law Journal*, Rimm's work was widely criticised as an unsophisticated and methodologically unsound study. Elab, a website dedicated to internet research, provide full background to the controversy at elab.vanderbilt.edu/research/topics/cyberporn/.

8    In October 2003, amid a flurry of concern that paedophiles were using internet chatrooms to target children for abuse, Microsoft pulled the plug on all its UK chatroom services. Microsoft representatives argued that the move was to safeguard youngsters from inappropriate online communication, but critics argued that the closure was largely driven by commercial motives – Microsoft abandoning chatrooms in favour of potentially more lucrative instant messaging services.

9    According to Magid (2003) the slow growth of mobile-phone ownership in the US was the consequence of several factors, including the continued reliability of American analogue phones, the multiplicity of (often incompatible) US phone systems and the relative expense of American cell phones compared to landline rivals.

10   The Wildseed range included, for example, graffiti-splattered faceplates for skateboarders that came with 'edgy, urban ringer tones and gritty icons'.

11   In 2002 a study produced for the British Home Office by researchers based at the University of Central Lancashire found that one in five schoolchildren used internet chat sites and one in eight used instant messaging programmes, with 13- to 14-year-olds accounting for the greatest proportion of both groups (Cyberspace Research Unit, 2002).

12   See, for example, Watson's (1997) analysis of the online fandom surrounding the band Phish.

13   The various contributions to Cassell and Jenkins (1998) show how a growth in girls' computer gaming in America was championed by a curious alliance of feminist activists (who wanted to change the 'gendering' of digital technology) and business interests (who wanted to create a new market for their products).

## 10 Conclusion

1    In a neat cross-media alliance with magazine publisher EMAP, those who attended the events were subsequently featured in advertorial spreads appearing in EMAP's youth-oriented lifestyle titles, *Heat*, *FHM*, *New Woman* and *Max Power*.

# FURTHER READING

Youth and the media is obviously an expansive field and only brief suggestions for further reading can be made here. For further sources related to more specific topics, readers should consult the references and notes provided in the relevant chapters of this book.

## THE HISTORICAL DEVELOPMENT OF YOUTH CULTURE AND THE COMMERCIAL YOUTH MARKET

Austin, Joe and Willard, Michael (eds) (1998) *Generations of Youth: Youth Cultures and History in Twentieth-Century America*, New York: New York University Press.
Brings together a selection of work on youth culture by American social historians and cultural studies scholars. Primarily a historical collection, though many of the contributions discuss the relation between youth culture and the institutions of the mass media.

Davis, John (1990) *Youth and the Condition of Britain: Images of Adolescent Conflict*, London: Athlone.
A historical account of the institutionalisation of adolescence in Britain, giving close attention to the role of the media in formalising 'youth' as a distinct age category during the 1950s and 1960s.

Fass, Paula (1978) *The Damned and the Beautiful: American Youth in the 1920s*, Oxford: Oxford University Press.
Explores the rise of American youth culture during the 1920s and 1930s, with particular attention to the developing 'campus culture' and the emerging leisure and entertainment industries.

Fowler, David (1995) *The First Teenagers: The Lifestyle of Young Wage-Earners in Interwar Britain*, London: Woburn.
Examines the development of British youth culture during the 1920s and 1930s, showing how a distinctive youth market had begun to take shape during the inter-war years.

Frank, Thomas (1997) *The Conquest of Cool: Business Culture, Counterculture and the Rise of Hip Consumerism*, Chicago: University of Chicago Press.
An insightful analysis of the relationship between the 1960s counter-culture and the American advertising industry. Frank shows how the 'creative revolution' of 1960s advertising mobilised images of 'youthful' hip in its attempt to address developing consumer markets.

Hesmondhalgh, David (2002) *The Cultural Industries*, London: Sage.
Although not specifically focused on 'youth media', provides a systematic account of the nature and development of the modern cultural industries more generally. Considers the development of the contemporary entertainment and information business sectors, drawing on a range of effective illustrative examples. An indispensable introduction to the field.

Hollander, Stanley C. and Germain, Richard (1993) *Was There a Pepsi Generation Before Pepsi Discovered It?: Youth-Based Segmentation in Marketing*, Chicago: American Marketing Association.
Charts the emergence of a commercial youth market in the United States during the 1920s and 1930s.

Osgerby, Bill (1998) *Youth in Britain Since 1945*, Oxford: Blackwell.
A historical survey of the key shifts in young people's social, economic and cultural experiences since the Second World War that gives close attention to the development of the commercial youth market and related media during the 1950s and 1960s.

Palladino, Grace (1996) *Teenagers: An American History*, New York: Basic Books.
A concise, yet informed, account of the development of modern American youth culture, with some close attention to the growth of the commercial youth market during the 1950s and 1960s.

Rollin, Lucy (1999) *Twentieth Century Teen Culture By the Decades: A Reference Guide*, Westport, CT: Greenwood Press.
Somewhat simplistic, but a readable overview of the history of American youth culture.

## THE THEORETICAL ANALYSIS OF YOUTH CULTURE

Back, Les (1996) *New Ethnicities and Urban Culture: Racisms and Multiculture in Young Lives*, London: UCL Press.

An exploration of 'race' and youth culture which focuses on the development of new identities and ethnicities. Provides a systematic analysis of the relationship between racism, community and social identities for young people in the African and south Asian diasporas.

Bennett, Andy and Kahn-Harris, Keith (eds) (2004) *After Subculture: Critical Studies in Contemporary Youth Culture*, London: Palgrave Macmillan.
A collection of diverse studies dealing with new developments in youth culture research. Contributions include analyses of popular music, clubbing, body modification and the internet.

Fornäs, Johan and Bolin, Göran (eds) (1995) *Youth Culture in Late Modernity*, London: Sage.
Collects a range of contrasting theoretical approaches to the nature, formation and dynamics of youth culture and subculture. Especially valuable are the numerous contributions that explore the relation between youth culture and the commercial market. Though the case-studies generally relate specifically to Swedish cultural history, many of the themes and issues explored are pertinent to the wider analysis of youth culture and its relation to the media.

Hall, Stuart and Jefferson, Tony (eds) (1976) *Resistance Through Rituals: Youth Subcultures in Post-War Britain*, London: Hutchinson.
The classic formulation of 'subcultural' theory. The neo-Marxist approach dates the collection, but it remains a theoretical landmark and many of the contributions represent useful introductions to the history of subcultural groups such as Teddy boys, mods and skinheads.

McGuigan, Jim (1992) *Cultural Populism*, London: Routledge.
McGuigan squares-up to trends in cultural analysis during the 1980s that he presents as a drift towards a simple celebration of consumer sovereignty in the marketplace. Advocates of 'active audience' theory will inevitably take issue with McGuigan's account, yet he makes a persuasive case for theorists to accord greater attention to the importance of political economy. The chapter on youth culture and consumption represents a thorough-going and thought-provoking critical survey of theoretical approaches to youth culture and its relation to commercial media.

McRobbie, Angela (2000) *Feminism and Youth Culture*, London: Macmillan.
A selection of essays produced by Angela McRobbie at various points in her career as one of Britain's pre-eminent cultural theorists. The anthology not only represents a thorough-going engagement with the construction and experience of gender within youth culture, but also bears testimony to important shifts in emphasis within cultural and media studies – away from the 1970s focus on the 'ideological power' of the text, towards a growing emphasis on polysemy and the active agency of audiences.

Miles, Steven (2000) *Youth Lifestyles in a Changing World*, Buckingham: Open University Press.
A critical examination of the changing nature of young people's position in contemporary society. Emphasises the notion of 'lifestyle' as a productive avenue for understanding young people's relationship with the media, consumerism and social change.

Muggleton, David (2000) *Inside Subculture: The Postmodern Meaning of Style*, Oxford: Berg.
Drawing on a series of interviews Muggleton analyses the nature and significance of subcultural style in contemporary society, arguing that they exhibit both modern and postmodern sensibilities – with a stress on postmodern fluidity and fragmentation running alongside a modernist emphasis on authenticity.

Redhead, Steve, Wynne, Derek and O'Connor, Justin (eds) (1997) *The Clubcultures Reader: Readings in Cultural Studies*, Oxford: Blackwell.
Gathers a range of studies of youth cultures and music during the 1990s, from rave and disco to house and northern soul. Combining description and theory, many of the contributions suggest dimensions of postmodern 'fluidity' and 'mutability' within the 1990s music scene.

Skelton, Tracey and Valentine, Gill (eds) (1998) *Cool Places: Geographies of Youth Cultures*, London: Routledge.
An edited collection that draws together a variety of studies that focus on the complexities of contemporary youth cultures, their spatial representations and interactions with the media.

Thornton, Sarah (1995) *Club Cultures: Music, Media and Subcultural Capital*, London: Polity.
Basing her study on an analysis of the rave scene of the late 1980s and early 1990s, Thornton examines how club culture was transformed into a self-conscious 'subculture' through the intercession of the national press and 'niche media' (such as the music and style press). Drawing on the work of Pierre Bourdieu, she also coins the term 'subcultural capital' to denote the hierarchies subcultural members establish through their patterns of media use.

Thornton, Sarah and Gelder, Ken (eds) (1996) *The Subcultures Reader*, London: Routledge.
An anthology that brings together key writings on subcultures from the Chicago School to the present. A useful general introduction also maps out the field of subcultural studies.

Willis, Paul (1990) *Common Culture: Symbolic Work at Play in the Everyday Cultures of the Young*, Milton Keynes: Open University Press.
Examines the capacity of young people to be 'creative' consumers of commercial products and media. Moves away from earlier notions of

subcultural 'resistance' towards ideas of meaningful symbolic creativity in everyday life.

## MEDIA 'EFFECTS' AND YOUNG AUDIENCES

Barker, Martin and Petley, Julian (eds) (2001) (2nd edn) *Ill Effects: The Media/Violence Debate*, London: Routledge.
Provides a thorough-going critique of theories of media 'effects', showing how such approaches fail to understand both the nature of the modern media and their relationship with audiences. The second edition includes discussion of the 'ill effects' attributed to the internet, suggesting that such concerns may be a prelude to the imposition of tighter controls on new media.

Buckingham, David (ed.) (1993) *Reading Audiences: Young People and the Media*, Manchester: Manchester University Press.
An anthology of qualitative studies covering young audience's engagement with a range of media, including television, comics, video and popular fiction. Collectively, they challenge simplistic views of young people as the passive victims of a pernicious media and suggest a more complex set of dialogues between young audiences and media texts.

Cumberbatch, Guy and Howitt, Dennis (1989) *A Measure of Uncertainty: The Effects of the Mass Media*, Broadcasting Standards Council, Research Monograph Series, No. 1, London: John Libbey.
Now a bit dated, but still represents a thorough critique of the research evidence on mass media effects, setting key studies in the context of the development of mass communications research.

Harris, Jessica (2001) *The Effects of Computer Games On Young Children – A Review of the Research*, RDS Occasional Paper, No. 72, London: Home Office, Research, Development and Statistics Directorate.
Funded by the British Home Office, a thorough and balanced survey of existing research on the 'effects' of computer games on young audiences.

## MORAL PANICS, MEDIA AND YOUTH

Acland, Charles (1995) *Youth, Murder, Spectacle: the Cultural Politics of 'Youth in Crisis'*, Oxford: Westview Press.
Examines media representations of youth and violence in America during the 1990s, with close analysis of newspaper photos, daytime television talk shows and Hollywood youth films.

Cohen, Stanley (2002) (3rd edn) *Folk Devils and Moral Panics: the Creation of the Mods and Rockers*, London: Routledge.

Cohen's study of the mods and rockers moral panic of the early 1960s was a foundational text – both in terms of its analysis of the development of subcultural groups and its attention to the media's active role in shaping social phenomena. The third edition includes a new introduction in which Cohen revisits the theory of moral panic and explores the way the concept has been used since it was originally developed during the 1970s. Cohen also tracks the history of moral panics over the last thirty years, commenting on the demonisation of young offenders and asylum seekers and on the *News of the World*'s 'name and shame' campaign against paedophiles.

Critcher, Chas (2003) *Moral Panics and the Media*, Buckingham: Open University Press.
Critically evaluates the value of moral panic models in the analysis of contemporary social, cultural and political life, with a range of original (and timely) case-studies.

Goode, Erich and Nachman, Ben-Yehuda (1994) *Moral Panics: The Social Construction of Deviance*, Oxford: Blackwell.
Giving particular consideration to the American experience, explores the history and nature of moral panics from the Renaissance witch-craze to the US drug panic of the 1980s.

Pearson, Geoffrey (1983) *Hooligan: A History of Respectable Fears*, London: Macmillan.
An excellent survey of the way successive generations of media commentators have voiced strikingly similar fears of social breakdown and moral degeneration, whether directed against the 'hooligans' of nineteenth-century London or the muggers of the modern inner-city.

Springhall, John (1998) *Youth, Popular Culture and Moral Panics: Penny Gaffs to Gangsta Rap, 1830–1996*, London: Macmillan.
An engaging and insightful study of the history of controversy surrounding the commercial media's putatively negative effects on young people. A history of anxiety is traced from the fears prompted by Victorian 'penny gaff' theatres to the hand-wringing responses to contemporary 'gangsta' rappers and computer games. Springhall examines why emergent media forms become the locus for wider social anxieties and explores why critics so frequently portray the media as a corrupter of the rising generation.

## GLOBALISATION AND 'YOUTH MEDIA'

Amit-Talai, Vered and Wulff, Helena (eds) (1995) *Youth Cultures: A Cross-Cultural Perspective*, London: Routledge.
A valuable collection of ethnographically-based studies of youth cultures in various national contexts, from Nepal and Canada, to the

Solomon Islands and Algeria – with some particularly useful contributions dealing with issues of globalisation, media and consumption practices.

Mitchell, Tony (1996) *Popular Music and Local Identity: Rock, Pop and Rap in Europe and Oceania*, London: Leicester University Press.
Examines notions of 'cultural imperialism' through a study of the 'hybridity' of local forms of pop, rock and rap music in four countries marginal to the 'world music' phenomenon, showing how vernacular cultures become 'hybridised' in the production and consumption of popular music.

Nayak, Anoop (2003) *Race, Place and Globalization: Youth Culture in a Changing World*, Oxford: Berg.
Considers issues of youth, locality and global change. Examines the ways young people's lives are being transformed by patterns of social and economic development, combined with migration, settlement and new urban cultures.

Pilkington, Hilary (ed.) (2002) *Looking West?: Cultural Globalization and Russian Youth Culture*, University Park, PA: Pennsylvania State University Press.
Charts how post-Soviet Russia's opening up to the West has been reflected in the cultural practices of its young people. Contributions suggest Russian youth have a 'pick and mix' attitude to Western media that reflects a receptiveness to the global alongside a commitment to the local.

Ralph, Sue, Langham Brown, Jo and Lees, Tim (eds) (1999) *Youth and the Global Media*, Luton: University of Luton Press.
This collection brings together edited sessions from the 29th Manchester International Broadcasting Symposium, which took place in 1998. The papers cover such topics as new media, music broadcasting, images of children and young people, and cultural diversity in youth broadcasting.

Wallace, Claire and Kovatcheva, Sijka (1998) *Youth in Society: the Construction and Deconstruction of Youth in East and West Europe*, Basingstoke: Macmillan.
Explores how different ideas of youth were constructed in east and west Europe in the course of modernisation under both Communism and welfare capitalism. Assesses how modern concepts of youth have been de-constructed and re-constructed by changes in state policies, the labour market, education and popular media.

Zolov, Eric (1999) *Refried Elvis: the Rise of the Mexican Counterculture*, Berkeley: University of California Press.
Shows how American rock 'n' roll became a major influence in Mexican politics, society and culture – from the arrival of Elvis in

Mexico during the 1950s, to the emergence of a full-blown counterculture during the late 1960s. Above all, however, Zolov's
account stands as an excellent case-study of the 'glocalisation' of
global 'youth media'.

## YOUTH AND FILM

Benton, Michael, Dolan, Mark and Zisch, Rebecca (1997) 'Teen Films: An
Annotated Bibliography', *Journal of Popular Film and Television*, 25(2)
Summer: 83–88.
An extensive inventory of academic writing dealing with 'teen'
cinema.

Doherty, Thomas (2002) (2nd edn) *Teenagers and Teenpics: the Juvenilization
of American Movies in the 1950s*, Philadelphia: Temple University
Press.
A wry and engaging account of the development of the American
'teenpic' industry during the 1950s. Doherty chronicles the progressive 'juvenilization' of Hollywood in response to the growing teenage
market. Included in the second edition is an expanded treatment of
'teenpics' since the 1950s, especially those produced during the age
of AIDS.

Gateward, Frances and Pomerance, Murray (eds) (2002) *Sugar, Spice and
Everything Nice: Cinemas of Girlhood*, Detroit: Wayne State University
Press.
A lively anthology of essays discussing the construction of teen femininity in a variety of youth-orientated films. Contributors consider
issues of production, reception and textual meanings in movies
stretching from *The Wizard of Oz* (1939) to *Spiceworld: The Movie*
(1997).

Lewis, Jon (1992) *The Road to Romance and Ruin: Teen Films and Youth Culture*,
London: Routledge.
Explores the relationship between youth culture and film, though the
discussion of 'teen films' themselves is rather limited.

Romney, Jonathan and Wootton, Adrian (eds) (1988) *Celluloid Jukebox:
Popular Music and the Movies Since the 1950s*, London: BFI.
Anthology of essays that consider the relationship between pop music
and cinema. Also includes interviews with Quentin Tarantino, David
Byrne, Penelope Spheeris, Ry Cooder and Wim Wenders.

Shary, Timothy (2002) *Generation Multiplex: the Image of Youth in Contemporary
American Cinema*, Austin: University of Texas Press.
A meticulous survey of representations of teenagers in American
cinema during the 1980s and 1990s. Shary explores how various
genres and sub-genres represent teens and their concerns, and how
they have both mirrored and shaped societal expectations and fears
about teen identities and social roles.

# YOUTH AND TELEVISION

Banks, Jack (1996) *Monopoly Television: MTV's Quest to Control the Music*, Boulder, CO: Westview.

Examines the historical development of music video as a commodity, analysing the structures within which music videos have been produced, distributed and exhibited on MTV. Account is given to the ownership and control of MTV and the role of record companies in the finance and production of music video.

Bodroghkozy, Aniko (2001) *Groove Tube: Sixties Television and the Youth Rebellion*, Durham, NC: Duke University Press.

Engrossing account of American primetime television's response to youth culture during the 1960s.

Davis, Glyn and Dickinson, Kay (eds) (2004) *Teen TV in the 1990s: Genre, Consumption and Identity*, London: BFI.

An anthology dedicated to a broad range of television programmes produced for and watched by teenagers, with coverage of shows such as *Dawson's Creek*, *Buffy the Vampire Slayer* and Australia's *Heartbreak High*. The studies examine how these dramas construct and reaffirm distinct concepts of 'youth'.

Goodwin, Andrew (1993) *Dancing in the Distraction Factory: Music Television and Popular Culture*, London: Routledge.

Examines the early development of MTV and the emergence of music videos.

Kaplan, E. Ann (1987) *Rocking Around the Clock: Music Television, Postmodernism and Consumer Culture*, London: Routledge.

Now very dated (case-studies include close analyses of videos by Billy Idol, Paul Young and Pat Benatar). But this represents an early (often insightful) attempt to apply postmodern theories to the analysis of music videos and MTV.

Lury, Karen (2001) *British Youth Television: Cynicism and Enchantment*, Oxford: Oxford University Press.

One of the first books to focus on the phenomenon of (post)modern 'youth television'. Lury argues that during the 1990s British 'youth television' addressed its audiences through a blend of 'cynicism and enchantment'.

# YOUTH AND POPULAR MUSIC

Bennett, Andy (2000) *Popular Music and Youth Culture*, London: Macmillan.

Bennett provides a comprehensive survey of the relationship between youth culture and popular music. Initial chapters provide a concise survey of existing critical work on youth culture and popular musi~

Original ethnographic research on Bhangra and European hip-hop offer fresh insights on the way young people appropriate pop music as a cultural resource.

Burnett, Robert (1996) *The Global Jukebox: The International Music Industry*, London: Routledge.
Now a little dated, but still a solid account of the development and operation of the international music industry. Examines the relationship between local and global cultures and between global conglomeration and the diversity of music production and consumption.

Frith, Simon and Goodwin, Andrew (eds) (1990) *On Record: Rock, Pop and the Written Word*, London: Routledge.
One of the first, and still the most comprehensive, surveys of critical approaches to pop music. An excellent guide to the shifting approaches and emphases in the field. Includes classic sociological analyses of 'deviance'; studies of technology; subcultural and feminist readings; semiotic and musicological essays; and close readings of stars, bands, and the fans themselves.

Hesmondhalgh, David and Negus, Keith (eds) (2002) *Popular Music Studies*, London: Arnold.
A readable introduction to key debates in the field of popular music. Includes coverage of textual analysis, production, consumption and everyday life. Also offers an international perspective, with contributions from writers based in North and South America, Europe, Japan, Australia, New Zealand and South Africa.

Negus, Keith (1999) *Music Genres and Corporate Cultures*, London: Routledge.
Explores the relationship between economics and culture within the music industry. Analyses the contrasting strategies adopted by major corporations like Sony and Polygram in managing different genres, artists and staff. Argues that popular music is shaped by the industry, but stresses the way music production takes place within a broader culture – and so is never totally under the thumb of the large corporations.

Rose, Tricia (1994) *Black Noise: Rap Music and Black Culture in Contemporary America*, Hanover, NH: Wesleyan University Press.
Although now somewhat dated, Rose's analysis of the nature and development of rap music and hip-hop culture remains a classic. Offers a particularly incisive account of gendered identities within the world of rap.

Ross, Andrew and Rose, Tricia (1994) (eds) *Microphone Fiends: Youth Music and Youth Culture*, London: Routledge.
A collection of essays and interviews that explore musical history; with commentaries on disco, heavy metal and rap music, together with case-studies of Riot Grrrls, Brazilian funk and British rave.

Sharma, Sanjay, Hutnyk, John and Sharma, Ashwani (eds) (1996) *Dis-Orienting Rhythms: the Politics of the New Asian Dance Music*, London: Zed Books.

Assesses the role that contemporary south Asian dance music has played in the formation of the cultural identities of British Asian youth. Also contextualises these developments within the wider nexus of cultural politics in the fractured spaces of postcolonial Britain.

## YOUTH AND NEW MEDIA

Cassell, Justine and Jenkins, Henry (eds) (1998) *From Barbie to Mortal Kombat: Gender and Computer Games*, Cambridge, MA: MIT Press.

Explores the growing attempts to market computer games to young women. Contributors examine how assumptions about gender, games, and technology shape the design, development, and marketing of games.

Howard, Sue (ed.) (1998) *Wired-Up: Young People and the Electronic Media*, London: UCL Press.

Includes studies of young people's use of a wide range of electronic media forms (including television, video, computer games and the telephone). Considers diverse issues that include the gendered nature of media consumption, the role of parental regulation and the significance of narrative, realism and morality.

Livingstone, Sonia (2002) *Young People and New Media: Childhood and the Changing Media Environment*, London: Sage.

Combines a comprehensive literature review with original empirical research on young people's use of new media. Provides a sophisticated discussion of the complex relationship between the media and childhood, the family and the home.

Newman, James (2004) *Videogames*, London: Routledge.

An accessible introduction to the history of videogames that provides a thorough survey of the shifting nature of the games industry and its markets.

Roberts, Donald and Foehr, Ulla (2003) *Kids and the Media in America*, Cambridge: Cambridge University Press.

Probably the most systematic empirical survey of American children and adolescents' use of the media to be produced within the last thirty years.

Sefton-Green, Julian (ed.) (1998) *Digital Diversions: Youth Culture in the Age of Multimedia*, London: UCL Press.

Explores the diverse ways young people engage with the media in the digital age, giving particular attention to youth's capacity as active social agents in the creation of culture. It collects an international range of empirical accounts describing the ways in which young people utilise and appropriate new technology.

# FURTHER RESOURCES

## ACADEMIC JOURNALS

### Journal of Popular Music Studies
Presents research on popular music throughout the world and approached from a variety of perspectives. A publication of the International Association for the Study of Popular Music, an international organisation established to promote the scholarly analysis of popular music. The IASPM website can be found at www.iaspm.net/.

### Journal of Youth Studies
A scholarly journal devoted to a theoretical and empirical study of young people's experiences. Launched in 1998, the journal is multidisciplinary and international in approach. Its contributions are diverse, but it often includes articles dealing with youth culture and its relation to the media and the commercial market.

### Popular Music
An international multidisciplinary journal covering all aspects of popular music, from the formation of cultural identities through popular music to the workings of the global music industry.

### Young: Nordic Journal of Youth Research
Launched in 1993, an interdisciplinary journal of youth research that forms part of the network Nordic Youth Research Information (NYRI). Deals with a broad range of issues affecting young people, but frequently includes empirical research and theoretical discussion related to youth culture,

lifestyle and the media. Full-text articles are available online from Vol. 1 (1993) to Vol. 10 (2000) at www.alli.fi/nyri/young/.

### Youth Studies Australia

A quarterly journal focused on issues facing young Australians. Covers a broad range of issues and areas, though often includes contributions dealing with youth culture, subcultures and the media.

## MAGAZINES AND PERIODICALS

The daily operation of the music industry can be followed in trade publications such as:

(in the UK) *Music Week* – www.musicweek.com/title.asp
(in the US) *Billboard* – www.billboard.com/bb/index.jsp

General coverage of contemporary popular music can be found in:

*Mojo* – www.mojo4music.com/
*NME* – www.nme.com/
*Q* – www.q4music.com/nav?page=q4music
*Rolling Stone* – www.rollingstone.com/
*Spin* – www.spin.com/
*The Wire* – www.thewire.co.uk/

Coverage of rap and hip-hop can be found in magazines such as:

*The Source* – www.thesource.com
*Vibe* – www.vibe.com/

Coverage of dance music and club culture can be found in:

*Mixmag* – www.mixmag.net/

Coverage of fashion, design and youth culture can be found in:

*Dazed and Confused* – www.confused.co.uk/frameset.htm
*The Face* – at the cutting edge of youth culture and style during the 1980s and early 1990s, but falling circulation meant that in May 2004 the magazine went into suspension pending a re-launch, re-sale or possible closure.
*i-D* – www.i-dmagazine.com/index2.php

## ONLINE RESOURCES

ClickZ Network – www.clickz.com/stats/ (formerly known as Cyberatlas) Market research dealing with internet trends and developments. Includes many articles related to the youth market and young people's use of new media.

The Media and Communications Studies Site — www.aber.ac.uk/media/index.html

Internet resources related to the analysis of media and communications. Links to articles, bibliographies and other material related to youth culture and popular music can be found at www.aber.ac.uk/media/sections/music.html.

MobileYouth — www.mobileyouth.org/

Established in 2001, mobileYouth is a market research agency dealing with the youth market and its use of mobile devices, technologies and services. Subscription gives access to a wealth of data and resources.

Popcultures.Com — Sarah Zupko's Cultural Studies Center — www.popcultures.com/

Online resources related to the study of popular culture and the media. With many links to material dealing with pop and rock music available at www.popcultures.com/articles/music.htm.

William and Gayle Cook Music Library, Indiana University — Worldwide Internet Music Resources

Online index of music journals, magazines, newspapers and periodicals available at www.music.indiana.edu/music_resources/journals.html.

# REFERENCES

Abbott, Chris (1998) 'Making Connections: Young People and the Internet', in Julian Sefton-Green (ed.), *Digital Diversions: Youth Culture in the Age of Multimedia*, London: UCL Press, pp. 84–105.

Abrams, Mark (1959) *The Teenage Consumer*, London: Press Exchange.

—— (1961) *Teenage Consumer Spending in 1959*, London: Press Exchange.

Acland, Charles (1995) *Youth, Murder, Spectacle: the Cultural Politics of 'Youth in Crisis'*, Oxford: Westview Press.

Adams, Michael (1994) *The Best War Ever: America and World War II*, Baltimore: Johns Hopkins University Press.

Adamski, Wladyslaw and Grootings, Peter (eds) (1989) *Youth, Education and Work in Europe*, London: Routledge.

Adorno, Theodor (1991) (orig. pub. 1941) 'On Popular Music', in Theodor Adorno, *The Culture Industry: Selected Essays on Mass Culture*, London: Routledge.

*Advertising Age* (1951) 'Everybody Talks About Youth Advertising . . .', 26 February.

Aglietta, Michel (1979) *A Theory of Capitalist Regulation: the US Experience*, London: Verso.

Allen, John (1992) 'Post-Industrialism and Post-Fordism', in Stuart Hall, David Held and Tony McGrew (eds), *Modernity and Its Futures*, Cambridge: Polity Press/Open University, pp. 169–220.

Allen, Sheila (1968) 'Some Theoretical Problems in the Study of Youth', *Sociological Review*, 16(3): 319–331.

Amin, Ash (1994) 'Post-Fordism: Models, Fantasies and Phantoms of Transition', in Ash Amin (ed.), *Post-Fordism: a Reader*, Oxford: Blackwell, pp. 1–39.

Anderson, Alison and Miles, Steven (1999) '"Just Do It?" Young People, The Global Media and the Construction of Consumer Meanings', in

Sue Ralph, Jo Langham Brown and Tim Lees (eds), *Youth and the Global Media*, Luton: University of Luton Press, pp. 105–113.

Anderson, Craig and Bushman, Brad (2001) 'Effects of Violent Video Games on Aggressive Behaviour, Aggressive Cognition, Aggressive Affect, Physiological Arousal, and Pro-social Behaviour: a Meta-Analytic Review of the Scientific Literature', *Psychological Science*, 12(5) September: 353–359.

Appadurai, Arjun (1996) *Modernity at Large: Cultural Dimensions of Globalization*, Minneapolis: University of Minnesota Press.

Ashton, David, Maguire, Malcolm and Spilsbury, Mark (1990) *Restructuring the Labour Market: the Implications for Youth*, Basingstoke: Macmillan.

Austin, Joe and Willard, Michael (1998) 'Angels of History, Demons of Culture', in Joe Austin and Michael Willard (eds), *Generations of Youth: Youth Cultures and History in Twentieth-Century America*, New York: New York University Press, pp. 1–20.

Back, Les (1996) *New Ethnicities and Urban Culture: Racisms and Multiculture in Young Lives*, London: UCL Press.

Baker, Houston (1993) *Black Studies, Rap, and the Academy*, Chicago: University of Chicago Press.

Bandura, Albert (1973) *Aggression: a Social Learning Analysis*, London: Prentice-Hall.

Bardens, Dennis (1954) 'Russia has her "Teddy Boy" Problem, Too', *Picture Post*, 12 June: 32–33.

Barker, Chris (1999) *Television, Globalization and Cultural Identities*, Milton Keynes: Open University Press.

Barker, Martin (ed.) (1984) *The Video Nasties: Freedom and Censorship in the Media*, Pluto Press: London.

—— (1989) *Comics: Ideology, Power and the Critics*, Manchester: Manchester University Press.

—— (1997) 'The Newsom Report: A Case Study in "Common Sense"', in Martin Barker and Julian Petley (eds), *Ill Effects: the Media / Violence Debate*, London: Routledge, pp. 12–31.

Barnard, Stephen (1989) *On the Radio: Music Radio in Britain*, Milton Keynes: Open University Press.

Baudrillard, Jean (1983) *Simulations*, New York: Semiotext.

—— (1985) 'The Ecstasy of Communication', in Hal Foster (ed.), *Postmodern Culture*, London: Pluto Press, pp. 126–135.

Beck, Ulrich (1992) *Risk Society: Towards a New Modernity*, London: Sage.

Becker, Howard (1963) *Outsiders: Studies in the Sociology of Deviance*, London: Free Press of Glencoe.

Belson, William A. (1978) *Television Violence and the Adolescent Boy*, Farnborough, Hants: Saxon House.

Bennett, Andy (1999a) 'Subcultures or Neo-Tribes?: Rethinking the Relationship Between Youth, Style and Musical Taste', *Sociology*, 33(3): 599–617.

—— (1999b) 'Hip Hop Am Main: the Localization of Rap Music and Hip Hop Culture', *Media, Culture, Society*, 21: 77–91.

—— (2000) *Popular Music and Youth Culture: Music, Identity and Place*, Basingstoke: Macmillan.

—— (2002) 'Researching Youth Culture and Popular Music: a Methodological Critique', *British Journal of Sociology*, 1(53): 451–466.

—— and Kahn-Harris, Keith (eds) (2004) *After Subculture: Critical Studies in Contemporary Youth Culture*, London: Palgrave Macmillan

Bennett, Catherine (1993) 'Game Boys and Girls', *The Guardian*, 2 December.

Benton, Michael, Dolan, Mark and Zisch, Rebecca (1997) 'Teen Films: an Annotated Bibliography', *Journal of Popular Film and Television*, 25(2) Summer: 83–88.

Benwell, Bethan (ed.) (2003) *Masculinity and Men's Lifestyle Magazines*, Sociological Review edited monographs, Oxford: Blackwell.

Berkowitz, Leonard (1962) *Aggression: a Social Psychological Analysis*, New York: McGraw-Hill.

Bernard, Jessie (1961) 'Teen-Age Culture: an Overview', *The Annals of the American Academy of Political and Social Science*, 338, November: 1–12.

Best, Steven and Kellner, Douglas (1998) 'Beavis and Butt-Head: No Future for Postmodern Youth', in Jonathon Epstein (ed.), *Youth Culture: Identity in a Postmodern World*, Oxford: Blackwell, pp. 74–99.

Bhabha, Homi (1990) 'The Third Space', in Jonathan Rutherford (ed.), *Identity: Community, Culture, Difference*, London: Lawrence and Wishart, pp. 207–221.

Bhattachariya, Nilanjana (2002) 'The Global Sounds of the Asian Underground', *Lines*, www.lines-magazine.org/Art_Aug02/Nila.htm, August.

Bjurström, Erling (1997) 'The Struggle for Ethnicity: Swedish Youth Styles and the Construction of Ethnic Identities', *Young: Nordic Journal of Youth Research*, 5(3): 44–58.

Blair, Tony (1997) *New Britain: My Vision of a Young Country*, London: Westview.

Blond, Francis (1962) *The American Invasion*, London: Anthony Blond.

Bocquet, José-Lois and Adolphe, Philippe Pierre (1997) *Rap Ta France*, Paris: Flammarion.

Boëthius, Ulf (1995) 'Youth, the Media and Moral Panics', in Johan Fornäs and Göran Bolin (eds), *Youth Culture in Late Modernity*, London: Sage, pp. 39–57.

Boucher, Manuel (1998) *Rap – Expressions Des Lascars: Significations et Enjeux du Rap Dans la Société Française*, Paris: Harmattan.

Bourdieu, Pierre (1984) *Distinction: a Social Critique of the Judgment of Taste*, London: Routledge.

Boyd, John (1973) 'Trends in Youth Culture', *Marxism Today*, 17(12) December: 375–378.

Brah, Avtar (1996) *Cartographies of Diaspora: Contesting Identities*, London: Routledge.

Brake, Michael (1985) *Comparative Youth Culture: the Sociology of Youth Culture and Youth Subcultures in America, Britain and Canada*, London: Routledge.

Br-Asian Media Consulting (2004) 'FAQs', www.brasian.com/faq.html, 3 January.

Brierly, Sean (1995) *The Advertising Handbook*, London: Routledge.

Briggs, Adam and Cobley, Paul (1999) '"I Like My Shit Sagged": Fashion, "Black Musics" and Subcultures', *Journal of Youth Studies*, 2(3): 337–352.

Brinkley, Ian (1998) 'Underworked and Underpaid', in Jonathan Rutherford (ed.), *Young Britain: Politics, Pleasures and Predicaments*, London: Lawrence & Wishart, pp. 39–50.

Buckingham, David (1993a) 'Introduction: Reading Audiences – Young People and the Media', in David Buckingham (ed.), *Reading Audiences: Young People and the Media*, Manchester: Manchester University Press, pp. 1–23.

—— (1993b) *Children Talking Television: the Making of Television Literacy*, London: Falmer Press.

—— (1996) *Moving Images: Understanding Children's Emotional Responses to Television*, Manchester: Manchester University Press.

*Business Week* (1946) 'Teen-Age Market: It's "Terrif"', 8 June: 72–73.

—— (1999) 'Generation Y', 15 February.

—— (2002) 'A Teen Dream for Investors', 15 July.

—— (2003) 'The CEO of Hip-Hop', 27 October.

Butler, Judith (1990) *Gender Trouble: Feminism and the Subversion of Identity*, London: Routledge.

—— (1991) 'Imitation and Gender Insubordination', in Diana Fuss (ed.), *Inside/Out: Lesbian Theories, Gay Theories*, New York: Routledge, pp. 13–31.

—— (1995) 'Melancholy Gender/Refused Identification', in Maurice Berger, Brian Wallis, Simon Watson (eds), *Constructing Masculinity*, London: Routledge, pp. 21–36.

Calcutt, Andrew (1998) *Arrested Development: Popular Culture and the Erosion of Adulthood*, London: Cassell.

Caldwell, John (2002) 'The Business of New Media', in Dan Harries (ed.), *The New Media Book*, London: BFI, pp. 55–68.

Campbell, Neil (2004) 'Introduction: on Youth and Cultural Studies', in Neil Campbell (ed.), *American Youth Cultures*, Edinburgh: Edinburgh University Press, pp. 1–30.

Cannon, David (1994) *Generation X and the New Work Ethic*, Demos Working Paper, London: Demos.

Carby, Hazel (1986) 'It Jus Be's Dat Way Sometime: the Sexual Politics of Women's Blues', *Radical America*, 20(4): 8–22.

Cassell, Justine and Jenkins, Henry (eds) (1998) *From Barbie to Mortal Kombat: Gender and Computer Games*, Cambridge, MA: MIT Press.

Centre for Contemporary Cultural Studies (1982) *The Empire Strikes Back: Race and Racism in Seventies Britain*, London: Hutchinson.

Chapple, Steve and Garofalo, Reebee (1977) *Rock 'n' Roll Is Here to Pay: the History and Politics of the Music Industry*, Chicago: Nelson-Hall.

Chibnall, Steve (1985) 'Whistle and Zoot: the Changing Meaning of a Suit of Clothes', *History Workshop*, 20: 56–81.

—— (1996) 'Counterfeit Yanks: War, Austerity and Britain's American Dream', in Philip Davies (ed.), *Representing and Imagining America*, Keele: Keele University Press, pp. 150–159.

Chudacoff, Howard (1989) *How Old Are You?: Age Consciousness in American Culture*, Princeton: Princeton University Press.

—— (1999) *The Age of the Bachelor: Creating an American Subculture*, Princeton: Princeton University Press.

Cieslik, Mark and Pollock, Gary (eds) (2002) *Young People in a Risk Society: the Restructuring of Youth Identities and Transitions in Late Modernity*, Aldershot: Ashgate.

CITF (Creative Industries Task Force) (2001) *Creative Industries Mapping Document 2001*, London: Department of Culture, Media and Sport.

Clarke, Gary (1990) (orig. pub. 1981) 'Defending Ski-Jumpers: a Critique of Theories of Youth Subcultures', in Simon Frith and Andrew Goodwin (eds), *On Record: Rock, Pop and the Written Word*, London: Routledge, pp. 81–96.

Clarke, John and Jefferson, Tony (1976) 'Working Class Youth Cultures', in Geoff Mungham and Geoff Pearson (eds), *Working Class Youth Culture*, London: Routledge & Kegan Paul, pp. 138–158.

——, Critcher, Chas and Johnson, Richard (eds) (1979) *Working Class Culture: Studies in History and Theory*, London: Hutchinson.

——, Hall, Stuart, Jefferson, Tony and Roberts, Brian (1976) 'Subcultures, Cultures and Class: a Theoretical Overview', in Stuart Hall and Tony Jefferson (eds), *Resistance Through Rituals: Youth Subcultures in Post-War Britain*, London: Hutchinson, pp. 9–74.

Clecak, Peter (1983) *America's Quest for the Ideal Self: Dissent and Fulfilment in the 60's and 70's*, Oxford: Oxford University Press.

Cloward, Richard and Ohlin, Lloyd (1961) *Delinquency and Opportunity: a Theory of Delinquent Gangs*, London: Routledge & Kegan Paul.

Cohen, Albert (1955) *Delinquent Boys: the Culture of the Gang*, Glencoe, IL: Glencoe Free Press.

Cohen, Phil (1972) 'Subcultural Conflict and the Working Class Community', *Working Papers in Cultural Studies*, No. 2, Birmingham: University of Birmingham.

—— and Ainley, Pat (2000) 'In the Country of the Blind?: Youth Studies and Cultural Studies in Britain', *Journal of Youth Studies*, 3(1): 79–95.

Cohen, Stanley (2002) (3rd edn) *Folk Devils and Moral Panics: the Creation of the Mods and Rockers*, London: Routledge.

Coleman, James (1961) *The Adolescent Society: the Social Life of the Teenager and its Impact on Education*, Glencoe: Free Press.

Coleman, John C. (1992) 'The Nature of Adolescence', in John C. Coleman and Chris Waren-Adamson (eds), *Youth Policy in the 1990s: the Way Forward*, London: Routledge, pp. 8–27.

Condry, Ian (1999) 'The Social Production of Difference: Imitation and Authenticity in Japanese Rap Music', in Heide Fehrenbach and Uta Poiger (eds), *Transactions, Transgressions, Transformations: American Culture in Western Europe and Japan*, New York: Berghahn Books, pp. 166–184.

—— (2002) 'Japanese Hip-Hop and the Globalization of Popular Culture', in George Gmelch and Walter Zenner (eds), *Urban Life: Readings in the Anthropology of the City*, Prospect Heights, IL: Waveland Press, pp. 357–387.

Connor, Ben (2003) 'Good Buddha and Tzu: Middle-class Wiggers from the Underside', *Youth Studies Australia*, 22(2) June: 48–54.

Connor, Steven (1989) *Postmodernist Culture: an Introduction to Theories of the Contemporary*, Oxford: Blackwell.

Cosgrove, Stuart (1984) 'The Zoot Suit and Style Warfare', *History Workshop*, No. 18: 77–91.

COTS (1997) *The California 'Youthquake'*, Sacramento: California Office of Traffic Safety.

Coupland, Douglas (1991) *Generation X: Tales for an Accelerated Culture*, New York: St. Martin's Press.

Crane, Diana (2002) 'Culture and Globalization: Theoretical Models and Emerging Trends', in Diana Crane, Nubuko Kawashima, Ken'ichi Kawasaki (eds), *Global Culture: Media Arts, Policy and Globalization*, London: Routledge, pp. 1–28.

Critcher, Chas (2000) ' "Still Raving": Social Reaction to Ecstasy', *Leisure Studies*, No. 19: 145–162.

—— (2003) *Moral Panics and the Media*, Buckingham: Open University Press.

Cross, Brian (1992) *It's Not About a Salary: Rap, Race and Resistance in Los Angeles*, London: Verso.

Cumberbatch, Guy (1989) 'Violence in the Mass Media: the Research Evidence', in Guy Cumberbatch and Dennis Howitt, *A Measure of Uncertainty: the Effects of the Mass Media*, Broadcasting Standards Council, Research Monograph Series, No. 1, London: John Libbey.

—— (2002) 'Media Effects: Continuing Controversies', in Paul Cobley and Adam Briggs (eds), *The Media: an Introduction*, Harlow: Pearson, pp. 259–271.

——, Maguire, Andrea and Woods, Samantha (1993) *Children and Video Games: an Exploratory Study*, Birmingham: University of Aston in Birmingham, Communications Research Group.

Cunningham, Helen (1995) 'Moral Combat and Computer Game Girls', in Cary Bazalgette and David Buckingham (eds), *In Front of the Children: Screen Entertainment and Young Audiences*, London: BFI, pp. 188–200.

—— (1998) 'Digital Culture: the View from the Dance Floor', in Julian Sefton-Green (ed.), *Digital Diversions: Youth Culture in the Age of Multimedia*, London: UCL, pp. 128–148.

Currie, Dawn (1999) *Girl Talk: Adolescent Magazines and Their Readers*, Toronto: University of Toronto Press.

Cyberspace Research Unit (2002) *Young People's Use of Chat Rooms: Implications for Policy Strategies and Programs of Education*, Preston: University of Central Lancashire, Cyberspace Research Unit.

*Daily Mail* (2002) 'The Silent Tears of Despair', 26 April.

*Daily Mirror* (1976) 'Foul Mouthed Yobs', 2 December.

—— (1991) 'Teenage Sex: The Shocking Truth', 24 November.

—— (2003a) 'Video Nasty ... With Special Thanks to the Met Police's SO19 Squad', 7 January.

—— (2003b) 'Don't Let Music Take the Rap', 7 January.

Datamonitor (2003) *Young Adults' Consumption Behaviour*, London: Datamonitor.

Davies, Bernard (1976) 'Youth Cultures: Myths and Political Realities', *Youth in Society*, No. 16, March/April.

Davies, Hunter (1978) *The Beatles: the Authorized Biography*, London: Granada.

Davis, Glyn and Dickinson, Kay (eds) (2004) *Teen TV in the 1990s: Genre, Consumption and Identity*, London: BFI.

Davis, John (1990) *Youth and the Condition of Britain: Images of Adolescent Conflict*, London: Athlone.

Davis, Nanette (1999) *Youth Crisis: Growing Up in the High-Risk Society*, Westport, CT: Praeger.

Dawson, Michael and Bellamy Foster, John (1996) 'Virtual Capitalism: the Political Economy of the Information Highway', *Monthly Review*, 48, July/August: 40–58.

de Certeau, Michel (1984) *The Practice of Everyday Life*, Berkeley: University of California Press.

Decker, Jeffrey (1994) 'The State of Rap: Time and Place in Hip Hop Nationalism', in Andrew Ross and Tricia Rose (eds), *Microphone Fiends: Youth Music and Youth Culture*, London: Routledge, pp. 99–121.

Denski, Stan and Sholee, David (1992) 'Metal Men and Glamour Boys: Gender Performance in Heavy Metal', in Steve Craig (ed.), *Men, Masculinity and the Media*, London: Sage, pp. 41–60.

Department of Employment (1971) *British Labour Statistics Historical Abstract 1886–1968*, London: HMSO.

Department of Health and Human Services (1998) *Trends in the Well-Being of America's Children and Youth*, Washington: Department of Health and Human Services.

Dery, Mark (1996) *Escape Velocity: Cyberculture at the End of the Century*, London: Hodder & Stoughton.

DiversityInc (2001) 'Why Are Marketers Ignoring the Graying Hip-Hop Generation?', *Blinks.net*, www.blinks.net/artman/publish/printer_75.shtml, 3 October.

Doherty, Thomas (2002) (2nd edn) *Teenagers and Teenpics: the Juvenilization of American Movies in the 1950s*, Philadelphia: Temple University Press.

Downes, David (1966) *The Delinquent Solution: a Study in Subcultural Theory*, London: Routledge & Kegan Paul.

Drotner, Kirsten (1992) 'Modernity and Media Panics', in Michael Skovmand and Kim Christian Schröder (eds), *Media Cultures: Reappraising Transnational Media*, London: Routledge, pp. 42–62.

Du Gay, Paul (1997) 'Introduction', in Paul du Gay (ed.), *Production of Culture: Cultures of Production*, London: Sage/Open University, pp. 1–10.

——, Hall, Stuart, Janes, Linda, Mackay, Hugh and Negus, Keith (1997) *Doing Cultural Studies: the Story of the Sony Walkman*, London: Sage.

Durkin, Kevin (1995) *Computer Games, Their Effects on Young People: a Review*, Sydney: Office of Film and Literature Classification.

Dwyer, Claire (1998) 'Contested Identities: Challenging Dominant Representations of Young British Muslim Women', in Tracey Skelton and Gill Valentine (eds), *Cool Places: Geographies of Youth Cultures*, London: Routledge, pp. 50–65.

Dyer, Richard (1997) *White*, London: Routledge.

Dyson, Michael (1996) *Between God and Gangsta Rap: Bearing Witness to Black Culture*, Oxford: Oxford University Press.

Early, Frances H. (2001) 'Staking Her Claim: Buffy the Vampire Slayer as Transgressive Woman Warrior', *Journal of Popular Culture*, 35(3) Winter: 11–17.

Easton, Paul (1989) 'The Rock Music Community', in Jim Riordan (ed.), *Soviet Youth Culture*, Bloomington: Indiana University Press, pp. 45–80.

*Ebony* (2003) 'The Half-Billion-Dollar Hip-Hop Empire of Russell Simmons', July.

Edwards, Tim (1997) *Men in the Mirror: Men's Fashion, Masculinity and Consumer Society*, London: Cassell.

Ehrenreich, Barbara, Hess, Elizabeth and Jacobs, Gloria (1987) 'Beatlemania: Girls Just Want to Have Fun', in Barbara Ehrenreich, Elizabeth Hess and Gloria Jacobs, *Re-Making Love: The Feminization of Sex*, London: Virago, pp. 10–38.

Eisenstadt, S.N. (1956) *Generation to Generation: Age Groups and Social Structure*, Glencoe: Free Press.

Elmer-Dewitt, Philip (1995) 'Cyberporn', *Time*, 3 July.

Erikson, Erik (1950) *Childhood and Society*, New York: Norton.

Escobar, Edward (1996) 'Zoot-Suiters and Cops: Chicano Youth and the Los Angeles Police Department During World War II', in Lewis Erenberg and Susan Hirsch (eds), *The War in American Culture: Society and Consciousness During World War II*, Chicago: University of Chicago Press, pp. 284–312.

Eyerman, Ron and Jamison, Andrew (1998) *Music and Social Movements: Mobilizing Traditions in the Twentieth Century*, Cambridge: Cambridge University Press.

Facer, Keri and Furlong, Ruth (2001) 'Beyond the Myth of the "Cyberkid": Young People at the Margins of the Information Revolution', *Journal of Youth Studies*, 4(4): 451–469.

Fass, Paula (1978) *The Damned and the Beautiful: American Youth in the 1920s*, Oxford: Oxford University Press.

Featherstone, Mike (1987) 'Lifestyle and Consumer Culture', *Theory, Culture and Society*, 4(1): 55–70.

—— (1995) *Undoing Culture: Globalization, Postmodernism and Identity*, London: Sage.

Fernando, S.H. (1995) *The New Beats: Exploring the Music Culture and Attitudes of Hip-Hop*, Edinburgh: Payback Press.

Finard and Co. (1998) *Finard Retail Review*, July.

Fiske, John (1989a) *Understanding the Popular*, Boston: Unwin Hyman.

—— (1989b) *Reading the Popular*, Boston: Unwin Hyman.

—— (1992) 'The Cultural Economy of Fandom', in Lisa Lewis (ed.), *The Adoring Audience: Fan Culture and Popular Media*, London: Routledge, pp. 30–49.

Flores, Juan (1994) 'Puerto Rican and Proud, Boyee!: Rap Roots and Amnesia', in Andrew Ross and Tricia Rose (eds), *Microphone Fiends: Youth Music and Youth Culture*, London: Routledge, pp. 89–98.

Ford, Rosemary and Phillips, Adam (1999) 'Media May Be Global, But Is It Youth?', in Sue Ralph, Jo Langham Brown and Tim Lees (eds), *Youth and the Global Media*, Luton: University of Luton Press, pp. 143–149.

Fornäs, Johan, Lindberg, Ulf and Sernhede, Ove (1995) *In Garageland: Rock, Youth and Modernity*, London: Routledge.

Fowler, David (1995) *The First Teenagers: the Lifestyle of Young Wage-Earners in Interwar Britain*, London: Woburn.

Fox, Stephen (1985) *The Mirror Makers: a History of American Advertising and Its Creators*, New York: Vintage.

Frank, Lisa and Smith, Paul (eds) (1993) *Madonnarama: Essays on Sex and Popular Culture*, Pittsburgh: Cleis Press.

Frank, Thomas (1997) *The Conquest of Cool: Business Culture, Counterculture and the Rise of Hip Consumerism*, Chicago: University of Chicago Press.

Frazer, Elizabeth (1987) 'Teenage Girls Reading *Jackie*', *Media, Culture and Society*, 9: 407–425.

Frith, Simon (1978) *The Sociology of Rock*, London: Constable.

—— (1983) *Sound Effects: Youth, Leisure and the Politics of Rock 'n' Roll*, London: Constable.

—— (1993) 'Youth/music/television', in Simon Frith, Andrew Goodwin and Lawrence Grossberg (eds), *Sound and Vision: the Music Video Reader*, London: Routledge, pp. 67–84.

Furlong, Andy and Cartmel, Fred (1997) *Young People and Social Change: Individualization and Risk in Late Modernity*, Buckingham: Open University Press.

Gaines, Donna (1991) *Teenage Wasteland: Suburbia's Dead End Kids*, New York: Pantheon Books.

—— (1994) 'Border Crossing in the USA', in Andrew Ross and Tricia Rose (eds), *Microphone Fiends: Youth Music and Youth Culture*, London: Routledge, pp. 227–234.

Games Investor (2003) 'The Games Industry: Past, Present and Future', www.gamesinvestor.com/History/history.htm.

Garnham, Nicholas (1998) 'Political Economy and Cultural Studies: Reconciliation or Divorce?', in John Storey (ed.), *Cultural Theory and Popular Culture: a Reader*, Harlow: Pearson, pp. 600–612.

Garratt, Sheryl (1984) 'All of Us Loves All of You', in Sue Steward and Sheryl Garratt (eds), *Signed, Sealed and Delivered: True Stories of Women in Pop*, London: Pluto Press, pp. 140–151.

—— (1998) *Adventures in Wonderland: A Decade of Club Culture*, London: Headline.

Gateward, Frances and Pomerance, Murray (eds) (2002) *Sugar, Spice and Everything Nice: Cinemas of Girlhood*, Detroit: Wayne State University Press.

Gauntlett, David (1995) *Moving Experiences: Understanding Television's Influences and Effects*, Academia Research Monograph 13, London: John Libbey.

Gendron, Bernard (1986) 'Theodor Adorno Meets the Cadillacs', in Tania Modleski (ed.), *Studies in Entertainment*, Bloomington, Indiana: Indiana University Press, pp. 18–38.

George, Nelson (2000) *Hip Hop America*, London: Penguin.

Giddens, Anthony (1990) *The Consequences of Modernity*, Cambridge: Polity.

—— (1991) *Modernity and Identity: Self and Society in the Late Modern Age*, Cambridge: Polity.

Gilbert, Eugene (1957) *Advertising and Marketing to Young People*, New York: Printer's Ink.

Gilbert, James (1986) *A Cycle of Outrage: America's Reaction to the Juvenile Delinquent in the 1950s*, Oxford: Oxford University Press.

Gillard, Patricia, Wale, Karen and Bow, Amanda (1998) 'The Friendly Phone', in Sue Howard (ed.), *Wired-Up: Young People and the Electronic Media*, London: UCL Press, pp. 135–152.

Gillespie, Marie (1995) *Television, Ethnicity and Cultural Change*, London: Routledge.

—— (2000) 'Transnational Communications and Diaspora Communities', in Simon Cottle (ed.), *Ethnic Minorities and the Media*, Buckingham: Open University Press, pp. 164–178.

Gillett, Charlie (1983) *The Sound of the City: the Rise of Rock and Roll*, London: Souvenir.

Gillis, John (1974) *Youth and History*, New York: Academic Press.

Gilroy, Paul (1987) *'There Ain't No Black in the Union Jack': the Cultural Politics of Race and Nation*, London: Hutchinson.

—— (1993a) *The Black Atlantic: Modernity and Double Consciousness*, London: Verso.

—— (1993b) *Small Acts: Thoughts on the Politics of Black Cultures*, London: Serpent's Tail.

—— (1997) 'Diaspora and the Detours of Identity', in Kathryn Woodwood (ed.), *Identity and Difference*, London: Sage, pp. 296–343.

Giroux, Henry (1996) *Fugitive Cultures: Race, Violence and Youth*, London: Routledge.

—— (1997) *Channel Surfing: Race Talk and the Destruction of Today's Youth*, Basingstoke: Macmillan.

Gladwell, Malcolm (1997) 'Annals of Style', *New Yorker*, 17 March.

Goode, Erich and Nachman, Ben-Yehuda (1994) *Moral Panics: The Social Construction of Deviance*, Oxford: Blackwell.

Gotlieb, Joanne and Wald, Gayle (1994) 'Smells Like Teen Spirit: Riot Grrrls, Revolution and Women in Independent Rock', in Andrew Ross and Tricia Rose (eds), *Microphone Fiends: Youth Music and Youth Culture*, London: Routledge, pp. 250–274.

Grayson, Richard S. (1998) 'Mods, Rockers and Juvenile Delinquency in 1964: the Government Response', *Contemporary British History*, 12(1): 19–47.

Greenfield, Karl Taro (1994) *Speed Tribes: Children of the Japanese Bubble*, New York: Boxtree.

Grossberg, Lawrence (1987) 'The Politics of Music: American Images and British Articulations', in *Canadian Journal of Political and Social Theory*, 11(1–2): 144–151.

—— (1994) 'Is Anybody Listening? Does Anybody Care? On Talking About "The State of Rock"', in Andrew Ross and Tricia Rose (eds), *Microphone Fiends: Youth Music and Youth Culture*, London: Routledge, pp. 41–58.

Grossman, David (1995) *On Killing: the Psychological Cost of Learning to Kill in War and Society*, Boston, MA: Little Brown & Co.

—— and DeGaetano, Gloria (1999) *Stop Teaching Our Kids to Kill: a Call to Action Against TV, Movie and Video Game Violence*, New York: Crown.

*Guardian, The* (1988) '"White Employed Youth" Profile Puzzles Theorists', 10 June.

—— (1995) 'Blair Wants "To Make UK Young Again"', 4 October.

—— (2001) 'Arts Industry Worth £100bn', 14 March.

—— (2001) 'Loyalty Pledge to Britain Urged For All Cultures', 12 December.

—— (2002) 'Those Crazy Kids', 11 February.

—— (2003) 'Minister Labelled Racist After Attack on Rap "Idiots"', 6 January.

Guevara, Nancy (1996) 'Women Writin', Rappin', Breakin'', in William Eric Perkins, *Droppin' Science: Critical Essays on Rap Music and Hip Hop Culture*, Philadelphia: Temple University Press, pp. 49–62.

Gunter, Barrie and Farnham, Adrian (1998) *Children as Consumers: a Psychological Analysis of the Young People's Market*, London: Routledge.

Hall, G. Stanley (1904) *Adolescence: its Psychology and its Relations to Physiology, Anthropology, Sociology, Sex, Crime and Education*, 2 Vols, New York: D. Appleton & Co.

Hall, Stuart (1983) 'The Great Moving Right Show', in Stuart Hall and Martin Jacques (eds), *The Politics of Thatcherism*, London: Lawrence and Wishart, pp. 19–39.

—— (1987) 'Minimal Selves', in Lisa Appignanesi (ed.), *Identity*, ICA Documents 6, London: Institute of Contemporary Arts.

—— (1988) 'Brave New World', *Marxism Today*, October: 24–29.

—— (1990) 'Cultural Identity and Diaspora', in Jonathan Rutherford (ed.), *Identity: Community, Culture, Difference*, London: Lawrence and Wishart, pp. 222–237.

—— (1992a) 'New Ethnicities', in James Donald and Ali Rattansi (eds), *'Race', Culture and Difference*, London: Sage, pp. 252–259.

—— (1992b) 'The Question of Cultural Identity', in Stuart Hall, David Held and Tony McGrew (eds), *Modernity and its Futures*, Oxford: Polity Press, pp. 273–327.

—— (1992c) 'What Is This "Black" in Black Popular Culture?', in Gina Dent (ed.), *Black Popular Culture*, Seattle: Bay Press, pp. 21–33.

—— and Jacques, Martin (eds) (1983) *The Politics of Thatcherism*, London: Lawrence and Wishart.

—— and Jefferson, Tony (eds) (1976) *Resistance Through Rituals: Youth Subcultures in Post-War Britain*, London: Hutchinson.

—— and Whannel, Paddy (1964) *The Popular Arts*, London: Hutchinson Educational.

——, Critcher, Chas, Jefferson, Tony, Clarke, John and Roberts, Brian (1978) *Policing the Crisis: Mugging, the State and Law and Order*, London: Macmillan.

——, Hobson, Dorothy, Lowe, Andrew and Willis, Paul (eds) (1980) *Culture, Media, Language*, London: Hutchinson.

Halloran, James (ed.) (1970) *The Effects of Television*, London: Panther.

Halton, Kathleen (1964) 'Changing Faces', *Sunday Times Magazine*, 2 August: 12–20.

Hamblett, Charles and Deverson, Jane (1964) *Generation X*, London: Anthony Gibbs & Phillips.

Hannerz, Ulf (1989) 'Notes on the Global Ecumene', *Public Culture*, 1(2): 66–75.

Harris, Jessica (2001) *The Effects of Computer Games On Young Children – A Review of the Research*, RDS Occasional Paper, No. 72, London: Home Office, Research, Development and Statistics Directorate.

Harvey, David (1989) *The Condition of Postmodernity: an Enquiry into the Conditions of Cultural Change*, Oxford: Basil Blackwell.

Haseen, Tabasam (2002) 'Bollywood Blues', *Spiked*, 2 May, www.spiked-online.com/Articles/00000006D8FB.htm.

Healy, Murray (1996) *Gay Skins: Class, Masculinity and Queer Appropriation*, London: Cassell.

Hebdige, Dick (1976) 'The Meaning of Mod', in Stuart Hall and Tony Jefferson (eds), *Resistance Through Rituals: Youth Subcultures in Post-war Britain*, London: Hutchinson, pp. 87–98.

—— (1979) *Subculture: the Meaning of Style*, London: Methuen.

—— (1987) *Cut 'n' Mix: Culture, Identity and Caribbean Music*, London: Comedia.

—— (1988a) 'Introduction', in Dick Hebdige, *Hiding in the Light: on Images and Things*, London, Routledge, pp. 7–16.

—— (1988b) 'Hiding in the Light: Youth Surveillance and Display', in Dick Hebdige, *Hiding in the Light: on Images and Things*, London: Routledge, pp. 17–36.

—— (1988c) 'Towards a Cartography of Taste, 1935–1962', in Dick Hebdige, *Hiding in the Light: on Images and Things*, London: Routledge, pp. 45–76.

Hechinger, Grace and Hechinger, Fred (1962) *Teen-age Tyranny*, New York: Morrow.

Hellmann, John (1997) *The Kennedy Obsession: the American Myth of JFK*, New York: Columbia University Press.

Hermes, Joke (2002) 'The Active Audience', in Paul Cobley and Adam Briggs (eds), *The Media: an Introduction*, Harlow: Pearson, pp. 282–293.

Hesmondhalgh, David (2002) *The Cultural Industries*, London: Sage.

Hill, Andrew (2002) 'Acid House and Thatcherism: Noise, the Mob, and the English Countryside', *British Journal of Sociology*, 53(1): 89–105.

Hill, John (1991) 'Television and Pop: the Case of the 1950s', in John Corner (ed.), *Popular Television in Britain: Studies in Cultural History*, London: BFI, pp. 90–107.

Hills, Matt (2002) *Fan Cultures*, London: Routledge.

Hind, John and Mosco, Stephen (1985) *Rebel Radio: the Full Story of British Pirate Radio*, London: Pluto Press.

Hine, Thomas (1999) *The Rise and Fall of the American Teenager*, New York: Avon.

Hodge, Bob and Tripp, David (1986) *Children and Television: a Semiotic Approach*, Cambridge: Polity.

Hodkinson, Paul (2002) *Goth: Identity, Style and Subculture*, Oxford: Berg.

—— (2003) '"Net.Goth": Internet Communication and (Sub) Cultural Boundaries', in David Muggleton and Rupert Weinzierl (eds), *The Post-Subcultures Reader*, Oxford: Berg, pp. 285–298.

Hoggart, Richard (1957) *The Uses of Literacy*, London: Chatto and Windus.

Hollander, Stanley C. and Germain, Richard (1993) *Was There a Pepsi Generation Before Pepsi Discovered It?: Youth-Based Segmentation in Marketing*, Chicago: American Marketing Association.

Hollingshead, August (1949) *Elmstown's Youth: the Impact of Social Classes on Adolescents*, New York: Wiley.

Huq, Rupa (1996) 'Asian Kool?: Bhangra and Beyond', in Sanjay Sharma, John Hutnyk and Ashwani Sharma (eds), *Dis-Orienting Rhythms: the Politics of the New Asian Dance Music*, London: Zed Books, pp. 61–80.

—— (2003) 'Global Youth Cultures in Localized Spaces: the Case of the UK New Asian Dance Music and French Rap', in David Muggleton and Rupert Weinzierl (eds), *The Post-Subcultures Reader*, Oxford: Berg, pp. 195–208.

Hutnyk, John (2000) 'Magical Mystical Tourism', in John Hutnyk, *Critique of Exotica: Music, Politics and the Culture Industry*, London: Pluto Press, pp. 87–113.

Hyder, Rehan (2004) *Brimful of Asia: Negotiating Ethnicity on the UK Music Scene*, Aldershot: Ashgate.

International Labour Office (1988) *Year Book of Labour Statistics*, Geneva: International Labour Office.

International Telecommunications Union (2003) 'Internet Indicators: Hosts, Users and Number of PCs', www.itu.int/ITU-D/ict/statistics/at_glance/internet02.pdf.

Jackson, Peter, Lowe, Michelle, Miller, Daniel and Mort, Frank (2000) 'Introduction: Transcending Dualisms', in Peter Jackson, Michelle Lowe, Daniel Miller, and Frank Mort (eds), *Commercial Cultures: Economies, Practices, Spaces*, Oxford: Berg, pp. 1–7.

——, Stevenson, Nick and Brooks, Kate (2001) *Making Sense of Men's Magazines*, Cambridge: Polity.

Jackson, Stevi (1996) 'Ignorance is Bliss, When You're Just Seventeen', *Trouble and Strife*, 33, Summer: 50–60.

Jameson, Frederic (1984) 'Postmodernism or the Cultural Logic of Late Capitalism', *New Left Review*, 146: 53–92.

—— (1988) 'The Politics of Theory: Ideological Positions in the Postmodernism Debate', in Frederic Jameson, *The Ideologies of Theory Essays, Volume 2*, London: Routledge, pp. 103–113.

Jenkins, Henry (1992) *Textual Poachers: Television Fans and Participatory Culture*, London: Routledge.

—— (2002) 'Interactive Audiences?', in Dan Harries (ed.), *The New Media Book*, London: BFI, pp. 157–170.

Jephcott, Pearl (1967) *A Time of One's Own*, Edinburgh: Oliver and Boyd.

Johansson, Thomas and Miegel, Frederik (1992) *Do the Right Thing: Lifestyle and Identity in Contemporary Youth Culture*, Malmo: Graphic Systems.

Johnson, Richard (1997) (orig. pub. 1986) 'What is Cultural Studies Anyway?', in John Storey (ed.), *What Is Cultural Studies?: a Reader*, London: Arnold, pp. 75–114.

Jones, Simon (1988) *Black Culture, White Youth: the Reggae Tradition from JA to UK*, Basingstoke: Macmillan.

Joyce, Michael (1998) 'New Stories for New Readers: Contours, Coherence and Constructive Hypertext', in Ilana Snyder (ed.), *Page to Screen: Taking Literacy into the Electronic Era*, London: Routledge, pp. 163–182.

Kahn, Richard and Kellner, Douglas (2003) 'Internet Communication and Oppositional Politics', in David Muggleton and Rupert Weinzierl (eds), *The Post-Subcultures Reader*, Oxford: Berg, pp. 299–314.

Kaplan, E. Ann (1987) *Rocking Around the Clock: Music Television, Postmodernism and Consumer Culture*, London: Routledge.

—— (1993) 'Madonna Politics: Perversion, Repression, or Subversion? Or Masks and/as Master-y', in Cathy Schwichtenberg (ed.), *The Madonna Connection: Representational Politics, Subcultural Identities, and Cultural Theory*, Boulder, Colorado: Westview Press, pp. 149–165.

Karla, Virinder and Hutnyk, John (1998) 'Visibility, Appropriation and Resistance', *Eastern Eye*, 13 March.

Katz, Alyssa (1998) 'Buffy the Vampire Slayer', *Nation*, 6 April: 35–36.

Katz, Cindi (1998) 'Disintegrating Developments: Global Economic Restructuring and the Eroding of Ecologies of Youth', in Tracey Skelton and Gill Valentine (eds), *Cool Places: Geographies of Youth Cultures*, London: Routledge, pp. 130–144.

Katz, Jon (1996) 'The Rights of Kids in the Digital Age', *Wired*, 4.07, July: 123.

Kaur, Raminder and Kalra, Virinder (1996) 'New Paths for South Asian Identity and Musical Creativity', in Sanjay Sharma, John Hutnyk and Ashwani Sharma (eds), *Dis-Orienting Rhythms: the Politics of the New Asian Dance Music*, London: Zed Books, pp. 217–231.

Kearney, Mary Celeste (1998a) 'Producing Girls: Rethinking the Study of Female Youth Culture', in Sherrie Innes (ed.), *Delinquents and Debutantes: Twentieth Century American Girls' Cultures*, New York: New York University Press, pp. 285–310.

—— (1998b) 'Don't Need You': Rethinking Identity Politics and Separatism from a Grrrl Perspective', in Jonathon Epstein (ed.), *Youth Culture: Identity in a Postmodern World*, Oxford: Blackwell, pp. 148–188.

—— (2004) (forthcoming) 'Teenagers and Television', in Horace Newcomb (ed.), *The Museum of Broadcast Communications' Encyclopedia of Television*, Chicago: Fitzroy Dearborn.

—— (2005) (forthcoming) 'Recycling Judy and Corliss: Transmedia Exploitation Practices and the Teen-Girl Entertainment Market, 1940s–1950s', in John McMurria (ed.), *Screen Teens: Film, Television and Youth Culture*.

Kehily, Mary Jane (1999) 'More Sugar?: Teenage Magazines, Gender Displays and Sexual Learning', *European Journal of Cultural Studies*, 2(1): 65–89.

Kellner, Douglas (1995) *Media Culture: Cultural Studies, Identity and Politics Between the Modern and the Postmodern*, Routledge: London.

—— (1997) 'Overcoming the Divide: Cultural Studies and Political Economy', in Marjorie Ferguson and Peter Golding (eds), *Cultural Studies in Question*, London: Sage, pp. 102–119.

Klein, Naomi (2000) *No Logo: No Space, No Choice, No Jobs — Taking Aim at the Brand Bullies*, London: Flamingo.

Kumar, Krishna (1995) *From Postindustrial to Postmodern Society: New Theories of the Contemporary Worlds*, Oxford: Blackwell.

Laing, Dave (1985) *One Chord Wonders: Power and Meaning in Punk Rock*, Milton Keynes: Open University Press.

Langham Brown, Jo, Ralph, Sue and Lees, Tim (1999) 'Foreword', in Sue Ralph, Jo Langham Brown and Tim Lees (eds), *Youth and the Global Media*, Luton: University of Luton Press, pp. ix–xiv.

Laurie, Peter (1965) *The Teenage Revolution*, London: Anthony Blond.

Lazer, William (1967) (orig. pub. 1963) 'Life Style Concepts and Marketing', in Eugene Kelly and William Lazer (eds), *Managerial Marketing: Perspectives and Viewpoints*, Homeward, IL: Irwin, pp. 33–41.

Leary, Timothy (1994) *Chaos and Cyber Culture*, Berkeley: Ronin.

Leblanc, Lauraine (1999) *Pretty in Punk: Girls' Gender Resistance in a Boys' Subculture*, New Brunswick: Rutgers University Press.

Lee, Stacey (1996) *Unravelling the 'Model Minority' Stereotype: Listening to Asian American Youth*, New York: Teachers College Press.

Lee, Jennifer and Zhou, Min (eds) (2004) *Asian American Youth: Culture, Identity, and Ethnicity*, London: Routledge.

Leech, Kenneth (1973) *Youthquake: Spirituality and the Growth of a Counter-culture*, London: Sheldon Press.

Lent, John (ed.) (1999) *Pulp Demons: International Dimensions of the Postwar Anti-Comics Campaign*, Madison: Fairleigh Dickinson University Press.

Leonard, Marion (1998) 'Paper Planes: Travelling the New Grrrl Geographies', in Tracey Skelton and Gill Valentine (eds), *Cool Places: Geographies of Youth Cultures*, London: Routledge, pp. 101–118.

Leonard, Mark (1997) *Britain™: Renewing Our Identity*, London: Demos.

Leslie, Peter (1965) *Fab: The Anatomy of a Phenomenon*, London: Macgibbon & Kee.

Levine, Harry and Reinarman, Craig (1988) 'The Politics of America's Latest Drug Scare', in Richard Curry (ed.), *Freedom at Risk: Secrecy, Censorship, and Repression in the 1980s*, Philadelphia: Temple University Press, pp. 251–258.

Levinson, Marc (1995) 'It's an MTV World', *Newsweek*, 24 April: 44–49.

Levy, Pierre (1997) *Collective Intelligence: Mankind's Emerging World in Cyberspace*, Cambridge: Perseus.

Lewis, Justin (1990) *Art, Culture and Enterprise: the Politics of Art and the Cultural Industries*, London: Routledge.

Lewis, Peter (1978) *The Fifties*, London: Heinemann.

Liebes, Tamar and Katz, Elihu (1990) *The Export of Meaning: Cross-cultural Readings of 'Dallas'*, Oxford: Oxford University Press.

Liechty, Mark (1995) 'Media, Markets and Modernization: Youth Identities and the Experience of Modernity in Kathmandu in Nepal', in Vered Amit-Talai and Helena Wulff (eds), *Youth Cultures: a Cross-Cultural Perspective*, London: Routledge, pp. 166–201.

*Life* (1959) 'A New $10-Billion Power: the US Teenage Consumer', 31 August: 78–85.
—— (1969) 'The Woodstock Rock Trip', 15 September: 14–23.
Lipsitz, George (1994) 'We Know What Time It Is: Race, Class and Youth Culture', in Andrew Ross and Tricia Rose (eds), *Microphone Fiends: Youth Music and Youth Culture*, London: Routledge, pp. 17–28.
Livingstone, Sonia (2002) *Young People and New Media: Childhood and the Changing Media Environment*, London: Sage.
—— and Bovill, Moira (1999) *Young People, New Media: Final Report of the Project, 'Children, Young People and the Changing Media Environment'*, LSE Report, London: London School of Economics and Political Science.
Lloyd, Fran (1993) *Deconstructing Madonna*, London: Batsford.
LongAcre (2001) '3i Invests in Ministry of Sound', LongAcre Press Release, 9 August.
Look-Look (2002) 'Who We Are', www.look-look.com/looklook/html/Test_Drive_Who_We_Are.html, 14 October.
Lopiano-Misdom, Janine and de Luca, Joanne (1998) *Street Trends: How Today's Alternative Youth Cultures Are Creating Tomorrow's Mainstream Markets*, New York: HarperCollins.
Lull, James (1995) *Media, Communication, Culture: a Global Approach*, Cambridge: Polity.
Lupton, Deborah (1999) *Risk*, London: Routledge.
Lury, Karen (2001) *British Youth Television: Cynicism and Enchantment*, Oxford: Oxford University Press.
Lyotard, Jean François (1984) *The Postmodern Condition: a Report on Knowledge*, Manchester: Manchester University Press.
McCann, P. (1997) 'Ulrika Has It. William and Nicola Do Not. Welcome to Middle Youth', *The Independent*, 11 November.
McCann-Erickson Worldwide (1989) *The New Generation: the McCann-Erickson European Youth Study, 1977–87*, London: McCann-Erickson.
McChesney, Robert (1999) *Rich Media, Poor Democracy: Communication Politics in Dubious Times*, Urbana, IL: University of Illinois Press.
Macdonald, Dwight (1958) 'A Caste, a Culture, a Market', *New Yorker*, 22 November.
MacDonald, Robert (ed.) (1997) *Youth, the 'Underclass' and Social Exclusion*, London: Routledge.
McGuigan, Jim (1992) *Cultural Populism*, London: Routledge.
McLuhan, Marshall (1964) *Understanding Media*, New York: McGraw-Hill.
McNair, Brian (2002) 'New Technologies and the Media', in Paul Cobley and Adam Briggs (eds), *The Media: an Introduction*, Harlow: Pearson, pp. 180–192.
McRobbie, Angela (1978) 'Working Class Girls and the Culture of Femininity', in Women's Studies Group, *Women Take Issue*, London: Hutchinson, pp. 96–108.

—— (1981) 'Settling Accounts With Subcultures', in Tony Bennett, Graham Martin, Colin Mercer and Janet Woollacott (eds), *Culture, Ideology and Social Process: a Reader*, London: Batsford Academic/ Open University Press, pp. 111–124.

—— (1982) '*Jackie*: an Ideology of Adolescent Femininity', in Bernard Waites, Tony Bennett and Graham Martin (eds), *Popular Culture: Past and Present*, London: Croom Helm, pp. 263–284.

—— (1989) 'Second-Hand Dresses and the Role of the Ragmarket', in Angela McRobbie (ed.), *Zoot Suits and Second-Hand Dresses: an Anthology of Fashion and Music*, London: Macmillan, pp. 23–49.

—— (1991) '*Jackie* and *Just Seventeen*: Girls' Comics and Magazines in the 1980s', in Angela McRobbie, *Feminism and Youth Culture: From 'Jackie' to 'Just Seventeen'*, London: Macmillan, pp. 135–188.

—— (1994a) 'Shut Up and Dance: Youth Culture and Changing Modes of Femininity', in Angela McRobbie, *Postmodernism and Popular Culture*, London: Routledge, pp. 168–169.

—— (1994b) 'The Moral Panic in the Age of the Postmodern Mass Media', in Angela McRobbie, *Postmodernism and Popular Culture*, London: Routledge, pp. 198–219.

—— (1997) 'The Es and the Anti-Es: New Questions for Feminism and Cultural Studies', in Marjorie Ferguson and Peter Golding (eds), *Cultural Studies in Question*, London: Sage, pp. 170–186.

—— (1998) *British Fashion Design: Rag Trade or Image Industry?*, London: Routledge.

—— (1999a) 'Pecs and Penises: the Meaning of Girlie Culture', in Angela McRobbie, *In the Culture Society: Art, Fashion and Popular Music*, London: Routledge, pp. 122–131.

—— (1999b) '*More!*: New Sexualities in Girls' and Women's Magazines', in Angela McRobbie, *In the Culture Society: Art, Fashion and Popular Music*, London: Routledge, pp. 46–61.

—— (1999c) 'Bridging the Gap: Feminism, Fashion and Consumption', in Angela McRobbie, *In the Culture Society: Art, Fashion and Popular Music*, London: Routledge, pp. 31–45.

—— (2002) 'Clubs to Companies: Notes on the Decline of Political Culture in Speeded Up Creative Worlds', *Cultural Studies*, 16(4): 516–531.

—— and Garber, Jenny (1976) 'Girls and Subcultures: an Exploration', in Stuart Hall and Tony Jefferson (eds), *Resistance Through Rituals: Youth Subcultures in Post-War Britain*, London: Hutchinson, pp. 209–222.

—— and Thornton, Sarah (1995) 'Rethinking "Moral Panic" for Multi-Mediated Social Worlds', *British Journal of Sociology*, 46(4), December: 559–574.

Maffesoli, Michael (1996) *The Time of The Tribes: the Decline of Individualism in Mass Society*, London: Sage.

Magid, Larry (2003) 'The US Perspective', Unpublished Conference Paper, Childnet International/Internet Association, Japan, 'Children, Mobile Phones and the Internet: The Mobile Internet and Children', Tokyo.

MAI (1999) *Millennium Youth 1999*, London: Market Assessment Publications.

Mailer, Norman (1961) 'The White Negro', in Norman Mailer, *Advertisements for Myself*, London: Andre Deutsch, pp. 269–289.

Malbon, Ben (1999) *Clubbing: Dancing, Ecstasy and Vitality*, London: Routledge.

Marshall, Sarah and Borrill, Carol (1984) 'Understanding the Invisibility of Young Women', *Youth and Policy*, 9, Summer: 36–39.

Massey, Doreen (1993) 'Power-Geometry and a Progressive Sense of Place', in Jon Bird, Barry Curtis, Tim Putnam, George Robertson and Lisa Tickner (eds), *Mapping the Futures: Local Cultures, Global Change*, London: Routledge, pp. 59–69.

—— (1998) 'The Spatial Construction of Youth Cultures', in Tracey Skelton and Gill Valentine (eds), *Cool Places: Geographies of Youth Cultures*, London: Routledge, pp. 121–129.

May, Kirse Granat (2002) *Golden State, Golden Youth: the California Image in Popular Culture, 1955–1966*, Chapel Hill: University of North Carolina Press.

Mazón, Mauricio (1984) *The Zoot-Suit Riots: the Psychology of Symbolic Annihilation*, Austin: University of Texas Press.

Medhurst, Andy (1988) 'Def Sentences', *The Listener*, 29 September 1988: 16–17.

—— (1995) 'It Sort of Happened Here: the Strange, Brief Life of the British Pop Film', in Jonathan Romney and Adrian Wootton (eds), *Celluloid Jukebox: Popular Music and the Movies Since the 1950s*, London: BFI, pp. 60–71.

Medved, Michael (1992) *Hollywood Versus America: Popular Culture and the War on Traditional Values*, New York: HarperCollins.

Mendonca, Luciana (2002) 'The Local and the Global in Popular Music: the Brazilian Music Industry, Local Culture, and Public Policies', in Diana Crane, Nubuko Kawashima, Ken'ichi Kawasaki (eds), *Global Culture: Media Arts, Policy and Globalization*, London: Routledge, pp. 105–117.

Merchant, Jacqueline and MacDonald, Robert (1994) 'Youth and the Rave Culture, Ecstasy and Health', *Youth and Policy*, 45, Autumn: 16–38.

Merriden, Trevor (2001) *Irresistible Forces: the Business Legacy of Napster and the Growth of the Underground Internet*, Oxford: Capstone.

Milavsky, Ronald J. (ed.) (1982) *Television and Aggression: a Panel Study*, London: Academic Press.

Miles, Steven (2000) *Youth Lifestyles in a Changing World*, Buckingham: Open University Press.

—— (2002) 'Consuming Youth: Consuming Lifestyles', in Steven Miles, Alison Anderson, and Kevin Meethan (eds), *The Changing Consumer: Markets and Meanings*, London: Routledge.

——, Cliff, Dallas and Burr, Vivien (1998) ' "Fitting In and Sticking Out": Consumption, Consumer Meanings and the Construction of Young People's Identities', *Journal of Youth Studies*, 1(1): 81–96.

Miller, Daniel (1992) '*The Young and the Restless* in Trinidad: a Case of the Local and the Global in Mass Consumption', in Eric Hirsch and Roger Silverstone (eds), *Consuming Technologies: Media and Information in Domestic Spaces*, London: Routledge, pp. 163–182.

Millwood Hargreave, Andrea (2003) *How Children Interpret Screen Violence*, London: BBC/BBFC/BSC/ITC.

Mintel Publications (1988) *Youth Lifestyle*, London: Mintel.

Mitchell, Tony (1996) *Popular Music and Local Identity: Rock, Pop and Rap in Europe and Oceania*, London: Leicester University Press.

—— (2003) 'Australian Hip Hop as a Subculture', *Youth Studies Australia*, 22(2) June: 40–47.

Mitteraurer, Michael (1992) *A History of Youth*, Oxford: Blackwell.

Modell, John (1989) *Into One's Own: From Youth to Adulthood in the United States 1920–1975*, Berkeley: University of California Press.

Morris, G. (1993) '. . . So What Is This Asian Kool?', *Select*, August: 46.

Mort, Frank (1988) 'Boys Own? Masculinity, Style and Popular Culture', in Rowena Chapman and Jonathan Rutherford (eds), *Male Order: Unwrapping Masculinity*, London: Lawrence & Wishart, pp. 193–225.

—— (1996) *Cultures of Consumption: Masculinities and Social Space in Late Twentieth-Century Britain*, London: Routledge.

—— (1997) 'Paths to Mass Consumption: Britain and the USA Since 1945', in Mica Nava, Andrew Blake, Iain MacRury and Brian Richards (eds), *Buy This Book: Studies in Advertising and Consumption*, London: Routledge, pp. 15–33.

Muggleton, David (1997) 'The Post-subculturalist', in Steve Redhead, Derek Wynne and Justin O'Connor (eds), *The Clubcultures Reader: Readings in Cultural Studies*, Oxford: Blackwell, pp. 185–203.

—— (2000) *Inside Subculture: the Postmodern Meaning of Style*, Oxford: Berg.

—— and Weinzierl, Rupert (eds) (2003) *The Post-Subcultures Reader*, Oxford: Berg.

Murdock, Graham (1997) 'Cultural Studies at the Crossroads', in Angela McRobbie (ed.), *Back to Reality? Social Experience and Cultural Studies*, Manchester: Manchester University Press, pp. 58–73.

—— and Golding, Peter (1977) 'Capitalism, Communication and Class Relations', in James Curran, Michael Gurevitch and Janet Wollacott (eds), *Mass Communications and Society*, London: Edward Arnold.

—— and McCron, Robin (1973) 'Scoobies, Skins and Contemporary Pop', *New Society*, 23(547) 29 March: 690–692.

Murray, Robin (1989) 'Fordism and Post-Fordism', in Stuart Hall and Martin Jacques (eds), *New Times: the Changing Face of Politics in the 1990s*, London: Lawrence and Wishart, pp. 38–53.

Musgrove, Frank (1974) *Ecstasy and Holiness: Counter Culture and the Open Society*, London: Methuen.

Negroponte, Nicholas (1995) *Being Digital*, London: Coronet.

Negus, Keith (1992) *Producing Pop: Culture and Conflict in the Popular Music Industry*, London: Edward Arnold.

— — (1998) 'Cultural Production and the Corporation: Musical Genres and the Strategic Management of Creativity in the US Recording Industry', *Media, Culture and Society*, 20: 359–379.

—— (1999) *Music Genres and Corporate Cultures*, London: Routledge.

Neville, Richard (1970) *Playpower*, London: Jonathan Cape.

Newman, James (2004) *Videogames*, London: Routledge.

*New Musical Express* (1998) 'The Labour Government's War On You', 14 March.

Newsom, Elizabeth (1994) *Video Violence and the Protection of Children*, Report of the Home Affairs Committee, London: HMSO.

Newsome, Rachel (2001) 'Youth Culture Has Eaten Itself (With the Help of Virgin, Nike and Gap)', *Independent on Sunday*, 19 August.

*Newsweek* (1984) 'Year of the Yuppie', 31 December.

—— (1996) 'Why London Rules', 4 November.

Nissen Jörgen (1998) 'Hackers: Masters of Modernity and Modern Technology', in Julian Sefton-Green (ed.), *Digital Diversions: Youth Culture in the Age of Multimedia*, London: UCL Press, pp. 149–171.

Nixon, Sean (1996) *Hard Looks: Masculinities, Spectatorship and Contemporary Consumption*, London: UCL.

—— (1997) 'Circulating Culture', in Paul du Gay (ed.), *Production of Culture: Cultures of Production*, London: Sage/Open University, pp. 221–220.

O'Donnell, Mike and Sharpe, Sue (2000) *Uncertain Masculinities: Youth, Ethnicity and Class in Contemporary Britain*, London: Routledge.

Office of National Statistics (1999) *Annual Abstract of Statistics*, London: HMSO.

Ogren, Kathy (1989) *The Jazz Revolution: Twenties America and the Meaning of Jazz*, New York: Oxford University Press.

Osgerby, Bill (1998) *Youth in Britain Since 1945*, Oxford: Blackwell.

—— (2001) *Playboys in Paradise: Masculinity, Youth and Leisure-style in Modern America*, Oxford: Berg.

Owen, Susan A. (1999) 'Buffy the Vampire Slayer: Vampires, Post-modernity, and Postfeminism', *Journal of Popular Film and Television*, 27(2) Summer: 24–31.

Palladino, Grace (1996) *Teenagers: an American History*, New York: Basic Books.

Parsons, Talcott (1942) 'Age and Sex in the Social Structure of the United States', *American Sociological Review*, 7(5): 604–616.

—— (1943) 'The Kinship System of the Contemporary United States', *American Anthropologist*, 45: 22–38.

Pastore, Michael (2000) 'Young Americans Take Their Spending Online', *CyberAtlas*, 19 September, cyberatlas.internet.com/big_picture/ demographics/article/0,,5901_463961,00.html.

—— (2001) 'Marketing to the Net's Future Means Marketing to Youths', *CyberAtlas*, 2 August, cyberatlas.internet.com/big_picture/demo graphics/article/0,,5901_859111,00.html.

—— (2002) 'Internet Key to Communication Among Young', *CyberAtlas*, 25 January, cyberatlas.internet.com/big_picture/demographics/article/0,,5901_961881,00.html.

Pearson, Geoffrey (1983) *Hooligan: a History of Respectable Fears*, Macmillan: London.

—— (1984) 'Falling Standards: a Short, Sharp History of Moral Decline', in Martin Barker (ed.), *The Video Nasties: Freedom and Censorship in the Media*, London: Pluto Press, pp. 88–103.

Peiss, Kathy (1987) *Cheap Amusements: Working Women and Leisure in Turn-Of-The-Century New York*, Philadelphia: Temple University Press.

Perkins, William Eric (1996) *Droppin' Science: Critical Essays on Rap Music and Hip Hop Culture*, Philadelphia: Temple University Press.

Philo, Simon (2004) '"Teensomething": American Youth Programming in the 1990s', in Neil Campbell (ed.), *American Youth Cultures*, Edinburgh: Edinburgh University Press, pp. 155–181.

Pilkington, Hilary (1994) *Russia's Youth and Its Culture: A Nation's Constructors and Constructed*, London: Routledge.

—— (ed.) (2002) *Looking West?: Cultural Globalization and Russian Youth Culture*, University Park, PA: Pennsylvania State University Press.

Pini, Maria (1997) 'Women and the Early British Rave Scene', in Angela McRobbie (ed.), *Back to Reality?: Social Experience and Cultural Studies*, Manchester: Manchester University Press, pp. 152–169.

—— (2001) *Club Cultures and Female Subjectivity: the Move from Home to House*, London: Palgrave.

Polhemus, Ted (1994) *Streetstyle: From Sidewalk to Catwalk*, London: Thames and Hudson.

—— (1996) *Style Surfing: What to Wear in the 3rd Millennium*, London: Thames and Hudson.

—— (1997) 'In the Supermarket of Style', in Steve Redhead, Derek Wynne and Justin O'Connor (eds), *The Clubcultures Reader: Readings in Cultural Studies*, Oxford: Blackwell, pp. 148–151.

Potter, Russell (1995) *Spectacular Vernaculars: Hip-hop and the Politics of Postmodernism*, Albany: State University of New York Press.

Provenzo, Eugene (1991) *Video Kids: Making Sense of Nintendo*, Cambridge, MA: Harvard University Press.

Quart, Alissa (2003) *Branded: the Buying and Selling of Teenagers*, London: Arrow.

Redhead, Steve (1990) *The End of the Century Party: Youth and Pop Towards 2000*, Manchester: Manchester University Press.

—— (1991) 'Rave Off: Youth, Subcultures and the Law', *Social Studies Review*, 6(3): 92–94.

—— (ed.) (1993) *Rave Off: Politics and Deviance in Contemporary Youth Culture*, Aldershot: Avebury.

——, Wynne, Derek and O'Connor, Justin (eds) (1997) *The Clubcultures Reader: Readings in Cultural Studies*, Oxford: Blackwell.

Reeves, J.L. and Campbell, R. (1994) *Cracked Coverage: Television News, The Anti-Cocaine Crusade and the Reagan Legacy*, Durham, NC: Duke University Press.

Reich, Charles (1971) *The Greening of America*, Harmondsworth: Penguin.

Reimer, Bo (1995) 'Youth and Modern Lifestyles', in Johan Fornäs and Göran Bolin (eds), *Youth Culture in Late Modernity*, London: Sage, pp. 120–144.

Reinarman, Craig and Levine, Harry (1989) 'Crack in Context: Politics and Media in the Making of a Drug Scare', *Contemporary Drug Problems*, 16: 535–577.

—— —— (1995) 'The Crack Attack: America's Latest Drug Scare, 1986–1992', in Joel Best (ed.), *Images of Issues: Typifying Contemporary Social Problems* (2nd edn), New York: Aldine de Gruyter, pp. 147–186.

—— —— (eds) (1997) *Crack in America: Demon Drugs and Social Justice*, Berkeley: University of California Press.

Reisman, David (1950a) *The Lonely Crowd: a Study of the Changing American Character,* New Haven: Yale University Press.

—— (1950b) 'Listening to Popular Music', *American Quarterly*, 2, Winter: 359–371.

Rentoul, John (2001) *Tony Blair: Prime Minister*, London: Time Warner.

Rheingold, Howard (1994) *The Virtual Community: Finding Connection in a Computerized World*, London: Secker & Warburg.

Rideout, Victoria (2001) *Generation Rx.com: How Young People Use the Internet for Health Information*, Malno Park, CA: Henry J. Kaiser Family Foundation.

——, Foehr, Ulla, Roberts, Donald and Brodie, Mollyann (1999) *Kids and Media @ The New Millennium*, Malno Park, CA: Henry J. Kaiser Family Foundation.

Ritchie, Karen (1995) *Marketing to Generation X*, New York: Lexington.

Ro, Ronin (1998) *Have Gun Will Travel: the Spectacular Rise and Violent Fall of Death Row Records*, New York: Doubleday.

Roberts, Donald and Foehr, Ulla (2003) *Kids and the Media in America*, Cambridge: Cambridge University Press.

Roberts, Kenneth (1995) *Youth and Employment in Modern Britain*, Oxford: Oxford University Press.

Robertson, Roland (1995) 'Globalization: Time-Space and Homogeneity-Heterogeneity', in Mike Featherstone, Scott Lash and Roland Robertson (eds), *Global Modernities*, London: Sage, pp. 25–43.

Robins, Kevin (1996) 'Cyberspace and the World We Live In', in John Dorey (ed.), *Fractal Dreams: New Media in Social Context*, London: Lawrence & Wishart.

Rock, Paul and Cohen, Stanley (1970) 'The Teddy Boy', in Vernon Bogdanor and Robert Skidelsky (eds), *The Age of Affluence, 1951–1964*, London: Macmillan, pp. 288–318.

Roedigger, David (1998) 'What to Make of Wiggers: a Work in Progress', in Joe Austin and Michael Willard (eds), *Generations of Youth: Youth*

*Cultures and History in Twentieth-Century America*, New York: New York University Press, pp. 358–366.

Rose, Tricia (1994a) *Black Noise: Rap Music and Black Culture in Contemporary America*, Hanover, NH: Wesleyan University Press.

—— (1994b) 'A Style Nobody Can Deal With: Politics, Style and the Postindustrial City in Hip Hop', in Andrew Ross and Tricia Rose (eds), *Microphone Fiends: Youth Music and Youth Culture*, London: Routledge, pp. 71–88.

Roszak, Theodore (1969) *The Making of a Counter Culture: Reflections on the Technocratic Society and its Youthful Opposition*, Berkeley: University of California Press.

Rowntree, J. and Rowntree, M. (1968) 'Youth as Social Class', *International Socialist Journal*, 25, February: 25–58.

Rushkoff, Douglas (1994) *Cyberia: Life in the Trenches of Cyberspace*, London: Flamingo.

Russell, Kristian (1993) 'Lyssergia Suburbia', in Steve Redhead (ed.), *Rave Off: Politics and Deviance in Contemporary Youth Culture*, Aldershot: Avebury, pp. 91–174.

Rutter, M., Graham, P., Chadwick, O.F.D. and Yule, W. (1976) 'Adolescent Turmoil: Fact or Fiction?', *Journal of Child Psychology and Psychiatry*, 17: 35–56.

Samad, Yunas (1998) 'Media and Muslim Identity: Intersections of Generation and Gender', *Innovation*, 11(4): 425–438.

Sato, Ikuya (1991) *Kamikaze Biker: Parody and Anomy in Affluent Japan*, Chicago: University of Chicago Press.

Savage, Jon (1990) 'Tainted Love: the Influence of Male Homosexuality and Sexual Divergence on Pop Music and Culture Since the War', in Alan Tomlinson (ed.), *Consumption, Identity and Style: Marketing, Meanings and the Packaging of Pleasure*, London: Routledge, pp. 153–171.

Schade-Poulsen, Marc (1995) 'The Power of Love: Raï Music and Youth in Algeria', in Vered Amit-Talai and Helena Wulff (eds), *Youth Cultures: a Cross-Cultural Perspective*, London: Routledge, pp. 114–143.

Schiller, Herbert (1969) *Mass Communication and American Empire*, New York: Beacon.

Schrum, Kelly (1998) '"Teena Means Business": Teenage Girls' Culture and *Seventeen* Magazine, 1944–50', in Sherrie Inness (ed.), *Delinquents and Debutantes: Twentieth Century American Girls' Cultures*, New York: New York University Press, pp. 134–163.

Schwichtenberg, Cathy (ed.) (1993) *The Madonna Connection: Representational Politics, Subcultural Identities, and Cultural Theory*, Boulder, Colorado: Westview Press.

Scraton, Sheila (1987) '"Boys Muscle in Where Angels Fear to Tread" – Girls' Sub-cultures and Physical Activities', in John Horne, David Jary and Alan Tomlinson (eds), *Sport, Leisure and Social Relations*, London: Routledge & Kegan Paul, pp. 160–186.

Seabrook, John (2001) *Nobrow: the Culture of Marketing/The Marketing of Culture*, London: Methuen.

Sefton-Green, Julian (1998) 'Introduction: Being Young in the Digital Age', in Julian Sefton-Green (ed.), *Digital Diversions: Youth Culture in the Age of Multimedia*, London: UCL Press, pp. 1–20.

—— and Buckingham, David (1998) 'Digital Visions: Children's "Creative" Uses of Multimedia Technologies', in Julian Sefton-Green (ed.), *Digital Diversions: Youth Culture in the Age of Multimedia*, London: UCL Press, pp. 62–83.

Segrave, Kerry (1992) *Drive-In Theaters: a History From Their Inception in 1933*, Jefferson, N.C: Macfarland.

Shank, Barry (1996) 'Fears of the White Unconscious: Music, Race, and Identification in the Censorship of "Cop Killer"', *Radical History Review*, Fall: 124–145.

Sharma, Sanjay (1996) 'Noisy Asians or Asian Noise?', in Sanjay Sharma, John Hutnyk and Ashwani Sharma (eds), *Dis-Orienting Rhythms: the Politics of the New Asian Dance Music*, London: Zed Books, pp. 32–60.

——, Hutnyk, John and Sharma, Ashwani (eds) (1996) *Dis-Orienting Rhythms: the Politics of the New Asian Dance Music*, London: Zed Books.

Shary, Timothy (2002) *Generation Multiplex: the Image of Youth in Contemporary American Cinema*, Austin: University of Texas Press.

Sibley, David (1995) *Geographies of Exclusion*, London: Routledge.

Skeggs, Beverly (1993) 'Two Minute Brother: Contestation Through Gender, "Race" and Sexuality', *Innovation*, 6(3): 299–322.

Smith, A.C.H., Immirizi, Elizabeth and Blackwell, Trevor (1975) *Paper Voices: the Popular Press and Social Change, 1935–65*, London: Chatto and Windus.

Smith, Cyril (1966) *Young People: a Report on Bury*, Manchester: University of Manchester.

Smith, Paul (1997) 'Tommy Hilfiger in the Age of Mass Customization', in Andrew Ross (ed.), *No Sweat. Fashion, Free Trade and the Rights of Garment Workers*, London: Verso, pp. 249–262.

Smith, Richard J. and Maughan, Tim (1998) 'Youth Culture and the Making of the Post-Fordist Economy: Dance Music in Contemporary Britain', *Journal of Youth Studies*, 1(2): 211–227.

Snyder, Ilana (1998) 'Beyond the Hype: Reassessing Hypertext', in Ilana Snyder (ed.), *Page to Screen: Taking Literacy into the Electronic Era*, London: Routledge, pp. 125–143.

Springhall, John (1980) *Coming of Age: Adolescence in Britain, 1860–1960*, Dublin: Gill and Macmillan.

—— (1998) *Youth, Popular Culture and Moral Panics: Penny Gaffs to Gangsta-Rap, 1830–1996*, Basingstoke: Macmillan.

Stern, David, Finkelstein, Neal, Latting, John and Dornsife, Carolyn (1995) *School To Work: Research on Programs in the United States*, Bristol, PA: Falmer Press.

Stewart, Fiona (1992) 'The Adolescent as Consumer', in John Coleman and Chris Warren-Adamson (eds), *Youth Policy in the 1990s: The Way Forward*, London: Routledge, pp. 202–226.

Storey, John (2001) 'The Sixties in the Nineties: Pastiche or Hyperconsciousness?', in Bill Osgerby and Anna Gough-Yates (eds), *Action TV: Tough Guys, Smooth Operators and Foxy Chicks*, London: Routledge, pp. 236–250.

Strinati, Dominic (1992) 'The Taste of America: Americanization and Popular Culture in Britain', in Dominic Strinati and Stephen Wagg (eds), *Come on Down? Popular Media Culture in Post-war Britain*, London: Routledge, pp. 46–81.

*Sun, The* (1989) '11,000 Youngsters Go Drug Crazy at Britain's Biggest-Ever Acid Party', 26 June.

—— (2003) 'And Still The Gun Madness Goes On', 6 January.

—— (2003) '80% of Criminals Are On Drugs', 10 January.

*Sunday Times* (2002) 'Crime Pays When Advertising to Youth', 14 April.

Swiencicki, Mark A. (1998) 'Consuming Brotherhood: Men's Culture, Style and Recreation as Consumer Culture, 1880–1930', *Social History*, 31(4) Summer: 773–808.

Taylor, Alexander and Harper, Richard (2001) *The Gift of the Gab?: a Design Oriented Sociology of Young People's Use of 'MobilZe!'*, Guildford: Digital World Research Centre, University of Surrey.

Taylor, Ian (1981) *Law and Order: Arguments for Socialism*, London: Macmillan.

——, Walton, Paul and Young, Jock (1973) *The New Criminology*, London: Routledge and Kegan Paul.

Thompson, John (1995) *The Media and Modernity: a Social Theory of Modernity*, Cambridge: Polity Press.

Thornton, Sarah (1994) 'Moral Panic, the Media and British Rave Culture', in Andrew Ross and Tricia Rose (eds), *Microphone Fiends: Youth Music and Youth Culture*, London: Routledge, pp. 176–192.

—— (1995) *Club Cultures: Music, Media and Subcultural Capital*, London: Polity.

Thorup, John (1998) 'Where Is the Ironic Generation?: On Young Media Users' Visual Competencies', *Young*, 6(1): 34–57.

*Time* (1966) 'London: The Swinging City', 15 April: 30–34.

*Times, The* (1958) 'The Hooligan Age', 3 September.

—— (1967) 'Who Breaks a Butterfly on a Wheel?', 1 July.

—— (1968) 'The Restless Generation', 18 December.

Toop, David (2000) *Rap Attack 3: African Rap to Global Hip Hop*, London: Serpent's Tail.

Tootelian, Dennis and Gaedeke, Ralph (1992) 'The Teen Market: an Exploratory Analysis of Income, Spending and Shopping Patterns', *Journal of Consumer Marketing*, 9: 35–45.

TRU (2002a) 'Teens Spent $172 Billion in 2001', Teen Research Unlimited, Press Release, 25 January.

—— (2002b) 'Teen Research Unlimited', www.teenresearch.com/home. cfm, 14 October.

Turkle, Sherry (1995) *Life on The Screen: Identity in the Age of the Internet*, London: Weidenfeld & Nicolson.

Turner, Ralph (1969) 'The Theme of Contemporary Social Movements', *British Journal of Sociology*, 20(4) December: 390–405.

US Census Bureau (2001) *Census 2000*, Washington, DC: US Department of Commerce, Economics and Statistics Administration.

Veares, L. and Woods, R. (1993) 'Entertainment', *Leisure Futures*, 3, London: The Henley Centre for Forecasting Ltd., pp. 86–89.

Wallace, Claire and Kovatcheva, Sijka (1998) *Youth in Society: the Construction and Deconstruction of Youth in East and West Europe*, Basingstoke: Macmillan.

Ward, Andrew (1987) 'Gender Relations and Young People', *Cultural Studies*, 1(2) May: 211–218.

Warren, Michelle (2000) 'Youth is Hot, Go For Cool', *The Sunday Business Post*, 1 January.

Wasler, Robert (1993) *Running With the Devil: Power, Gender and Madness in Heavy Metal Music*, Hanover, NH: University Press of New England.

Watson, James (ed.) (1977) *Between Two Cultures: Migrants and Minorities in Britain*, Oxford: Blackwell.

Watson, Nessim (1997) 'Why We Argue About Virtual Community: a Case Study of the Phish.Net Fan Community', in Steven Jones (ed.), *Virtual Culture: Identity and Communication in Cybersociety*, London: Sage, pp. 102–132.

Weber, Max (1978) 'The Distribution of Power Within the Political Community: Class, Status, Party', in Max Weber (eds Guenther Roth and Claus Wittich), *Economy and Society: An Outline of Interpretive Sociology*, Berkeley: University of California Press.

Wei, William (1998) 'Hmong American Youth: American Dream, American Nightmare', in Joe Austin and Michael Willard (eds), *Generations of Youth: Youth Cultures and History in Twentieth-Century America*, New York: New York University Press, pp. 311–326.

Wertham, Fredric (1954) *Seduction of the Innocent*, New York: Rinehart.

West, Mark (1988) *Children, Culture and Controversy*, Hamden, CT: Archon Books.

Whitely, Sheila (2000) *Women and Popular Music: Sexuality, Identity and Subjectivity*, London: Routledge.

Widdicombe, Sue and Wooffitt, Robin (1995) *The Language of Youth Subcultures: Social Identity in Action*, Hemel Hempstead: Harvester Wheatsheaf.

Willcock, H.D. (1949) *Report on Juvenile Delinquency*, Mass Observation Report, London: Falcon Press.

Williams, Christopher, Chuprove, Vladimir and Zubock, Julia (2003) *Youth, Risk and Russian Modernity*, Aldershot: Ashgate.

Williams, Raymond (1961) *The Long Revolution*, Harmondsworth: Pelican.

Willis, Paul (1977) *Learning to Labour: How Working Class Kids Get Working Class Jobs*, London: Gower.

—— (1978) *Profane Culture*, London: Routledge and Kegan Paul.

—— (1979) 'Shop Floor Culture, Masculinity and the Wage Form', in John Clarke, Chas Critcher and Richard Johnson (eds), *Working Class Culture: Studies in History and Theory*, London: Hutchinson, pp. 185–200.

—— (1990) *Common Culture: Symbolic Work at Play in the Everyday Cultures of the Young*, Milton Keynes: Open University Press.

Wireless World Forum (2003) *mobileYouth 2003*, London: W2F.

Wolfe, Tom (1970) *Radical Chic & Mau-Mauing the Flak Catchers*, New York: Farrar, Straus & Giroux.

Women's Studies Group (1978) *Women Take Issue*, London: Hutchinson.

Wright, Robert (2000) 'I'd Sell You Suicide: Pop Music and Moral Panic in the Age of Marilyn Manson', *Popular Music*, 19(3): 365–385.

Wyatt, Justin (1994) *High Concept: Movies, Marketing and Hollywood*, Austin: University of Texas Press.

Wyn, Johanna and White, Rob (1997) *Rethinking Youth*, London: Sage.

Young, Jock (1971) *The Drugtakers: the Social Meaning of Drug Use*, London: Paladin.

Zoglin Richard (1995) 'A Company Under Fire', *Time*, 12 June: 37–39.

Zollo, Peter (1999) (2nd edn) *Wise Up to Teens: Insights Into Marketing and Advertising to Teenagers*, New York: New Strategist Publications.

Zolov, Eric (1999) *Refried Elvis: the Rise of the Mexican Counterculture*, Berkeley: University of California Press.

# INDEX

# eBooks – at www.eBookstore.tandf.co.uk

## A library at your fingertips!

eBooks are electronic versions of printed books. You can store them on your PC/laptop or browse them online.

They have advantages for anyone needing rapid access to a wide variety of published, copyright information.

eBooks can help your research by enabling you to bookmark chapters, annotate text and use instant searches to find specific words or phrases. Several eBook files would fit on even a small laptop or PDA.

**NEW:** Save money by eSubscribing: cheap, online access to any eBook for as long as you need it.

## Annual subscription packages

We now offer special low-cost bulk subscriptions to packages of eBooks in certain subject areas. These are available to libraries or to individuals.

For more information please contact webmaster.ebooks@tandf.co.uk

We're continually developing the eBook concept, so keep up to date by visiting the website.

## www.eBookstore.tandf.co.uk